Psychopathology:
Learning Theory,
Research, and Applications

PSYCHOPATHOLOGY: LEARNING THEORY, RESEARCH, AND APPLICATIONS

JACK SANDLER
University of South Florida
ROBERT S. DAVIDSON
Veterans Administration Hospital, Miami, Florida

Harper & Row, Publishers
New York, San Francisco, Evanston, London

Sponsoring Editor: George A. Middendorf. Project Editor: David Nickol.
Designer: Michel Craig. Production Supervisor: Stefania J. Taflinska.

Psychopathology: Learning Theory, Research, and Applications

Library of Congress Cataloging in Publication Data
Sandler, Jack, 1929–
    Psychopathology: learning theory, research, and
applications.
    1. Psychology, Pathological.   I. Davidson, Robert
S., joint author.   II. Title.   [DNLM: 1. Psycho-
pathology.   WM100   S217p   1973]
RC454.4.S26   616.8′9   73–2703
ISBN 0–06–045717–1

Contents

Preface   vii
Introduction   ix

Part One   Introduction   1
   1. Orientation: Philosophy, Science, and Methodology   2
   2. Classification: Conceptual Models   17

Part Two   Etiology   35
A. Theoretical Models
   3. Intrapsychic and Behavioral Models   37
B. Experimental Method and Data
   4. Classical Conditioning Techniques   83
   5. Operant Conditioning Techniques   99
   6. Other Behavioral Analogs: Operant Respondent
      Combinations   143

Part Three   The Modification of Pathological Behavior   179
A. Deceleration Methods
   7. Classical Conditioning Treatment Techniques   190
   8. Operant Behavior Modification Procedures:
      Deceleration Techniques   210
   9. Operant Behavior Modification Procedures: Aversive
      Techniques   231
B. Acceleration Methods
   10. Shaping Normal Behavior   261

Part Four   Broadening the Base of Behavior Modification   **299**
11. Stimulus and Response Generalization   302
12. Postlude   312
Index of Authors   357
Subject Index   363

Preface

Interest in pathological behavior, however this is defined, is as old as the first written records. Many early formulations, such as the focus on evil spirits (demonology), seem to us, today, to be complete anachronisms. However, this change from a primitive point of view to the "modern" approach did not come about overnight. As psychology began to take on the raiment of her sister sciences, the influence of environmental events upon human behavior came to the fore, thus enabling a more productive analysis of all forms of behavior, including pathological ones. As an example of this change, the current interest in learning processes has made available large advances in methodology, which have opened the door to a proliferating body of data relevant to an experimental analysis of behavior pathology. This book is an attempt to plot a course through some of the landmarks, historical and contemporary, along the behavior modification path of progress.

In many respects this book had its origins in our graduate training careers. Both authors are products of a behaviorally oriented clinical program, in which the experimental analysis of clinical phenomena was emphasized. "Abnormal" events were interpreted as special instances of the laws governing all forms of human behavior.

In carrying this orientation into our practicum experiences, we became increasingly disillusioned with the nonexperimentally derived rules and practices governing most clinical endeavors. As a result, we subsequently became largely involved with the experimental analysis of the causes of psychopathology, and later we gradually applied this knowledge to the treatment of clinical problems. We were fortunate, during this time, to be associated with colleagues who favored and stimulated this interaction between laboratory and clinic.

In the course of these efforts, and in the burgeoning body of literature related to the experimental analysis of psychopathology, it became increasingly clear that an adequate scientific foundation for *the study and modification of abnormal behavior has been advanced to the point where it could be seriously considered as a substitute for conventional approaches. This has already been shown by the inroads on tradition made by the behavior modification movement, and it also seems possible to consider a similar change with regard to theory dealing with the causes of pathological conditions. From our point of view, psychologists stand at the threshold of a revolution in clinical psychology, which is just now beginning to make available to the research-oriented clinician a theoretical system and applied armamentarium far superior to those currently in vogue.*

Such an analysis would present an approach that differs in several important ways from the standard abnormal psychology textbook. There would be few case studies, anecdotal reports, and narrative accounts. Instead, there would be an emphasis upon experimental models, scientific methodology, basic principles, and applications of these sources to the world of clinical events. Though there have been similar attempts in the past, it has been our conviction that these previous endeavors have been limited by the lack of relevant knowledge available. Thus, their impact on clinical theory and practice has been negligible.

With these views serving as a basic premise, we were then faced with the task of purveying these arguments into written form. Each author was initially assigned primary responsibility for different sections. These efforts were then reviewed and revised by the alternate author. The outcome thus represents an integrated product in every sense of the word. In addition, we have attempted to hew closely to the design described above.

In reviewing the final effort, we find that the level and orientation is directed toward the advanced undergraduate and beginning graduate student. Some prior knowledge of research methodology, learning theory, and clinical psychology will be of considerable benefit to the student.

There are many individuals who have made varying contributions all along the way. Where possible, we have made explicit recognition of this. In addition, we have learned from a variety of sources: teachers, patients, colleagues, and so on. It is an impossible task to delineate these varying influences, but clearly this book could not have been written without them. A number of individuals have read portions of drafts, and we should like to acknowledge the assistance of Richard LaBarba, Neil Schneiderman, Norman Spector, and a host of undergraduate and graduate students in this connection.

For the training that led to our current orientation, we owe thanks to Florida State University and the experimentally oriented Clinical Psychology graduate program, designed largely by Joel Greenspoon. Much of our own research reported here was supported by the Veterans Administration and NIMH grants. For the basic philosophy and technology, we are grateful to B. F. Skinner. For stimulation, love, and inspiration, we express thanks and dedicate this book to Bobbie and Joy.

Introduction

This book represents an attempt to synthesize contemporary behavior theory and the experiments that it has generated with the world of clinical events. Our view of behavior theory, simply stated, emphasizes the manner in which environmental events change human behavior, or influence learning. Our objective is to review some of the recent developments in behavior theory and to present a general analysis of the acquisition, maintenance, and modification processes influencing pathological conditions. Thus, we are primarily concerned with presenting a survey and analysis of the experimental literature that enables the isolation of those environmental conditions (variables) associated with the occurrence (causes) and cures (treatment, modification) of pathological states, however they are defined. Our focus will be restricted to learning systems, with particular emphasis upon operant conditioning principles.

Certainly it is true that a number of disciplines and methodologies have contributed to the study of psychopathology. All of these, however, have had their spokesmen and, for the most part, are based upon response-response methods—that is, attempts to correlate pathological conditions with other covarying phenomena (such as the biochemical basis of schizophrenia). The disadvantages of correlational analyses as compared with manipulative experimental procedures have been frequently enumerated (Spence, 1956; Kimmel, 1971), and this topic will be subsequently analyzed at some length. Suffice it to say for the present that the concept of research, as applied in this book, is more restricted than is true in the standard psychopathology text.

This book, then, is not intended to be an eclectic approach to the study and treatment of abnormal behavior. On the contrary, the data have been collected, reviewed, and analyzed within the orientation described. The overall approach emphasizes laboratory experiments with well-designed methodologies and the analysis of the data for clinical implications. Frequently, we will refer to research that we consider to be relevant in the above context, even though the investigator has not explicated this relationship and the study has not been incorporated into the standard clinical literature.

Structurally, the book opens with a general orientation toward a philosophy of science and the place of behavioral science within this context, with a special emphasis upon the functional analysis of relationships between independent variables and dependent variables. This paradigm involves the experimental manipulation of variables responsible for the initial acquisition or appearance of a particular problem condition as well as a determination of how such variables may contribute to its later modification. It is this group of formative variables that perhaps is most relevant to the causative base of psychopathology. Analysis of the historical trends in this area will bring the reader into contact with work initiated by investigators operating within a variety of behavioral systems, as well as with contemporary developments.

Maintenance and modification of pathological behavior, which may involve manipulation of the same or entirely different variables from those that contributed to the genesis of the problem condition, are discussed in a later section on behavior modification. Those modification practices and techniques that are designed to suppress or eliminate pathological behavior are discussed in one subsection. Another subsection is devoted to a discussion of attempts to increase the frequency of normal, constructive behavior with less emphasis on direct treatment of pathological conditions.

One final introductory note would seem to be in order. In some quarters the juxtaposition of the terms "research" and "psychopathology" is regarded as a terminological contradiction. A few hardy individuals have characterized themselves as experimental psychopathologists, but, in so doing, have run the risk of being excommunicated from the several mainstreams of psychology. Since their efforts most often employ lower organisms, and because of the abiding reluctance to accept such research as having much, if any, relevance to clinical events, clinicians generally dismiss these efforts as, at best, interesting tours de force. Occasionally, an investigator has roiled the waters, but the stir was soon replaced by a sea of Philistine tranquility.

Many experimentalists also minimize the importance of such endeavors. After all, scientists are interested in general principles and not in minor perturbations or deviations, which are the psychopathologists' stock-in-trade. Thus, castigated from the "pure" and the "applied," the psychopathologist himself, as the stepchild of the behavioral sciences, is an interesting study in the delay of gratification. This book, in a very real sense, owes its inception and whatever value it may have to these investigators, and is also an attempt to offer some long overdue reinforcement for those individuals who have made and will continue to make contributions to the field.

Psychopathology:
Learning Theory,
Research, and Applications

PART ONE / INTRODUCTION

The two chapters in Part One are addressed to a number of basic issues in the field of psychopathology. A brief review of the problems encountered in applying scientific procedures in psychology, in general, and psychopathology, in particular, is provided in Chapter 1.

Chapter 2 is largely concerned with a description of the problems attendant to traditional definition and classification practices. Alternative behavioral formulations are provided as substitutes for contemporary classification schemes.

Chapter 1 / Orientation: Philosophy, Science, and Methodology

Man has always had a deep and abiding interest in pathological behavior, not only because the unusual is intrinsically fascinating, but also because deviant acts make it necessary for society to attempt to control such behavior. By inference, it would appear that our present practices are the result of a long history of such endeavors. Thus, if an individual's behavior was regarded as undesirable by the group, various methods were introduced in an attempt to reduce the probability of any such future occurrence. In the process a series of conventions, rules, and finally laws were established, which more or less defined deviant behavior and established more permanent forms of control. Ultimately, these cultural practices were organized into institutional frameworks, thereby further increasing the probability that the prevailing systems would be maintained.

The definition of psychopathology, and the specific manner in which controls were implemented, differed from place to place and from time to time. Various cultures tolerated (and even promoted) certain forms of behavior (cannibalism, for example) that were prohibited by others. In Europe during the Middle Ages the number of pathological conditions was extensive, and they were harshly treated, since they were often equated with sin and regarded as the work of the devil. In our own times standards have been changing, both with regard to what is conventionally considered to be pathological (the sexual revolution, for example) and with regard to the forms of control (elimination of the death sentence for capital crimes, misdemeanor charges for possession of marijuana). For the most part, however, practical expedience, rather than systematic study and planning, characterize conventional efforts to deal with pathological behavior.

Simultaneously, during the course of history a philosophy of human nature evolved that stressed a fundamental disparity between man and the world of inanimate events.

> *The notion that man is, in his barest essence a free agent propelled by self-initiated forces that defy, by their very nature, prediction or scientifically ordered description customarily applied to inanimate events is deeply engraved not only in the thoughts and values of Western civilization but, to some extent, at least in man's self-conceptualizations throughout the history of human societies. (Immergluck, 1964, p. 270)*

As part and parcel of this process, certain values have evolved that represent the traditional view of man's nature, and this evolution has influenced the study of pathological behavior. So it is claimed, for example, that man is free to choose a course of conduct, or that an individual can initiate action and make spontaneous and capricious changes. Many of these notions appear to be compellingly conclusive on the basis of our observations of our own and our neighbor's behavior. However, these views occur as a function of tradition and private experience rather than objective analysis.

Independent of social practices, a science of human behavior has emerged with its own emphasis upon systematic analysis and controlled observation, rather than tradition, practical expedience, and private experience. In the process a considerable amount of information has been obtained, which also has relevance to an understanding of pathological behavior. Unfortunately, however, the knowledge derived from the scientific approach is not always compatible with our conventional views. Such disagreements between science and tradition have frequently occurred in the past. At one time, for example, church dogma was in direct conflict with the increasing evidence in support of a heliocentric theory of the solar system. Similarly, the theory of evolution was denounced when first proposed, because it conflicted with certain cherished notions about man's origins. Perhaps the present conflict will be resolved, as were these earlier disagreements. In the meantime, however, a number of problems, which are important to an experimental analysis of psychopathology, have resulted from these differences. Before some of these problems are considered, a brief discussion of the scientific enterprise might be helpful.

THE SCIENTIFIC ENTERPRISE

Science is often characterized as the search for order in nature. The scientist, of necessity, assumes that the events in which he is interested, whether the movement of heavenly bodies, muscle reflexes, the structure of cells, or group cooperation, can ultimately be described within a lawful context: general principles that state the relationships between these events and their causal determinants. His ultimate goal is the positing of a probability statement—that is, given a particular set of circumstances, we can predict certain consequences. Even so-called disorderly phenomena, for example, hurricanes, cancerous processes, suicide, can ultimately be analyzed, despite their *apparent* unlawfulness. The basic assumption of lawfulness in nature is related to the concept of determinism, which asserts that all events occur as a function of antecedent conditions, or are "caused" by these conditions. The search for general relationships is almost always tied to controlled observations (for example, the experiment) that provide a specific example of the relationship between the events in which the scientist is interested. If there is an irreducible core of the scientific method, which may include hypotheses, theory construction, further tests, laws, models, etc., it is the controlled observation, or the experiment.

When the relationship between events is analyzed in the classical experiment (in the simplest case), an attempt is made to control all possibly relevant conditions while manipulating one (the independent variable) and observing its effect on the event in question (the dependent variable). If a steady state has been achieved prior to the introduction of the independent variable and this manipulation results in a significant change in the dependent variable, then a very elegant and parsimonious experiment has been conducted with a successful outcome (Sidman, 1960b). For example, a person may want to test a switch in an electrical circuit. A power source may be connected to a light in order to conveniently make this simple test. With the switch in the off position, a steady state is achieved (light off). After the switch is turned on, the light is illuminated. Several switch manipulations convince us that "light on" is a function of "switch on." A simplified functional analysis has thus been completed. This process can be repeated by others, who are now provided with an objective definition of the events investigated and the procedures employed. Subsequent to repeated demonstrations of a given cause-and-effect relationship, the experiment and its findings enter the public domain and contribute to the establishment of a *general* relationship between the events analyzed. Theories may be constructed after data collection within an area allows analysis and comparison of functionally related variables.

There are many variations to this basic experimental design, some of which will be reviewed later in this chapter, but several implications should already be apparent: Science proceeds slowly from the simple to the complex, threading its route through a subject matter as cautiously as a man jumping from stone to stone over a rushing river. The reservoir of scientific knowledge is not static, but subject to change with many self-corrective techniques as well as with each new well-done experiment. Equipped with the basic faith of a universal determinism and armed with an experimental methodology, the scientist sets out on a pilgrimage toward the pot of gold at the end of his rainbow—the prediction and control of natural events.

THE SCIENTIFIC STATUS OF PSYCHOLOGY

Where does the study of behavior, abnormal or otherwise, fit into this scheme of sciences? A definition of the proper subject matter of psychology would seem to be in order. Aside from its nonscientific pursuits, psychology is the experimental science of observable (or potentially observable) behavior. Since all the above rules and tenets of science apply equally to psychology, the variables that are to contribute grist to the mill of psychological science must be observable, measurable, and replicable.

Some writers (Stevens, 1939) have posited that a science of psychology involves special problems, since the behavior of the experimenter may be a part of the subject matter or may otherwise bias the conduct of research. These objections, however, may be raised in the areas of biology and physiology as well. Such problems appear to be pseudoproblems as long as the experimenter clearly focuses upon objective, observable variables, whether the variables form part of the behavior of other organisms or whether the experimenter chooses to focus only upon his own behavior (as did Ebbinghaus, 1885).

As in the case of the other sciences, many psychologists similarly assume that human behavior can be described within some lawful context, and that this lawfulness will be revealed as the variables influencing human behavior are isolated through experimentation. As we have seen, to function as a scientist, the psychologist must share the faith of any scientist in the universal determinism of his subject matter. If behavior *appears* to be capricious and uncontrolled, it may be only that the controlling variables are historical (and therefore not currently observable) or multifarious and subtle and, consequently, not obvious to the observer.

This extension of science into the world of human affairs, however, has not been accomplished without a great deal of furor and debate. The difficulty is that this view of human behavior is clearly at odds with the traditional concept of man, which regards behavior as the result of "self-initiated forces" rather than the product of specifiable antecedent conditions. Psychology has thus been faced with the problem of resolving two apparently incompatible notions. The difference between these two orientations is frequently cast in terms of the free will versus determinism controversy. Thus, one popular variation of the free-will doctrine argues that people engage in "good" or "bad" behavior because they choose to do so.

A. Grünbaum (1952) analyzes the antideterministic position in terms of the four major arguments that are advanced against the possibility of a scientific study of man. The antideterminist argues that (1) the uniqueness of individual behavior, (2) the complexity of human behavior, (3) the goal-seeking nature of human behavior, and (4) the necessity for assuming responsibility for one's actions raise doubt about the possibility of a true science of psychology. Although Grünbaum considers these to be specious arguments, he recognizes that the validity of the deterministic position must be established on empirical grounds. In the meantime, however, antideterminism has created serious problems in the development of a science of human behavior.

It is beyond the scope of this book to analyze this controversy and the entire sphere of influence exercised by antideterminism, but several of its ramifications are relevant to our interests. L. Immergluck (1964) regards the antideterministic position as the last outpost of vitalism and animism; animism is the practice of attributing causes to fictitious inner agents as explanatory devices, and one variation of it may be termed mentalism. The end result of this antideterministic influence is that each of us has strong preconceived biases about the whys and wherefores of human behavior, which may interfere with a scientific analysis of the variables influencing behaviors. So we say, for example, that the alcoholic can stop drinking if he simply exercises self-control, the balky student would improve if he weren't stubborn, thus directing our attention away from the actual determinants. It is often difficult, even for the sophisticated behavioral scientist, to escape these biases, since he is as much a product of cultural conditioning as the layman.

Thus, psychology, like any other science, has had to coin new terms to use in place of the commonsense terms. The great advantage of this endeavor, despite its unpopularity, is that it decreases our preconceived biases regarding the degree to which we can exercise voluntary control over events and reduces surplus connotations. The reduction of such biases, however, appears to deprive man of his own cherished notions about "human nature." The more we attribute to deterministic principles, the less there is to explain on the basis of individual choice and inner determinants (Skinner, 1959).

Despite many such obstacles, progress during the past thirty years suggests that a true science of human behavior, cast in deterministic terms, with an effective methodology, and a refined language system, is beginning to emerge. Concurrently, and perhaps even more importantly, resistance to such an endeavor is gradually dissipating, although there is still considerable reluctance to accept this doctrine completely. Our increasing attempts at social planning implicitly support the belief that such changes in the environment will result in constructive changes in man's behavior.

PSYCHOPATHOLOGY AND SCIENCE

Before embarking on a journey into the maze of psychopathology, let us consider how science can be an improvement over conventional approaches to the study of abnormal behavior. The history of mankind's attempts to deal with deviancy is, after all, a long one.

In no one field has there been more resistance to scientific analysis than in the study of psychopathology. Paradoxically, it is not so much an antideterministic position that has retarded progress, as it is the wrong kind of determinism. History is replete with a myriad of notions that state purported relationships between certain events, on the one hand, and deviancy, on the other. These notions can be differentiated in terms of folk wisdom, pseudoscientific views, and pseudodeterministic views.

Among the first, for example, one might include the statements that "poverty breeds crime" and "alcoholism runs in families." Even a brief consideration of these putative relationships reveals their inadequacy as predictive statements. Not all poor people are criminals, and not all criminals come from economically deprived circumstances. Similarly, many alcoholics had parents who were teetotalers, and the presence of alcoholic parents may result in abstention in the offspring. These, then, are simply rules of thumb that state low-level correlations, which have, therefore, limited predictive power. The existence of an *element* of truth in a general statement does not provide the scientist with a satisfactory, predictable relationship between events. The scientist hopes to achieve better than chance predictive power; else why bother to invest time and effort in his pursuit of knowledge and refinement? When our predictions are wrong as often as they are right, the statement or relationship from which the prediction is derived must be rejected or revised. The popular literature is replete with defective generalizations about pathological conditions. Unfortunately, these generalizations are often accepted without critical appraisal and frequently dictate the manner in which society attempts to control deviancy. It is conceivable, for example, that we could eliminate poverty and still not eliminate crime.

Many people, of course, recognize that such statements do not actually posit one-to-one relationships. It sometimes appears, however, that once we have established such rules of thumb, we are satisfied that we have achieved an important insight, and this satisfaction discourages a more thorough analysis of the problem.

Similarly, with regard to pseudoscientific notions, we have been told that deviancy is the result of almost everything from the changing phases of the moon (hence the word lunacy) to bumps on the head. Unfortunately, despite the superabundance of, such speculations, they have not been accompanied by a comparable degree of scientific documentation. On the contrary, perhaps because human behavior is so multifaceted, almost any statement expressing a relationship between alleged causes and pathological effects has found support in some quarters.

Finally, many clinical systems may be considered pseudodeterministic in the sense that they attribute causes to fictitious inner agents that operate in a metaphysical sense (Immergluck, 1964). Frequently, in clinical psychology this position is cast in mentalistic terms. Thus, the person who deviates from the acceptable pattern is "mentally ill." Many authorities have decried the use of such terminology as a holdover from an earlier period in which physical infirmity was regarded as a product of natural forces and abnormal behavior as a product of supernatural forces. Nevertheless, such concepts continue to be invoked, and the search for causal agents is conducted somewhere inside the individual (usually in the brain), where tradition tells us they reside. Once the focus of attention is directed toward the hypothesized mental events, the observables are relegated to a subordinate position, thus reducing the probability of isolating antecedent conditions (Skinner, 1959, p. 189).

Stuart (1970) has argued that such an approach to human behavior is "genotypic"; that is, it is essentially concerned with explanation of behavior in terms of subsurface dynamics or personality states, as contrasted with the "phenotypic" approach, which emphasizes observable actions and is therefore of higher scientific caliber.

Although we shall return to this issue, let us for the moment recognize that these traditional views have a powerful, compelling appeal for most of us, pervading many areas of psychopathology and deluding us into believing that because we have applied a familiar label or expressed a simple relationship, we have isolated a causative agent.

SCIENTIFIC METHODS IN
PSYCHOPATHOLOGY AND CLINICAL PSYCHOLOGY

In psychology the study of pathology has been advanced largely by clinical psychologists. Clinical psychology arose as a discipline early in this century, when psychologists became involved in the problems attendant to the diagnosis and treatment of patients in mental hospitals. World Wars I and II provided an additional impetus to this development, when large numbers of psychologists were called upon to analyze and treat disorders caused or augmented by the trauma of war. This movement, however, has also fallen short of establishing valid, scientifically documented, general principles.

Early in its history clinical psychology adopted from psychoanalysis and other historical antecedents the analytical strategy that seemed most logically appropriate to the treatment of pathological behavior—the case study method. This procedure focuses upon the individual patient or client and attempts to reconstruct from his history the data pertinent to his current problems. The case study usually consists of information from interviews, observation, and standardized tests designed to reveal the developmental history of the patient's psychopathology, thus constituting a retrospective analysis. At its best, in the hands of an extremely perceptive clinician, this approach may reveal prognostic indicators and general antecedent conditions, but only rarely can it reveal specific antecedent, or "causal," stimulus configurations, or even current maintaining stimuli, both of which would be helpful in treatment. At its worst the case study method provides a wealth of material irrelevant to the current behavior needing treatment or modification. Sometimes, apparently because of the focus upon allegedly important features of the patients' behavior, practitioners of this method mistakenly conclude that the causes of pathology have been discovered, as when, for example, presumed traumatic historical events are inferred (but not documented).

Since this method lacks the controlled observations and manipulations of the laboratory, it clearly must proceed outside the pale of experimental analysis. Nevertheless, the wise experimentalist or psychopathologist periodically takes the pulse of contributions from case studies, which often suggest interesting behaviors and independent variables of which they could be a function.

Another clinical strategy, the controlled field observation, is frequently the method used by investigators conducting more formalized observations in clinical settings. This method was borrowed in essence from anthropology and sociology, where it may be impossible to manipulate independent variables that affect large groups of people. This is not to say that such manipulation is impossible, for many psychologists are now performing experimental analyses of the behavior of groups but, as it is most often used, the method in question has at its core the correlation of events, frequently of behaviors. Thus, the field study may generate interesting notions about correlated (covarying) response classes, but without the isolation and manipulation of the independent variables that control behavior, the method cannot assume its place among the exact sciences. On some occasions clinical investigators have attempted to extend this method to include the measurement (but not the manipulation) of an independent variable. For example, the independent variable may consist of a particular class membership (such as schizophrenic versus normal, anxious neurotic versus undifferentiated schizophrenic, rigid versus scattered, or authoritarian versus creative-artistic), but since membership in any of these classes depends upon *behavior,* the investigator is still left with the question of specifying the independent variable to be manipulated.

For these and other reasons the methodological contribution of clinical psychology, to date, has not been a particularly impressive one, and few of the variables influencing pathological behavior have been isolated by such analyses. Consider one area of inquiry, which has witnessed extensive investigation: Over forty years of effort have been expended in an attempt to isolate those family conditions responsible for pathology—that is, what family variables are related to psychosis, drug addiction, delinquency, etc.? A recent review of this literature concludes, however, that *no* factors that differentiate between those families revealing high rates of pathological behaviors and the families of normal members have been experimentally isolated (Frank, 1965).

Small wonder, then, that considerable confusion continues to exist among the lay public and professionals alike regarding the circumstances responsible for pathological conditions, and that, too often, myths and legends continue to exert considerable influence upon the manner in which practitioners and social agencies attempt to cope with these problems.   .

THE VALUE OF THE EXPERIMENTAL APPROACH

Clinical psychologists have long recognized the need for improved methods of analysis in the field, and have wrestled with the problem since the study of abnormal behavior was first initiated. In addition to the obstacles previously mentioned, one very real difficulty involves an ethical dilemma. Controlled experimentation in this area would require the manipulation of variables for the purpose of demonstrating their effect on pathological behavior, and few, if any, psychologists would advocate the imposition of experiences that may be disabling to the individual.

Yet at least several alternatives are available, as demonstrated by the successful manner in which they have been routinely used in medical and pharmacological research, which involves similar problems.

Research on infrahumans is one readily available possibility, and in fact, the literature is replete with animal studies that are relevant to an understanding of psychopathology. However, for many reasons, some of which have already been described, this approach has had little impact on clinical theory and treatment. In addition, restricted research on humans can be undertaken when the risk of undesirable consequences is minimal or nonexistent. Of course, such research requires prior knowledge of the probable effects of the experimental procedure, and this knowledge, although available to a limited extent for some time, has been utilized only within the past few years. (Moreover, the argument of possible danger is a matter of degree and could conceivably be invoked in almost any experiment involving human subjects.) When a general pathological condition is of interest, examples that have little or no relevance outside the experimental situation may be investigated. Thus, forms of phobic behavior may be analyzed through the use of a response controlled by an avoidance contingency using noise or mild shock. Finally, psychologists can employ treatment techniques (that is, techniques to modify undesirable behavior) that use variables related to experimental procedures or represent, at the very least, analogies of systematic attempts to modify similar forms of behavior in the laboratory setting. Here again, it has not been until recently that such attempts have been seriously undertaken.

Despite the availability of these alternatives, they have been used only to a limited extent. For the most part the study of behavior pathology has been conducted by methodologies that are not, strictly speaking, experimental; that is, a dependent variable has not been controlled and the effects of an independent variable upon that dependent variable systematically examined. Case histories, field studies, questionnaire techniques, etc., appear in the literature in abundance. Often these are retrospective in nature. Thus, the human subject may be examined for the purpose of recon-structing the circumstances that were ostensibly responsible for the pathological condition. Many of these endeavors (and here we would include factor-analytic studies) are, at best, response-response methodologies, which establish a correlation between two behavioral events but tell us little about the functional relationship between behavior and its controlling variables. Often these methods involve even more serious shortcomings, which cast doubt upon the conclusions (Fontana, 1966).

It is only through the traditional experiment that a functional analysis of relationships can be obtained. The manipulation of inde-pendent variables ultimately may enable the investigator to estab-lish the necessary and sufficient conditions responsible for the behavior under investigation. In addition to providing a clearer specification of the nature of relationships, functional analyses have the added advantage of enabling regulation or elimination of those conditions responsible for undesirable outcomes (since the effect of the independent variable can be clearly determined).

Sometimes, especially in the early stages of science, func-tional and nonfunctional approaches complement one another. In the study of psychopathology, however, psychology has been over-burdened with the nonfunctional approach. This is probably a conse-quence of pressures exerted by society for finding quick answers to the many bewildering questions that exist in the area. Case histories and questionnaire methods can certainly be implemented with less difficulty than the more laborious and time-consuming functional analysis. They thrive, perhaps, because of our desperate search for "immediate" and simplistic solutions. However, forty or fifty years of such efforts have now been expended with only marginal returns for the investment, and we can only speculate on the degree to which our knowledge might have advanced if our time and skills had been distributed more equitably between the two approaches.

In brief, the study of pathological processes has not reached a satisfactory level of scientific maturity via those methods that have been employed most often for this purpose. Nevertheless, this has been the history of our efforts in the field of pathological behavior, and it has resulted in a bewildering state of affairs, sweeping gen-eralizations, conflicting viewpoints, incompatible conclusions, and enigmas. For example, it has been said that common general prin-ciples underlie all forms of human behavior and that abnormal processes are qualitatively different from normal processes; that schizophrenia is caused by too much mothering and that it is caused by not enough mothering (Ward, 1970); that illegal forms of deviant behavior should be punished, since the perpetrator is responsible for his crime, and that such acts are the result of environmental conditions rather than moral corruption. Much has been said about the depriving mother, the rejecting mother, the schizophrenogenic mother, etc., but we still appear to be no closer to a functional identification of causes and effects than when we started.

If these conflicts are to be resolved and the study of pathological behavior is to provide us with knowledge of social utility, greater emphasis must be placed upon controlled experiments and less effort expended upon those methodologies that have been shown to be relatively unproductive. When such a program is undertaken, the lawfulness underlying the various forms of psychopathology may eventually be uncovered. When this information is integrated into general laws, we will be able to apply knowledge that will enable man to exert control over the causes and to effect cures of pathological conditions.

In the following chapters the study of behavior pathology has been organized primarily around information derived from experimental analyses of a functional nature. The emphasis is upon laboratory experiments of behavioral processes, with reasonably well-defined methodologies, that reveal predictable relationships between antecedent conditions and pathological behavior and include attempts to apply this knowledge to the clinical environment. Interpretations and theoretical arguments are limited and are advanced within a systematic conditioning and learning point of view, rather than by invoking clinically based theories, which have long suffered from a surplus of speculation and a shortage of systematic data (Dinsmoor, 1960).

FURTHER METHODOLOGICAL CONSIDERATIONS

Earlier in the chapter a brief outline of the manner in which the scientific method is used to obtain knowledge was advanced. The purpose then was to contrast the procedures of science with the adequacy of the knowledge obtained through common sense and private experience. The actual scientific process is much more complex and variegated than indicated, and the current purpose is to elaborate on this topic and demonstrate the manner in which scientific procedures are related to the study of pathological behavior. In particular, the focus will now turn to an extended discussion of methodology, since this is of critical importance in the development of an experimentally based analysis of psychopathology.

As was previously indicated, the goal of the scientific method is to generate laws that state the relationships between various events. Some examples are the laws governing the movement of physical objects, the laws governing genetic inheritance, and the laws governing biological evolution. The behavioral pathologist hopes to establish similar laws regarding the causes and cures of pathological behavior. The adequacy of a law, however, is determined by its experimental foundation, and herein lies the source of much confusion and controversy.

The reader may recall the earlier description of the classical experimental model as one in which all relevant variables are held constant save one (the manipulated variable). Such a method reveals the functional relationships between the event investigated and its controlling variables. For example, an animal's heart rate may be controlled to the extent that it shows very little variability, suggesting that all relevant variables are controlled. (The animal is at rest; distracting stimuli are removed; etc.) Injection of the animal with a drug such as amphetamine (the independent variable) may produce a regular and consistent increase in heart rate for as long as the drug is active in the animal's system. This provides a hypothetical example of one kind of successful experiment.

Of course, not all experiments are designed according to this basic model, since the possible variations of this basic theme are great. For example, when the experimenter doubts that all relevant variables have been properly controlled (or, occasionally, that they can be controlled), he may prefer to introduce and remove the independent variable several times. This is known as the reversal procedure, and if it results regularly in departures from and returns to the initial steady state, it is an even more powerful demonstration that these effects may be ascribed only to the manipulated independent variable. Thus, in the preceding example if the experimenter has any reason to believe that variables other than the presence or absence of the drug may have affected heart rate, he may inject the drug several times to resolve this problem.

When the expected returns to the initial steady state in the dependent variable do not occur, the independent variable may be applied to several successive dependent variables in a concurrent design (called multiple base-line design by Baer *et al.,* 1968). In the hypothetical example the same drug might be administered on several occasions and its effects observed on other dependent variables, such as respiration rate, blood pressure, metabolic rate, or rate of bar-pressing activity. If the results reveal that all the dependent variables have been similarly manipulated, even though at different times this method may demonstrate the control of the independent variable without requiring a return to the original steady state.

In addition, several independent variables may be manipulated within the context of one experiment. As long as they can be either manipulated serially, superimposed upon a particular dependent variable one at a time, or randomly alternated, their effects may be judged independently of each other.

Still another variation may consist of dimensionalizing an independent variable by presenting it in increasing, decreasing, or randomized orders of magnitude, intensity, etc. Thus, several other drugs in addition to amphetamine could be injected into the organism and their differential effects observed (some drugs may produce decreases rather than increases in heart rate), or the dose level (amount injected) could be manipulated to produce a dose-response curve.

Taken together, these procedures represent some of the possible forms of functional analysis of the relationships between variables. Such methods are standard in well-established sciences such as physics and physiology, but they are still not in wide use in experimental psychopathology. The more popular experimental method is the statistical procedure developed by F. Galton, K. Pearson, and R. A. Fisher (Boring, 1950). With this approach the effects of an independent variable on a treated group (the experimental group) are generally compared with an untreated control group. Results are typically presented in terms of a probability statement; that is, the differences between the two groups are analyzed to determine whether or not they could have arisen purely by chance (the null hypothesis). When this possibility is remote, the differences are attributed to the independent variable.

In exploratory stages of scientific research, when knowledge of the effective range of an independent variable may be limited, the experimenter may use the statistical design. Thus, if it were not possible to generate steady states of heart rates in humans, the effects of amphetamine on the average heart rate in one group could be compared with the average heart rate in an untreated control group. In addition, it is often necessary to use a group design in clinical trials of treatments that could conceivably generate various outcomes, or to combat problems of dropout in follow-up (Paul, 1969a).

There are, of course, many variations of the statistical method. For example, several independent variables of several levels may be analyzed within one experiment (factorial design), which enables the analysis of more complex interactions than might be possible in the steady-state design. The statistical design also has the practical advantage of taking less time than the steady-state method, which may have to be temporally extended in the search for control or steady-state conditions. On the other hand, the statistical design has the disadvantages of emphasizing statistical control rather than experimental control: Sometimes large numbers of subjects are required; possibly useful data may have to be sacrificed; and little information is revealed about an individual subject. This last is particularly relevant to the clinician. In the sense that the steady-state design emphasizes functional relationships that apply to individual subjects, it would seem to be more compatible with the interests of the applied practitioner than the statistical design.

Here, then, are representative experimental strategies that, until recently, have had limited service in the field of psychopathology. Granted that the problems inherent in the subject matter are complex, dynamic, and evanescent, the challenge is in the use of procedures that offer solutions to these problems. However, there is no shortcut substitute for an approach that employs an experimental analysis that starts at the relatively simple level and that gradually builds to the more complex. The terms "experimental analysis" and "functional analysis" will be used to denote one of the classes of experimental design just reviewed.

THE OPERANT PARADIGM

Some of the most creative solutions to the scientific analysis of human behavior have been proposed by B. F. Skinner (1938, 1953). Although we shall examine Skinner's views throughout the book, several introductory comments are appropriate at this point. Skinner has long maintained that the basic datum of psychology is the probability that a particular response will occur. Most often this means that an investigator will be analyzing response frequency as the dependent variable. The paradigm also requires appropriate control conditions for generating stable rates of behavior. Once such control conditions are in effect, the experimenter is ready to begin a functional analysis of the relationships between independent and dependent variables. Thus, the experimenter can introduce independent variables, as in the manner described previously, and observe the ensuing changes in response frequency.

Skinner has contended further that the analysis of behavior must be initiated at a relatively simple level and proceed systematically to the more complex. This explains why Skinner emphasized such an easily instrumented and reliably measured response as the bar press in lower organisms, especially in the formative years of his theory. It is a simple matter to obtain a laboratory animal, exercise the appropriate control conditions (such as food deprivation and stable test environment), and demonstrate the manner in which the frequency of the bar-press response can be modified. In the process much information may be accumulated regarding the antecedent conditions or independent variables of which changes in bar-press frequency are a function.

It is no accident, of course, that this procedure lent itself to the analysis of what Skinner considered to be critical variables: the consequences of behavior. Through their efforts, Skinner and his associates confirmed and extended the basic learning principles of reward, extinction, and punishment. Thus, the major response-consequence arrangements and their concomitant effects were formulated. Those arrangements that resulted in an increase in response frequency were defined as reinforcing operations and fell into two categories: positive reinforcement in which a response *produced* a stimulus or event, and negative reinforcement in which a response *eliminated* or removed a stimulus or an event. In addition, previously neutral stimuli that acquired reinforcement properties were termed conditioned positive or negative reinforcers. Response-consequence arrangements that resulted in a *decrease* in response frequency were also divided into two categories: extinction, in which a previously reinforcing arrangement was terminated, and punishment, in which the production of a stimulus resulted in response decrement.

In such investigations, then, the concept of functional analysis came to denote the continuous transaction between a response and the related environmental consequences. Thus, an adequate analysis of behavior requires, first, the specification of the response, then, the isolation of the relevant determinants. (Does the behavior produce positive reinforcement? produce an aversive stimulus? eliminate an aversive event? etc.) Finally, the question of how this continual interaction influences the final outcome must be answered.

The more detailed and extensive the analysis of this continuing transaction is, the greater the predictive value of the information derived from the analysis will be.

Skinner maintained that virtually all forms of human behavior are shaped and influenced by environmental events; that is, that behavior is "instrumental" in a person's adjusting to environmental contingencies, including those responses that have traditionally been considered to be "voluntary" and under the person's control. Although such environmental influences might be subtle and obscure, a proper analysis would explicate this characteristic. For this reason Skinner termed such instrumental behaviors operants, which implies an active organism operating on and responding to the environment. Obviously, this position represents one variation of determinism with its emphasis upon response consequences as the major variables influencing the course of responding. It is also a theory of learning, since the major focus of analysis is the changes in behavior (for example, increases or decreases in response rate) that occur as a function of the specified variables.

As the system was elaborated and the principles became more general, similar functional analyses were made of increasingly more complex operant responses. Thus, it was determined that many classes of responses reveal stable characteristics when the appropriate control and measurement restrictions are implemented. This, in turn, enabled a functional analysis of the probability or rate of response of such behaviors. In recent years, for example, creative experimentalists have applied functional analyses to verbal behavior (Salzinger, 1959; Krasner, 1958), physiological responses (Brady, 1962), drug reactions (Brady, 1956, 1957; Dews, 1962), social interactions (Azrin & Lindsley, 1956), and many other clinical behaviors.

It would appear, then, that the basic paradigm is potentially applicable to many classes of behavior, including those traditionally regarded as outside the purview of learning theory. Although the question of generality is still, of course, a source of debate, many of the clinical phenomena previously interpreted by traditional strategies have already been analyzed by means of reinforcement principles. In subsequent chapters an attempt will be made to demonstrate the manner in which such an approach can be implemented in the experimental analysis of pathological behavior.

Chapter 2 / Classification: Conceptual Models

Clinicians have expended a great deal of effort in the search for a universally acceptable definition of abnormal behavior. Many different criteria have been proposed, and various models have been offered, but to date no completely satisfactory resolution of the problem has emerged. What is patently clear, however, is that the definition of psychopathology is almost as widely divergent as the number of people who have applied the term. Virtually every dimension of behavior from ducks following a human to college students wearing long hair has been regarded as abnormal by someone. The literature is replete with discussions of this issue, and it is hardly necessary to recapitulate the various arguments. The interested reader is referred to a variety of sources (Buss, 1966; Coleman, 1964; Jahoda, 1958; Scott, 1958), which provide detailed discussions of the topic.

The persistence of this effort is readily explained. Perhaps the first step in the systematic analysis of any phenomenon is the definition of its parameters. This requirement, however, is more easily satisfied when dealing with physical rather than behavioral events. Meteorologists, for example, can propose a generally accepted standard for defining a hurricane without fear of serious contradiction. Thus, one of the characteristics is wind velocity of seventy-five miles per hour. However, many different standards have been employed in dealing with such phenomena as alcoholism, phobias, and depression, including standards with ethico-legal, philosophical, medical, and social bases, and often the standards that arise out of these independent lines of interest are incompatible with one an other.

For example, one popular criterion of abnormality is the degree to which an individual deviates from the norms of his society. This criterion has the advantage of recognizing that behavior considered abnormal within one cultural context, such as cannibalism, may be normal within another cultural context. There are, however, difficulties in applying this standard, aside from those involved in defining cultural norms. For example, if it were to be accepted as the universal criterion, participation in the Nazi extermination program would be regarded as normal behavior. In fact, this was the very defense maintained by the accused during the war crimes trials. The International Commission established to investigate these activities, however, drew a distinction between responsibility to the state (read "cultural norms") and responsibility to a "higher ethic" (read "international social norms"). Thus, a definition of abnormal behavior based upon norms in one culture cannot be expected to apply to all dimensions of behavior or to all cultures.

A second alternative is to focus attention upon only those examples of psychopathology that are so extreme as to be regarded as abnormal by the vast majority of people. The criterion here might be in terms of the "severity" of the condition. To so restrict the definition, however, would neglect the multitude of cases that are less extreme but make up the bulk of pathological behaviors.

In actual practice some form of "maladaptive" criterion seems to be employed most often in the judging of behavior pathology. For example, when an individual's behavior prevents him from functioning effectively at home, in school, or on the job, social agencies, in one form or another, characterize the behavior as pathological. Thus, a housewife's fear of flying would probably be regarded as a minor inconvenience and pass unnoticed. In a pilot, however, the same behavior would prevent him from earning a living, possibly leading to other serious problems, and thus would require treatment. Similarly, bed-wetting in an infant is considered routine, but it is considerably more serious in a teen-ager. Unfortunately, these informal standards are subject to considerable error. As E. Goffman (1961) points out,

> Ordinarily the pathology which first draws attention to the patient's condition is conduct that is "inappropriate" in the situation. But the decision as to whether a given act is appropriate or inappropriate must often necessarily be a lay decision, simply because we have no technical mapping of the various behavioral subcultures in our society, let alone the standards of conduct prevailing in each of them. (p. 363)

Thus, in most cases the behavior that comes to the attention of the practitioner has already been filtered by an ambiguous and questionable process.

More recently, Rosenhan (1973) has provided even more striking evidence that calls into serious question generally accepted practices for identifying insanity. Thus, eight normal volunteer subjects gained admission to twelve different hospitals and were labeled as insane simply on the grounds that they complained about "hearing voices." Despite the fact that by all objective indices the volunteers never displayed aberrant behavior, the pseudopatients were never detected by the hospital staffs. As Rosenhan asserts, "Any diagnostic process that lends itself to massive errors of this sort cannot be a very reliable one" (p. 179).

For these and other reasons several authors have suggested that the question of definition be postponed until there is general agreement regarding the definition of effective or well-adjusted behavior. L. I. O'Kelley and F. A. Muckler (1955) propose, for example, that our primary concern should be with the isolation of determinants of behavior, rather than with exploring the "essence" of abnormality. There is much to be said for this position, and it is certainly in keeping with the current focus upon establishing relationships between independent and dependent variables. In terms of the orientation presented in Chapter 1, our highest priority should be the establishing of an objective conceptual framework, from which implications for psychopathology will emerge.

There are, no doubt, other alternative approaches to the problem of defining deviancy, and efforts will probably continue within a variety of contexts, depending upon individual biases. Recently, for example, a number of behavior therapists have circumvented the problem by focusing their treatment efforts upon improving normal behavior while virtually ignoring a formal definition of the patient's abnormal behavior. (See Chapter 10.)

Despite the many problems and the vagueness of the rules of thumb, codes, standards, etc., one should not overlook the fact that they have been established. Further, in any attempt to deal with pathological behavior, one must also propose some limits in order to distinguish between pathological and normal behavior. Of course, any such distinction is arbitrary. Behaviors identified as pathological in this text include examples from a variety of frameworks; emphasis is placed upon cases where it can be demonstrated that some deviation from a norm or expected response rate occurred as a consequence of, or was modified by, an experimental treatment. Thus, in the chapters dealing with the causes of abnormal behavior, deviant conditions are sometimes defined in terms of a decrease in learning rates (for example, impaired avoidance conditioning or breakdown in discrimination learning), a departure from an observed norm (for example, a high rate of inappropriate sexual behavior), or a correspondence to a generally accepted clinical phenomenon (for example, a high rate of withdrawal from a nonthreatening stimulus or a high rate of self-punishment despite nonpunishing alternatives). Later explication of a proposed conceptual model will reveal a schema that may resolve some of the problems mentioned.

CLASSIFICATION MODELS

Every science in its infancy has taken on the task of establishing a taxonomy, or classification, since the process of abstracting similar characteristics from differing events promotes the analysis of relationships between variables. Classification schemes were established relatively early in the development of physics and chemistry, since the relationships between the physical phenomena and the variables that affected them seemed readily apparent and were supported by the evidence from experiments.

In psychology, however, there has been considerable difficulty in establishing a consensually validated classification system that would be relevant for a scientific analysis. This is probably, at least in part, due to the fact that classifications of behavior are too easily formulated. We are constantly aware of the similarities and differences in human behavior, and these observations are readily categorized. Thus, we have at our disposal a multitude of adjectives, such as shy, withdrawn, loquacious, meek, arrogant, aggressive, and outspoken, to describe personal characteristics. Such a conventional taxonomy, however, has only limited usefulness in a scientific analysis, and a great deal of time and effort has been invested in psychology, particularly in the area of personality analysis, in order to establish a more reliable classification system. This has produced the popular approach of classifying individuals according to such dimensions as introversive-extroversive, dominant-submissive, compliant-authoritarian. Frequently, these classifications are made on the basis of an individual's response to questionnaire or self-report forms, or occasionally, observer analyses. The assumptions underlying such attempts at classification are: (1) Homogeneous behaviors imply homogeneity of determinants, and (2) different classes of behavior are affected by different determinants (Patterson, 1964).

The process of abstracting similarities and differences in behavior may be conducted on several levels. Some terms, such as "assaultive," "inactive," and "socially isolated," are fairly closely tied to actual behavior; that is, they would probably reveal a reasonably high degree of reliability from observer to observer. Thus, they can usually be translated to a reliable objective measure. Other terms, such as "paranoid," "latent homosexual," and "hallucinations," seem to be somewhat further removed from the empirical observation, and their use thus increases the possibility of observer variability. Finally, there are those terms, such as "neurotic," "psychotic," "character disorder," "psychopath," "hysteric," and "schizophrenic," that actually represent theoretical categories and thus encompass a wide range of events. These terms, then, are the furthest removed from the actual behavioral observation and, as such, may be particularly prone to observer variability.

Terms at the behavioral end of the continuum reflect a phenotypic bias and thus are essentially concerned with what a person *does,* that is, behavioral description. Terms at the other end of the continuum reflect a genotypic bias and are essentially concerned with what a person *is,* that is, explanations of behavior in terms of subsurface dynamics or theoretical constructs (Stuart, 1970).

The question of which approach to use is particularly important in psychopathology, inasmuch as classification has critical implications for the individual being classified. As E. Zigler and L. Phillips (1961) point out, classification of abnormal behavior has often taken the form of diagnosis, which has direct bearing upon questions relating to etiology, treatment, and prognosis. In other words, to restate the basic assumptions underlying classification, homogeneous patterns of deviance should be the result of similar causes, and different treatment programs might be developed for different classes of pathology (Patterson, 1964).

Since most classification attempts in the area of behavior pathology have been constructed within a genotypic framework, it might be instructive to briefly review the history of such endeavors.

THE MEDICAL MODEL

From ancient to contemporary times most attempts at abstracting similarities in psychopathology, for the purpose of classification, have been based upon the disease-entity model borrowed from the medical profession. This model was initially patterned upon a taxonomic scheme that identified single symptoms or clusters of symptoms (syndromes). These symptoms were, in turn, correlated with a specific causal agent, ran a predictable course, and were modifiable or not depending upon the availability of treatment methods. Within the medical realm this model has been very useful, simplifying treatment practices and contributing to improved methods of disease control. There is some reason to believe that the model is not completely satisfactory for complex syndromes, such as multiple sclerosis, and the disease-entity model is now being replaced, at least in some quarters, by a process, or systems, approach. For the most part, however, this approach has enabled a standardized strategy for the treatment and prevention of many medical conditions. Perhaps because of its striking success and unquestioned utility with medical disease entities, this same model has also been the most popular approach to the classification of pathological behaviors. As we shall see, however, this generalization from one field to another has resulted in numerous problems.

Historically, the Greek physician Hippocrates introduced a genotypic bias when he employed the disease-entity model in the classification of pathological behavioral conditions, basing his system upon a hypothetical imbalance of the four basic "humors" manufactured in the body. Certain pathological states were assumed to be caused by an excess of certain kinds of humor. Thus, the melancholy individual suffered from an excess of black bile, the apathetic individual from an excess of phlegm, etc. Though this approach represented a significant advance over earlier primitive views, which correlated psychopathology with the work of demons, there is, of course, no evidence to support this notion. There are, however, lingering remnants of both approaches even today that are reflected in the contemporary bias of hypothesizing alleged internal events as the causes of pathological behavior.

Although the disease-entity model has a long history, it was the relatively recent contribution made by Kraepelin that most firmly entrenched the system and resulted in the standard psychiatric classification currently in use. Kraepelin's system (based almost entirely on observations of hospitalized patients) reflected the genotypic view that psychopathology is correlated with brain pathology and that syndromes of mental abnormality group themselves together with sufficient regularity to enable the practitioner to regard them as being parallel to specific disease entities, such as measles or malaria. As Emil Kraepelin said,

> *Judging from our experience in internal medicine, it is a fair assumption that similar disease processes will produce identical symptom pictures, identical pathological anatomy and an identical etiology. . . . Cases of mental disease originating in the same cause must also present the same symptoms and pathological findings. (Diefendorf, 1921)*

It was Kraepelin, then, who first classified behavioral disorders in terms of manic-depressive psychoses (disorders characterized by frequent mood changes) and dementia praecox, both of which were considered the result of organic impairment. Later, he added the concept of neurosis to his nomenclature in order to include those milder disorders considered to be largely of "psychogenic," or environmentally determined, origin. With some minor revision (for example, the substitution of the term "schizophrenia" for the term "dementia praecox") this classification system has continued to be employed up to the present time, thus coming to represent the contemporary nosology for mental disorders—the science of classifying diseases.

Let us briefly consider the manner in which this classification procedure is typically implemented (American Psychiatric Association, 1965). The present classification system divides mental disorders into three major categories: disorders caused by brain impairment (organic disorders); mental deficiency, especially if present from birth and without a demonstrable organic connection; and disorders of psychogenic (nonorganically acquired) origin. Each of these major categories is further divided into subclassifications. The last category, for example, is further divided in terms of psychotic disorders, psychosomatic disorders, psychoneurotic disorders, and personality disorders, again with further subclassifications in each of these categories. In all there are some fifty classifications in the psychogenic category alone. Each of these disorders is defined in terms of alleged specific signs or symptoms. Psychotic disorders, for example, are ostensibly characterized by some degree of personality disintegration and failure to correctly test and evaluate external reality. When such a general reaction is accompanied by shallow, inappropriate affect, unpredictable giggling, silly behavior and mannerisms, delusions, often of a somatic nature, hallucinations, and regressive behavior, the diagnosis of hebephrenic schizophrenia is formulated.

The chief characteristic of the neuroses is " 'anxiety' which may be directly felt and expressed or which may be unconsciously and automatically controlled by the utilization of defense mechanisms" (American Psychiatric Association, 1965). Neurotic disorders are considered less extreme than the psychoses in terms of reality loss and personality disintegration.

In theory, when a patient is referred for diagnosis (a practice that is in itself highly questionable, since it usually involves a subjective definition of psychopathology), a psychiatric and psychological examination is usually undertaken for the purpose of correlating specific behavioral patterns with the appropriate classification. In other words, inferences from patient *behavior* are made for the purpose of applying a theoretical (genotypic) label. An observation of patient hostility, for example, may be important largely because it contributes to the diagnosis of paranoid schizophrenia.

Such practices, of course, are common to all science. Their use in psychopathology, however, has created considerable difficulty.

Consider some of the problems involved in this process. First with regard to the disease-entity system in general, in a few isolated cases stable functional relationships have been demonstrated between anatomical or physiological causal agents and behavior pathology. Some of the best examples of this successful application of the disease-entity model have been paresis, a behavioral disorder with associated central nervous system deterioration based upon dissemination through the blood stream of the syphilitic treponema pallium, and hydrocephalis, a disorder of behavior development based upon hypersecretion of glial cells in the brain. In each of these conditions pathological behavior is associated with a known disease process.

In the vast majority of behavior disorders, however, the relationship to the medical disease model is dubious. As opposed to the two examples of organic disorders, most of the behavioral aberrations to be discussed here and by far the largest number of disorders found in the population at large fall into the class commonly called functional (or psychogenic) disorders. As N. Cameron (1944) said over twenty-five years ago,

> *All current attempts at classification of functional personality disorders are unsatisfactory; this is true for the neuroses as well as for the psychoses. No causal organisms have been implicated, hence we cannot fall back upon them as we can in the specific infectious diseases. There are no characteristic organic lesions, as there are in the systemic diseases; and the*

central nervous system exhibits no consistent changes that can be correlated with the syndromes as in neurological disorders. Physiological and biochemical studies do not support the older assumptions that fundamentally different metabolic processes underlie different forms of personality disorder. It is important for persons working in the abnormal field to realize that the current official psychiatric classifications are not based upon final and convincing scientific evidence. (pp. 870–871)

There are further logical arguments that point out the fallacies inherent in the medical disease-entity model of behavior pathology. As T. S. Szasz (1960) has said, there is a basic epistemological error in assuming a symmetrical analogy between neurological and/or physiological causal agents and the symptoms they give rise to, and antecedent stimuli and consequent responses in behavior pathology.

Another difference concerns the rather more clearly defined and generally accepted model of physical normality (an intact and functioning organism) as opposed to the model of *behavioral* normality, which, as has been indicated, may have as many variations as the number of authors who propose definitions of it.

Not all users of the Kraepelinian system, of course, subscribe to his organic bias. Many contemporary writers and practitioners continue to employ psychiatric nomenclature, but their views regarding the relative contribution of organic and psychological factors differ from Kraepelin's. When organic processes are minimized, especially as in the neuroses and the personality disorders, some form of "mental trauma" is hypothesized as the critical circumstance. Thus, the diagnosis of neurosis is usually interpreted as the end result of mental disease or illness. Such forms of mentalism have also fallen under heavy attack (Szasz, 1960) and, as we have seen earlier, are subject to serious criticisms.

In any event, regardless of which variation of the genotypic model one selects, certain sources of error are involved, and these must be recognized. As long as our subject matter is restricted to observable, measurable behavior, classification is possible, though still complex. But when unmeasurable processes or subjective states are required portions of the subject matter, the task of the taxonomist is hopeless, for who can say what variables affect them? It would seem an impossible dream to attempt a science based upon hypothetical variables (MacCorquodale & Meehl, 1948). Restricting the subject matter to behavior is a complex task in itself, since behavior requires not only a biological organism, but also an analysis of what the organism does, which may change from moment to moment.

A second difficulty with the Kraepelinian type of model is that it postulates qualitative differences between groups of patients (Stuart, 1970) as well as, implicitly if not explicitly, qualitative differences between normal and abnormal. Such a practice is incompatible with the assumption of common general principles underlying all behavioral phenomena. Practitioners of the conventional model, for example, often regard laboratory studies of abnormal behavior as having little relevancy to "genuine" abnormal behavior. Thus, examples of self-aversive stimulation in lower organisms are regarded as being qualitatively different from masochistic behavior in humans, where theory requires the acknowledgment of a superego or conscience. In its most extreme form this position holds that any attempt to impose a scientific framework on abnormal behaviors violates the cardinal principle that such phenomena can only be understood *in situ*. Otherwise, their essential characteristics are destroyed. If this criterion had been imposed upon medical research, most of mankind's medical cures would never have been discovered.

This position stems from a misunderstanding of the scientific method and has contributed to the schism between the experimental psychopathologist and the practitioner. Any attempt to understand natural phenomena within an experimental framework must necessarily introduce "artificial" controls. Appreciation of the importance of such practices, however, would enable the practitioner to suggest areas in which a closer approximation of relevant clinical circumstances could be achieved.

In addition to these considerations, throughout its long history the attempt to establish the reliability and validity of the conventional diagnostic system has been singularly unsuccessful (Zigler & Phillips, 1961). Finally, recent criticism has focused upon the manner in which conventional diagnosis may actually contribute to patient problems, rather than provide useful information (Rotter, 1960; Menninger, 1963; Sarbin, 1967; Stuart, 1970). The substance of these arguments is reflected in the following statement:

> [*The*] *mere assignment of a diagnostic label to a patient may prejudice his therapeutic experience and/or the course of the response which he receives from the social community. If the labels were shown to have high reliability and validity, exposure to this "secondary deviance" (deviance imposed by social institutions and of which the patient is essentially innocent) might be warranted. But dispositional diagnostic labels do not have this scientific character.* (*Stuart, 1970, p. 116*)

In the light of these considerations, despite its unquestioned popularity, the medical model for classifying behavior disorders appears to have little to recommend its further use. For these reasons we have chosen to abandon the conventional textbook method of using the terms employed in psychopathology. The reader will find little or no use of such terms as "neurotic," "psychopathic," and "schizophrenic." An alternative classification system is offered later in the chapter.

THE STATISTICAL MODEL

One alternative to the medical model in the search for a more refined schema is the statistical model. This approach usually involves the analysis of responses on a test, some particular behavioral variable, or behavioral observations. The extent of deviation from standardized norms characterizes the degree of pathology (McQuitty, 1954). One variation of this approach involves the technique of factor analysis, in which particular "factors" are isolated for the purpose of identifying core behavioral characteristics. For example, D. C. Piercy and J. E. Overall (1968) obtained clinician ratings of patients based upon a psychiatric rating scale and isolated four major classes of behavior disorders: thinking disturbance, psychomotor activation, direction of aggression, and mood. Ostensibly, if such dimensions are adequate and extensive enough, all patients can be classified in a similar manner, thus providing a classification based upon each individual's particular pattern of deviancy on these factors. H. J. Eysenck (1961c) has written a skillful argument in defense of the statistical model, and his own efforts have inspired the collection of a large body of data.

G. R. Patterson (1964) has applied a similar approach to the classification of childhood disorders. "The procedure involved three steps: collection of referral and observation data in the clinic setting, factor analysis of this matrix, and analysis of factor profiles to determine homogeneous classes" (p. 337). Although these efforts were not completed at the time of reporting, five factors were identified as potential major categories of disordered behavior within which all of the observations could be subsumed: hyperactive, withdrawn, immature, aggressive, and anxious. These dimensions were then used to construct a profile, which suggested certain homogeneous groups of childhood disorders.

Although this model at least offers the possibility of objective measurement and dimensional analysis (which may be of great heuristic value), it also involves several difficulties. For one, social norms are implicit in the model, and many would question whether social conformity is the best criterion of normality. Second, many of the statistical techniques rely upon correlational analyses in the establishing of pathological regularities. Thus, regardless of the reliability and validity of the concepts, this model provides, at best, only limited knowledge of any relevant independent variables. Finally, as Buss (1966) has mentioned, the statistical model involves the additional problem of advancing criteria for the *direction* of deviation on any pathological dimension. On a measure of intelligence, for example, if an IQ of 100 is "normal," are both extremely high and extremely low scores considered abnormal? Creativity, productivity, and rates of many responses may present similar problems. Thus, when this classification model is advanced, the question of establishing points beyond which behavior is regarded as pathological must also be considered.

A Behavioral Classification System: The Frequency Model

Perhaps because of the growing disenchantment with conventional classification, a number of writers (Ferster, 1965; Staats & Staats, 1963; Bandura, 1969; Kanfer & Saslow, 1969) have proposed a third alternative for classifying behavior disorders, which may be termed the frequency model. Essentially, this approach focuses upon the

> *attempt to identify classes of dependent variables in human behavior which would allow inferences about the contemporary controlling factors, the social stimuli, the physiological stimuli, and the reinforcing stimuli of which they are a function. In the present early stage of the art of psychological prognostication, it appears most reasonable to develop a program of analysis which is closely related to subsequent treatment. A classification which implies a program for behavioral change is the only one which has not only utility but the potential for experimental verification.* (Kanfer & Saslow, 1969, p. 419)

In this fashion the identification of similar causes (independent variables) underlying homogeneous patterns of deviance and the relating of different treatment programs to different classes of behavior pathology can be experimentally validated.

Essentially, such a strategy classifies pathological behavior in terms of behavioral excesses (inappropriate behavior) or behavioral deficits, *as these excesses or deficits deviate from the reinforcing practices of the community.* Simply stated, the two major classes of deviancy are defined by: (1) the presence of behavior that the community regards as undesirable and (2) the absence of behavior that the community regards as desirable. There is, of course, a close correspondence between this model and the maladaptive criterion examined earlier. There are, however, two important differences. First, the conventional definition *implies* some deviance from community standards. The behavioral model *explicates* this condition and, as we shall see, offers a method that enables its empirical determination. Second, in the conventional model the maladaptive criterion serves merely as a starting point from which hypothesized internal variables are inferred (thus, hostility is an expression of tension reduction, or delusions are equated with schizophrenia), and treatment is directed to the resolution of the inferred internal state. In the behavioral model classes of deviance are interpreted in terms of potentially verifiable antecedent conditions (that is, the causes of psychopathology) and testable treatment techniques. Thus, both models would characterize a pilot's fear of flying as abnormal behavior, since such a deficit would impair gainful employment, a practice that is reinforced by the individual's community. Similarly, community standards would define bed-wetting in a teen-ager as inappropriate behavior. On the other hand, long hair, jeans, and sandals might be appropriate (reinforced) in a hippie commune, but would be frowned upon in a Wall Street office. In the context of the frequency model, however, this criterion could be objectively defined through an analysis of each community's practices, and the focus would be upon the isolation of variables influencing the behavior.

For the most part, since community standards are usually reasonably well defined, a *general* classification system can also be constructed. Thus, such terms as "depression," "autism," "catatonia," "phobias," and "sexual impotence" all encompass conditions characterized by the absence or reduced rate of behaviors generally regarded as desirable. Any or all of these terms can be further dimensionalized as appropriate for any one individual. The term "withdrawal," for example, may be objectively defined as a reduced or zero rate of facial expression, hand shake, head nodding, verbal behavior, etc. S. W. Bijou (1963) has similarly redefined the "mentally retarded" individual in terms of a limited repertoire of behavior, and the task of behavioral research is to investigate the observable or potentially observable conditions that may produce retarded behavior, not retarded mentality.

Other conditions, such as hyperactivity, compulsions, rituals, self-abuse, and crying, may be considered excessive behaviors in terms of either (1) their frequency, (2) their intensity, (3) their duration, or (4) their occurrence in situations where their socially sanctioned frequency approaches zero (Kanfer & Saslow, 1969). For example, *any* display of hallucinations might constitute a pathological condition, since this form of behavior is virtually never reinforced in our culture, whereas fastidiousness may be acceptable under certain conditions until it becomes compulsive, that is, occurs with excessively high frequency.

Again, any term denoting excess can be analyzed in terms of its relevancy for any one individual. Thus, the impulsive person may be objectively defined in terms of a high rate of credit-charging behavior or a high rate of aggressive motor behavior. Furthermore, since many forms of pathological behavior have a verbal dimension, they can be similarly analyzed. For example, stuttering may be considered as an excess of dysfluencies. Obsessions, psychosomatic complaints, etc., also represent an abnormally high rate of certain forms of pathological verbal behavior.

There is, of course, no hard-and-fast distinction between the classes of deviancy. A high rate of alcoholic behavior, for example, will often be accompanied by deficits of a social, vocational, and sexual nature. In such instances, the major classification is made on the basis of the behavioral dimension that is most relevant to treatment.

It may be obvious, at this point, that the frequency model for classifying pathological behavior is congruent with a learning-theory approach. Thus, in general, deficits represent those circumstances in which treatment is designed to *increase* the frequency of responses that are not present to a sufficient degree in the individual's behavior repertoire, whereas behavioral excesses represent a category of pathological behavior in which treatment is designed to reduce or *decrease* the frequency of the target behavior. Furthermore, learning theory may offer the means by which causal circumstances may be inferred. Finally, the frequency model is congruent with the ultimate goal of treatment: returning the patient to his own environment. The model explicitly acknowledges the criterion of reinforcing practices in the community and enables an objective analysis of what these reinforcing practices are.

Goldfried and D'Zurilla (1969), for example, provide an excellent demonstration of the use of a behavioral model for the purpose of identifying community standards relative to competency in a college population. Thus, significant people in the college environment (students, teachers, etc.) defined a large, representative sample of concrete problem conditions that are usually encountered by college freshmen during their first quarter. Competency was defined by the individual student's ability to adjust to these experiences.

Although we shall discuss these issues at some length in subsequent chapters, let us briefly consider the manner in which the principles may be implemented by referring to two examples from the authors' clinical experiences. Both of these instances involved two children who were diagnosed as autistic, with the predominant characteristic being a complete lack of speech. Quite obviously, both children revealed serious deficits in terms of verbal communication, which would suggest similar etiological circumstances. Treatment, then, might emphasize some form of speech training. Extensive interviews with the parents and other informed individuals, however, revealed quite different developmental backgrounds. In one case the child had vocalized at an early age and only later became completely mute. The father indicated that the child's failure to continue vocalizing occurred after he had beaten the child on several occasions for imitating noises at the father's place of business. On the other hand, the second child showing the same topography or deficit had apparently received a great deal of attention from a housekeeper for nonverbal forms of communication, such as gestures and grunts, during early stages of language development and never acquired any form of normal speech pattern.

This method of analysis, then, provided us with clues that seemed to be relevant to the etiology of these pathological conditions, as well as information that enabled the formulation of an effective treatment program. If the frequency model for classifying disordered behavior can be employed by others in a similar fashion, its value in clinical practice will be established.

Relation of the Frequency
Model to Experimental Methodology

The use of the frequency model in classifying behavior pathology also enables the experimentally oriented clinician to apply a rigorous method for analyzing the variables that influence the patient's behavior as well as for analyzing the effectiveness of his clinical procedure: That method is the single-organism functional analysis described in Chapter 1. This is a logical consequence of the use of the frequency classification model, since the core of the method involves testing independent variables against the base rate of occurrence of the behavior in question. In the clinician's terms measurement of the base rate (that is, the frequency of response occurrence under natural conditions) is the first step in any functional analysis and may be regarded as the diagnostic evaluation. (For example, how often does the negativistic child comply with requests? How often does the phobic individual engage in the feared activity?) Thus, a reliable measurement of the frequency of occurrence of the significant behaviors in a patient's repertoire would provide a descriptive, dynamic, and useful assessment.

Once the appraisal of the pertinent base rates has been made, the clinician can select the behavior or behaviors that represent the most critical problems and focus upon these in treatment. Thus, each patient may serve as a "subject" in an experiment. The clinician must make a judgment as to the independent variables that are most relevant to the modification of the behavior in question. The independent variables represent treatment; that is, they are the factors responsible for any behavior modification that is produced. In selecting the treatment variable or variables, the clinician should depend upon prior experimental work, so that he can employ variables that have proved effective in modifying the same or similar behaviors in the past.

Once the independent variable has been programmed and a reliable change in the behavior observed, the clinician's immediate goals in terms of a constructive change in the patient's behavior have been satisfied. In order to meet the goals of the scientist, however, several additional steps would be necessary to complete an acceptable research design and to provide evidence regarding the effectiveness of his procedures. The primary requirement is to demonstrate that the obtained modification was not due to concomitant variation of any other variables. This requirement may be met in several ways. For example, a standard group design could be employed in which a group of patients with similar problems or target behaviors could be treated with the same independent variable and compared to an untreated control group. In this fashion the rate of "spontaneous change" in behavior can be evaluated. Such statistical designs have some utility when base rates cannot be sufficiently controlled, but their main flaw (at least from the clinician's point of view) is that they do not allow focusing upon individual cases. These designs also require more subjects per group in inverse relation to the magnitude of the behavioral change produced by the independent variable.

A slightly more powerful design (technically a concurrent, or multiple base-line, design) might compare the effect of the same independent variable over several different dependent variables. If several different behaviors within the individual are selected, this would allow the clinician to continue to focus upon a single case. Thus, for example, several different dimensions of a child's hyperactivity may each be treated by the same variable. To the extent that all the behaviors are similarly modified, the effect may be attributed to the independent variable with increased reliability.

As stated earlier, the functional design using reversals is perhaps the most elegant available. In this procedure the independent variable is introduced, then removed and introduced again. To the extent that the rate of the dependent variable (problem behavior) returns to base rate following each such removal, the effects are said to be reversible.

If the second introduction of the independent variable achieves the same effect as the first, and the second removal is again followed by a return to base rate, then the presentation of the independent variable has been systematically demonstrated to be sufficient to produce the behavioral change in question.

One great advantage of the single-subject base-line design is that changes in continuously recorded base rates are the criteria of successful modification or treatment. Conversely, when changes in the response rate are not observed, the experimental clinician can immediately revise his efforts to find an effective independent (treatment) variable. The analysis is thus self-corrective.

One disadvantage, however, involves an ethical dilemma: Once a constructive change in the patient's behavior has occurred, is the clinician justified in returning the patient to his "former state" in the interests of science? This conflict can be resolved by introducing the appropriate variable contingent upon other behaviors via the multiple base-line design. For example, several different measures of hyperactivity in a child can be sequentially treated. This design may also resolve the dilemma presented by irreversibility (a treatment effect that persists).

Finally, an assessment must be made of the degree to which constructive changes in the patient's behavior under treatment conditions will generalize to his natural environment. This can be facilitated through the explicit use of variables that will enhance such an effect (Schaefer & Martin, 1969).

One example of the manner in which the proposed model may be implemented is provided by a patient who refused to join the ward group in eating his meals in the cafeteria. The patient was diagnosed as a paranoid schizophrenic, and his behavior was characterized by social withdrawal, suspicion, hostility, and self-imposed isolation in his own room. Attempts to change the patient's behavior (largely through coaxing on the part of the nursing staff) were virtually unsuccessful.

In conjunction with a general behavior modification program, the nursing staff was requested to observe the frequencies with which the patient engaged in certain behaviors. For example, over a twelve-day period the patient initiated no social contacts (except when necessary to secure his medication), rarely emerged from his room, and ate no meals with the rest of the ward. Apparently he survived on stolen bits of food.

The next step was to decide upon a procedure that would result in constructive changes in behavior. Thus, access to his room was selected as a potential reinforcer to be made contingent upon eating with the ward group in the dining room. Gradually increasing requirements were programmed, and regular attendance and eating of meals in the dining room was the projected treatment goal. Accordingly, the patient was informed that he would have to approach the dining room at mealtime before being allowed back into his bedroom. When the patient failed to comply with these requirements and prematurely returned to his room, he found the door locked. After several such incidents, he eventually approached the meal line, after which he was immediately allowed to reenter his room. In succeeding steps the patient was required to increasingly engage in those responses involved in appropriate dining behaviors. This procedure, termed shaping behavior by successive approximations to the final form, was developed in the laboratory with animals (Skinner, 1953). The analysis of the patient's ongoing behavioral repertoire and the use of a high-frequency behavior (staying in his room) to reinforce behaviors occurring at low or zero frequency are associated with D. Premack (1959).

At the end of two weeks the patient was regularly going to the dining room, eating full meals, and occasionally engaging in social interaction with other patients. The latter behavior was not directly modified, but occurred as a by-product of shaping meal attendance and eating. The treatment of this case is, of course, in marked contrast to the standard treatment. The fact that this patient carried a psychiatric diagnosis of schizophrenia may well have produced efforts by the staff to modify his "paranoid ideation" or his "delusions of persecution," which may have led him to believe people were "out to get him" and to take preventative measures, such as staying in his room.

This case is presented as an example of the application of the frequency model and functional analysis of pathological behavior. It required technical, but not necessarily methodological, sophistication.

SPECULATION AND THE CLINICAL POINT OF VIEW

Now that the frequency and functional-analysis models of behavior pathology have been elaborated, a logical consequence is the consideration of the speculative use of these models. In the sections and chapters to come, there will be a number of areas in which all the rigorous criteria of an elegant experiment are simply lacking. In many of these cases the authors may speculate, as clinicians and philosophers are wont to do, regarding the function of particular variables in the naturalistic environment. Sometimes the speculation may involve little more than extrapolation or generalization from one response system to another. On the other hand, there will be occasions calling for comment regarding combinations of variables that have never been put to experimental tests. In either case there will be some attempt to state clearly how much speculation and how much empirically supported generalization is involved.

Perhaps it should also be reiterated that this book is primarily empirically oriented, and analysis will usually be restricted to those areas characterized by experimental support. However, since data collection from such a systematic viewpoint is relatively new to clinical psychology, there will obviously be vacant areas that have not yet acquiesced to experimental control. Some of these areas include displacement of pathological behaviors by reinforcement of normal responses, complex combinations of reinforcing and punishment contingencies, and schedules designed to lead to stimulus and response generalization in the natural environment.

PART TWO / ETIOLOGY
A. Theoretical Models
B. Experimental Methods and Data

In this section the major systems that have had an important impact on the experimental analysis of psychopathology are presented. In order to provide an organized perspective, the relevant systems are divided into two categories: the intrapsychic approach (as represented by psychoanalysis) and the behavioral approach. The latter is further subdivided into classical conditioning theory, operant conditioning theory, and several models that involve general behavior theory principles.

These divisions are arbitrary in the sense that there are varying degrees of correspondence, as well as shades and nuances of differences, between the systems. On some dimensions the differences within behavioral models are greater than the differences between behavioral theory and intrapsychic theory. For example, most of the theories, intrapsychic as well as behavioral, involve the concept of conflict, in the sense that competing experiences and/or competing response systems are regarded as fundamental determinants in the etiology of behavioral irregularities or anomalies. This is less nearly true, however, in the case of those operant investigators who have analyzed pathological processes as extensions of "normal" processes, rather than in the context of behavioral irregularities. Thus, the behavior produced in these latter arrangements does not represent a "departure from the norm" but is rather a systematic extension of the variables involved.

The various systems also differ, both within and between

themselves, in the range and nature of events studied. Early theorists such as S. Freud and I. P. Pavlov attempted to analyze relatively broad dimensions of pathological behavior. Recent approaches are more restricted in their focus, which, especially in the case of operant investigators, often reflects an inductive bias. Also, Freud's observations of pathological phenomena were made under clinical conditions. Pavlov initiated the tradition of observing experimental analogs of pathological behavior. Thus, a distinction between intrapsychic and behavioral models may be made on these grounds, except that contemporary classical and operant conditioners have also applied their principles to clinical events.

One popular distinction is frequently made on the basis of research generated. Thus, the intrapsychic model is considered to fall at one end of the continuum, and all of the behavioral systems are thought to occupy varying positions at the other end of the spectrum. However, some behavioral theories are also attempts at analyzing Freudian concepts, especially those of the J. Dollard and N. E. Miller school.

Let us bear in mind, then, that as we explore the various positions, hard-and-fast distinctions blur the congruences and areas of overlap. The discussions of the behavioral models are divided into two segments. In the first segment the various theories are presented. In the second, the research findings that are relevant to the different theoretical models are presented.

A / THEORETICAL MODELS
Chapter 3 / Intrapsychic and Behavioral Models

THE INTRAPSYCHIC MODEL: PSYCHOANALYSIS

It may appear paradoxical to initiate a review of the experimental psychopathology literature with a discourse on psychoanalysis. The two approaches have often been cast in polarized terms, as being based upon different assumptions and promoting different practices.

Although this is, in part, a valid assessment, it ignores the important congruences that also exist. Both orientations share a common deterministic foundation, and much of the experimental psychopathology literature has been strongly influenced, implicitly if not explicitly, by psychoanalysis.

Nevertheless, there are difficulties in analyzing psychoanalytic theory within a scientific framework. In Freud's writings, for example, it is difficult to separate the descriptive content of a concept or expression from its "dynamic" meaning. But perhaps the greatest obstacle in the path of such an endeavor is the paucity of rigorously formulated statements that are amenable to experimental inquiry. Despite the fact that the cornerstone of the Freudian position is the alleged relationship between real or imagined infantile sexual trauma, on the one hand, and adult neuroses, on the other, one is hard put to find explicit statements that may be put to the test.

Fortunately, many writers have attempted to elaborate analytic theory for the purpose of formulating cause-and-effect relationships. There are still others who have attempted to provide an experimental foundation for Freudian theory. Where possible, we have isolated those theoretical statements that are most directly relevant to such an analysis. Occasionally, some violence to the extensive use of metaphor in the Freudian literature has necessarily resulted.

PATHOLOGICAL BEHAVIOR

The Causes of Neurosis

Aside from his profound influence on personality theory, in general, Freud also had a powerful effect on the study of psychopathology. Certainly, he contributed a massive inferential architecture intended to house and explain abnormal as well as normal behavior. The house Freud designed, however, suffered from a number of serious gaps and weaknesses in its theoretical architecture.

In formulating his theory, Freud began with a secure foundation of determinism which emphasized personality development as a function of the interaction between biological processes and the environment. This transaction was alleged to be fraught with difficulty for the developing child. Thus, according to the Freudian model, the infant is primarily concerned with the immediate gratification of libidinal urges. Any disruption or irregularity in this process could result in psychopathology. Of particular importance were the events subsumed under the concept of the Oedipus complex. Here, forbidden impulses or drives were believed to enter most directly into conflict with social prohibitions, thereby creating conditions that resulted in anxiety—that is, a fear of the punishment (loss of the object that provides sexual gratification) that might occur as a result of libidinal expression. According to Freud, attempts are then made to reduce this anxiety by various defense mechanisms (fundamentally repression), which distort reality by denying the urges and relegating them to the unconscious. When repression fails in this endeavor, the libido seeks gratification in neurotic symptom formation.

Thus, the general outline of a cause-and-effect relationship between antecedent conditions and psychopathology was formulated. The varying forms of neuroses are allegedly determined by the character and intensity of the trauma-inducing experiences, and the stage of psychosexual development at which they occur. The symptoms that result (that is, the neurotic behavior) were regarded as substitutes for more socially desirable sources of gratification.

This application of determinism to aspects of human behavior that had previously been ignored underscored Freud's great contribution to psychology. Unfortunately, from the standpoint of scientific analysis, Freud's system for explaining the relationships was cloaked in mentalism. The events that resulted in neurotic behavior were regarded as products of the individual's fantasy life and were thought to operate at the unconscious level (Pumpian-Mindlen, 1952). Psychopathology, as Freud viewed it, was a function of unconscious processes that defended against anxiety created by emotional conflict. (This view is reflected in the popular approach that equates abnormal behavior with an emotional disturbance, or an "emotional block." Anything from thumb-sucking and bed-wetting to alcoholism and schizophrenia are regarded as "emotional illnesses," the roots of which are to be found in childhood conflict.) Furthermore, it was the presumed psychic apparatus mediating these processes that occupied Freud's attention, rather than the *objective* referents of the relationship between trauma and neurosis (E. Jones, 1953). Thus, he proposed that antecedent conditions were followed by effects upon the psyche, with its divisions of personality structures and mental spheres, and that the psyche served as an intervening agent in influencing subsequent behavior. Antecedent events, then, did not directly influence behavior, but were always followed by various effects upon the psyche (the mental apparatus, including ideas, feelings, complexes, cathexes, and the oft-reified trilogy: the id, the ego, and the superego), which mediated the relationship between important experiences in childhood and their end product—neurotic behavior. In other words, the mental apparatus was the intervening agent that was largely responsible for the manifestation of inappropriate behavior or the inhibition of appropriate behavior.

It was in this manner that Freud explained the "gaps" between the relevant childhood events and the neurotic behavior he encountered in his adult patients.

There is much that has been omitted in this account; however, even this brief review serves to underscore the many topics in experimental psychopathology that have been influenced by psychoanalysis. Before considering this issue, let us briefly summarize the status of Freudian theory as a scientific enterprise.

The dialogue between Freudian advocates and antagonists is a long and wordy one (Ellis, 1950). In terms of sheer number the balance is in favor of the critics. There are those who maintain that psychoanalysis cannot be assessed by conventional scientific procedures (Pumpian-Mindlen, 1952) and that this is one of its virtues. There are others, however (including many prominent psychoanalysts), who take an alternative point of view (Lehrman, 1960), and at least within a behavioral context, the argument is in favor of those approaches that are amenable to a functional scientific analysis. To the objection that such a pursuit runs the risk of violating Freudian concepts, the answer is that it is a risk worth taking if psychoanalysis is not to be ruled out of the mainstream of contemporary behavioral science.

The difficulties involved in the use of mentalistic explanatory devices have been described and require no further elaboration. Suffice it to say that, in the case of psychoanalysis, such a strategy leaves unresolved the question of how such covert entities as the psyche and unconscious processes such as repression are to be observed or manipulated. To further complicate matters, the resort to psychic explanatory constructs became an end in itself, and the individual's behavior was frequently relegated to a minor role, or impossibly concealed within inferences regarding the mental apparatus. As the system was elaborated, the disparity between Freud's conceptual framework and objective events increased, creating further problems for systematists. Hence the endless arguments over such terms as "drive," "instinct," and "anxiety."

Finally, despite the alleged relationship between childhood trauma and adult neurosis, "Freudian theory is markedly deficient in providing a set of relations; rules by which one can arrive at any precise expectations of what will happen if certain events take place" (Hall & Lindzey, 1957, p. 71). Thus, it is impossible to generate testable predictions about the relationships and to apply the criterion of quantitative proofs characteristic of other sciences (Skinner, 1959).

Despite these serious drawbacks, Freud's many contributions to the study of human behavior and psychopathology are also apparent. G. A. Kimble (1961) summarizes the relationship between psychoanalysis and learning theory in the following fashion: The most general similarity is the commonly shared assumption that behavior is determined in part by the events in an organism's past. Hence the congruence between the psychoanalytic emphasis upon early experiences and the continuing experimental effort to isolate historical cause-and-effect relationships.

There are numerous other more restricted comparisons: Freud's approach to motivation and adjustment is related to the concept of homeostasis; the pleasure principle paraphrases the law of effect; some of Freud's views regarding personality development can be translated into learning theory; psychodynamic processes (friction between the id and the superego) resemble many of the features encompassed by various conflict models; the concept of anxiety is central to both psychoanalysis and a number of learning theories; some of the basic phenomena of learning (stimulus generalization, secondary reinforcement) are represented, at least approximately, in psychoanalytic thought (Kimble, 1961).

To these particulars, one might add the relationship between psychoanalytic concepts and the social-learning model, the frustration-aggression model, and the trauma-punishment model.

Finally, there is no doubt that Freudian principles heavily influenced several generations of Western thought regarding the effects of certain child-rearing practices on emotional disturbance. Furthermore, many of these issues continue to be of contemporary importance. In a general sense, then, much of the material in the following sections is related, if sometimes distantly, to psychoanalytic propositions.

In recognition of the putative value of the Freudian system, there has been a continuing interest in applying objective analysis to the kinds of events that Freud was interested in. This has generally taken two forms. Investigators, particularly social scientists, have attempted to examine the universality of Freudian concepts. Is there, for example, a prototypical psychosexual development as specified by Freud? Here the evidence has been largely contradictory (Orlansky, 1949; Sears, 1951; Caldwell, 1964). Other investigators have attempted to analyze the alleged relationships between antecedent events (the independent variables) and consequent pathological effects as specified by Freud. Here again, several difficulties are encountered. In general, advocates of the Freudian approach have been more interested in justifying psychoanalytic theory than in testing it. Furthermore, there is an overabundance of case study material and retrospective analyses, with their attendant limitations, and only a few genuine experiments. Also, as we have seen, Freud's excessive use of metaphor makes translation into empirical statements difficult and arbitrary. Nevertheless, there are a number of critical propositions that may be regarded as testable hypotheses. In view of our previously stated biases, we will restrict our attention to the experimental demonstration of such statements.

The relevant psychoanalytic principles can be organized along two dimensions. There are the relatively circumscribed statements regarding the etiology of various pathological conditions, and there is the more general issue of defense mechanisms. Each of these will be independently analyzed, for convenience purposes.

With regard to the causes of psychopathology, let us examine the following representative statements as examples of testable hypotheses, in the sense that a relationship between independent and dependent variables is specified, and consider the supporting evidence.

Perhaps the most important general propositions may be stated in this fashion: Maladaptive effects arise as a consequence of the prevention of the various forms of sexual gratification (Freud, 1930, p. 47). Or, again, if powerful inhibitors are present during the establishment of object choice, sexual inhibitions will arise, resulting in neurosis (Fenichel, 1934). Thus, the strong suppression of affection by the cross-sex parent could create an inhibition of reactiveness to the opposite sex in general, and under the heightened genital excitation of puberty, the person would seek the same sex members as sexual partners to avoid the anxiety induced by sexual impulses toward opposite sex members (Sears, 1951, p. 47).

Maladaptive effects may also occur as a consequence of premature genital experiences that are manifested before social controls can be introjected, resulting in perversion and neurosis in which the individual continues to seek further inappropriate sexual gratification (Freud, 1930, pp. 94–98).

Finally, pathology may also be the result of restricted exposure to the same sex parent during childhood, thus leading to inadequate sexual identification and homosexuality (Freud, 1930, p. 86).

Unfortunately, there has been virtually no attempt to refine these statements into a testable format for the purpose of providing empirical support. The one major exception is in the area of child-rearing practices. Considerable effort has been expended for the purpose of explicating the alleged relationships between certain childhood experiences and their effect on abnormal behavior. For example, Freud argued that all children displayed an inborn need to suck and the manner in which this oral drive is satisfied is an important determinant of personality characteristics. When oral gratification is thwarted, as in the case of arbitrary scheduling of bottle feeding, as opposed to child-regulated breast feeding, the child will develop an "oral pessimistic" character manifested by anxiety, insecurity, aggressiveness, and impatience. (From here it was a relatively simple matter to infer that the presence of such behavior in the adult was caused by the alleged experiences, thus providing "proof" for the theory. Thumb-sucking is still popularly regarded as a sympton of oral deprivation.)

Similar statements were formulated, both by Freud and by his followers, with regard to the relationship between harsh elimination training practices, and the so-called anal traits of obstinacy, orderliness, and parsimony.

Of the many such references in the literature (Caldwell, 1964), however, only a handful represent experimental attempts to test these hypotheses. The remainder (which report largely negative findings) display the many methodological flaws usually attendant to retrospective analyses (Caldwell, 1964).

Let us briefly consider the several experimental analyses of these propositions. Perhaps the earliest of these was D. Levy's study (1934), in which puppies separated from their mothers and fed by means of an eyedropper were found to chew and suck at each other's bodies between meals more than nondeprived puppies did. S. Ross (1951) similarly found that bottle- and dropper-fed puppies revealed a higher incidence of nonnutritive sucking than puppies nursed by their mother did. On the other hand, A. Davis *et al.* (1948), in studying a similar relationship in human infants, observed that such effects occurred after the infants acquired a well-articulated sucking response. In other words, only *after* infants had received oral gratification for sucking *and the oral gratification was withdrawn* was there evidence of maladaptive behavior.

Evidence from other quarters provides still additional cause for questioning the psychoanalytic argument. H. W. Bridger and B. Birns (1968) showed that sucking in neonates is influenced by arousal level, and L. P. Lippsett *et al.* (1966) conditioned the sucking response in neonates, all of which casts doubt on the "inborn need for gratification" hypothesis. In any event, no further *direct* evidence of an experimental nature in support of any of the above hypotheses appears in the literature. In this regard, the Freudian argument remains unverified, and the issue of disrupted sexual development as the fundamental cause of adult neuroses is still moot, despite the popular support for such a position.

One may, of course, refer to indirect attempts at experimental validation formulated within the context of alternative theories. For example, let us compare the Freudian position with social-learning theory in analyzing certain parent-child relationships that both systems regard as critical determinants of psychopathology. For purposes of comparison some revision of terminology is required.

Let us assume that Freud's argument regarding the importance of the "depriving" parent represents a close parallel to A. Bandura and R. H. Walter's (1962) concept of the rejecting parent. As we have seen, Freud maintained that children who are "rejected" at certain stages of development will develop pathological reactions. Bandura and Walters agree, in principle, but their analysis suggests that such transactions are far more complex than is implied by Freud's argument. Thus, these authors argue that virtually no child is completely deprived or completely rejected, nor is there (probably) any child who hasn't experienced some form of deprivation. In the vast majority of instances, children are exposed to some combination of rewarding and depriving experiences. Thus, the effects of rejection will depend upon the extent to which one of these types of parental responses predominates (Bandura and Walters, 1962).

Furthermore, when a child is prevented from achieving adequate sexual gratification, the effects of *this* experience "are inevitably modified by the effects of the rewards that are dispensed from time to time, particularly during the child's early years, in almost every family situation" (Bandura and Walters, 1962). What is important, here, is that an alternative theoretical position provides us with an opportunity to explore the range of potential variables that are relevant to the "rejection-deprivation" experience, that is, combinations of rewarding and punishing experiences. When these potential variables are considered, as we shall see, it becomes apparent that the effects of such parent-child interactions on pathological behavior depend upon a host of factors that Freud never considered.

In a similar vein, Freud's concept of identification may be analyzed within the framework of social-learning theory; his concept of infantile trauma may be considered as an extension of punishment theory, etc. These alternatives are considered more fully in subsequent sections, where we shall again see that, when Freud's arguments are evaluated in this manner, the evidence is even more damaging than is the lack of data in support of his statements (Green, 1967).

Suffice it to say that the relationship between early psychosexual trauma and subsequent pathological behavior is far more complex than Freud recognized, and the question of disrupted sexual drives as a fundamental determinant of deviant behavior remains unsupported.

It is difficult to understand why proponents of psychoanalysis have ignored repeated appeals to provide experimental support for their position (Orlansky, 1949; Sears, 1943; Ellis, 1950). Experimental analysis of many psychoanalytic propositions, although difficult, is well within the limits of our scientific capabilities, and it is becoming increasingly apparent that the neglect of this responsibility is resulting in the replacement of the psychoanalytic theory of the neuroses by those approaches that are based upon a scientific foundation.

The Defense Mechanisms
in Relation to Behavioral Pathology

A second contribution that psychoanalysis has made to the study of psychopathology is encompassed by the theory of defense mechanisms. Although the concept has attracted widespread attention and elaboration beyond the Freudian system, we will restrict our focus to those processes and statements that are critical to psychoanalysis and/or have been experimentally attacked.

The importance of defense mechanisms for students of pathological behavior rests on Freud's recognition of the "adaptive" nature of human behavior in the face of traumatic circumstances. As we have seen, Freudian theory regards neurotic behavior as adaptive mechanisms that are evidence of repression—the visible upshot of unconscious causes (Munroe, 1955). The concept implies the expression of various attempts to reduce the threat of punishment aroused by forbidden impulses. Under such conditions, for example, an individual may deny or distort the impulse; he may resort to immature modes of obtaining gratification; he may attribute his own impulses to others; or he may attempt to satisfy his impulses in indirect ways. In the Freudian system all of these modes of responding are regarded as unconscious attempts to escape from the anxiety experienced by the more direct expression of the forbidden impulses.

The concept of defense mechanisms serves to underscore the fundamental dilemma in the psychoanalytic system. On the one hand, Freud's description of such dynamic processes has a powerful, dramatic appeal to the student of human behavior. It seems almost self-evident that individuals often attempt to deal with threatening events in a circumlocutious fashion (for example, by denying the "truth" about themselves). Although such attempts may represent forms of escape and avoidance behavior, Freud's explanatory system does not enable the conventional scientific tests of proof and disproof. Thus, some translation into an objective framework is required, at which point, however, the concepts lose their definitive character (Sears, 1944, p. 306).

All of the various mechanisms suffer from this limitation (some perhaps more than others) and, in this sense, defy empirical formulation. Consequently, there are no direct experimental efforts that shed light on the "dynamic" (unconscious conflict) nature of the defense mechanisms. The studies we will refer to, which have frequently been regarded as tests of the defensive processes, actually represent attempts to verify the *objective* components of the defensive processes and are more appropriately considered in the context of the behavioral models presented in subsequent chapters.

According to Freud, the fundamental defense mechanism is

repression, that is, the process by which forbidden impulses and their attendant memories and ideas are denied and relegated to the unconscious. In this fashion Freud explained his patients' inability to recall and express traumatic experiences and impulses. In the ensuing fifty years since Freud first formulated his theory of repression, there have been over two hundred studies designed to provide an experimental foundation for the concept. Unfortunately, little sound experimental knowledge has been advanced in this endeavor. As indicated, part of the reason for this sad state of affairs rests on the fact that the principle, as stated by Freud, is difficult to translate into objective terms. Sears (1944), for example, suggests that Freud's concept of the unpleasant, itself, refers to ideas or experiences associated with the threat of loss of love, a highly individual matter, and not to events regarded as unpleasant by conventional standards. For example, trauma in the Freudian system is defined as a fantasized threat to libidinal gratification. Trauma in the experimental literature is most often operationally defined as an electric shock—an unconditioned aversive event. The former may appear to be more "relevant" in terms of analyzing human behavior, but the latter represents an event amenable to empirical analysis. Furthermore, in the Freudian literature there is no attempt to define repression independent of the repression process itself.

When it is assessed in this manner, the concept cannot be verified. There is some evidence suggesting that rewarded experiences are remembered more accurately than unpleasant experiences, but this research makes only tangential contact with the Freudian concept, and even here the evidence is contradictory. We must conclude, then, that the repression principle remains unsupported by conventional scientific standards.

If, however, the repression process is defined in terms of punishment theory, we can at least analyze certain possibly relevant cause-and-effect relationships and at the same time satisfy the requirements of scientific rigor. Thus, early sexual behavior may indeed involve aversive experiences that undoubtedly result in a changed individual. However, the nature of the change, including the repression (forgetting) of associated stimuli, its permanence, its extent, and other features of the relationship can be determined empirically without recourse to the concept of unconscious anxiety. As we shall see in subsequent chapters, when considered in this manner, the cause-and-effect relationships again are more complex than those specified by Freud.

The situation is similar with regard to the concepts of regression and fixation. Freud recognized that individuals, when faced with threatening events, might resort to behavior that was successful at earlier stages of development. Similarly, individuals might continue to display "immature" behavior, which was highly successful at an earlier time, long after it has been inappropriate to new situations. These modes of responding were identified, respectively, as regression and fixation. Again, it is possible to provide an experimental analysis of such behavior without reference to their "dynamic" properties (Karsh, 1970).

Much of the experimental literature that is relevant in this connection stems from learning-theory research with lower organisms and will be reviewed in subsequent chapters. Suffice it to say that such modes of behavior can be easily understood and verified within learning theory. Thus, organisms will continue to display responses that have been rewarded, even after the reward has been withdrawn and even though new responses are required as determined by the relevant variables such as length of reward training, amount of reward, distribution of reward, and the presence of associated stimuli (Wilcoxon, 1952). Organisms will also regress, or return to earlier modes of responding, when current modes of responding are unsatisfactory or aversive, their responses again depending upon the relevant variables. All of this can be understood without reference to the concept of impaired psychosexual development.

If by the term "displacement" we mean the process whereby behavior that is present in one circumstance occurs under other circumstances (Miller, 1948b) or the transfer to alternative forms of gratification when earlier forms of gratification are no longer available, this, too, can be analyzed by behavioral principles focusing upon the relevant variables.

Probably the most difficult mechanism to analyze on a behavioral level is projection. Here threatening impulses are ostensibly defended against or reduced by attributing such thoughts and impulses to others. Experimental translations of this process have involved an analysis of the relationship between various threatening experiences (deprivation, fear, etc.) and their influence on judgment. Even disregarding the question of the relevancy of such efforts for the concept of projection, the findings are so sparse and ambiguous as to provide virtually no evidence of a definitive nature (Holmes, 1968).

EVALUATION

Psychopathologists have attempted to assess the contribution of psychoanalysis almost since its inception. There is little question that Freud had a profound influence on contemporary thought, and his system occupies, perhaps even today, the dominant position in clinical psychology and psychiatry. It was Freud who pointed out the critical problems of human behavior, and it is to these problems that an applied science of psychology should be addressed. The paradoxes, the inconsistencies, the irrationalities—these are the aspects of human behavior that psychology should come to grips with.

But the durability of such a theory must ultimately be measured in terms other than its literary and philosophical appeal. The criterion of scientific proof remains the *sine qua non* for advancing knowledge, and eventually all cause-and-effect arguments must be put to such a test. If Freud suggested certain relationships, it remains for others to apply the scientific criterion to his pronouncements. As we have seen, it is in this critical area that psychoanalysis has been found wanting. In O. H. Mowrer's (1960) terms, "We accepted a psychoanalytic theory long before it had been adequately tested and thus embraced as 'science' a set of presuppositions which we are painfully having to repudiate" (p. 302).

In the ever continuing effort to advance psychological knowledge, Freud's act was the curtain raiser; others were left with the task of specifying the precise nature of the relationships that he suggested. Attention will now be directed toward learning models of behavior pathology. These models, based upon long traditions of laboratory research with animals, represent a more scientific approach to etiology than Freud was able to complete in his lifetime.

BEHAVIORAL MODELS:
THE CLASSICAL CONDITIONING MODEL

Pavlov

Just as Freud was the leading figure in the development of the intrapsychic model of psychopathology, the classical conditioning model owes its influence largely to Pavlov. Both men formulated a system designed to encompass a broad spectrum of abnormal as well as normal behavioral processes. Pavlov differed from Freud, however, in two important respects. For one, Pavlov's theory relied upon hypothetical neural constructs, whereas Freud emphasized hypothetical psychic processes. For another, Pavlov's strategy involved, first, establishing behavioral regularities in lower organisms, identifying irregularities (that is, abnormal behavior), and finally, applying this knowledge and theory to the world of clinical events in humans. Freud's procedure was restricted to clinical observations of pathological behavior in humans and "theory construction" without benefit of laboratory tests.

Pavlov's interest in pathological behavior evolved out of his studies of the conditioned reflex. His discovery of the conditioned reflex provided psychology with some of its most important principles and widely used means of studying the acquisition and modification of behavior. As a careful, rigorous scientist, Pavlov explored many facets of the principles that he established. In this fashion he attempted to isolate the necessary and sufficient conditions for a conditioned reflex, the variables that influenced it, and special extensions into a number of areas, including those observations that he regarded as experimental analogs of abnormal behavior.

His contributions in this area may be differentiated in terms of the neural theory that he proposed and the experimental analysis of *behavioral* events, which ultimately led to the study of experimental neurosis. The latter will be considered in the section dealing with research.

In explaining pathological behavior, Pavlov referred to the two fundamental processes alleged to govern all cortical events, excitation and inhibition (Pavlov, 1927). "By and large 'excitation' refers to the arousal of the cortex and the general facilitation of processes of learning, remembering, and performing. Inhibition, in its broadest meaning, refers to a process within the central nervous system which interferes with the ongoing perceptual, cognitive and motor activities of the organism" (Eysenck & Rachman, 1965, p. 33).

The two major determinants governing pathological behavior are: (1) the "type" of nervous system (inferred from behavior) and (2) exposure to certain conflict-inducing (excitation versus inhibition) experiences. It is the interaction between the two that determines the character, nature, and extent of the pathological behavior. Both determinants were analyzed within the context of the neural excitation-inhibition principle.

With regard to the type of nervous system, almost from the start Pavlov was impressed with the "temperamental" differences observed in his canine subjects, which he attributed to differences in neural processes. Although his early observations were restricted to the study of physiology, differences between dogs in terms of conditioned salivary responding later began to attract his attention. B. M. Teplov (1964) suggests that Pavlov gradually evolved a position that ultimately ascribed such differences to properties of the nervous system of which they were an index.

A tentative typology based upon such differences was formulated as early as 1910 by one of Pavlov's students. Subjects were divided into three groups: (1) active, nervous, sensitive dogs, in which the excitatory process was regarded as dominant, (2) unexcitable dogs, in which the inhibitory process was believed to dominate, and (3) dogs alleged to reveal a balance of excitatory and inhibitory characteristics (the majority).

With some minor revisions a typology along these lines was more clearly formulated in the late 1920s and early 1930s. "Sanguine" animals, in which the excitatory process predominates, were energetic and highly reactive under quick changes of stimuli, "but with the slightest monotony of the environment they became dull, drowsy, and inactive" (Pavlov, 1927, p. 286). At the other extreme were "melancholic" animals in which the inhibitory process predominated as reflected by their restrained, cowering temperament. "When restrained in the experimental apparatus, their reflex activity is extremely regular and stable" (Pavlov, 1927, p. 286).

> *In between the extremes just described can be found numerous intermediate types which present a greater balance between excitation and inhibition, types on the whole better adapted to the natural conditions of life and therefore more biologically resistant.*
>
> *It is obvious that a large number of animals cannot be placed definitely in any of these . . . types, but broadly speaking all the dogs which we used could be divided into two*

> *groups—those with an excessive or moderate tendency to excitation, and those with an excessive or moderate tendency to inhibition. (Pavlov, 1927, p. 289)*

That Pavlov believed such a typology could be applied to man as well as dogs is clearly suggested by Teplov (1964, p. 19) and by W. H. Gantt (1942).

Pathology occurred when dogs of the extreme types were exposed to an experience involving conflict between the processes of excitation and inhibition, since their "unbalanced" systems were more susceptible to breakdown under stress. "If at a locus of the cortex, excitation and inhibition come into conflict at high intensity, the neural elements concerned may be unable to bear the strain, and may consequently be thrown into a pathological state" (Pavlov, 1927, p. 289). Thus, the excitable dog developed positive conditioned responses with ease and inhibitory conditioned responses with difficulty or not at all. Under stress dogs of this type developed behavior compared by Pavlov to the symptoms of neurasthenia. At the other extreme are dogs of the inhibitable type. In these dogs conditioned responses are formed with difficulty, but the inhibitory response, once formed, is very stable. Under strain these animals, according to Pavlov, respond with an experimental neurosis resembling hysteria (Kimble, 1961).

Later in his life Pavlov (1955) became interested in applying these principles to the analysis and modification of behavioral disturbances in psychiatric patients. Thus, Pavlov regarded the negativism, stereotypy, catalepsy, and apathy observed in schizophrenics as a function of irradiation of cortical inhibition caused by overstraining and weakening of the excitatory process, as in the second instance above. The behavior observed in manic-depressive reactions was thought to be the consequence of stress superimposed on an excitatory system.

Critique. Pavlov's contribution to the experimental analysis of pathological behavior stands unquestioned, and we will subsequently review the line of investigation that evolved out of his efforts in this area. However, it is more difficult to assess the impact of his theory on the study of psychopathology, although it seems reasonably safe to say his emphasis upon innate temperamental predisposers had *relatively little* influence on clinical theory and practice—perhaps this was because of the existence of the rival, more popular Freudian model, perhaps because of the traditional American emphasis upon environmentalism, perhaps because the relationship between his experimental analogs and clinical phenomena was obscure. Pavlov's theoretical model never achieved a wide degree of acceptance outside of Eastern European psychology (with several important exceptions). "For all that, Pavlov surely deserves credit for breaking ground in applying studies of animal behavior to the problem of human disorders; and the interest he stimulated has led a number of other investigators to follow this same line of inquiry" (Dinsmoor, 1960).

Eysenck

H. J. Eysenck clearly falls in the category of those theorists who ascribe to a Pavlovian emphasis upon constitutional predisposers, since the concept of neurological dispositions, which is the cornerstone of the Pavlovian model, plays an equally important role in Eysenck's system. Thus, Eysenck argues that the cortical processes of excitation and inhibition determine the individual's degree of conditionability. Individuals in whom inhibitory processes occur quickly, strongly, and persistently, and in whom excitatory processes occur slowly, weakly, and nonpersistently, thus resulting in retarded conditionability, will reveal extroverted characteristics. High degrees of introversion are found in people in whom the reverse is true (Eysenck & Rachman, 1965, p. 33).

Eysenck and his colleagues have combined the theory of constitutional predisposers with a factor-analytically based classification scheme. On the basis of this effort, they have isolated several response dimensions that are presumed to identify various pathological conditions. Thus, psychoticism-neuroticism represents one such factor; introversion-extraversion represents a second, and so forth. When an individual is classified in terms of the various factor combinations, several general pathological conditions can be explicated. For example, an individual who is high in neuroticism and high in extraversion will often reflect the characteristics of the psychopath, that is, criminal, destructive, antisocial tendencies. A person who is high in neuroticism and high in introversion will be characterized by conditions in which anxiety is a major component, such as phobias, obsessions and compulsions, and generalized anxiety.

This system, in turn, offers suggestions with regard to etiology. Thus, dysthymic persons (neurotic introverts) in whom excitatory processes predominate display easily conditioned fear responses. Conditions in which the neurotic extraversive characteristics are present are inferred to be a function of an inability to form quick and strong conditioned responses (Eysenck, 1961b).

> We see introverted and highly emotional people as being constitutionally predisposed to develop dysthymic neuroses, that is to say, anxiety states, obsessional and compulsive habits of behaviors, phobias, and so forth; we see extroverted and highly emotional people as predisposed to develop psychopathic, criminal, and hysterical reactions. Whether these predispositions are to be translated into actual behaviors depends, of course, on the particular environment in which the person finds himself, and the schedule of reinforcement which he encounters during his life. Thus, both biological-heredity and social-environmental influences come into play in determining

the final conduct which we observe and which, in the case of the neurotic or the criminal, brings him in touch with some social agency or other. (Eysenck & Rachman, 1965, p. 58)

Thus, it is obviously a biosocial theory in the sense that it stresses both the biological nature of the organism and the social influences that impinge upon the organism and lead to certain types of responses (Eysenck & Rachman, 1965, p. 58).

Critique. Eysenck has perhaps even more ardently applied the "innate temperament" model to the field of psychopathology than Pavlov did. Thus, Eysenck attempted to formulate the etiology of a variety of behavioral disorders as well as a reclassification of psychopathology within the model's framework. In view of his unflagging interest in this line of inquiry and the extent of literature produced by the Eysenck group, surely he must be considered one of the foremost proponents of this model. At the very least, his approach has had a continuing impact on the study of psychopathology, at least in certain quarters.

As we shall see in our subsequent review of Eysenck's evidence, however, the knowledge advanced by these efforts, although bearing on the issue of causative determinants, represents a departure from the prototypical experimental model described earlier. The difficulty in validating Eysenck's (as well as the Pavlovian) position is inherent in those theories that base their assumptions upon neurological predispositions; that is, such a reduction obscures the possibility of a completely behavioristic account and, in the extreme case, perhaps misdirects our attention away from isolating environmental determinants, while professing to isolate those determinants. Thus, although Eysenck accepts the importance of environmental events as determinants, there is little attempt to apply this concept beyond the acknowledgment of the classical conditioning paradigm. He asserts, for example, the importance of schedules of reinforcement, but does not attempt to accommodate this concept within the system.

Despite these limitations, of all those theorists who promote the intervening physiological determinant model for an analysis of pathological behavior, Eysenck stands out as one of the most important.

Wolpe
In contrast to Eysenck and Pavlov, in J. Wolpe's (1958) scheme neurological processes play a subordinate role to environmental events (except in certain instances) in the etiology of the neuroses (the only form of behavior pathology to which he addresses himself). Although agreeing with Pavlov on the importance of predisposing physiological conditions, Wolpe (1958) does not consider them to be essential determinants, and he specifically rejects the notion that neuroses occur as a function of damage to the nervous system. On

the contrary, he claims that pathological conditions can be considered completely as special examples of the principles governing all learned behavior. Thus, he accepts the importance of the Pavlovian paradigm, but not the neurological explanation that accompanied it.

Wolpe (1958) regards neurotic behavior as persistent, maladaptive responses characterized by anxiety, that is, conditioned fear. This definition was formulated largely in the context of his activities as a practicing therapist, whereas Pavlov's definition initially was formulated exclusively on the basis of his experimental work and only subsequently applied to clinical phenomena. Nevertheless, Wolpe (1958) maintains that "all human neuroses are produced, as animal neuroses are, by situations which evoke high intensities of anxiety" (p. 78).

The two principles that are invoked to explain the acquisition of such behavior are contiguity and drive reduction. Thus, classical conditioning, as exemplified by Pavlov's research, reveals how learning may occur "if a response has been evoked in temporal contiguity with a given sensory stimulus and it is subsequently found that the stimulus can evoke the response although it could not have done so before" (Wolpe, 1958, p. 19). These stimulus-response sequences depend upon the development of *functional* connections (synapses) between neurons appropriately in anatomical opposition (Wolpe, 1958). The reaction of the autonomic system follows such conditioned associations, and in the case of a disturbing state of affairs, the physiological concomitants of anxiety are associated to new conditions in the environment.

In addition to the classical conditioning principle, however, C. L. Hull's (1943) concept of drive reduction is also invoked to explain the organism's attempt to escape and/or avoid anxiety-arousing situations. For example, in situations in which a noxious stimulus is acting on an organism, not only will anxiety be produced and associated with contiguous events, but "out of the multitude of molar acts that may comprise the organism's response, the one that is learned is followed by the removal of the noxious stimulus and a termination of the drive created by that stimulus" (Wolpe, 1958, p. 81). Unfortunately, such effects may result in a breakdown of efficient behavior and/or the emergence of maladaptive behavior that alleviates or avoids the anxiety.

Given these principles, Wolpe further specifies the special circumstances that result in neurotic behavior. There are two basic situations that can evoke anxiety: exposure of the organism to ambivalent stimuli and exposure to noxious stimuli (Wolpe, 1958). The latter case may involve a relatively small number of severe noxious stimuli or a relatively large number of mildly noxious stimuli. Since the organism will always respond by attempting to escape such stimuli, the development of neurotic behavior further requires that such escape be prevented. In the animal neuroses this is accomplished through physical confinement; in the human neuroses, through psychological confinement, for example, by an increase in the aversive consequences of attempted escape behavior. Confinement assures continued contact with the noxious situation, thereby increasing the anxiety level as well as autonomic reactivity.

Wolpe argues that few human neuroses are produced as a consequence of direct exposure to a noxious experience, that is, a directly fear-arousing event such as a car accident. Nevertheless, the fear reaction that occurs under either direct circumstance (that is, either a few severe noxious events or many weak ones) is conditionable to any stimuli that happen to be present at the time, according to the Pavlovian principle.

Wolpe is less clear in the case of conflict-produced neuroses, arguing simply that "simultaneous, strong conflicting action tendencies somehow generate high degrees of anxiety within the nervous system" (Wolpe, 1958, p. 79).

The theory, of course, is most directly concerned with the etiology of phobias, where the stimulus antecedents can be ostensibly articulated in terms of the two situations described above. Other manifestations of anxiety reactions are also attributed to differences in the learning process. Free-floating anxiety, for example, is explained in terms of the degree to which those omnipresent properties of the environment (light, light and shade contrasts, amorphous noise, spatiality, and the passage of time) become connected to anxiety reactions, resulting in the patient's being persistently and apparently causelessly anxious. The more intense the anxiety evoked in the individual, the greater the probability that more stimulus aspects "would acquire *some* measure of anxiety conditioning" (Wolpe, 1958, p. 78).

Neurotic reactions that are not characterized by overt signs of anxiety, such as hysteria and the obsessions, are explained in terms of personality variables, similar to Eysenck's position. Thus, in some individuals, during stress, there may be sensory, motor, and ideational reactions, as well as the autonomic responses characteristic of anxiety. Such reactions occur with greater frequency in extroverted individuals for the following reason. Since the predominant characteristic in extroverts is the rapid generation and slow dissipation of reactive inhibition, when such individuals are exposed to stress, they respond with relatively low degrees of anxiety, thereby increasing the probability that contiguous stimuli will become conditioned to responses other than the anxiety response. The end result is the inhibition of those sensory, motor, and/or ideational responses, as revealed in "anesthesias, or disturbances of vision or hearing; of paralyses, pareses, tics, tremors, disturbances of balance, contractures or fits; or amnesias, fugues, or 'multiple personality' phenomena" (Wolpe, 1958, p. 85).

When the conditioning of such nonanxiety reactions is more complex and highly organized, obsessive-compulsive behavior may occur. The essential feature of such a reaction is its intrusiveness, its pervasiveness and influence in all of the patient's daily activities. Wolpe further distinguishes between anxiety-elevating **obsessions,** in which there is an immediate response to stimulation (via classical conditioning) in the form of increased anxiety, and anxiety-reducing obsessions, which are performed for the purpose of diminishing anxiety (escape behavior) characterized by tidying, hand washing, eating, buying, "activities which are of course 'normal' when prompted by usual motivations and not by anxiety; rituals like touching poles, perversions like exhibitionism and various thinking activities" (Wolpe, 1958, p. 91).

Critique. Although Wolpe is generally considered a proponent of the Pavlovian model, it is important to clarify his position in this regard. There are several dominant themes that have influenced his development as a behavioral therapist. For one, there were his experiments with an animal model. We will subsequently discuss his efforts in this area in detail; for now, it is important to recognize that Wolpe extended his work on the development of pathological reactions from lower organisms to the clinical arena. On the basis of these efforts he contended that the maladaptive behavior that emerged in his experiments could best be explained by classical conditioning and drive-reduction theory. Thus, classical conditioning operated during the initial circumstances, which gave rise to the pathological fear reactions, and maladaptive behaviors, such as phobias, were *maintained* because of their anxiety-reducing properties. As we shall see, alternative explanations can be offered in interpreting Wolpe's findings, but, in any event, in this sense Wolpe is only nominally a Pavlovian and perhaps belongs more appropriately in our subsequent treatment of other behavioral models, especially two-factor theory.

Wolpe also differs from Pavlov in another important way. Wolpe appears to be more enamored of the classical conditioning model as an explanation for the etiology of anxiety than as a mechanism through which innate predisposers are manifested. Although this difference is somewhat attenuated by Wolpe's attempt to explain "nonanxiety" pathological conditions as a function of "special conditions" (thus tempting one to consider them as predisposers in the Eysenckian sense), Wolpe has, for the most part, professed a strict environmentalist bias. By the same token, however, his attempt to correlate anxiety neurosis with the autonomic nervous system, and nonanxiety neurosis with other systems, invokes the use of intra-organismic concepts as explanatory mechanisms.

We will return to Wolpe's contributions to the study of pathological behavior in subsequent chapters, particularly his innovations in psychotherapy, which have had an even more profound impact on clinical psychology than his theory of the neuroses.

SUMMARY: THE PAVLOVIAN MODEL

Pavlov's quasi-neurological explanation of pathological behavior has never been widely accepted by Western psychologists, with the possible exception of Eysenck and his associates. Pavlov's thesis can be questioned on the grounds that conditioning is possible in the absence of the cerebral cortex, that the thesis is unable to explain certain facts of conditioning, and that what passes for physiology is often nothing more than the translation of behavioral facts into neurophysiological language (Kimble, 1961).

It is the *empirical* content of Pavlov's labors, however, that has been of considerable importance to general learning theory if not to the study of pathological behavior. Wolpe's theory clearly emphasizes this aspect of the Pavlovian model, and the experiments that buttress his argument are described in a subsequent chapter.

BEHAVIORAL MODELS:
THE OPERANT CONDITIONING MODEL

Skinner

Compared with the two previous systems, the impact of the operant model on the study of psychopathology is of more recent vintage. This is, at least in part, due to a preference by its proponents for first establishing basic principles underlying human behavior and, only then, extending those principles to applied or "special" areas.

With regard to theories of behavior pathology, although there is no one operant spokesman who holds a position comparable to Freud or Pavlov in their respective areas, most extensions of the operant model evolved out of the work of B. F. Skinner. Although the behavioral model proposed by Skinner (1938, 1953) was quite different from theirs, he credits both men with having an influence on his own position.

Like Freud and Pavlov, Skinner was interested in the interaction between the individual and the environment. But, unlike these men, Skinner regards this interaction as the quintessence of a science of human behavior. Since this process can be assessed completely within an empirical framework, it is unnecessary and, worse, possibly misleading, to hypothecate intrapsychic or physiological mechanisms as mediators of the process, in order to explain human behavior. On the contrary, Skinner (1953) proposes that a complete analysis of human behavior can be undertaken without reference to explanatory mechanisms at any level of discourse other than behavioral. Hence his emphasis upon the functional relationship between an organism and its environment, which can be analyzed in terms of independent variables and dependent variables (that is, behavior). When information about this relationship is available, we are provided with a perfectly adequate explanation of behavior without recourse to hypothesizing at any other level of conceptualization.

The basic operation that influences this interaction is described by the well-known principle of reinforcement (contingencies). Changes in human behavior (learning) can be explained in terms of the contingency or temporal correlation between a response and its environmental consequences. (See Table 1.) In general, if a response is followed by an event that results in an increase in the future probability of that response, reinforcement has occurred. Some rein-

TABLE 1. Five Most Common Types of Consequences That May Come to Control a Response[a]

CLASS OF STIMULUS[b]	CONTINGENCY WITH BEHAVIOR	NAME OF PROCEDURE[c]	EXPECTED OUTCOME
1. S+	Present on response	Positive reinforcement	Increase
2. S−	Present on response	Punishment	Decrease
3. S+	None (S+ terminated)	Extinction	Decrease
4. S−	Withdraw or postpone on response	Negative reinforcement	Increase
5. S−	None (S− terminated)	Extinction	Decrease

a Adapted from Holland and Skinner (1961).

b S+ and S− refer to classes of stimuli which are identified according to their functional relationship to behavior.

c Examples of each procedure and the contribution to the formation of pathological behavior are discussed in the text.

forcers strengthen behavior when they are *presented* and others when they are *removed* or *postponed*. Thus, the thirsty child eventually learns to go to the sink for a drink, since such behavior provides immediate reinforcement. Similarly, the automobile driver applies his brakes when approaching a red light, since this enables him to avoid a potentially dangerous event. These arrangements are defined, respectively, as positive and negative reinforcement.

Conversely, if the reinforcement relationship between a response and its consequence is terminated, this usually results in a decrease in response frequency and, ultimately, extinction. The punishment arrangement is one in which response probability is reduced as a function of a response-contingent event. Thus, the student who experiences little or no success may become a dropout. (That is, school attendance may be extinguished.) The parent who scolds a child for coming home late hopes thereby to decrease the frequency of such undesirable behavior (punishment).

Thus, whereas the Pavlovian learning model transfers environmental control over a response from the *preceding* unconditioned stimulus to an associated conditioned stimulus (both eliciting stimuli which precede responses), the operant learning model stresses the manner in which a response is controlled by the events that *follow* it. Although the procedures used in each case differ considerably, many of the terms and concepts are similar. For example, in both conditioning models an event that is not correlated with a particular response—that is, does not control the (future) probability of that response—is a neutral stimulus. In both systems an unconditioned stimulus is one that controls response probability prior to any formal conditioning, and a conditioned stimulus controls response probability after conditioning. The Skinnerian system, however, posits at least two main classes of conditioned stimuli: conditioned reinforcers, which control behavior by virtue of their association with unconditioned or primary reinforcers (money is perhaps the most commonplace example), and discriminative stimuli, which precede and signal the availability of either conditioned or unconditioned, positive and/or negative reinforcement. Thus, if a hungry organism receives food for responding only in the presence of a stimulus (say a green light), he will eventually respond only when the light is on. Similarly, if a shock-avoidance contingency is in effect only in the presence of a tone, the organism will engage in the appropriate behavior only during this condition. In like fashion, an employee may work diligently in the presence of his supervisor, but may loaf and engage in extraneous activities when the boss is on vacation. Such changes in behavior define the characteristics of stimulus discrimination and represent an extension of the reinforcement principle.

As the operant model has evolved, similar extensions and applications have been introduced, encompassing broader areas of human behavior and more complex events. With regard to pathological behavior, Skinner maintains that such behavior can be understood completely within the framework of the general laws governing all behavior, although special extensions of the principles might be required to explain phenomena that often appear to be paradoxical. Basically, however, the differences between normal and abnormal behavior are often a function of differences in individual reinforcement histories. Although Skinner himself has not explicated a formal model of psychopathology, he has stressed the importance of punishment as the source of many forms of pathological behavior (Skinner, 1953).

The punishment technique, argues Skinner, is the most common method employed by social agencies to achieve control over human behavior, probably because, from the standpoint of the *punisher,* it is immediately effective in reducing undesirable behavior (and therefore reinforcing to the punisher). Unfortunately, there are many problems attending to the use of punishment, which have not been carefully analyzed and are frequently overlooked by the administrators of punishment. For example, punishment rarely eliminates a response from a person's behavioral repertoire; it simply reduces the probability of the response's occurring in the presence of the punishing stimulus or associated stimuli (conditioned punishment). The *first* effect of punishment is that it elicits emotional responses (fear, anger) that may be incompatible with the punished behavior. Subsequently, the *second* effect is that the punished behavior itself may also evoke the opposed emotional responses.

As an effect of the severe punishment of sexual behavior, the early stages of such behavior generate conditioned stimuli giving rise to emotional responses which interfere with the completion of the behavior. One possible outcome then, is that punishment for sexual behavior may interfere with similar behavior under socially acceptable circumstances—for example, in marriage. In general, then, as a second effect of punishment, behavior which has consistently been punished becomes the source of conditioned stimuli which evoke incompatible behavior. (Skinner, 1953, p. 187)

The *third* effect of punishment occurs as a consequence of negative reinforcement. Those responses that enable the organism to escape punishment or avoid conditioned punishment are reinforced. "The most important effect of punishment, then, is to establish aversive conditions which are avoided by any behavior of 'doing something else' " (Skinner, 1953, p. 189). Thus, Skinner explains the repression process in terms of avoidance behavior. There is no need, then, to appeal to any event that does not have the dimensions of behavior. Punishment does not so much create a negative probability that a response will be made, but rather a positive probability that incompatible behavior (avoidance behavior) will occur.

In any event, the outcome of such an arrangement is conflict between the response that leads to punishment and the response that avoids it. In this fashion Skinner analyzes pathological conditions as the end result or by-product of punitive forms of control. Thus, we have escape and avoidance behavior in the form of withdrawal and phobias, in which the "unreasonable" fear has been displaced; anxiety, as the fear of a future event that, in the past, has preceded punishment; and anger or rage, as the possible emotional by-product of a punishing experience, which may be directed at the aversive agent, other people, or things in general. Whatever the specific form, the etiology is frequently considered to be of a punitive nature, especially if punishment is excessive and/or consistent.

Although Skinner has examined in detail the importance of punishment in relation to pathological behavior, he has also recognized that the causes of psychopathology are diverse and complex, and he remains primarily an analyst of positive reinforcement. Thus, he has made numerous suggestions regarding the manner in which positive reinforcement schedules and associated stimulus control events may produce pathological effects. For example, those schedules which result in high rates of responding (variable ratio) may be involved in such pathological outcomes as "compulsive" gambling, particularly if the number of wins are frequent at first and thinned out later. On the other hand, if positive reinforcements are thinned out too rapidly, extinction may occur and the rate of behavior may drop almost to zero. Under these circumstances, abulia, depression, or other behavioral deficits may follow.

Adventitious delivery of reinforcement may also result in pathological behavior. For example, Skinner has described the Kaingang Indians who dance and shout to "make" thunderstorms go away (Skinner, 1969). The fact that the storms frequently move off maintains the behavior. Many pathological forms of superstition and ritual may originate in similar fashion.

A number of these suggestions have been elaborated upon by

other reinforcement theorists, as we shall see in the following section.

Critique. Skinner's position regarding the study of the causes of pathological behavior must be considered in the broader context of his approach to a science of human behavior. Although vitally concerned with applied science, he has long maintained that the practical application of knowledge must be preceded by the establishment of general principles. In this sense he represents the "pure science" approach to solving problem conditions, and, indeed, his own research efforts attest to this. Nevertheless, he has, on many occasions, departed from his basic science interests to comment on practical affairs, his works including a treatise on the establishment of a model community designed to eliminate pathological behavior (Skinner, 1948).

Skinner has been the target of criticism from a number of quarters. Learning theorists have condemned his "antitheoretical" bias, and both learning theorists and applied psychologists have decried his attempts to explain human behavior largely on the basis of reinforcement principles. Skinner's reply to the former critics clearly reveals that his statements were restricted to those kinds of theories that attempted to explain behavior in terms of other than behavioral dimensions, such as the real nervous system, the conceptual nervous system, or the mind (Skinner, 1969).

His response, in the latter case, is to acknowledge that the facts of human behavior often result in embarrassing exceptions to the reinforcement principle. "Men sometimes act in ways which bring pain and destroy pleasure, have a questionable net utility, and work against the survival of the species" (Skinner, 1969, p. 5). The problem, here, is not that the principles are too simplistic to accommodate such complex events, but that our observations of such phenomena are usually made independent of the required information (that is, the relevant variables) necessary to explicate the manner in which the principles apply in such special instances. Once this information is available, we can interpret complex behavior more successfully. The argument, then, rests on empirical grounds, where, appropriately enough, all such questions ultimately are or should be decided.

Sidman

Although Skinner has long been interested in psychopathology, it is only within the past decade that other operant investigators have become seriously involved in the study of such behavior. Although most of their efforts have centered upon the treatment of pathological conditions (to be reviewed in a subsequent section), several writers have also concentrated on issues relevant to the study of the causes of psychopathology.

M. Sidman is one investigator who has clearly articulated an operant approach to the analysis of maladaptive behavior. As Sidman views it, the study of clinical events can be best accomplished by isolating the lawful relations that are involved and, thereby, uncovering the normal sources of pathological behavior (Sidman, 1960a). "Normal not according to any statistical criterion, but in the sense that they carry on a lawful existence independent of their pathological manifestations" (Sidman, 1960a, p. 61).

To accomplish this objective, experimental and clinical psychologists must overcome their tendency to equate the terms "abnormal" and "disorderly."

> *When an experimenter isolates a lawful behavioral phenomenon he is likely to consider that its very lawfulness removes it from the realm of clinical interest. Similarly, the clinician who does venture into the laboratory will, more often than not, try to demonstrate the absence of lawfulness in some behavioral phenomenon. Neither worker seems to give much thought to the possibility that maladaptive behavior can result from quantitative and qualitative combinations of processes which are themselves intrinsically orderly, strictly determined, and normal in origin. (Sidman, 1960a, p. 61)*

Abnormal behavior, then, can be understood as special examples of the general laws governing all learned behavior. Although particular experimental paradigms may be required, no unique rules, concepts, or analytical devices are necessary for explicating the causes of pathological behavior.

Sidman's analysis is largely restricted to experimental analogs of pathological behavior (for example, the maintenance of behavior that has no adaptive value, anxiety functionally defined as conditioned suppression, immobility effects, and self-aversive stimulation), and he makes no explicit attempt to apply his argument to pathology at the human level. Nevertheless, he maintains that such an enterprise has the necessary power and subtlety to uncover processes relevant to clinical phenomena (Sidman, 1960a, p. 67).

Critique. Sidman's position reflects Skinner's emphasis upon methodology and empiricism as opposed to theorizing in terms of nonbehavioral conceptual systems. His particular contribution rests on the attempt to apply general principles to so-called paradoxical behavioral phenomena. Although clinicians have long paid lip service to such an attempt, Sidman is one of the few writers who have made explicit suggestions with regard to how such an endeavor can be accomplished. Despite his contribution in this necessarily critical area, Sidman's paper has been almost completely ignored in the standard clinical literature.

Ferster

Another early associate of Skinner's, C. B. Ferster, is representative of the growing list of operant psychologists attempting to apply Skinner's principles to the study of pathological behavior.

For Ferster, no analysis of behavior that ignores the effects of the behavior on the environment is complete (Ferster, 1965). Thus, a functional analysis of any behavior, including pathological manifestations, requires the isolation of the environmental effects that influence the future course of the behavior. These effects are the variables that cause or determine the behavior. This approach is, of course, in contrast to the traditional emphasis upon inner determinants. Again, no special concepts or rules are required in such an analysis. Indeed, Ferster makes virtually no reference to abnormal behavior in his discussion, preferring to focus his attention, instead, upon the customary practices involved in labeling behavior as "abnormal." Thus, an individual's milieu might be analyzed to determine those practices that represent contingencies applied to particular forms of behavior. It then becomes "possible to classify an individual's behavioral repertoire by comparing it with the behavioral potential of the milieu" (Ferster, 1965, p. 12). Any discrepancies represent conditions that society identifies as abnormal.

Ferster has applied this theoretical position to the analysis of schizophrenic and autistic behavior. For example, the behavior of many psychiatric patients may be characterized as deficient in several respects; thus, they have restricted behavioral repertoires, which "are not producing the reinforcement of the world" (Ferster, 1958, p. 103). Similarly, autistic children are

> *individuals in whom normal performances have never developed. The normal development of their repertoire was temporarily arrested at some time. Such a deficit may occur because the repertoire of the child is weakened through the normal processes by which behavior can be suppressed or eliminated. All of the basic processes by which new performances are generated, strengthened, maintained, eliminated, punished, suppressed, or controlled by special aspects of the environment are relevant to an analysis of how a particular history could produce a behavioral deficit. (Ferster & DeMyer, 1961, p. 344)*

The longer the conditions obtain, the greater the difficulty in reinforcing normal behavior.

Some of the special circumstances that result in a deficient behavioral repertoire are: (1) an inadequate reinforcement history in which certain normal experiences did not obtain, so that those special skills necessary to obtain social reinforcements are not present, (2) inappropriate schedules of reinforcement, especially schedules in which inordinately large amounts of work are required to produce few social reinforcements, (3) punishment, which may distort a response so that it does not produce its customary reinforcing effect. In addition, avoidance behavior may be generated by punishment and become prepotent over the existing repertoire.

These general principles may be employed for the purpose of explaining the etiology of certain pathological conditions. For example, Ferster assumes that when appropriate reinforcement is minimal or altogether missing, this will result in a depleted behavioral repertoire. Thus, children who do not experience the commonplace forms of care and attention following their vocalizations (either contingently or noncontingently) might not develop early verbal repertoires. This, in turn, reduces the probability of social reinforcement, and an extinction cycle is established.

Ferster regards such extinction conditions as important determinants in many of the behavioral deficits observed in pathological conditions. Similarly, the sudden removal of regularly delivered reinforcement (as in the loss of a parent or other loved one) may result in even more dramatic effects. Depression or other types of behavioral deficits would be expected to occur under such circumstances. Autistic behavior in a child may develop following loss or illness of a parent, or any other hiatus between child and reinforcing agency (as with alcoholic or depressed parents, often-absent parents, schizophrenic or similarly disturbed parents, or inattentive parents).

The lack of reinforcement may also lead to an increasing frequency of behavior that relies on the aversive control of others for reinforcement. An example is provided by the largely ignored child who can attract attention only through temper tantrums. Many antisocial acts may be similarly acquired (Ferster, 1958).

Inappropriate reinforcement schedules may produce pathological behavior characterized by either high or low response rates. When the response requirements of a schedule are increased too rapidly, extinction will result. Thus, for example, assuming that a child can progress from saying one new word to twenty words per day may result in verbal decrement, rather than an increment, because the reinforcement schedule is too rapidly reduced. Similarly, assuming that a child can ride a bicycle by himself after learning to sit upon it may result in failure and the suppression of further bicycle-riding skills.

Reinforcement schedules may also acquire adventitious control over responses, which would then be expected to increase to high rates. For example, the person who has beginner's luck at cards may become a pathological gambler. In this case, adventitious reinforcement may have followed the first instance of the behavior, which was then increased and maintained at a high rate because of an unpredictable intermittent schedule of reinforcement.

Inappropriate stimulus control, according to Ferster, may be observed in any situation in which stimuli have not at some time been paired with reinforcement. For example, the first party a child attends may function as a totally novel stimulus—it disrupts the ongoing behavior and may be functionally equivalent to an aversive stimulus, suppressing appropriate behavior. This may be particularly true for the child who has received the majority of his reinforcement from parents or other adults. Consequently, the child's behavior **at the** party may seem entirely inappropriate to the circumstances.

This may be prevented by exposing the child to other children prior to parties (thereby, theoretically, providing reinforcement).

In the same fashion a person may be taught to respond appropriately to strangers through the reinforcement of appropriate responses to persons other than his family (friends first, strangers last), and one may be taught to speak through a gradual increase in the number of stimuli to be imitated or otherwise responded to verbally if these stimuli set the occasion for reinforcement.

Ferster also argues that aversive control is often functionally equivalent to extinction or removal of positive reinforcement. That is, both produce response decrements. Punishment by social agencies, such as parents, may produce this effect primarily because it sets the occasion for nonreinforcement. Ferster further believes, with Skinner, that extinction is a more powerful and long-lasting technique for removing a response from a behavioral repertoire than is punishment, which may have only temporary effects. In addition, punishment may have dangerous side effects, such as emotional and autonomic responses (anxiety), in the presence of preaversive stimuli, such as threats of punishment. Punishment may also increase the probability of escape and avoidance behavior (including counteraversive control), which may not serve the purpose of the punisher. And because punishment frequently yields more immediate effects than positive reinforcement, the frequency of the controlling agency's (for example, the parent's) use of aversive techniques may increase.

Critique. Ferster's efforts are perhaps representative of the progressive development of operant approaches from the world of pure research to the arena of clinical events. Ferster's background is very much that of the basic scientist, and his collaboration with Skinner produced one of the basic reference texts in the area (Ferster & Skinner, 1957). On the other hand, Ferster differs from both Skinner and Sidman in that a greater percentage of his recent interests has been devoted to applied activities. This interest reaches back at least ten years, during which time he outlined a response-frequency based classification model and offered some tentative suggestions with regard to the etiology and treatment of pathological behaviors. He is currently involved in the functional analysis of learning variables that influence and modify autistic behavior in children (Ferster & Simons, 1966). As in Sidman's case, these efforts have had, to date, relatively little impact on the clinical literature, although interest in them is increasing in the behavior modification field.

Sandler and Davidson
The views expressed by Skinner and other operant theorists suggest that a better understanding of pathological conditions can be accomplished by analyzing the interactions between (a) the variables involved in an individual's behavioral history and (b) those determi-

nants currently impinging upon the organism. With the knowledge of the former we can better predict how the latter will influence behavior. J. Sandler and R. S. Davidson (1971) have attempted to formulate such a model, beginning with the study of human behavior as determined by simple or unitary response consequences and then advancing to the more complex events involved in pathological behavior, which are assumed to be determined by multiple and complex response consequences.

Three separate components of the model are identified in terms of variables governing initial acquisition (stage 1), variables governing maintenance (stage 2), and current variables. Optimal understanding of any pathological condition can be obtained by explicating the variables involved in each stage, as well as the interactions between variables.

Acquisition of relatively "simple" forms of behavior may be explained in terms of positive or negative reinforcement (stage 1). Moreover, a number of individuals have argued that certain forms of psychopathology may be understood as extensions of such unitary determinants. Hence the view that interprets phobias as examples of avoidance behavior established by means of negative reinforcement.

However, few responses in the natural environment (and especially those defined as pathological) can be adequately explained by such a simplistic analysis. It is probably the case that such factors as reinforcement schedules and interactions between response consequences and associated stimuli are also present during or shortly after initial acquisition of behavior manifested in the natural environment. No adequate analysis of that behavior, then, can be accomplished without information relevant to these (stage 2) variables. Thus, an exploration of certain forms of pathology can be advanced on the basis of this information. For example, compulsive gambling may occur as a function of the schedule of reinforcement, and many forms of inappropriate behavior may be the result of stimuli associated with primary reinforcement, as in the case of fetishism.

Once again, however, although such information is critical for explaining the early history of a pathological condition, it is probably inadequate for the purpose of generalizing to clinical phenomena, especially to those conditions characterized by behavioral deficits. Some additional insight might be obtained, in this connection, by analyzing those response consequences encompassed by the terms "extinction" and "punishment." Thus, pathological conditions characterized by deficiencies (autism, schizophrenia, academic deficiencies, impotence, frigidity, etc.) may be the consequence of an extended deprivation (extinction) and/or punishment history. In any event, the effects of such arrangements can only be determined by explication of the variables relevant to acquisition (positive or negative reinforcement, schedule of events, associated stimuli) in conjunction with the relevant extinction/punishment variables. Under certain circumstances "unusual" interactions occur, for example, between positive reinforcement and an aversive event, thus resulting in the *maintenance* of behavior under extinction-like or apparently punishing circumstances. The end result might be revealed in masochistic or self-defeating behavior.

Although inclusion of such considerations improves the level of the model's sophistication, once again, considerable caution. must be exercised in advancing an analog to clinical phenomena at this juncture. It seems reasonable to assume that most pathological conditions are influenced by more complex, multiple response-consequence arrangements than those described above. Thus, a phobic condition initially acquired as a function of negative reinforcement may be subsequently influenced by positive reinforcement (in the form of attention and concern), punishment (in the form of ridicule and abuse), or extinction (the unavailability of positive reinforcement).

There is, of course, an infinite number of variations on the theme, and probably no one of them completely describes the history of any given form of pathological behavior in the natural environment. Nevertheless, it seems reasonable to assume that as the many permutations and combinations of variables are analyzed, closer and closer approximations to clinical phenomena will be observed (Sandler & Davidson, 1971). Thus, by analyzing the interaction between initial acquisition variables and subsequent variables, the stage-two component of the model might offer clues regarding the circumstances relevant to the maintenance of the problem condition.

Sandler and Davidson argue that with a proper analysis of the *history* of pathological conditions (including acquisition variables, associated stimuli, and secondary determinants), we are in a better position to predict behavior in any new situation which the individual may encounter (third-stage determinants), as for example meeting a traffic obstacle on a familiar route to work, or seeking treatment for a behavior disorder. Reactions to those experiences can be best understood by reference to the variables determining the individual's prior history. In each case the effect of the new (third stage) circumstances will be determined by its interaction with the ongoing behavior.

Critique. The argument advanced by Sandler and Davidson is clearly a programmatic one, requiring extensive analysis of the suggested combinations of variables in order to be realized. Lest this seem completely visionary, however, we might recognize that there is now, and has been for some time, considerable interest in the experimental analysis of the multiple determinants of behavior. Since these efforts will be subsequently reviewed in detail, we wish only to mention at this point that the model is potentially verifiable. The most urgent need at present is for the analysis of interactions between second-stage and third-stage determinants. Very little work has been reported in this area, and it would certainly flesh out the bones on the skeleton.

SUMMARY: THE OPERANT CONDITIONING MODEL

The reviews presented in this section suggest that operant theorists are now increasingly applying reinforcement principles to an analysis of the etiology of psychopathology. In keeping with their preference for a strict empirical-environmentalist framework, their efforts are characterized by the systematic extension of response-consequence arrangements from simple cases to those more complex events encompassed by the term "psychopathology."

The implications of this recent development for the study of behavior disorders are profound, perhaps revolutionary. Of all the various behavioral models that have been proposed, the one which breaks most sharply with tradition and current scientific practice in psychology is the operant model. Other theorists have argued in favor of a learning model, but they have continued to rely upon non-behavioral explanatory schemes. Operant theory carries this line of inquiry one step further by, first, acknowledging the environmental argument in reinforcement theory terms, and then, explicitly disavowing any reliance upon neural or mental processes. This has resulted in a breakdown of the distinction between behavioral regularities and irregularities, a rejection of the conventional classification system, and the advancement of unconventional therapeutic practices.

The response to these efforts has been swift and, at times, vitriolic, essentially questioning the validity of generalizing the reinforcement principle to complex behavioral processes. It has been suggested that the concept is tautological, is of limited interest beyond its value for animal trainers, and does not explain evidence of learning in the absence of response consequences (Breger & McGaugh, 1965). The rebuttals to these arguments have also been fast and furious (Rachman & Eysenck, 1966; Kanfer & Phillips, 1970; Wiest, 1967), and it wlil serve little purpose to recapitulate the various positions.

Suffice it to say that these issues are far from resolved. "In science, however, the theory that eventually gains acceptance is the one that provides the most experimental control over the subject matter" (Wiest, 1967, p. 223). We shall, then, put the argument to temporary rest until our subsequent consideration of the data.

VARIATIONS ON AT LEAST TWO
THEMES: OTHER BEHAVIORAL MODELS

We have seen how the two major learning models have been employed by their proponents in the analysis of pathological behavior. In addition to those arguments that have largely been advanced within the confines of one learning system, a number of theorists have offered alternative approaches to the experimental analysis of psychopathology. Some of these overlap with respondent conditioning and some with instrumental conditioning, but each represents enough of a departure to warrant separate consideration.

The following selections, although by no means exhaustive, are representative of those approaches which are also supported by experimental analyses. The systems differ with regard to their use of learning-theory concepts, their relationship to psychoanalytic principles, and their explicit involvement with psychopathological phenomena.

Dollard and Miller: The Conflict Model

The theory formulated by J. Dollard and N. E. Miller (1950) has often been described as an attempt to translate psychoanalytic principles into learning theory, although it does not encompass the intrapsychic processes postulated by Freud. Thus, their system seems to represent a bridge between psychoanalysis and general learning theory.

Whereas Freud considered motivation in the framework of libidinal forces seeking gratification (the pleasure principle), Dollard and Miller postulate a drive-reduction process. The drives that impel behavior may be of the approach variety (the search for food, for example) or of the avoidance variety (escape from pain). In addition to the primary drives related to the biological welfare of the organism, acquired drives may come to play the same functional role by virtue of their presence during drive reduction. Thus, special food preferences are acquired in the presence of hunger reduction, and special fears are acquired as a function of pain reduction.

The presence of a drive is a necessary precursor to learning, but other conditions must obtain for learning to actually occur. Although drives impel a person to respond, "cues determine when he will respond, and which responses he will make" (Dollard & Miller, 1950, p. 32). Furthermore, "the ease with which a response can be learned in a certain situation depends upon the probability that the cues present can be made to elicit that response" (Dollard & Miller, 1950, p. 36).

In any given situation an initial hierarchy of responses exists, with an order ranging from the most likely response to the least likely response. Sometimes this hierarchy is determined by biological conditions, and sometimes by earlier learning experiences. The probability that a response will be repeated and its position in the hierarchy is determined by the probability of reward. Those responses that are rewarded (that is, result in drive reduction) are reinforced and therefore elevated in the hierarchy; those that are not rewarded are lowered in the hierarchy.

Dollard and Miller apply these concepts to a conflict model to explain the causes of pathological behavior. When two or more drives are incompatible, conflict ensues. There may be conflict between primary drives, between acquired drives, or between both. Any given conflict situation may involve two or more approach drives (the organism must choose between two approach goals), two or more avoidance drives (the organism must respond to two avoidance alternatives), or a combination of approach and avoidance drives. In the last case there are drives directed toward a goal and drives directed away from a goal. Under such conditions the individual may be unable to reduce any of the conflicting drives "which therefore remain dammed up, active, and nagging" (Dollard & Miller, 1950, p. 13).

A commonplace example of such conflict pits anger against fear. When an individual is angered, the attempt to reduce this drive often takes the form of aggression toward the eliciting target. More often than not, however, such aggression also leads to punishment. Thus, the stimulus for aggression is also the stimulus for fear. If the fear drive is sufficiently intense and the anger drive relatively mild, conflict resolution will be in the form of fear reduction, and the avoidance response will rise in the response hierarchy. But if the anger drive is also intense, avoidance will not reduce the tension and discomfort created by the anger. A state of chronic, unresolved high drive ensues, and the individual will be stimulated by both the frustrated drive and fear.

Two consequences (symptoms) of such processes are postulated. The first involves those physiological reactions that are concomitants of high-drive states. The second involves those responses that prevent one from both thinking about one's anger and expressing aggression. Since the second consequence provides at least temporary relief from the disturbing situation, it is strongly reinforced, that is, rises in the response hierarchy. Subsequently, these responses may recur with even greater frequency and encompass a wider range of events and circumstances (Dollard & Miller, 1950).

Fear may also result in the repression of events associated with the feared target or activity. In some instances the drive itself is present, but the individual is unaware of the process. In other instances cues associated with the feared responding are repressed, and the object remains unlabeled, unrecognized, and relegated to the unconscious.

Since, in the Dollard and Miller system, language and awareness are critical cue determinants of adaptive behavior, processes that prevent such appropriate conceptual activity result in further difficulties. Thus, repression may provide a defense against fear, but it also reduces the probability that the individual will be able to discriminate between fear-provoking events and nonfear-provoking events. The fear responses are generalized to inappropriate situations. The fundamental difference between maladaptive behavior and normal behavior, then, is the individual's lack of awareness of conflict in the former instances. Since such conflicts are not accessible to realistic thought and intelligent resolution, the maladaptive behavior will persist because of its immediate drive-reduction function, and will not ordinarily be replaced by more adaptive alternatives (Dollard & Miller, 1950).

Like Freud, Dollard and Miller argue that neuroses are a defense against anxiety, and that the circumstances that result in such conditions are most prominent during childhood, since intense emotional, unconscious conflicts constitute the necessary basis for neurotic behavior, and childhood is rife with such "opportunities." Children are constantly exposed to conflicting demands during a time when their higher mental processes are immature. This is particularly true during feeding, cleanliness training, sex training, and the treatment of anger responses (Dollard & Miller, 1950).

Consider the typical manner in which the treatment of anger may generate difficulties.

> *Parents intuitively resent and fear its anger and the rage of a child, and they have the strong support of the culture in suppressing its anger. Direct punishment is probably used much more frequently when the child is angry and aggressive than in any other circumstance. More or less without regard to what the child is angry about, fear is attached to the stimuli of anger. (Dollard & Miller, 1950, p. 148)*

Thus, anxiety becomes attached to both the emotional cues produced by the anger and the cues associated with punishment.

> *It is this latter connection which creates the inner or emotional conflict. After this learning has occurred, the first cues produced by angry emotions may set off anxiety responses which "outcompete" the angry emotional responses themselves. The person can thus be made helpless to use his anger even in those situations where culture does permit it. He is viewed as abnormally meek or long-suffering. Robbing a person of his anger completely may be a dangerous thing since some capacity for anger seems to be needed in the affirmative personality. (Dollard & Miller, 1950, p. 148)*

Critique. In brief, then, Dollard and Miller are in fundamental agreement with Freud regarding the causes of psychopathology. The unconscious conflict between a learned fear, for example, and an innate or acquired drive is the cornerstone of the theory. Maladaptive behavior (phobias, compulsions, etc.) provides a partial resolution of the conflict by enabling immediate relief, but the long-range effects are more serious. Thus, these effects are "symptoms" of some critical disturbance at another level of analysis.

Initially, it was believed that the translation of mental-conflict terminology in drive theory would increase the model's scientific respectability. In this fashion Dollard and Miller hoped to combine the vitality of psychoanalysis with the laws of learning. Certainly, the Dollard and Miller school produced a continuing line of research based upon the conflict model. A considerable amount of data was generated, often with the implication that the analysis of incompatible reaction tendencies might provide analogs of pathological behavior. We will shortly consider some of the experimental efforts in this area as well as their relevancy for confirming the above.

On the other hand, a number of writers (Bandura, 1961; Mowrer, 1965) have argued that the Dollard and Miller position really did not provide an advance in behavior theory; rather it merely represents a translation of Freudian concepts into a behavioristic framework, while continuing to rely upon intrapsychic assumptions that differ in no essential way from Freud.

Nevertheless, Dollard and Miller's contribution represents an important historical milestone in providing a bridge between laboratory techniques and clinical phenomena.

Mowrer

O. H. Mowrer has made many contributions to the study of psychopathology, including some of the first attempts to apply learning principles to clinical phenomena. Mowrer has formulated a general theory of personality, analyzed special forms of maladaptive behavior (neuroses, anxiety, vicious circle behavior, phobias), conducted important research in the area, and more recently, attempted to reconstruct a moralistic approach to psychopathology.

His early effort to apply learning principles to pathological behavior (Mowrer, 1950) has been characterized as a two-factor theory, because of its analysis of learning in terms of both instrumental and respondent processes. At that time, Mowrer argued that instrumental processes govern voluntary events and represent the means by which the individual learns which responses produce pleasure and avoid pain. Thus, the individual responds through his effector mechanisms, attains his goal, and thereby increases the probability of similar responding in the future. Respondent processes govern involuntary, reflex events that result in sign learning; sign learning is the process by which previously neutral stimuli acquire conditioned stimulus properties.

Since most reflex events are related to potentially dangerous situations, sign learning is critical for the individual's survival. A knowledge of the signs associated with such situations is necessary if the individual is to respond quickly and efficiently and thus to maintain his biological integrity.

Indiscriminate and/or inappropriate sign learning interferes with adequate solution learning, thus restricting the individual's behavioral repertoire, and eventually contributing to a maladaptive behavior pattern. Consider the child who has been exposed to excessive punishment for aggressive or sexual behavior. This produces conditioned fear (anxiety) in the presence of those stimuli that accompany or signal such behavior. By not engaging in the forbidden act, the child is relieved of the anxiety conditioned to such situations. In the process, however, an inordinate number of stimuli may acquire the signs for danger, and instrumental processes may be employed for the purpose of reducing the constant threat. Solution learning then becomes largely a protective device, rather than an efficient learning mechanism, thus reducing the degree to which learning mechanisms can be used for effective trial-and-error learning; that is, fewer resources are available to deal with the changes required by changing environmental demands. For Mowrer the central factor in neurotic behavior is anxiety, a conditioned pain reaction that is aroused in the presence of "dangerous" stimuli. Behavior that circumvents the danger (defensive behavior) is reinforced, because of its immediate relief-giving properties, but provides no long-term solution. The neurotic, claims Mowrer, is an individual who has learned how not to learn (Mowrer, 1950, p. 526). Instrumental processes enable the individual to avoid the anxiety associated with the many danger signs in the environment, but in the process the source of the anxiety remains untouched. The child who is exposed to many painful experiences during socialization will attach anxiety to those situations necessary for normal development. If instrumental processes are employed in order to escape further anxiety, he will not learn effective coping mechanisms.

Subsequently, Mowrer revised his two-factor system by claiming that "all learning is sign learning and that solution learning is a derivative thereof" (Mowrer, 1960, p. 257). Furthermore, Mowrer asserted that sign learning mediated emotional reactivity. Thus, all behavioral events involve an association between the signs and the various emotions produced under different circumstances. When responding results in positive reinforcement, for example, the response-produced stimuli become associated with the emotion of hope. When the hoped-for event fails to occur (as in extinction), the response-produced stimuli become associated with the emotion of disappointment. Similarly, when responding results in a noxious event (as in punishment), the signs become associated with the emotion of fear. When the feared event fails to occur, the signs become associated with the emotion of relief. Mowrer stresses that these associations between signs and emotions occur as a consequence of pairing between the stimuli correlated with these various events and the emotional drives they arouse.

To explain pathological behavior in the light of his emphasis upon emotional learning, Mowrer invokes the concepts of shame and guilt. In the process of becoming socialized, children "develop attitudes of fear and hope, experience relief and disappointment" (Mowrer, 1960, p. 391). In addition, however, there is the "capacity to experience that fateful phenomenon known as guilt" (Mowrer, 1960a). Guilt is the emotion experienced when the organism performs a forbidden act and anticipates that he will be punished. Even though the fear of punishment may not be great enough to inhibit an act, that fear may be very lively indeed *after* the act is performed (Mowrer, 1960, p. 397). The organism then stands in dread of chastisement, which is, in itself, aversive and promotes escape and avoidance behavior.

The normal, healthy individual is one who accepts the penalties for engaging in forbidden behavior, as distinguished from the pathological individual who displays various forms of maladaptive behavior, including defensive behavior (lying, rationalizing, forgetting, etc.), aggressive behavior, withdrawal, etc. These, then, are modes of immediately alleviating one's guilt, but they are not directed at the source of the guilt itself.

More recently, Mowrer has elaborated further on these themes. The traditional analysis of sequences from disturbed emotion to maladaptive behavior is incorrect, claims Mowrer. In contrast to the traditional argument, his thesis is that

> *in psychopathology, the primary basic cause is deliberate, choice mediated behavior of a socially disapproved, reprehensible nature which results in emotional disturbance and insecurity (because the individual is objectively guilty, socially vulnerable, and, if caught, subject to criticism or punishment). The symptoms which then ensue represent ways in which the individual is trying to defend himself against and hide his disturbing and suspicion-arousing emotions (of moral fear and guilt). Thus, a deliberate misdeed is the original, or primary, cause, and emotional disturbance follows, which may then produce symptoms of a more or less behavioral type. (Mowrer, 1965, p. 243)*

Critique. Mowrer's recent pronouncements are difficult to assess. Even though he considers his revised system to be an improvement over his earlier theory, little seems to have been gained by reconceptualizing the four major response-consequence arrangements in emotion-learning terms. Adding the concepts of shame and guilt diverts our attention still further from the major issue at hand, that is, functionally identified causes and cures of pathological behavior.

The impact of his earlier two-factor theory is easier to assess. As we shall see, the two-factor theory has generated a great deal of research that has implications for the experimental analysis of behavior pathology. Moreover, a substantial number of behaviorally oriented clinicians advocate the two-factor theory as the best explanation for a number of clinical conditions, especially the classical forms of neuroses. Thus, it is now almost commonplace to interpret a phobia as an example of avoidance behavior, as explained by the two-factor theory.

Masserman

The continuing effort by some psychiatrists to provide an experimental foundation for psychoanalytic concepts is best represented by Wolpe and Jules Masserman. As we have seen, Wolpe's effort led, ultimately, to a rejection, out of hand, of the critical psychoanalytic notion of unconscious conflict in favor of a thoroughgoing behaviorism based upon learning theory. Jules Masserman's approach, on the other hand, may be characterized as an amalgam of behavioristic and psychoanalytical propositions in the context of a conflict model (Masserman, 1946).

It is in his experimental work (to be reviewed subsequently) that Masserman is more the behaviorist than the Freudian; it is in his theoretical explorations that he is more the Freudian than the behaviorist. For this reason we have chosen to focus our attention upon his efforts in the former area, by providing a theoretical analysis of his research projects.

Masserman argues that, for the most part, organisms maintain adequate adjustment with their environment.

> *If, however, the young animal is subjected to exceedingly severe conflicts between mutually excessive satisfactions or counterposed desires and aversions, it develops deeply ingrained inhibitions, fears, rituals, somatic disorders, social maladjustments, and other aberrations of behavior which become highly elaborate and more difficult to treat than those originating in childhood. (Masserman, 1966)*

Although Masserman appears to agree with Freud and Dollard and Miller regarding the etiological importance of a fear conflict, he differs from both by stating that equally serious and lasting neurotogenic efforts can also be induced by conflict between mutually exclusive satisfactions, such as food versus play (that is, approach-approach conflicts), exploration versus escape, or the slaking of thirst versus sexual gratification—that is, "situations that parallel the disruptive effects of prolonged indecisions as to available gratifications in human affairs" (Masserman, 1966, p. 12).

In addition to conflict as a causative agent, Masserman also acknowledges the impact of early deprivation. For example, children given adequate physical care in orphanages but deprived of individualized attention and love during the crucial first four years of life lose the capacity to form warm relationships and develop serious and persistent disturbances of behavior variously called "autism, protophrenia, or childhood schizophrenia" (Masserman, 1966, p. 28).

Although Masserman rejects Freud's emphasis upon neurosis caused by unconscious sexual conflict, the notion of pathological behavior as *symptomatic* is retained. This is, perhaps, more apparent in his earlier publications (which invoked the concept of defense mechanisms in the Freudian sense) than in his more recent efforts. Nevertheless, he continues to consider pathological behavior as a reflection of a disturbance at another level.

Critique. It is difficult to characterize Masserman as belonging to any one school or representing any one position. As we shall see, his experimental efforts bear little relationship to many of his theoretical pronouncements, which have never been well systematized. On the whole, however, Masserman's research clearly reflects the predominant theme of the conflict model, the importance of which he has explicitly acknowledged.

On the other hand, although he has accepted this model, he has not pursued it as diligently as have Dollard and Miller or Mowrer. Masserman is content to argue that deprivation and stress may produce pathological behavior, but he does not attempt either to specify the necessary and sufficient traumatic events or to relate these experiences to specific or general forms of psychopathology. Masserman's major contribution as an early investigator will be subsequently reviewed in the section on experimental methods.

Harlow: The Deprivation Model

History reveals a continuing interest in the effects of restricted experiences on pathological behavior. Even before the development of a scientific methodology, there were numerous anecdotes reporting the abnormal behavior of children separated from society and raised under feral conditions. The more recent attention given to the deleterious effects of deprivation on ghetto children reflects a current interest in this area.

Psychologists have contributed considerable information to this topic, often formulating their contributions in terms of sensory restrictions, social deprivation, etc. Although, to date, an integrated theory of the many observations relevant to psychopathology remains to be formulated, much of this information bears upon the issue of psychopathology, even when the investigators have not themselves been directly interested in psychopathological phenomena.

In theory, any departure from "normal" stimulation represents a form of deprivation, with complete separation, at birth, from all exteroceptive events representing the extreme case. Practically, however, all organisms experience some degree of sensory restriction, and no living organism is ever completely deprived. The issue is one of determining which forms of deprivations result in which forms of behavior pathology, and here we include a range of events that are not generally included under the term "sensory reduction" (which is usually restricted to studies of social isolation in normal, human, adult males). We have chosen the term "deprivation model" to encompass more of the possibly relevant arrangements, including early and extended isolation in infrahumans.

The work of Harry Harlow and his associates (Harlow & Zimmerman, 1959; Harlow & Harlow, 1962, 1965) probably best represents the systematic study of the effects of psychological deprivation on pathological behavior. In a long series of investigations extending over some twenty years, Harlow has demonstrated the manner in which various deprivation experiences in the rhesus monkey result in a host of pathological conditions, including anxiety, depression, self-injury, autistic behavior, inappropriate sexual patterns, impaired learning ability, inadequate social behavior.

Harlow (Harlow & Harlow, 1965) maintains that normal infant-mother affectional interactions in rhesus monkeys advance through a series of stages (roughly analogous to similar development in humans). The mother's behavior may be described in this fashion: (1) the stage of maternal attachment and protection, (2) the transitional or ambivalence stage, which is also described as the disattachment stage, and (3) the stage of separation or rejection. As the infant monkey develops, the mother's behavior changes from close attachment and protection, through progressive relaxation of control over the baby's activities (thereby encouraging and enabling increasing independence and fostering socialization), to ultimate separation.

The infant's development is normally characterized by stages that complement and advance the maternal stages. Initially, the infant monkey's behavior is largely reflexive, thus ensuring appropriate orientation to, and contact with, the mother as the source of nourishment and physical contact. As voluntary responses evolve, the comfort and attachment stage begins. In this stage the infant develops the mechanisms for establishing nonnutritional interactions as well as the mechanisms for following and imitating. This stage is followed by the security stage, in which there is an increase in exploratory behavior, a gradual reduction in the frequency of mother-child interactions, and an increase in the frequency of contact with other environmental objects. As contact with the environment (including age-mate association) increases, the infant enters into the separation stage, terminating the mother-child relationship with independent behavior. Harlow further suggests the development of a peer social system that advances through a similar series of stages, which are necessary for the development of adequate, independent social interactions (Harlow & Harlow, 1965).

In terms of psychopathology, being deprived of the experiences related to these stages may prevent the development of appropriate affectional social patterns and result in disordered behavior. In general, the earlier the deprivation and the longer it is maintained, the greater the probability of pathological effects. Of particular importance to Harlow is the experience of contact comfort. Thus, above and beyond the alleviation of hunger and thirst, one of the mother's chief functions is to provide contact comfort, in order to ensure normal affectional development. Indeed, Harlow considers this to be of such critical importance that "the primary function of nursing may be that of insuring frequent and intimate contact between mother and infant, thus facilitating the localization of the source of contact comfort" (Harlow & Zimmerman, 1959, p. 423). Infants deprived of contact comfort do not display adequate affectional behavior; on the contrary, they reveal heightened emotionality and autistic-like reactions in the presence of fear stimuli (instead of escaping to the mother and then exploring, as in the normal monkey) as well as other forms of maladaptive behavior.

Harlow further maintains that the contact-comfort experience is independent of drive reduction (that is, biological needs), which is a rather unusual position, since most learning psychologists explain the development of adequate social behavior as an extension of biological reinforcement.

Peer group experiences are also of critical importance in the development of normal behavior (Harlow & Harlow, 1962). Indeed, peer interactions may even compensate for contact-comfort deprivation. Thus, monkeys provided with adequate nutrition and contact comfort may still display serious pathology if deprived of the opportunity to interact with other peer animals. This is particularly evident in the mothering behavior of females who have been deprived of contact with peers. Such females will either avoid or attack their infants or do both.

Critique. Harlow's theoretical statements are predicated on the basis of research dealing with virtually total isolation (that is, more than just maternal deprivation is usually involved), a condition that occupies one end of the deprivation continuum. For this reason, as Harlow recognizes, generalizing to human behavior must be undertaken with extreme caution, although he has, on occasion, pointed out the similarity between his experimental model and similar analyses of the effects of maternal deprivation in human infants (Harlow *et al.,* 1972).

His focus upon contact comfort has caused some discomfort for drive-reduction theorists, who maintain that appropriate social behavior emerges from adequate earlier biological need reduction. On the other hand, Harlow's acknowledgment that infants deprived of contact comfort may still acquire adequate social patterns as a consequence of peer influences appears to be inconsistent with his thesis that contact comfort is a critical determinant of adult adjustment. In this connection the status of the contact-comfort concept still requires further analysis.

Regardless of the theoretical issues, however, one can scarcely deny Harlow's importance in imposing a systematic framework on a traditional, but loosely organized, area of inquiry. Much remains to be done, of course, in terms of isolating functional relationships between independent and dependent variables, but a good start has been provided by his efforts.

Bandura: The Social-Learning Model
It is a commonplace observation that children imitate the behavior, both good and bad, of adults. The importance of this phenomenon for the study of personality and pathological behavior has long been recognized by writers in these fields. Freud, for example, termed the process by which a child acquired the characteristics of a parent "identification."

More recently, the study of such imitation has been advanced within the confines of social-learning theory, as demonstrated by the work of Albert Bandura and his associates (Bandura & Walters, 1962). Bandura's model borrows heavily from reinforcement theory, but he also attempts to explain a number of dimensions of imitation learning which appear to defy analysis by reinforcement principles per se. For this reason Bandura's position represents a sufficient departure from strict reinforcement theory to warrant independent review.

Bandura makes a distinction between imitation *learning* and imitative *performance*. The former may occur as a function of exposure to a model even in the absence of reinforcement. Subsequently, when the imitative behavior is expressed, reinforcement contingencies may exert their effect. Thus, a strict reinforcement analysis fails to account for novel behavior, the learning of complex behaviors that appear the first time in their entirety, the learning of behavior that is not reinforced, and behavior that first appears long after it has been learned. To explain these phenomena, Bandura assigns a prominent role to representational mediators that are assumed to be acquired on the basis of a contiguity learning process (Bandura, 1969). "After modeling stimuli have been coded into images or words for memory representation they function as mediators for subsequent response retrieval and reproduction" (Bandura, 1969, p. 133). It is this cognitive process, then, that Bandura considers to be critical for the acquisition of imitative behavior in the natural environment.

The imitation process may be advanced in several ways. In one instance, observation of a model may result in the inclusion of a completely novel response in the observer's repertoire, either in terms of new behavior or in terms of an old response in the presence of new stimulus conditions. Thus, a child raised in a "disturbed" environment, exposed to adults displaying pathological behavior, may directly imitate such behavior. The model may also generate an inhibitory or disinhibitory effect. In the former case the individual *refrains* from making a response he might have made, and in the latter case he engages in behavior that would ordinarily be inhibited. "Many phobic behaviors, for example, arise not from injurious experiences with the phobic objects, but rather from witnessing others respond fearfully toward, or be hurt by, certain things" (Bandura, 1969, p. 167). Inhibited models may explain the imitation of avoidance behavior in children and the disposition to withdraw from stressful events rather than to cope with them. Similarly, observing a parent engage in behavior such as a temper tantrum, previously inhibited in the imitator, might serve as a cue for the expression of such behavior.

In addition to his theoretical statements, Bandura has made numerous contributions to the experimental analysis of psychopathology and has ardently rejected the disease-symptom approach, in favor of a behavioral orientation (Bandura, 1968). Thus, he argues that

> the persistence of the disease-demonology model and the need
> for invoking psychodynamic explanatory agents appear to be

largely due to lack of knowledge of the genesis of functional behavioral deviations. When the actual social learning history of maladaptive behavior is known, the basic principles of learning provide a completely adequate interpretation of many psychological phenomena, and explanations in terms of symptoms underlying disorders become superfluous. (Bandura, 1968, p. 298)

Although Bandura has not explicitly formulated a theory of the etiology of pathological behavior based upon a social-learning model, his recent efforts offer some suggestions for such an enterprise. Thus, an analysis of pathological conditions should include the manner in which the significant adults in an individual's life serve as the models for deviancy, either in terms of generating maladaptive behavior or in terms of inhibiting adaptive behavior.

Instead of classifying pathology in the conventional manner, with its emphasis upon subject variables or personal characteristics, Bandura advocates the scheme advanced by A. W. Staats and C. K. Staats (1966), which focuses upon the functional characteristics of the behavior, that is, the environmental determinants that help to explain "the acquisition and maintenance of deviant response patterns and to guide therapeutic practices" (Bandura, 1968, p. 298).

For example, many individuals are classified as abnormal because of deficient behavioral repertoires; that is, they lack the requisite skills for adequate social, academic, and vocational adjustment. These deficiencies may be of a relatively circumscribed nature, as in the "slow learner," the "social misfit," and the vocationally handicapped, or they may be more extensive, as exemplified by autism, mental retardation, and institutionalized psychosis. Although a number of learning variables may be involved in such conditions, models may also produce behavioral deficits. Since "stable complex patterns of behavior are in part socially transmitted through observation of competent models" (Bandura, 1968, p. 299), inadequate models may also produce deficits in the observer. Similarly, a deficit may be the result of inhibitory modeling processes, thus involving a different response history. Behavioral deficits frequently observed in schizophrenia, for example, may be explained in terms of inhibitory modeling processes. Inadequate self-grooming may occur as a function of inadequate models, and social withdrawal may be the result of inhibitory models that led the imitator to avoid stressful situations rather than cope with them. Similarly, modeling may also be involved in the display of inappropriate behavior—that range of pathological events that often seems to typify abnormal behavior. Inappropriate labeling, for example, is often exhibited by schizophrenics. Once again, the model relationship may explain the etiology of such effects. A good example is reported in a case study by T. Lidz *et al.* (1965), in which two schizophrenic brothers maintained that disagreement meant constipation.

This clearly inappropriate expression was primarily a result of exposure to a relatively bizarre social learning situation rather than an expression of "mental illness." Whenever the boys disagreed with the mother, she told them they were constipated and required an enema. The boys were then disrobed and given enemas, a procedure that dramatically conditioned an unusual meaning for the word "disagreement." (p. 295)

Bandura refers to other studies in the literature, which "provide ample evidence that delusions, suspiciousness, grandiosity, extreme denial of reality, and other forms of schizophrenic behavior are frequently learned through direct reinforcement and transmitted by parental modeling of unusually deviant behavior patterns" (Bandura, 1968, p. 295).

Critique. Bandura argues that reinforcement theory simply cannot explain all of the facts relevant to an analysis of the imitation process, since under natural conditions the behavior exhibited by models is typically reproduced in the absence of direct reinforcement. Instead of assuming an intrinsic reinforcer or generalized reinforcement pattern, Bandura reemphasizes the traditional distinction between imitative learning, which is influenced by contiguity variables, and imitative performance, which is influenced by reinforcement variables, with a contiguity representational process mediating between the two.

This position bridges the gap between earlier formulations in which modeling was regarded as a function of an "innate propensity" and those contemporary positions which analyze imitation as a reinforcement-determined phenomenon (Gewirtz & Stingle, 1968; Baer *et al.,* 1967). Although Bandura claims that his theory handles the facts better, proponents of the latter view are now attempting a detailed analysis of the modeling-imitation interaction in which the reinforcement variables that govern the process are explicated. They would probably further argue that a reliance upon cognitive explanations might be misleading if it directs our attention away from a behavioral analysis in pursuit of alleged hypothetical explanations.

Once again, we must look to further research for a clarification of these issues and a resolution of the differences.

SUMMARY: OTHER BEHAVIORAL MODELS

In this section we have reviewed several behavioral models that rely, to varying degrees, upon contiguity theory and reinforcement theory. In addition, however, they also make reference to hypothetical processes that differ from Pavlov's neural explanatory system. Furthermore, they differ from the operant system in that proponents of the latter specifically disavow any explanation based upon the conceptual nervous system, the real nervous system, or intrapsychic systems.

The approaches reviewed have achieved varying degrees of popularity. The theory that has been regarded most often as the best representative of the behavioral position on psychopathology is Dollard and Miller's. However, although their views are still very much in evidence, the influence of their approach to the analysis of pathological conditions has recently declined. Miller, himself, has turned his attention to other areas of inquiry since his last formal statement on learning-theory approaches to psychopathology (Miller, 1959).

The one common thread that appears to unify the various theories, regardless of how they attack this area of inquiry, is that, from the standpoint of a *behavioral* analysis, psychopathology is ultimately defined in terms of either some sort of behavioral deficit (that is, the absence of desirable behavior) and/or some sort of inappropriate behavior (that is, the presence of undesirable behavior). This is less clear in the Dollard and Miller system, which bears the vestiges of psychoanalysis, with its emphasis upon unconscious processes, and patently clear in Harlow's approach, with its emphasis upon impaired social development. What is also clear, however, is that the experimental models that these men have generated, whether based upon the concept of conflict, deprivation, or imitation, have had and will continue to have an important bearing on the study of the causes of psychopathology. It is to these efforts that our attention will be directed next.

In this section we have reviewed some of the major theoretical attempts to answer the question: "Why abnormal behavior?" The first major breakthrough in psychology occurred with Freud. Largely due to his influence psychologists began to focus their attention upon disruption or impairment of the biological-social transaction in order to find the causes of psychopathology. This was a radical departure from the previous theoretical emphasis upon biological impairment (usually of the central nervous system). Freud applied a deterministic frame of reference that acknowledged the importance of environmental factors in all facets of human behavior. Thus, he included aspects of human functioning that were previously ignored and in the process advanced a more sophisticated analysis of deviance; that is, the inclusion of "normal" dimensions of behavior reduced the dichotomy between the normal and the abnormal.

On the other hand, the cause-and-effect relationships specified by Freud were overdrawn, resulting in a host of popular but hastily drawn conclusions: Bottle feeding causes thumb-sucking; stopping a child from sucking his thumb will cause even more serious problems; a domineering mother will raise a homosexual (either latent or overt) son; harsh toilet training will cause stinginess, etc. Vestiges of many of these notions still abound in the popular women's literature. The explicit rejection of conventional scientific proof by many Freudians prevented these propositions from being put to the test. The heavy reliance upon unverifiable, hypothetical processes caused further embarrassment for psychoanalytic theorists.

With the growing disaffection with psychoanalysis and its emphasis upon unconscious conflict, and with the improvement in research methods, other views, which departed from analytic doctrine, were formulated. Most of these views also emphasized conflict as a critical determinant, and perhaps this was a logical development. Unfortunately, the kind of conflict postulated in these alternative systems also invoked mentalistics or nonverifiable physiological mechanisms, as in Pavlov's, Dollard and Miller's, and Mowrer's approaches. Although these theorists also provided experimental support for their positions, their efforts were often formulated in the context of verifying the theory and drew our attention away from the functional analysis of antecedent conditions and subsequent effects on pathological behavior. The end result was that one form of unsupported generalization was substituted for another, thus providing little knowledge of the necessary and sufficient conditions underlying behavior pathology.

On the other hand, the clearly experimental bias of these investigators helped establish a scientific basis for the study of psychopathology and resulted in the destruction of certain myths. Thus, they further contributed to the dissolution of the schism between the normal and the abnormal. Whereas Freud and most clinicians paid lip service to the universality of general principles, these investigators provided evidence in direct support of this argument, as we shall see when reviewing their laboratory models.

A second contribution of these investigators has been the reformulation of an answer to the question, "Why?" The conventional wisdom searched for a simplified explanation of the "disease" of psychopathology. If this disease could be isolated, then a cure could ultimately be found, in the same way that medical researchers have embarked on finding a cure for cancer. Although this doctrine continues to have considerable appeal in many quarters, a more sophisticated aproach to the study of the causes of psychopathology has emerged, largely through the efforts of writers such as Dollard and Miller and Mowrer. No longer can the question "Why?" be answered in terms of the disease process. A person does not suddenly contract the disease of deviancy, nor can a clinical observation of abnormal behavior provide the means by which such an inference is made. On the contrary, what these writers have verified has long been known in theory and often overlooked in practice: Pathological behavior is the end result of a whole complex history of events and variables. Furthermore, the study of these events can best be accomplished by resorting to the classical scientific strategy, which requires the study of simple processes before attacking complex, multivariable processes.

CONCLUSION

One final statement might now be considered. Theories may be evaluated in terms of their logical consistency, their heuristic value, their generality, their parsimony, their practical utility, etc. In the last analysis, however, all of these criteria, in turn, depend upon some measure of empirical support. Any theory, regardless of how elegant and appealing, must be capable of (potential) verification.

One corollary of this proposition is that the greater the degree to which a theory rests upon an experimental foundation, the greater is the degree of confidence that can be placed upon the predictions it generates. This is not to demean the value of nonexperimental observation; witness Darwin's contribution to knowledge. It simply means that our confidence in a theory is enhanced when the theory can be translated into experimental analysis. Furthermore, we have argued that this criterion is particularly important in the field of psychopathology, where science must compete with nonscientific tradition in the formulating of general principles.

No doubt the advocates of the various theories reviewed in this section would argue that their system meets this test. We will discuss this issue at length in the subsequent section, which reviews the experimental support. Several comments, however, may be made at this juncture, and a word about hypothetical constructs is indicated. A distinction may be made between operant theory and the other behavioral approaches along this dimension. This is, of course, not by accident. Skinner has long been recognized as an ardent critic of "hypothetical systems." Instead, he advocates a primarily inductive strategy designed to isolate general principles through the establishment of functional relationships between antecedent events and consequent effects.

Scientists have argued over the advantages and disadvantages of hypothesizing, and psychology has not escaped this controversy. Skinner has often been cast in the role of the antitheoretician, on one side of the conflict, with the rest of psychology on the other side. Perhaps these were fair odds in those halcyon days when Skinner was the only outspoken critic, hypothesizing was a popular pastime, and the crusade of strict empiricism was less favorably received than it is today. Although there have been numerous counterattacks, including the argument that Skinner also engaged in subtle and disguised forms of "theorizing" (which he never denied), one can scarcely deny that he has remained relatively consistent, in this regard, while the mainstream of psychology has also moved in this direction.

Chapter 4 / Classical Conditioning Techniques

Pavlov

In our review of Pavlov's theory we focused upon his explanation of pathological behavior in terms of disturbances at the cortical level. His efforts in this area were primarily designed to explicate his typological system and to confirm the neurological events alleged to be responsible for pathological behavior. "It becomes clear on considering all the pathological cases so far described, that the underlying cause of their development is in every instance the same. Broadly we can regard these disturbances as due to a conflict between the processes of excitation and inhibition which the cortex finds difficult to resolve" (Pavlov, 1927, p. 302).

Despite Pavlov's physiological orientation, however, it is possible to consider his experimental neurosis arrangements within the context of a behavioral analysis without resorting to hypothetical neural events. Let us review his efforts from this point of view.

When Pavlov first formulated the now familiar conditioning paradigm, the operations seemed reasonably straightforward and without analytical complications. Thus, the basic procedure involved (1) the measuring of some stimulus-physiological reflex, in which the stimulus had definable eliciting characteristics (for example, meat powder–salivation), (2) the subsequent pairing of the eliciting stimulus with a neutral stimulus (for example, a buzzer sounding for ten seconds prior to the presentation of the meat powder), and (3) over a series of such trials, the elicitation of the reflex with increasing magnitude and decreasing latency in the presence of the previously neutral stimulus. With this procedure an ineffectual stimulus acquired a property previously restricted to the unconditioned stimulus (UCS); thus, the procedure demonstrated a form of learning.

As the principle was increasingly applied to reflex systems other than the salivary response, however, and as other modes of reflex processes were studied (especially those involving electric shock), it became increasingly apparent that the procedures actually employed by subsequent investigators bore only a superficial resemblance to the initial Pavlovian paradigm, especially when the *consequences* of responding intruded into the arrangement. For example, one common respondent-conditioning procedure used by later investigators involved pairing a neutral stimulus with the shocking of an animal's leg. The shock, of course, elicited the leg flexion, and after sufficient pairing the previously neutral stimulus acquired a similar functional property. In some experiments the shock was administered on each trial, even though the animal displayed the conditioned response (CR). In other arrangements, however, if the animal displayed the conditioned response, he *prevented* the onset of shock; thus, the arrangement involved response consequences. "The differences between these two procedures did not seem important to the earliest investigators of conditioning, and the two procedures were used quite indiscriminately" (Kimble, 1961, p. 44).

As the significance of response consequences became evident, however, learning theorists began a long dialogue, the essential purpose of which was to clarify the differences between "respondent" processes and "instrumental" processes. It is beyond the scope of this book to detail this important and complex issue. The interested reader, however, may refer to Black's (1971) extensive review and analysis. Although this issue is far from resolved, most authorities agree that a distinction may be made on operational grounds. Kimble (1961), however, has described the difficulties involved in such a resolution, and the interested reader is referred to his discussion. For the present purposes we will consider only those arrangements in which the consequences of responding have no bearing on the experimental events, thus satisfying the requirements of classical conditioning. All those conditioning arrangements where there is reason to believe that response consequences influenced the experimental events (even in those cases where this possibility was neglected and obscured) will be considered examples of instrumental processes or combinations of instrumental and respondent processes.

Some understanding of the application of the term "neurosis" to the phenomena observed by Pavlov can be obtained if we consider the observations that preceded these pathological reactions.

In the course of developing the conditioned-response paradigm, Pavlov investigated a number of conditions which contributed to the establishment of the general principle. Thus, various auditory, visual, and tactual stimuli were conditionable when appropriately arranged in contiguity with the unconditioned stimulus eliciting the salivary reflex. Furthermore, in elaborating the paradigm, Pavlov found that his canine subjects could usually be trained to discriminate between those stimuli that were paired with the unconditioned stimulus (positive stimuli) and those that were not so paired (negative stimuli), even if both stimuli were in the same sense modality. Thus, one of two differently pitched tones might be presented in a series of trials. That tone paired with the unconditioned stimulus would acquire conditioned stimulus (CS) properties, thus eliciting salivation, and the alternate tone would not. As training progressed, increased efficiency would result, the animal always salivating in the presence of the positive tone and never salivating in the presence of the negative stimulus. Conditioned responses that were acquired under these arrangements revealed the predictable regularities Pavlov had come to expect of all his subjects regardless of temperament, even though they might be constitutionally different along the excitatory-inhibitory dimension.

Certain procedures, however, resulted in a disruption of the animal's behavior, and the degree and manner of disruption seemed to be related to the animal's temperament. Pavlov was interested in the investigation of these conditions because of their possible relationship to psychopathology.

Even prior to these observations, however, Pavlov reported a finding that, in retrospect, may have even more important implications for the study of psychopathological effects. When, under ordinary circumstances, strong shock or skin cauterization is "applied, the organism responds by a violent motor reaction directed towards removal of the noxious stimulus or to its own removal from it" (Pavlov, 1927, p. 29). (Today we recognize such reactions as examples of escape behavior.) Under other circumstances, however, such noxious stimuli are transformed into conditioned stimuli for the alimentary reflex. When this is accomplished, "not even the tiniest and most subtle objective phenomenon usually exhibited by animals under the influence of strong, injurious stimuli can be observed in these dogs. No appreciable changes in the pulse or respiration occurs in these animals, whereas such changes are always most prominent when the noxious stimulus has not been converted into an alimentary conditioned reflex" (Pavlov, 1927, p. 30).

Pavlov's interest in such phenomena was restricted to his observation that even a noxious stimulus could be transformed into a CS, thus demonstrating the potency of the conditioning paradigm. Although the importance of such effects for understanding certain dimensions of pathological behavior, for example, masochistic behavior (Sandler, 1964), now seems clear, it was those procedures resulting in discrimination breakdown that first captured Pavlov's attention as examples of experimental neurosis.

An experiment by N. R. Shenger-Krestovnikova (1921) in 1914 provides one example of such a neurosis. Here, a round circle of light served as the positive stimulus (paired with the UCS) and an elliptical circle of light as the negative stimulus. After the discrimination was acquired, the experimenter gradually decreased the eccentricity of the ellipse until it was almost circular. After three weeks of training, which would usually have been expected to result in improved efficiency, the animal's behavior deteriorated so that it was now occasionally salivating to the negative stimulus, and eventually the discrimination disappeared completely.

> *At the same time, the whole behavior of the animal underwent an abrupt change. The hitherto quiet dog began to squeal in its stand, kept wriggling about, tore off with its teeth the apparatus for mechanical stimulation of the skin, and bit through the tubes connecting the animal's room with the observer, a behavior which never happened before. On being taken into the experimental room the dog now barked violently, which was also contrary to its usual custom; in short it presented all the symptoms of a condition of acute neurosis. (Pavlov, 1927, p. 29)*

Only when the first discrimination task was again presented was the animal's behavior appropriate to the task, but even this required twice the length of training time originally involved.

Other arrangements also resulted in experimental neuroses. In one experiment, for example, dogs with the two extreme temperaments were presented with progressively longer delays between onset of the conditioned stimulus and the unconditioned stimulus. The inhibited dogs tolerated delays up to five minutes, but excitable dogs reached a state of general excitation at delays of two minutes and at three-minute delays began moving violently, howling, and barking. Retraining of the excitable dogs was accomplished using a five-second delay, but each attempt to introduce delays of three minutes or more resulted in general excitation.

In still another procedure the sudden introduction of a "strong" conditioned stimulus after an inhibited dog had been trained with a weak one resulted in disruptive behavior.

A purely fortuitous circumstance provided additional information, which Pavlov also considered relevant to experimental neurosis. In 1924 Pavlov's laboratory was inundated by a city-wide flood, which constituted a terrifying experience for his canine subjects, although all the animals were rescued. Subsequently, further conditioning efforts with an inhibited dog trained prior to the flood were unsuccessful. The animal was now restless, showed a complete absence of conditioned reflexes, and refused to eat in the experimental environment, even when his deprivation level was increased. The animal would respond only in the presence of the experimenter, and all conditioned reflexes disappeared as soon as he departed. Pavlov attributed this pathological reaction to the trauma of the flooding experience. By alternately appearing and disappearing, the experimenter gradually reinstated the conditioning.

Comment. We have seen the major observations of experimental neurosis reported by Pavlov. Here, in the very earliest examples of experimentally induced behavior disorders, we first encounter a conceptual problem that reappears time and time again in the literature and is still unanswered: Does the term "experimental neurosis" refer to the outcome of an arrangement that produces impairment in efficiency, as defined by the experimental procedure, or must there also be additional evidence of anomalies accompanying that impairment, either in or outside the experimental environment, before we can regard the effect as a genuine behavior disorder? Furthermore, to what extent can the experimental results be generalized to human behavior in the natural environment?

Pavlov, himself, was unclear on these points. P. Broadhurst (1961) suggests that Pavlov believed the term "experimental neurosis" should be restricted to the observation of a disruption in conditioning, although other reviewers (Dworkin, 1939; Franks, 1956) have reached different conclusions.

Perhaps Pavlov was uncertain as to whether other behavioral disorders were necessary concomitants of the experimental effect in experimental neurosis. The only clearly dramatic examples of extensive disturbance were revealed by the Shenger-Krestovnikova experiment, although milder behavior disorders were also reported as a consequence of the delay procedure.

A stronger case can be made for the argument that Pavlov considered pathology at the human level to be a function of circumstances analogous to those involved in the experimental neurosis arrangements. One scarcely invests some twenty years of research, as Pavlov did in his later life, for the purpose of disproving a theory. Thus, Pavlov related an excitatory temperament to manic-depressive psychoses, and an inhibitory temperament to schizophrenia and certain neurotic disorders (Frolov, 1937).

In any event, Pavlov's views and findings never had the impact on applied practices that he anticipated. For one thing, it was hard to accept the notion that the many varieties of psychopathology could be attributed to a breakdown in discrimination or to lengthening delays in the CS-UCS interval. For another, Pavlov's efforts in this connection were obscured by the more interesting and appealing views expressed by "dynamic" psychology à la psychoanalysis.

Finally, Pavlov never succeeded in isolating the necessary and sufficient conditions responsible for the experimental neurosis effects (nor, as we have seen, was he able to substantiate his claims regarding neural dysfunction). As he himself suggested, all of the animals serving as subjects had prior and differing histories, which may have had a profound effect upon the obtained results. Such variables may even have contributed to those behavioral differences that led Pavlov to postulate "innate temperamental differences." A more convincing demonstration of the alleged variables might have been provided by the use of the reversal procedure described earlier. Some of Pavlov's conclusions regarding the causes of experimental neurosis appear to be influenced by informal correlational analyses rather than a systematic functional analysis. Thus, he attributed certain experimental effects to alleged temperamental differences (which may have emerged after or during the experiment) without systematically analyzing this relationship.

Despite these shortcomings and the limited impact of Pavlov's efforts on applied pursuits, other investigators pursued this line of inquiry and contributed additional knowledge to the experimental neurosis literature. If nothing else, Pavlov formulated a method and a technology that provided the means for evaluating the etiology of certain behavioral irregularities and demonstrated the first analog of clinical events, however obscure the resemblance. To whatever degree the similarity between experimental neuroses and clinical events has improved since his early efforts, the line of endeavor owes its inception to his insights.

Krasnogorski: Experimental Neurosis in Children
Pavlov's work on experimental neurosis met with something less than unrestrained enthusiasm in clinical psychology. Although other investigators continued to analyze experimental neurosis in animals, their efforts had virtually no impact on clinical theory and practice during the next thirty years. (One important exception is A. Salter's publication "Conditioned Reflex Therapy," which appeared in 1949.) Initially, however, both in Russia and the United States, there were several attempts to apply the Pavlovian model to experimental neurosis in children. The Russians hewed very closely to the procedures outlined by Pavlov, but the early American work (where the report is sufficiently detailed to enable a careful analysis of the procedures) strongly suggests that instrumental processes were at work, even though they may have been obscured by the experimenter's bias or overlooked because of unfamiliarity with instrumental conditioning principles. The examples provided by J. B. Watson, M. C. Jones, and others fall into this category. For this reason we have chosen to present these early American studies in the section on operant-respondent combinations, rather than in terms of their conventional classical conditioning interpretation.

Perhaps the purest Pavlovian example of experimental neurosis in children is provided by N. I. Krasnogorski, a colleague of Pavlov's. In an article entitled "The Conditioned Reflexes and Children's Neuroses," published in 1925, Krasnogorski described a series of studies undertaken in 1907, which resulted in effects resembling those reported by Pavlov.

The first of these represented a breakdown in discrimination, accompanied by a general behavioral disturbance. A six-year-old boy served as the subject. During feeding periods the sound of 144 metronome beats was accompanied by feeding and "occasioned the conditioned motor reflex" (the opening of the mouth), and the sound of 92 metronome beats served as the negative stimulus (no food was paired with it). After differential training was established, the negative stimulus was changed to 108 beats, with no appreciable change in conditioning effects. When the negative stimulus was increased to 120 beats, the discrimination was maintained, but response latencies increased. "At the same time we observed an important change in the behavior of the child; having always been easy to deal with and quiet during the experiments, he now became irritable and refused to go to the laboratory" (Krasnogorski, 1925, p. 757). Finally, the child was required to discriminate between 144 beats and 132. "During the work which now began, we were informed from the child's ward that the patient had become nervous; he had always been well-behaved; now he cried often, beat the other children and said he wanted to leave the hospital" (p. 757). The record of events and change may be observed in Table 2.

A similar effect was observed in a second child who was trained to make a difficult discrimination on the skin. "When we had formed too many active and inactive places on the child's skin, systematically accompanying by food the first and not the latter, the child became restless; it would refuse to come in for the experiments; the intensity of the conditioned reflexes and the exactness on local differentiation were diminished" (Krasnogorski, 1925, p. 758).

Krasnogorski also reported an example of experimental neurosis as a consequence of the delay procedure. The "opening-of-the-mouth reflex" in a six-year-old child was formed by presenting food five seconds after a metronome had started. After the reflex was conditioned, the delay was suddenly increased to thirty seconds. "After several such stimulations, the conditioned reflex lost its stability and rapidly disappeared." The child began to yawn and to be sleepy, and as result of these experiments, developed an intensive inhibition. A replication of the procedure a second time resulted in a successful reflex delay. When the delay was now increased to sixty seconds, "the reflex disappeared again; the child began to sleep during the experiments, and refused to go to the laboratory" (Krasnogorski, 1925, p. 760). After the child had rested for a week, delayed conditioning for as long as forty seconds was reestablished.

As with Pavlov, Krasnogorski interpreted these results as a consequence of conflict between excitation and inhibition. Thus, as the differentiations became more difficult, the usual conditioned-reflex activity disappeared, and an intensive inhibition developed. On the basis of such observations, Krasnogorski argued that

> *the intensive conflicts between irradiation and inhibition form a favorable soil for the origin of different neuroses in childhood. We know how serious neuroses can develop as a result of such catastrophic collisions of inhibiting the powerful sexual reflex in adults. Thus, the intensive conflict between stimuli and inhibition in children sometimes produces a disturbance of the balance which influences the whole behavior of the child and is*

TABLE 2. Findings for Four Months[a]

Date, 1924	No. of Stimu-lation	Time	Stimulation	Condi-tioned Reflex	Latent Period	Remarks
3/6	91	12:04	Metronome 144	+	0.4	Goes to the experi-
	92	12:07	Metronome 144	+	0.5	ment quickly and
	93	12:13	Metronome 144	+	0.4	laughing, gets into
	94	12:15	Metronome 144	+	0.5	the apparatus by himself
4/4	159	3:05	Metronome 144	+	1.2	A calm, well-bal-
	10	3:07	Metronome 92	0	—	anced, and quiet
	160	3:09	Metronome 144	+	1.5	child
	161	3:11	Metronome 144	+	1.0	
	11	3:14	Metronome 92	0	—	
	162	3:17	Metronome 144	+	1.3	
5/21	267	1:09	Metronome 144	+	0.9	After the experiment
	268	1:12	Metronome 144	+	0.9	laughs and talks
	6	1:15	Metronome 108	0	—	
	269	1:18	Metronome 144	+	...	
5/28	275	2:48	Metronome 144	+	1.2	
	7	2:51	Metronome 108	0	—	
	276	2:54	Metronome 144	+	0.7	
	277	2:57	Metronome 144	+	0.7	
	1	3:00	Metronome 120	+	2.0	
	278	3:03	Metronome 144	+	0.6	
5/31	280	2:01	Metronome 144	+	0.8	Refuses going to the
	281	2:04	Metronome 144	+	0.9	experiment; walks
	282	2:07	Metronome 144	+	0.8	and mounts slowly
	283	2:12	Metronome 144	+	1.0	to the apparatus; after the experi-ment is silent

the cause of the development of serious neuroses. This is the origin of most neuroses in children. (Krasnogorski, 1925, p. 766)

Comment. Krasnogorski's conclusions may be called into question on two counts. First, they clearly represent extrapolations beyond the data. Second, his procedures are quite different from Pavlov's, despite his statements to the contrary. Neither the UCS nor the unconditioned response (UCR) is clearly specified, although enough information is available to suggest that he was not dealing with a purely respondent event. Finally, it is of interest to note that Krasnogorski's use of the term "inhibition" connotes a behavioral flavor, as compared with Pavlov's reference to *cortical* inhibition.

Date, 1924	No. of Stimulation	Time	Stimulation	Conditioned Reflex	Latent Period	Remarks
6/8	321	12:38	Metronome 144	+	1.2	Goes to the experiment silently and gets into the apparatus; report from the ward of a change in the patient's behavior; he has become taciturn
	322	12:41	Metronome 144	+	0.7	
	4	12:44	Metronome 120	0	—	
	323	12:47	Metronome 144	+	1.0	
	324	12:50	Metronome 144	+	1.5	
	1	12:53	Metronome 132	+	1.7	
	325	12:56	Metronome 144	+	0.9	
6/18	330	12:40	Metronome 144	+	1.2	Is rude, fights with other children; insists on being discharged from hospital; doctor's report from the ward that his behavior is insupportable; he is extremely excited, fights, and is disobedient
	6	12:43	Metronome 120	+	5.3	
	331	12:47	Metronome 144	+	2.0	
	2	12:50	Metronome 132	+	3.0	
	3	12:53	Metronome 132	+	2.0	
	332	12:56	Metronome 144	+	0.9	
6/22	348	1:04	Metronome 144	+	...	Yawns, is sleepy, closes his eyes; at 1:17 falls asleep for the first time after five months of experimenting; at 1:23 awakes from a knock at the door
	12	1:07	Metronome 132	+	1.1	
	13	1:10	Metronome 132	+	0.5	
	14	1:15	Metronome 132	+	1.4	
	349	1:25	Metronome 144	+	0.8	

a From Krasnogorski (1925).

Liddell

The two major contributors in the United States to the Pavlovian experimental neurosis literature were H. S. Liddell and his associates at Cornell and W. H. Gantt at Johns Hopkins.

Liddell, in particular, attempted to systematically expand the scope of the Pavlovian model to encompass a wider range of conditioning events and a more genuine analog of clinical phenomena. The examples provided by Liddell can again be best understood by first considering the work that preceded the experimental neurosis efforts.

Whereas Pavlov conditioned the salivary reflex in dogs, Liddell conditioned a motor-reflex response in sheep and, to a lesser degree, in goats, pigs, dogs, and rabbits. The reflex employed was leg flexion, usually flexion of one of the subject's forelegs, obtained by applying a mild electric shock (UCS). To complete the paradigm, various conditioned stimuli (metronome, darkness, etc.) were presented in advance of the shock. Such a procedure typically resulted in progressive and regular acquisition of the conditioned response. Liddell's most frequent arrangement involved a discrimination between positive and negative stimuli presented at fixed time intervals or in rhythmic patterns, which, according to Liddell, required inhibition of the conditioned response in the presence of the negative stimulus.

In the course of these efforts, a subject would occasionally display aberrant reactions similar to those reported by Pavlov, including oversensitivity to stimulation, agitation, fast and exaggerated leg flexions, and rapid and irregular breathing (Anderson & Liddell, 1935). These irregularities were usually accompanied by pathological behavior in the nonexperimental environment as well as in the laboratory condition (Anderson & Parmenter, 1941). As a consequence of these observations, Liddell turned his attention to the systematic investigation of experimental neurosis. It is to his credit that the series of studies conducted at Cornell showed a steady improvement in experimental design, statistical control, and instrumentation. Thus, in his later efforts cardiographs and cardiotachometers were used to measure heart rate and heart response patterns. Also, conditioning procedures and their pathological effects were maintained for five or six years, far beyond the length of time undertaken by Pavlov.

In addition to the difficult discrimination and the long delay procedures reported by Pavlov, Liddell and his associates used extinction procedures, and training with a positive conditioned stimulus alone but presented on rigid temporal schedules to produce experimental neurosis (Liddell, 1950).

Liddell claimed it was the last arrangement that produced the most reliable and genuine forms of experimental neurosis up to that time. Thus, by 1950 Liddell could assert that

> *although sheep and goats do not worry as we do, they can nevertheless be brought into states of chronic unrelieved tension severe enough to alter their behavior not only in the laboratory, but in pasture and barn for years or for life. Such patterns of self-maintaining tension correspond to Pavlov's descriptions of the experimental neurosis and closely resemble the clinical manifestations of anxiety. (Liddell, 1950, p. 182)*

The basic requirement for demonstrating these effects was to present conditioning trials at constant intervals. Furthermore, different intertrial intervals (ITI) resulted in different behavioral manifestations.

Long intervals (five to seven minutes between trials) resulted in an excitatory breakdown, as evidenced by overreaction and chronic agitation. When the interval between trials was reduced to two minutes, an inhibitory breakdown occurred, resulting in a chronic state of "concealed" vigilance or rigid, stereotyped behavior. The differences between these neurotic patterns were attributed to alleged differences in central nervous system responsivity; the agitated state was related to sympathetic processes, and the immobility state was related to parasympathetic processes.

In one of his more interesting elaborations, Liddell (1951) conditioned eight young goats simultaneously in the presence of their mother, while their siblings were conditioned in isolation. A two-minute ITI procedure was used, in which ten seconds of darkness (CS) was followed by a shock to the foreleg (UCS). "Tonic immobility," or restricted movement, was produced in the isolated animals but not in the controls. Furthermore, one of the isolates stopped feeding and died.

In a similar experiment (Liddell, 1954) the neurotic behavior was again produced in the goats, two years after the initial conditioning, by simply restraining the animals in a harness for two hours each day and presenting the conditioned stimulus alone every six hours.

Comment. There is little doubt that the Liddell group anticipated many subsequent developments in the experimental psychopathology field. In addition to replicating and extending Pavlov's findings, Liddell employed an instrumental response in pigs, which was later adopted by Masserman (1943); he developed a punishment paradigm (response-contingent shock) to produce experimental neurosis; and he investigated an avoidance procedure. His studies on conditioning in isolation represent an attempt to analyze the importance of social variables on classically conditioned experimental neurosis. Finally, it does not seem too far-fetched to consider Liddell's work on ITIs as being parallel to the use of fixed-interval schedules in similar efforts reported by several operant investigators (Morse & Kelleher, 1970; see Chapter 5).

Although Liddell's efforts were incompletely developed, certainly a considerable amount of data has been generated, which suggest numerous possibilities for further research. Unfortunately, despite Liddell's sedulous arguments regarding these efforts, clinicians have largely ignored the implications of his work for understanding behavior pathology.

Eysenck

Perhaps the most elaborate extension of Pavlovian principles into the area of psychopathology has been conducted by H. S. Eysenck and his associates. This effort, however, differs in several important respects from other classical conditioning approaches. Thus, although Eysenck accepts the Pavlovian neurological model and the concept of classical conditioning, his own research endeavors have been largely involved with the relationship between personality type and conditionability. Eysenck argues that those neurotics who condition rapidly (dysthymic-introvertive) are presumed to reflect the influence of a predominance of cortical excitation; those neurotics in whom conditioning is unstable (hysterical-extroverted) reflect a preponderance of cortical inhibition.

Numerous studies have been conducted that support such a thesis (Eysenck, 1965). Thus, the Eysenck group has shown that the eye blink reflex and the galvanic skin reflex are more rapidly conditioned in introverts than in extroverts, although these findings have been called into question.

In any event, in Eysenck's system, the classical conditioning principle is used to *define* pathological characteristics, rather than as an explanatory device that helps to uncover the manner in which pathology is *acquired.* Thus, although an ardent proponent of learning theory, Eysenck's own research has focused upon the correlation between inferred physiological processes and psychometrically defined behavioral characteristics.

On the other hand, his continued interest in learning-theory approaches to psychopathology has generated other functional analyses. Perhaps the clearest example is a study reported by S. Rachman (1966a), a longtime associate of Eysenck's. In this study Rachman attempted to demonstrate the acquisition of a sexual fetish via the classical conditioning paradigm. The unconditioned stimulus consisted of colored photograph slides of attractive female nudes, and the conditioned stimulus consisted of a colored slide of a pair of black, knee-length women's boots, a common fetishistic object. The fetish response was defined as changes in penis volume when the last slide was shown, as measured by means of a phallo-plethysmograph.

After the neutral properties of the CS and several other similar objects were determined, three subjects were given eighteen conditioning trials, in which the CS was presented for fifteen seconds, followed by thirty seconds of a nude slide, with five-minute rests interposed after each block of six trials. Trials were presented from one to three minutes apart. After five successive plethysmographic reactions were obtained, an extinction procedure was introduced. In addition, Rachman also tested for spontaneous recovery of the conditioned response one week later and for stimulus generalization.

The first subject reached the conditioning criterion in thirty trials and revealed similar reactions (stimulus generalization) to two other fetishistic stimuli (different colored boots of various shapes). This reaction was extinguished in nineteen trials but was recovered one week later in the next testing procedure. This time the response was extinguished in fourteen trials. The second subject reached criterion in sixty-five trials and generalized to one stimulus; the response was extinguished in thirty-nine trials. Once again, spontaneous recovery of the conditioned response was manifested in the following week's test, and the conditioned reaction was still present after twenty extinction trials. Another twelve trials were required four days later for extinction. The third subject reached the criterion in twenty-four trials and generalized to two other stimuli; the response was extinguished in thirteen trials. The response was spontaneously recovered one week later and was reextinguished in ten trials.

> *Three of the major phenomena of conditioning were demonstrated. There seems to be little question, therefore, that sexual arousal can be conditioned to previously neutral stimuli. Whether sexual CRs can be so easily acquired to other types of stimuli is an open question. It is conceivable that common fetishes (e.g., boots, hair, fur) are, as a consequence of naturally occurring conditioning, particularly sensitive stimuli. (Rachman, 1966a, p. 296)*

Subsequently, Rachman and Hodgson (1968) replicated this study while controlling for pseudoconditioning. Thus, in one condition the unconditioned stimulus was presented prior to the CS. The results confirmed the earlier report of conditioned fetishism while excluding the possibility that pseudoconditioning was a determinant of the effects.

Comment. Little needs to be added to Rachman's statements, except to reiterate the position argued by Eysenck and other behavior theorists: A strict learning interpretation of many forms of pathological behavior may adequately explain the relevant etiological events. Thus, Rachman's model provides an excellent programmatic approach to the functional analysis of pathological behavior, since both acquisition and extinction of the sexual response were brought under stimulus control.

Asthma As a Classically Conditioned Phenomenon

No account of psychopathology is complete that does not attempt to account for the relationship between psychological variables and somatic dysfunction. It has long been known that various experiences evoke physiological reactions, and Freud's first explorations into psychoanalysis were an attempt to explain such relationships, although he restricted his early statements to conversion hysteria (in which an emotional event was assumed to have caused a psychic disturbance manifested by a physical anomaly involving the "voluntary" organs). Eventually, a "science" of psychosomatics evolved, which analyzed such conditions as colitis, ulcers, hypertension, asthma, and neurodermatitis as symptomatic of early emotional trauma. Much was written about the ulcer personality and the asthma personality, although little was accomplished in the way of isolating the necessary and sufficient conditions involved in the acquisition and modification of these disorders. It was still not known which traumatic events produced which kinds of disorders, and why the same kind of trauma produced certain disorders in one person and not in another.

At the same time, information based upon a learning-theory model suggested that classical conditioning principles might offer some answers to these questions. The assortment of psychosomatic-like conditions induced by Pavlovian procedures, for example, has been limited only by the ingenuity of the investigators and the restrictions of the principle. Suffice it to say that there is abundant evidence that almost every physiological index of emotional responsivity is amenable to classical conditioning (Kimble, 1961). Franks (1961) provides a review of the literature on classically conditioned psychosomatic disorders, but one good example of such research is revealed in a study of learned asthma in the guinea pig (Ottenberg *et al.*, 1958).

The procedure involved intraperitoneal injections of fresh, undiluted egg white (UCS) three times in a one-week period. After two weeks had elapsed, sensitization, revealed as respiratory distress, developed, and the animals were subsequently exposed to a diluted mist of egg-white spray.

> *The sequence of respiratory signs was as follows: rapid breathing, restlessness, chewing, ruffling of the fur, then labored breathing with the use of accessory muscles of respiration, prolonged expiration, gasping, coughing, dilation of alai nasi, and finally cyanosis and convulsion. The severity in individual asthmatic attacks varied and all of the animals did not have attacks on each trial. (Ottenberg* et al., *1958)*

Subsequently, those animals that displayed the highest frequency of asthma attacks continued to display such distress when merely placed in the experimental chamber (CS) without the egg-white spray. Furthermore, as time elapsed, the severity of the attacks diminished. "Extinction was apparent in all after 13 trials. This we define as learned asthma" (Ottenberg *et al.*, 1958, p. 397).

Figure 1 reveals the changes that took place during extinction. Note that over 80 percent of the animals continued to display the asthma response through the first seven trials.

Earlier, B. Noelpp and I. Noelpp-Eschenhagen (1952) induced asthma attacks in guinea pigs by pairing a sound (conditioned stimulus) with a histamine spray (unconditioned stimulus). After only five trials respiratory distress was conditioned to the sound. Similar findings were reported more recently by D. R. Justesen *et al.* (1970) and E. Dekker *et al.* (1957) induced asthma attacks in humans by presenting conditioned stimuli selected on the basis of the individual's clinical history.

Comment. The classical conditioning of psychosomatic processes represents an important extension of the Pavlovian paradigm. There is, at present, a considerable amount of literature related to this

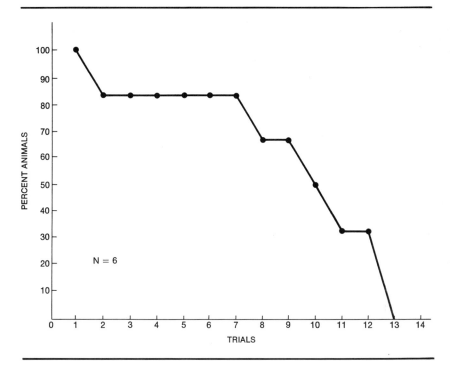

Figure 1. *Extinction curve of learned asthma. The responses are expressed as the percentage of animals that had learned asthmatic attacks on consecutive daily trials. (From Otterberg et al., 1958)*

area of inquiry, although, once again, it has had only a limited impact on clinical practice and theory. On the other hand, an interest in coupling conditioning procedures with personality analysis has been promoted by a number of theorists. Another plausible line of reasoning, however, would regard psychosomatic conditions to be exclusively learned phenomena, and differences in conditionability a function of as yet unexplicated learning variables.

Conclusion

The investigations reviewed in this chapter reflect two major themes in the classical conditioning approach to psychopathology. The more purely Pavlovian position incorporates the model within a typology or "temperament theory" framework. The second position (exemplified by the last two studies) focuses almost exclusively upon the classical conditioning procedure as a possible paradigm for explaining the acquisition of pathological conditions, without recourse to physiological constructs. Rachman's findings, for example, explain fetishism independent of any introversion-extroversion interpretation.

Although neither of these two views has had any great popularity with or support from students of psychopathology, the typology position is the more tenuous of the two, perhaps because of the contradictory evidence. However, even the status of the second position is ambiguous. For one thing, in the earlier research on experimental neurosis the full power and rigor of an experimental analysis was not applied. "What many of these investigators have studied is what collection of varied procedures leads, on occasion, to what varied collection of results" (Dinsmoor, 1960, p. 301). More recent efforts provide stronger evidence in support of the classical conditioning paradigm. Thus, in a study that will be reported in detail later, N. E. Schneiderman *et al.* (1971) demonstrated the manner in which neurotic behavior could be induced and removed several times (reversal procedure), so that the correlation between independent and dependent variables was more than anecdotal. Thus, the full potential of classical conditioning procedures still remains to be realized. For another thing, the initial Pavlovian procedure was restricted to involuntary reflexes, and clinical events often encompass voluntary (instrumental or operant) components; extensions of the Pavlovian model into the arena of clinical phenomena have, implicitly if not explicitly, acknowledged this (McGuire *et al.*, 1965). Thus, although there is a strong resemblance between the Rachman procedure and the Pavlov procedure, a detailed analysis would also reveal some important differences. Few contemporary learning theorists would ascribe to John B. Watson's earlier thesis that the classical conditioning principle is the building block of all behavior, and perhaps the most ardent critics of this position are learning theorists themselves. Operant theorists were quick to point out the restricted nature of the classical conditioning paradigm, and other, more general behavior theorists have neutralized the importance of classical conditioning in favor of other concepts. More recently, a movement has emerged among learning theorists and researchers to attempt to accommodate the principles and procedures from both classical conditioning and operant conditioning approaches. It is too early to pass judgment on this development, but if history serves as any measure, scientific advances often occur in this fashion.

Chapter 5 / Operant Conditioning Techniques

As we have seen, Skinner and others have made occasional reference to the application of operant principles in the analysis of pathological behavior. Although there are few operant investigators who are popularly identified as experimental psychopathologists, a considerable amount of research within the operant paradigm has direct relevancy for a behavioral analysis of the causes of psychopathology. The studies cited in this chapter, although by no means exhaustive, represent those efforts that are clearly attempts to analyze clinical phenomena, as suggested by the investigators, or appear to have clear-cut implications for clinical events, even though the investigators make no such claim. In general, the operant bias is expressed in these endeavors in the attempt to isolate functional relationships between variables, rather than provide experimental support for a given hypothesis established on the basis of intervening variables or constructs.

As in the case of other behavioral systems, the operant approach may be identified by those procedures that characterize the system.

Skinner laid the groundwork via the positive-reinforcement paradigm, which was essentially an elaboration of earlier work by E. L. Thorndike. A food-deprived animal is placed in an enclosure with a modified telegraph key projecting into the chamber. The animal must press the key to obtain food, thus defining the reinforce-

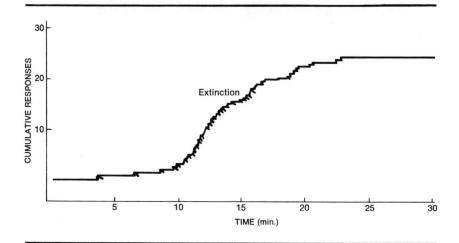

Figure 2. *Stylized record of bar-press response frequency as a function of continuous, immediate reinforcement contingent upon the response, followed by extinction. Each downward deflection represents the delivery of reinforcement. (Adapted from Reese, 1966)*

ment contingency. The acquisition of the bar-press response as a function of response consequences can then be analyzed.

Procedurally, the bar-press response is "shaped" by successive approximations of the response, and the entire course of acquisition may be charted on a cumulative recorder. The typical acquisition process in such a procedure is revealed in Figure 2. Extinction is analyzed by the termination of the response-reinforcement contingency, with the typical result revealed in Figure 2.

In such an arrangement the effects of such variables as the delay of reinforcement, the magnitude of reinforcement, the length of reinforcement history, and conditioned reinforcement on both acquisition and extinction are readily analyzed and directly revealed.

A major advance from the basic paradigm was afforded by the investigation of reinforcement frequency and pattern, that is, the schedule of reinforcement. Skinner identified four different classes of reinforcement schedules, each of which produced a characteristic acquisition effect and influenced the results obtained in extinction. Thus, initially in training, reinforcement usually occurs after each response (continuous reinforcement, CRF); such reinforcement typically results in a high frequency of responses early in an experimental session and progressive and longer response delays (as a result of satiation). In addition, extinction occurs rapidly. These effects can be modified with a schedule of "intermittent" reinforcement (Ferster & Skinner, 1957). When reinforcement is presented after X number of responses (fixed ratio), the rate increases, and pausing is generally restricted to the postreinforcement period. When reinforcement is administered after a random number of responses

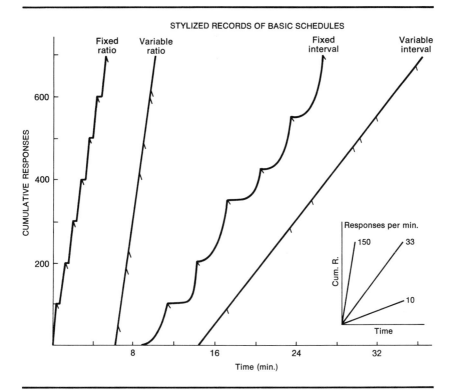

Figure 3. *Stylized records of responding under basic schedules of reinforcement. Diagonal marks indicate reinforcement; the slope of various response rates is indicated at lower right. Fixed Ratio: high rate, with brief pause following reinforcement and abrupt change to terminal rate. Variable Ratio: high sustained rate, no pausing after reinforcement. Fixed Interval: low overall response rate due to pause following reinforcement; length of pause increases with length of interval; gradual increase to high terminal rate as interval ends. Variable interval: low sustained rate, no pausing after reinforcement. (Adapted from Reese, 1966)*

(variable ratio), a high stable rate emerges with few or no pauses. When reinforcement is delivered after a fixed interval of time, the result is a "scalloping" effect in which there is a pause and low response rate after reinforcement, followed by a gradual increase to a very high rate at the end of the interval. When the time interval varies in a random manner (variable interval), an intermediate, stable response rate with few or no pauses is produced. A stylized presentation of the four basic schedules and respective effects appears in Figure 3. Of course, in each instance the transition from CRF to intermittent reinforcement must be gradual and systematic in order to circumvent extinction. When the transition is accomplished, resistance to extinction is considerably enhanced, sometimes resulting in sustained performance for months, depending upon the animal's prior reinforcement history. More recently, operant investigators have become involved in the analysis of complex schedules combining two or more of the above schedules.

Although the initial operant paradigm was restricted to positive reinforcement procedures, Skinner and others have explored the manner in which the principles of response consequences might also encompass other phenomena analyzed by traditional learning theorists, such as stimulus discrimination and generalization, and escape and avoidance behavior. In a typical discrimination procedure an exteroceptive stimulus is present during reinforcement periods and is absent during nonreinforcement periods. The relationship between a discriminative stimulus (S^D) and a reinforcing contingency is revealed by an increase in response frequency under such (S^D) conditions and a decrease in response frequency when the stimulus for nonreinforcement (S^Δ) is presented. The concept of the discriminative stimulus has achieved considerable importance with the increasing attempt to apply such laboratory-derived principles to the world of human events. This concept, together with the concept of conditioned reinforcement, may ultimately provide important knowledge regarding the degree to which the operant model will enable the analysis of human behavior in the natural environment.

Further important advances have been made through the experimental analysis of aversive events. Punishment may be defined as any procedure that involves the administration of a response-contingent event resulting in a reduction in response frequency. The typical arrangement involves, first, the acquisition of a response, usually via a positive-reinforcement procedure (although punishment of negatively reinforced behavior has also been recently analyzed as described below), and the subsequent superimposition of a response-contingent aversive stimulus.

The investigator is thus provided with a powerful analytical procedure enabling him to explore the effects of such traditional punishment variables as intensity of punishment, delay of punishment, and duration of punishment as they interact with already explicated positive-reinforcement variables.

Negative reinforcement may be defined as any of those procedures that generate escape or avoidance behavior. Traditionally, the study of such phenomena involves a preaversive stimulus that overlaps or terminates in shock. The subject can either turn off the shock (escape) or avoid it by responding during the preaversive stimulus. Sidman (1953) has demonstrated the acquisition of such avoidance behavior in the absence of an exteroceptive stimulus. Here, shocks are programmed to occur on some temporal basis, and each response postpones the shock for a given interval. Under these conditions response frequency typically increases, thus describing another important component of the acquisition process. There are, of course, many variations on these major themes, some of which have important implications for the experimental analysis of patho-logical behavior and are described below.

Estes and Skinner: Anxiety and the Conditioned-Suppression Paradigm

As we have seen, one of the constantly recurring themes in the clinical literature is the importance of anxiety in understanding abnormal behavior. In some systems, especially of the drive-reduction variety such as Wolpe's, anxiety occupies a central position (McAllister and McAllister, 1971). Despite the popular status of the term, other investigators have argued that the research findings that are frequently cited as support for this position can be explained by the observed changes in experimental stimulation (Schoenfeld, 1950).

These differences are far from resolved, and we shall return to this controversy later. For the present let us consider the manner in which operant investigators have contributed information regarding the functional analysis of events that are frequently interpreted within an anxiety framework.

An early study by W. K. Estes and Skinner (1941) provides one relevant experimental paradigm. These investigators were interested in demonstrating the manner in which a previously neutral event acquires aversive properties, which are manifested by disruption of ongoing behavior.

In the first stage of the study, the bar-press response in rats was maintained by periodic food reinforcement. Under these circumstances a relatively constant response rate emerged during experimental sessions. Subsequently, a series of tone-shock combinations was introduced into the experimental session. The tone was presented for three minutes followed by unavoidable shock. The food-reinforcement schedule remained in effect at all times. Initial disruption of ongoing behavior was restricted to the postshock period. In the next stage the number of tone-shock combinations was increased to two per session, and the length of tone duration was increased to five minutes. After several such conditions, responding in the presence of the tone declined. By the third day of the experiment, responding practically ceased during the tone, a phenomenon described as conditioned suppression. (See Figure 4.)

Estes and Skinner (1941, p. 392) concluded that "the principle result . . . was the conditioning of a state of anxiety to the tone, where the primary index was a reduction in the strength of the hunger-motivated lever-pressing behavior." (Also of interest was the observation that not only was responding maintained at full strength during the no-tone period, but there was a "compensatory" increase in periodic rate following the period of depression. The implications of this finding will be more thoroughly discussed in subsequent sections.)

Comment. Aside from the value provided by the empirical demonstration itself (note that anxiety is equated with the operations that

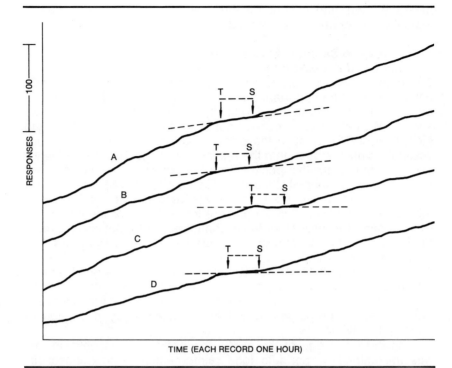

RESPONSES

100

TIME (EACH RECORD ONE HOUR)

Figure 4. *Reduction in rate of responding during successive periods of anxiety. Averaged curves for six rats on four consecutive days. T----S represents the tone-shock sequence. By the third day responding practically ceases during the presentation of the tone. (From Estes & Skinner, 1941)*

produced conditioned suppression), there appear to be other reasons to consider the conditioned-suppression paradigm as a representative analog of the "anxiety" phenomenon. Thus, observation of the subjects during the preaversive stimulus reveals additional anxiety-like reactions. These include increases in "freezing," urination, defecation (Brady & Hunt, 1955), heart rate and blood flow (Stebbins & Smith, 1964), and 17-hydroxycorticosteroid levels (Mason *et al.,* 1957).

One final bit of evidence might make the story more complete: the observation of experimentally induced conditioned supression in humans. Mulder *et al.* (1967) provide us with one such attempt, in a procedure that was a systematic replication of the Estes-Skinner study. Human subjects were reinforced for lever pulling on a fixed-ratio schedule. After stable rates emerged, the tone-shock sequence was introduced. Although the evidence for conditioned suppression was meager (out of twenty-five subjects, four suppressed, nine withdrew from the experiment, and twelve did not suppress), some interesting effects were observed. For example, statements made by the subjects who withdrew suggested that it was not the shock per se that was the determining factor but the "anxiety" experience during the preaversive period that they found most disconcerting.

In conducting such research with humans, Mulder *et al.* (1967) warn, it is important to remember that we are dealing with the variables involved in individual reinforcement histories as well as with manipulating the aversive conditions, which may partially explain the variability reported by investigators using human subjects in the conditioned-suppression paradigm (Sachs & May, 1969).

Sidman: Further Elaborations on the Estes-Skinner Theme
In an early formal statement regarding the general application of operant principles to pathological phenomena, Sidman (1960a) described several studies that extended the Estes-Skinner paradigm into a number of areas. Each of these studies provides information relevant to an analysis of certain forms of pathological phenomena, including anxiety, self-punishment, and superstitious behavior. A review of these efforts also provides some insight into the experimental practices employed by operant investigators in isolating the variables that influence behavior.

Replication of the Estes-Skinner procedure with rhesus monkeys confirmed the conditioned-suppression effect, as shown in Figure 5.

Even when the parameters and the frequency of the stimulus-shock sequence were modified and extended, the animals continued to display conditioned suppression (that is, no responding during the preshock stimulus and an immediate return to "normal" responding after each unavoidable shock). When the shock was presented on an intermittent basis, however, the conditioned-suppression effect deteriorated: Responding between stimuli was uneven; suppression sometimes continued after the shock had been delivered; lever pressing occurred during the stimulus period prior to suppression and, on occasion, continued at a low steady rate until the subject received the shock.

Sidman suggested that such a breakdown in the typical experimental effects reflects some of the characteristics of psychopathology, an observation similar to Pavlov's and others. Committed to the argument that the "anomalies which began to appear in the behavioral records appeared to be disorderly only because we were not at the time able to identify the controlling variables" (Sidman, 1960a, p. 64), Sidman proceeded to analyze the variables that might provide for an orderly demonstration of the disordered behavior. Two variables were selected for further study: (1) duration of preshock stimulus, and (2) duration of on-time, when the stimulus was presented, in proportion to off-time, when it was not presented. (These dimensions correspond to the length of the CS interval and the length of the intertrial interval in classical conditioning terminology.) Various combinations were employed with the general finding that the relationship between these dimensions controlled the degree of conditioned suppression. Thus, an animal would press the lever at a

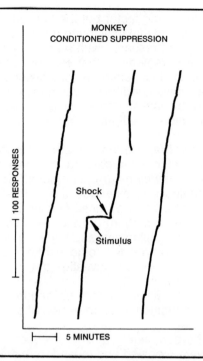

MONKEY
CONDITIONED SUPPRESSION

100 RESPONSES

Shock

Stimulus

5 MINUTES

Figure 5. *An illustration of the Estes-Skinner conditioned-suppression phenomenon. Responses are recorded cumulatively with the pen automatically resetting to the bar line after every 450 responses. The introduction of the clicking noise (stimulus) is indicated by the slight oblique downward displacement of the pen at the first arrow. The shock, which immediately follows termination of the tone, occurs at the point where the pen displacement is rectified, indicated by the second arrow. (From Sidman, 1960a)*

very slow rate during the preshock stimulus, but only if there were relatively long intervals of silence between stimulus periods. For example, when twenty-four minutes of silence alternated with six-minute stimulus periods, conditioned suppression resulted. However, when the nonstimulus intervals were reduced to two minutes and the stimulus periods were constant, "the animal [responded] considerably more often during a 6-minute clicking period" (Sidman, 1960a, p. 64), as revealed in Figure 6.

The general conclusion drawn from these studies was that "animals manifest anxiety only to the extent that they can afford to do so in terms of reinforcement cost" (Sidman, 1960a, p. 64).

Sidman was also one of the first investigators to apply the conditioned-suppression paradigm to avoidance behavior. His results here were equally interesting and important. In a typical arrangement monkeys were exposed to shock at regular intervals (shock-shock

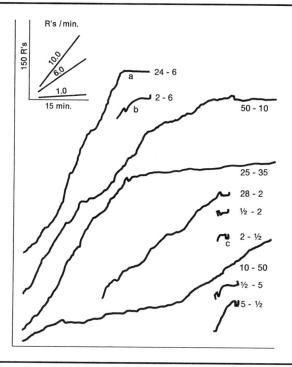

Figure 6. *Sample cumulative records made in tests with periods of clicking and of silence of various lengths. The first number of each pair designates the number of minutes of silence; the second, the number of minutes of clicking. The oblique downward displacement of each curve indicates the point at which clicking was introduced. (From Sidman, 1960a)*

interval). Each lever press postponed (avoided) the scheduled shock for a given interval (response-shock interval). Under these conditions stable avoidance responding was generated within a relatively short time. When five-minute stimulus-unavoidable shock pairs were alternated with five-minute periods of the avoidance arrangement, the animal's response rate first increased in both the stimulus and the nonstimulus periods. Eventually, there was a return to the normal rate during stimulus-off, but the higher rate during stimulus-on was maintained (the reverse of the Estes-Skinner effect). Finally, when the avoidable shock contingency was removed, lever pressing extinguished during the silence periods, but persisted for a long time during the stimulus-on periods, a phenomenon that Sidman termed conditioned facilitation. Thus, the same experimental arrangement (tone-shock procedure) resulted in completely opposite effects, conditioned suppression and conditioned facilitation, when superimposed over different reinforcement histories. In the latter instance "from an adaptive point of view, the facilitation of lever pressing makes no more sense than does suppression. The shock is inevitable, and the animal's high response rate during the stimulus represents only so much wasted energy. It would take very little stretching of the imagination to class this behavior as pathological" (Sidman, 1960a, p. 64). One is irresistibly drawn to the analogy of the many examples of similar forms of pathological behavior in the clinical literature.

In order to examine this apparent facilitation anomaly, Sidman analyzed the relation between the aversive events and their effect on behavior. In each stimulus period the monkey received only one shock. Thus, only an extremely small proportion of responses were actually punished; the remainder of the responses were largely successful. In other words,

> *avoidance of shock still reinforces lever pressing, even though the relation is a spurious one. The monkey's behavior during the stimulus period is nonadaptive because the rules of the environment have·changed, and the changes have not yet elicited appropriate response modification. The occasional shocks only serve as false discriminative cue to keep the animal behaving in a fashion appropriate to the former circumstances.* (Sidman, 1960a, p. 66)

Another point that appears relevant concerns the temporal relations between the shock and the response immediately preceding it, a dimension that may vary from a very brief period to a relatively long period. This dimension may have enhanced the maintenance of behavior even though the effect was achieved purely as a function of the vagaries of the response, rather than through any formal experimental control.

It appears, then, that the establishment of a response that persisted, despite the fact that the only consequence was an unavoidable shock, was a function of a combination of historically real and currently adventitious contingencies. Such a phenomenon "requires an organism with a particular type of behavioral history, and it requires a unique set of current circumstances which serve to perpetuate the processes that stem from the history even after they are no longer relevant to the demands of the environment" (Sidman, 1960a, p. 66).

One further extension of these efforts provided Sidman with additional information of a clinically relevant nature. In attempting to analyze the relationship between behavioral history and current circumstances, he trained a monkey to pull a chain for food reinforcement and to press a lever to postpone shock. Both contingencies were simultaneously available, and the monkey had the option of working on either. After the animal adjusted to these circumstances, sometimes pulling on the chain, sometimes pressing the lever, the avoidable shock arrangement was withdrawn, and clicker-shock

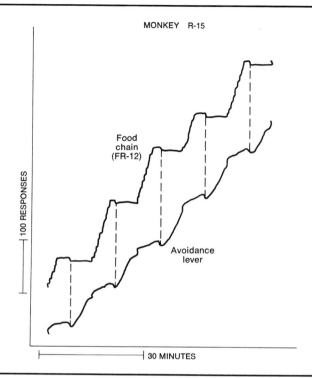

Figure 7. *Concurrent cumulative records for chain pulling and lever pressing. The portions of the records displaced obliquely downward denote clicking periods that preceded shock. The broken lines connect temporally corresponding points (introduction of clicking) on each curve. (From Sidman 1960a)*

sequences were introduced. Now the only shocks received were unavoidable and occurred at the end of the clicking period. Rather than suppression of the chain-pulling response (expected on the basis of the conditioned-suppression effect), *both* responses increased during the stimulus periods, as shown in Figure 7.

Even when the food-reinforcement contingency was eliminated, the animal continued to pull the chain at a high rate during the stimulus periods. Further investigation suggested that this effect occurred because of the interdependence between the two responses; that is, "the food-reinforced behavior was being controlled in some way by the avoidance contingency, even though no such control was demanded by the experimental arrangement" (Sidman, 1960a, p. 67).

Such "inappropriate" responding was explained in terms of adventitious reinforcement resulting in superstitious behavior. Thus, a response may be correlated only by chance with a reinforcing state of affairs, but the organism responds *as if* the relationship were a contingent one. Analysis of the monkey's response pattern revealed, for example, that the two responses occurred in sequential patterns. When this alternation pattern was disrupted (by requiring more responses on the chain pull via a change in reinforcement schedule), the superstitious avoidance component of the chain-pull response was disrupted, and a conditioned-suppression procedure did not result in an increase in this response.

Comment. In addition to the evidence marshaled in support of his thesis that seemingly unusual, paradoxical behavior patterns may be analyzed as an extension of normal, regular processes, there is much grist for the clinical mill in Sidman's report. He has provided a method for analyzing (as well as some tentative answers to) the questions that have long plagued clinical investigators, especially those concerning the wide range of reactions to the same events. Thus, ultimately he provides a method for possibly explaining why some individuals under certain circumstances display maladaptive behavior and others, under the same circumstances, do not. Sidman has shown that the same effects may occur as a consequence of differing reinforcement histories, and that different effects may emerge from approximately the same histories. Perhaps equally important, his analysis of the conditioned-suppression paradigm might be regarded as a prototype for clinical investigations into cause-and-effect relationships. "Unusual" conditioned-suppression effects were ultimately seen as being determined by the interaction between selected variables. One combination of variables produced one effect, and another combination of the same variables resulted in a different effect, thus resolving the mystery. Although generalization to the human level must be done with caution, perhaps a similar analysis might help to clarify the inconsistencies that have been observed in the conditioned-suppression paradigm with humans.

Finally, Sidman's work is perhaps the first attempt at a functional analysis of the interaction between historical determinants and later variables. As discussed earlier, it is our thesis that many of the answers related to the experimental analysis of clinically relevant phenomena can be accomplished in just this fashion.

Azrin and Holz: Discriminative and
Suppressive Properties of Punishment

Of the various operant investigators who have studied basic processes relevant to clinical phenomena, Nathan Azrin and his colleagues have provided some of the most impressive efforts (Azrin & Holz, 1966). In his earlier research Azrin focused upon the effects of punishment on positively reinforced behavior, thus elucidating some of the complex issues involved in punishment paradigms, and contributing much information to problems that have been traditionally vexing.

Although he has only on occasion related these basic processes to the realm of clinical events, there is little question that

Azrin's work has important clinical implications, especially for understanding the etiology and modification of various forms of pathological behavior. More recently, Azrin has also contributed much information relevant to the modification of clinical conditions.

Of his many investigations in the punishment area, one of the most interesting is a study revealing the manner in which events that are ordinarily punishing exerted a completely opposite influence (Holz & Azrin, 1961). Under certain circumstances, for example, animals may work to produce stimuli that were previously "punishing."

Initially, two food-deprived pigeons were reinforced for disk pecking on an intermittent basis. After response rates stabilized, each response was punished by a shock sufficient to suppress the nonpunishment rates by 50 percent. When this was accomplished, the animals were run for an additional session each day in which no response consequences were present. As might be predicted, the animals' responses extinguished in the latter case. There were, then, two base lines (the extinction condition and the reinforcement shock condition) against which the effects of an independent variable could be ascertained. Subsequently, when the shock was withdrawn from the reinforcement-shock sessions, the animals' rates declined. Furthermore, when punishment was introduced into the extinction session, their rates *increased* and were maintained for as long as the shock was administered, as shown in Figure 8.

Increase in response rate also occurred when shock was introduced independent of responses. Thus, in each case a previously punishing stimulus was now correlated with an increment in behavior. Finally, when a relatively nonaversive shock was associated with extinction in a third pigeon, independent assessment revealed that the shock had acquired discriminative properties for the absence of reinforcement, just as in the previous instances, where it had acquired discriminative properties for the presence of reinforcement.

W. C. Holz and Azrin contend that similar arrangements may obtain in the natural environment, where the possibility of accidental interactions between reinforcing and nonreinforcing events may exist. Thus, a parent may apply reinforcement to a child after punishment; if so, the punishment would be (inadvertently) paired with reinforcement and could be expected to acquire a discriminative property. A similar process may occur in any natural situation involving more than one response consequence.

Comment. Azrin and his colleagues have provided additional evidence of changing effects of events on behavior as a function of the manipulation of stimulus dimensions or as a function of the interaction between behavioral determinants. Thus, shock may exert a punishing effect or a discriminative effect, depending upon its physical characteristics and its interaction with other relevant variables (Holz & Azrin, 1962). In humans the same "noise" stimulus may exert a punishing effect, a negatively reinforcing effect, or a discriminative

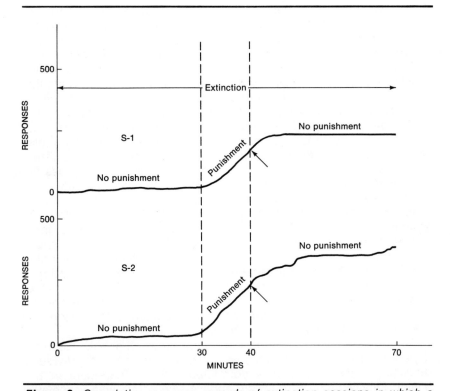

Figure 8. *Cumulative-response records of extinction sessions in which a ten-minute punishment period was introduced. The records include a thirty-minute period before the introduction of punishment and a thirty-minute period after the punishment. The arrows point out the additional increase in rate that occurred immediately upon the termination of punishment. (From Holz & Azrin, 1961)*

effect, depending upon its relation to other behavioral determinants (Azrin, 1958). And finally, again in humans, the same stimulus, noise, may serve as a punishing stimulus, when response contingent, and as a conditioned reinforcer, when paired with positive reinforcement (Ayllon & Azrin, 1966).

The importance of such findings for the analysis of "bizarre" or unusual behavior seems clear. The advertent or inadvertent manipulation of stimulus dimensions and/or response-consequence interactions may thus produce changes in the ordinary (normal) effects of various behavioral events. "These results provide an experimental basis for interpreting clinical phenomena such as 'masochism' wherein an individual 'seeks out' punishment and does nothing to avoid it" (Ayllon & Azrin, 1966, p. 418).

To this we would add that these results might also serve as a partial explanation, for patterns of behavior which stand in stark contrast to "normal" sources of gratification. Thus, even traditional psychopathologists have recognized the complex combination of response consequences that characterize such perversions as sexual masochism. O. Fenichel (1945), for example, states that "certain experiences may have so firmly established the conviction that sexual pleasure must be associated with pain that suffering has become the prerequisite for sexual pleasure" (p. 357). Similarly, the incorrigible child, the antisocial individual, in fact, many examples of repeated exposure to punishing events may fall into this category.

Where the Azrin and Holz analysis differs from the past is in the explanatory possibilities that their model offers. Such behavior has been typically explained in terms of a hypothetical process within the organism, that is, the need to punish oneself to allay guilt. A more parsimonious answer may be provided by the further analysis of the interaction between punishing and positively reinforcing events, which has typically been ignored in most clinical reports. Such a framework would require, at least as a minimum, the analysis of the schedule of reinforcing events, the schedule of punishing events, and as we shall see, the relationships between these events and associated (conditioned or discriminative) stimuli.

Sandler and Davidson: Other Forms of Masochism
The operant analysis of interactions between current events and prior history, as relevant to the study of psychopathology, may be conducted along a number of different paths. Whereas Azrin and his colleagues demonstrated the clinical implications of arrangements involving punishment superimposed over positively reinforced baselines, Sandler and Davidson attempted to analyze the interaction between punishment and negatively reinforced behavior. Such arrangements provide an excellent opportunity for generating clinically relevant phenomena (Sandler, 1964), because of the special features involved. A study by these investigators supports this argument (Sandler *et al.*, 1966a).

Marmoset monkeys were trained to bar press in a discrete trial, signal-shock-avoidance procedure, involving one hundred trials per session. In such an arrangement responses may occur at any time during a session, but only lever presses during a trial terminate the preshock signal and avoid the shock. Under these circumstances animals typically reduce their between trial responses to a minimum, responding once per trial, shortly after the preshock stimulus is presented.

After this pattern evolved and stabilized, the subjects were punished for all responses by shock of low, intermediate, or high intensity. For example, animals in the latter condition now had the option of responding and receiving a shock of an intensity almost equal to the avoidable shock, or of not responding and receiving the avoidable shock. The most adaptive behavior was to respond only once per trial, thereby minimizing exposure to both the response shock and the avoidable shock. The least adaptive behavior was to re-

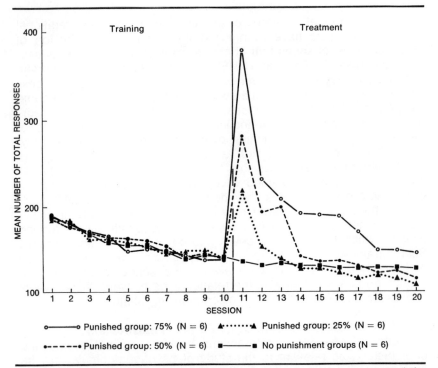

Figure 9. *Mean total response rates for the three punished groups and the three combined nonpunished groups during initial avoidance sessions and the punished avoidance sessions. (From Sandler et al., 1966a)*

spond at a high rate between trials and to stop responding within trials, thus producing nonavoidable shocks as well as avoidable shocks. The results are shown in Figure 9.

Although all the animals displayed some degree of maladaptive behavior, the monkeys in the high-intensity punishment condition were the least adaptive. Furthermore, when these conditions were maintained through the next ten sessions, the subjects in the other two groups displayed an increase in adaptive behavior, while progress in the high-shock group was restricted to a moderate reduction in between trial responding.

In the final stage of the experiment, the avoidable shock was withdrawn (extinction), but the response shock was maintained. Under these circumstances *any* lever presses were maladaptive, since responses produced shock, and the absence of responding resulted in no aversive consequences. The animals in the high-intensity punishment group extinguished rapidly, but the subjects in the other two groups continued to respond (thereby producing unnecessary shock) for a considerable period of time, as shown in Figure 10.

Subsequently, Sandler *et al.* (1966c) demonstrated that such behavior may be maintained *indefinitely* if punishment conditions and nonpunishment conditions are randomly alternated, and may be

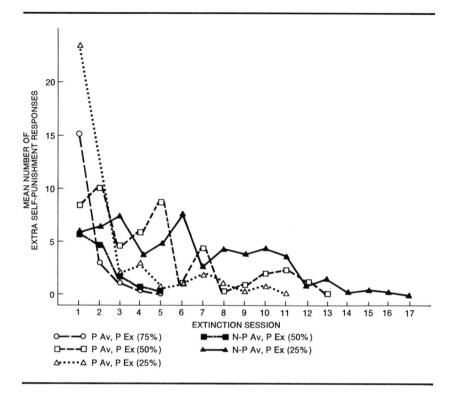

Figure 10. *Mean extra self-punishing response rates for the five punished groups during each extinction session. (From Sandler et al., 1966a)*

maintained if a nonpunishing avoidance response alternative is made available (Sandler & Davidson, 1967).

Comment. Clearly, then, self-punishing "maladaptive" behavior can occur as the consequence of an interaction between current aversive events and a prior avoidance history. Furthermore, manipulation of the appropriate variables will result in the durable maintenance of self-punishing effects. Once again, an analogy may be drawn between such behavior and clinical phenomena with similar characteristics, from the dramatic examples of self-destructive activities to more subtle forms such as cigarette smoking and accident-prone behavior. Although such problem conditions no doubt involve other variables as well, to the extent that all or many examples of clinical phenomena involve self-punishing components, the analogy may be relevant. The validity of the parallel between the experiments and clinical phenomena, of course, is still moot. The answer to this question will be provided only by further experimentation involving closer and closer approximation to the clinical events. In any event, if we take Sandler and Davidson's work together with the Azrin and Holz material, we may observe similar patterns of maladaptive behavior that have emerged as a consequence of different reinforcement histories.

Morse and Kelleher: Schedule-Induced "Pathology"

Perhaps the most elegant examples of operant interactions resulting in maladaptive behavior are provided by W. H. Morse and R. T. Kelleher (1970). These investigators have produced a great deal of information regarding the manner in which the schedule of events modulates and determines behavior. In the course of their efforts, Morse and Kelleher have demonstrated that the effects of drugs on behavior depends upon the type of schedule controlling the behavior, as well as the manner in which different schedule histories modulate the effects of ordinarily punishing events. One of their earlier studies is representative of these efforts (Morse *et al.,* 1967). Squirrel monkeys were placed in a restraining chair facing a leash. Strong shock administered to the monkey's tail every sixty seconds frequently elicited a leash-pulling response, which was recorded through a switch and lever. In addition, if the first leash-pulling response occurred within thirty seconds after a shock was presented, it also produced the next shock. If no response was elicited, the shock was delivered after sixty seconds, as before. Initially, the response-produced shock resulted in a burst of responses. Subsequently, the arrangement was modified so that in one condition shock only occurred thirty seconds after a response, thus reversing the response-shock relations; that is, now all shocks were produced by responses, whereas previously, the shocks resulted in responding. Under these circumstances most responses occurred *prior* to the shock in contrast to the previous case in which response frequently was highest after the shock, as shown in Figure 11.

Eventually, the response characteristics that emerged were comparable to response patterns generated by fixed-interval positive reinforcement. In other words, the animals' response rates appeared to be maintained by a strong shock, presented at fixed-intervals, since this was the only programmed consequence of such behavior, whereas the absence of responding would have removed all aversive consequences.

Similar effects were generated by procedures in which response-contingent shock was superimposed over other shock-escape procedures and shock-avoidance procedures. In one case, for example, shocks were postponed for decreasing intervals with successive responses. Thus, the first nine responses postponed shock for thirty seconds; responses ten through nineteen postponed shocks for twenty-seven seconds, etc. Finally, shocks were no longer postponed after one hundred responses. The result of these manipulations was a stable pattern of positively accelerated responding between shocks. Furthermore, in most of these studies these effects were maintained over long periods of time (Morse & Kelleher, 1970).

These results have been replicated and extended in a number

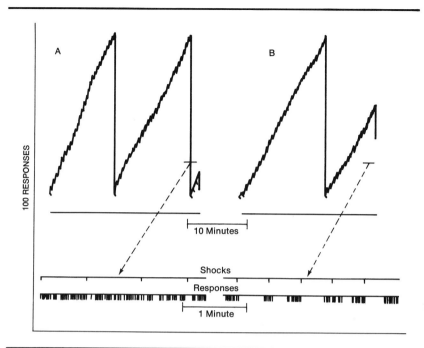

Figure II. *Response patterns under the schedule in which shocks occur every sixty seconds or following the first response thirty seconds after the last shock. A: Session 5; B: Session 26. Cumulative response records recorded on the ordinate. Responses and shocks during the terminal part of the session are shown as recorded on a faster speed paper tape. The heavy horizontal line on the cumulative record indicates the paper tape. The deceleration in responding following shock in session 5 has changed to an acceleration in responding before shock in session 26. (From Morse et al., 1967)*

of additional studies. J. W. McKearney (1968), for example, trained monkeys to postpone shock and then introduced a fixed-interval response-shock schedule. When the shock-postponement schedule was eliminated (as in extinction), a fixed-interval response pattern emerged in which the response-produced shock at the end of the interval was the only consequence maintaining the behavior. "In the course of these experiments the three monkeys responded over 800,000 times, producing over 3,000 intense electric shocks" (McKearney, 1968, p. 1250).

R. Stretch *et al.* (1968) provided additional confirmation in a similar series of investigations. Finally, Kelleher and Morse (1968) demonstrated the maintenance of a fixed-interval response pattern terminating only in strong shock, as a consequence of, first, training monkeys to respond for food reinforcement, then introducing the shock schedule, and finally, withdrawing the food contingency.

Comment. The investigations discussed here have several important implications. First, they elaborate the operant paradigm to encompass events involving multiple response consequences, perhaps reflecting some of the characteristics of behavior that occur in the natural environment. Second, they provide evidence that "the way in which behavior is affected by even a strong stimulus is not invariant" (McKearney, 1968, p. 1251), but rather a function of the schedule of event presentation and the ongoing behavior at the time the schedule is imposed. (See our earlier discussion of two- and three-part schedules p. 64.) Third, they provide a learning model for interpreting pathological behaviors, especially in terms of revealing how "normal" antecedents may interact with subsequent events to produce abnormal effects, and how these effects may be maintained by the schedule of events, even in the absence of the initial behavioral determinants. Regardless of whether or not we are concerned with pathology, "much of the behavior of an individual is multiply determined and not maintained by only consequent events. Even in the simplest sort of experimental situations, interactions inherent in the situation tend to develop some schedule control" (Morse & Kelleher, 1970, p. 174).

Schaefer: Head Banging in Monkeys

A not uncommon but little understood pathological condition is head banging, a term that encompasses a wide variety of events including hitting one's head against objects, striking one's head or face by oneself, etc. Examples of such self-injurious behavior often appear in mild form in children at early stages of their development and later disappear (extinguished, suppressed?). In some instances, however, head banging increases in frequency and intensity.

Such behavior is often interpreted as a function of brain damage, the need for self-stimulation, frustration, etc. At least as plausible a view suggests that head banging is learned as a function of environmental events. In this context, the behavior is an operant maintained most typically by the attention it evokes from other people.

Evidence in support of such a position is provided in a study by H. H. Schaefer (1970). Two male rhesus monkeys (seven years old and two years old) served as the subjects. Initially, the experimenter seated himself in front of one of the monkey's cages and used food pellets to reinforce successive approximations of the head-banging response (raising the paw, positioning the paw above the head, bringing the paw down upon the head, etc.).

During the next ten days, the sole supply of food was presented contingent upon every tenth head-hitting response (Fixed Ratio 10) during repeated brief sessions in the course of the day. During these periods phrases such as "Poor boy!" "Don't do that!" and "You'll hurt yourself!" were associated with contingent reinforcement inter-

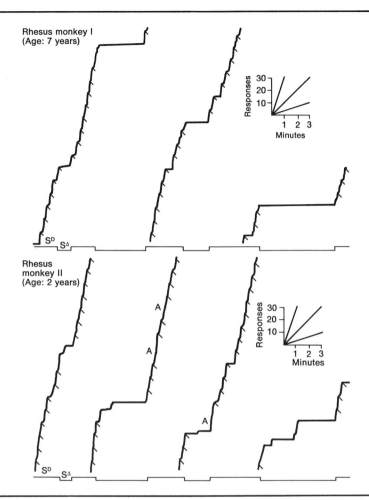

Figure 12. *Discrimination formation after ten days for two rhesus monkeys seven and two years of age; head hitting was reinforced in the presence of the spoken words ("Don't do that!" etc.). (From Schaefer, 1970)*

vals (S^D). The absence of these expressions signaled the withdrawal of reinforcement (S$^\Delta$).

Figure 12 shows the cumulative records for the two monkeys at the end of the tenth day of discrimination training. Both animals hit themselves promptly upon the presentation of the discriminative verbal cues, although the younger monkey's performance was the more precise of the two. On the other hand, the older monkey displayed a higher response rate and continued to hit itself when the food schedule was not implemented.

The animals were then placed on a free-feeding schedule for several days. When they were satiated with food, the experimenter repeated the above procedures. "To a naive onlooker it might well have appeared that the experimenter showed extreme 'compassion' or 'attention' during the S^D periods, while he was 'indifferent' during the S^Δ period" (Schaefer, 1970, p. 113). No hitting responses were displayed by the older animal, although the younger monkey responded a total of sixty times in S^D and forty times in S^Δ. Subsequently, a brief attempt to condition head banging against the cage wall was unsuccessful.

Schaefer also reported several additional observations. For example, the younger monkey showed the head-hitting response in the presence of individuals other than the experimenter, including members of audiences at professional meetings. Such generalization, however, was not observed in the older monkey.

Comment. In this, the first and only experimental demonstration of the acquisition of head banging, several operant principles are explicated. It seems quite clear that the target behavior was acquired as a function of response consequences, maintained by controlling stimuli associated with response consequences, and produced in the nonexperimental environment (at least in one instance) in line with the principle of stimulus generalization.

One, of course, may question the adequacy of the analogy to similar clinical phenomena. (Schaefer argues that since the response produced head lacerations, the condition qualifies as a clinical analog.) However, that issue is of less importance than the fact that forms of self-injury can be demonstrated completely as a function of environmental manipulation. There are additional data supporting the notion that head banging in humans, once acquired, may be maintained by social reinforcement. It only remains to be demonstrated that, as in the Schaefer case, initial acquisition can also be explained by learning theory.

Excessive Consummatory
Rates: Several Experimental Models
The work reviewed in the previous studies reflects one of the dominant themes in the operant analysis of pathological behavior: the importance of aversive events. Other investigators have contributed information that is also relevant in this connection. As we have indicated, one of the characteristics of certain forms of pathology is the presence of excessively high rates of responding. This is clearly the case in such conditions as compulsions and obsessions, but it may also be a concomitant of many other phenomena, for example, phobias, alcoholism, and obesity. The popular assumption, of course, is that the individual is "compelled" by some inner force to engage in these behaviors, usually because this serves to reduce anxiety. We have already reviewed several tentative suggestions regarding the manner in which learning principles may be applied to the analysis of such phenomena. D. R. Williams and P. Teitlebaum (1956) have provided another relevant aversive paradigm with rats.

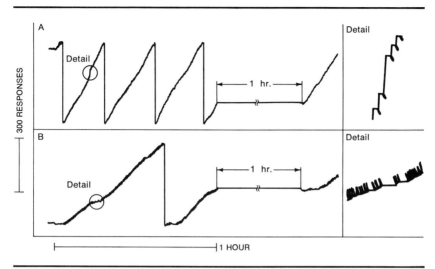

Figure 13. *Cumulative response records showing forced drinking during a typical two-hour session. The pen moves upward with each lick and toward the right as time elapses. Each shock period is indicated by a small (one-eighth inch) downward displacement of the pen. (A) Drinking of a liquid nutrient showing several licks after each shock. (B) Drinking of a quinine solution showing single licks after each shock. (From Williams and Teitlebaum, 1956)*

A Sidman avoidance procedure was implemented for the purpose of generating high rates of liquid ingestion. By licking fluid dispensed through a tube attached to a "drinkometer," the rat was able to postpone the delivery of shock. In this fashion, the investigators succeeded in forcing ingestion of liquids that were normally refused and in producing abnormally high rates of liquid consumption.

After escape training, in which rats licked immediately after shock in order to terminate the ongoing shock schedule, high rates of licking were differentially reinforced; that is, high rates resulted in fewer shocks than did low rates. Figure 13 reveals the changes in behavior as a consequence of the experimental arrangement.

Under ordinary circumstances satiated rats refused to drink water. In addition, quinine solutions were rejected. In the Williams and Teitlebaum procedure, rates of both water and quinine drinking increased drastically as a consequence of the avoidance contingency, even though the rats were satiated. When the shock was withdrawn, drinking behavior immediately declined.

Similar effects have been reported in the literature on polydipsia (literally: excessive drinking) as a function of a number of reinforcement variables. J. L. Falk, for example, observed a three- to fourfold increase in normal water ingestion in animals when food was delivered on intervals longer than thirty seconds (Falk, 1961) and water under a fixed-ratio schedule (Falk, 1966).

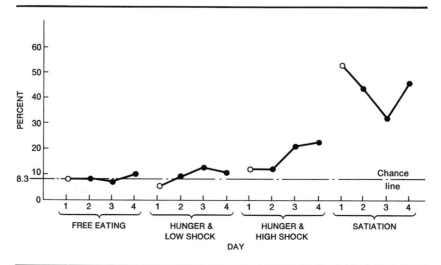

Figure 14. *Daily percentage of the total number of pellets removed that were taken during the first five seconds of each procedure. (From Ullman, 1951)*

These observations support the argument that pathologically high response rates may be caused by learning variables or by interactions between learning variables alone; one need not refer to the concept of inner dynamics. It seems reasonable to assume, however, that in most *clinical* instances such behavior is a function of unexplicated combinations of response consequences, complex schedules, discriminative stimuli, and conditioned reinforcers. These are often difficult, if not impossible, to isolate in the natural environment. Consequently, recourse to experimental analogs that analyze such complex determinants may shed light on this position.

A. D. Ullman (1951), for example, conducted a most interesting study revealing the acquisition of compulsive eating in rats that were food deprived to 80 percent of their ad-lib weight. In four consecutive daily, twenty-minute, free-eating sessions, the number of pellets removed from a trough was recorded (base line). In the next four sessions "low shock" was administered to the animals throughout the first five seconds of each minute for a total of twenty shocks per session. This was followed by four sessions of "high shock" similarly administered. Prior to the next four high-shock sessions, the animals' regular dry diet was reinstated, in addition to which the animals were provided with a wet mash at least five hours prior to the session (satiation condition). The results were analyzed in terms of the percentage of total number of pellets removed during the first five seconds in each session.

As Figure 14 reveals, there was an initial reduction in response rates in the first shock session, followed by a progressive increment. In addition, "almost every pellet removed from the trough was actually eaten by the animals. On some occasions the animal was already actually eating a pellet when the shock came on, dropped it, and took another. This happened infrequently; for the most part animals kept their noses in the trough and ate as many as four pellets during a single 5-second shock interval'' (Ullman, 1951, p. 578).

Not only did pellet removal and eating increase during the shock conditions, but in the high-shock sessions six of the eight animals took more pellets during the first shock interval than during any other five-second interval. Even though the total number of pellets taken was reduced during the satiation condition, the response still occurred with considerable frequency, the highest percentage again occurring during the first shock interval.

The author explains this compulsive eating in terms of an additive drive-reduction process. Perhaps a more parsimonious explanation might emphasize the acquired escape-avoidance properties of the eating response, although this can only be confirmed by replication designed specifically to investigate this process.

Comment. These findings illustrate several points relevant to the study of pathological behavior, aside from their obvious implications for the analysis of alcoholism, to be discussed subsequently. For one, the Williams and Teitlebaum study suggests that avoidance arrangements may produce subtle effects, ordinarily overlooked, but which, when properly analyzed, add important information to our understanding of pathological effects. Thus, the conventional use of aversive arrangements in parental discipline may introduce undesirable side effects, which are obscured by the occurrence of more clearly defined changes in behavior. Finally, these studies once again reveal how the same or similar effects may occur as a consequence of different antecedent conditions.

Aggression: Several Experimental Models

Much has been written about aggression as a fundamental behavioral characteristic. Although some theorists (especially ethologists) argue that aggression represents an adaptive mode of behavior (in terms of species survival, for example), the study of aggression by psychopathologists has focused upon the undesirable consequences of aggression for either the aggressor, the target of aggression, or both. Operant theorists would further maintain that aggressive behavior, especially at the human level, occurs as a function of environmental events, usually of an aversive nature. Hence Skinner's continuing objection to the use of punishment on the grounds that it may generate counteraggression.

Even informal observation suggests that when a parent disciplines a child, this is often followed by the child's being aggressive toward other children or inanimate objects. Furthermore, it has long been noted that animals exposed to shock will frequently respond by biting inanimate objects as well as parts of their own body. Although the relationship between pain and aggression is no doubt far more

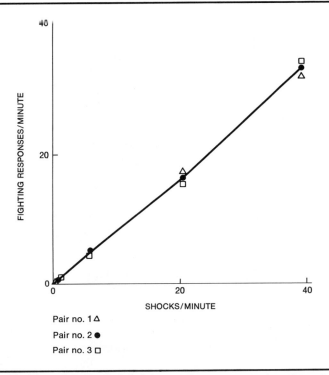

Figure 15. *The elicitation of fighting responses as a function of the frequency of presentation of foot-shock for each of three pairs of rats. (From Ulrich & Azrin, 1962)*

complex than this simplified model would suggest (Solomon, 1964), several investigators have analyzed the manner in which painful experiences may produce aggressive behavior.

The research model often used in this connection involves fighting behavior elicited by shock. A study by R. E. Ulrich and Azrin (1962) is representative. Normally docile, nonaggressive rats were placed in an experimental chamber, which had transparent sides and a grid floor. In the absence of shock, the subjects explored the chamber. "Soon after shock was delivered, however, a drastic change in the rats' behavior took place. They would suddenly face each other in an upright position, and with the head thrust forward and the mouth open they would strike vigorously at each other" (Ulrich & Azrin, 1962, p. 512). Figure 15 shows that the frequency of fighting behavior increased from zero responses in the absence of shock to thirty-three fighting responses per minute when shock was presented thirty-eight times per minute. Figure 16 shows that increases in shock intensity also produced an increase in fighting behavior.

At low intensities chance factors exerted an important effect, and defining a fighting response became arbitrary. At the higher in-

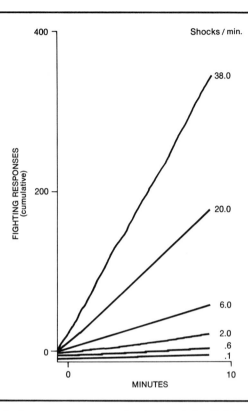

Figure 16. *Typical curves for one pair of rats of the fighting responses at various frequencies of presentation of shock. (From Ulrich & Azrin, 1962)*

tensities, however, the attack movement was unmistakable. The slight decrease in fighting frequency at the highest shock intensity was the result of tetany induced at this level. Similar results were obtained with several other species.

These findings have been replicated and extended by others. D. A. Powell *et al.* (1969), for example, examined the effects of prior aversive experiences on shock-induced aggression. These experiences consisted of either (a) free operant avoidance training, (b) shock-induced aggression, or (c) unavoidable shocks. In addition, a yoked design was used to ensure that all animals received the same shock schedule. The results revealed that an avoidance history and a dominant fighting history increased the probability of shock-induced aggression.

Thus, although pain-elicited aggressive behavior appears to have many of the characteristics of a reflex, as Ulrich and Azrin suggest (and as demonstrated by Powell *et al.,* 1969), it is possible that this apparently reflexive fighting also has instrumental properties. Certainly, the evidence suggests that various prior experiences influence such behavior.

In addition to the pain-elicited aggression model, psychologists have also analyzed the effects of changes in positive-reinforcement consequences on aggression, especially changes in reinforcement schedules. It has long been known, for example, that the sudden withdrawal of positive reinforcement frequently produces attack behavior. Such observations provide the cornerstone for "frustration" theory (Amsel, 1971). In operant terms these arrangements may be considered examples of an extinction paradigm where an animal with a well-reinforced response is suddenly placed on extinction for that response, resulting in extinction-induced aggression (Azrin et al., 1966). Aggression can even be induced when the reinforcement occurs on an intermittent basis, rather than being completely eliminated. A study by W. D. Gentry (1968) provides a good example.

Six pigeons were employed as subjects, three of which were food-deprived and served as "target" animals. Preliminary observations during nonreinforcement conditions established the absence of any attack behavior. Subsequently, three of the experimental animals were trained to peck a key for food. The food was delivered according to progressively increasing ratio requirements that reached a terminal value of one reinforcement per fifty responses (FR-50), after which point the target bird was reintroduced into the experimental chamber. In the following phase the response key was taped over and the reinforcement mechanism made inoperative. This procedure was replicated one time. Figure 17 shows the results of the experiment for one pair of animals.

Although there were differences in magnitude between the three pairs, all three subjects showed the same pattern of increasing attack during the FR-50 reinforcement condition and reduced attack during the nonreinforcement condition. When aggression was exhibited, "the experimental bird attacked the target animals by pecking its head and throat and pulling out its feathers. The target bird rarely fought back and often made 'defensive' movements, e.g., turning its head away from the experimental bird. The aggression was so intense in two pairs of animals that it resulted in injury to the target pigeons" (Gentry, 1968, p. 815). These attacks usually occurred during the postreinforcement pause, which is a general concomitant of Fixed Ratio responding.

Finally, a recent preliminary investigation adds one more tentative observation to this review. G. L. Peterson (1971) investigated the effects of reinforcement schedules on aggression in children. In the procedure that produced the clearest evidence of the effect, eight five-year-old boys and eight five-year-old girls served as subjects. Each child was led into an experimental room in which there was a Bobo clown and a stimulus-reinforcement box. After three minutes in which a base line of aggressive behavior (such as elbowing, kicking, punching, and pushing the Bobo clown) was recorded, the child was taken to another room and shown a number of desirable objects. The subject was then returned to the experimental room and informed that if he responded on the stimulus-reinforcement appa-

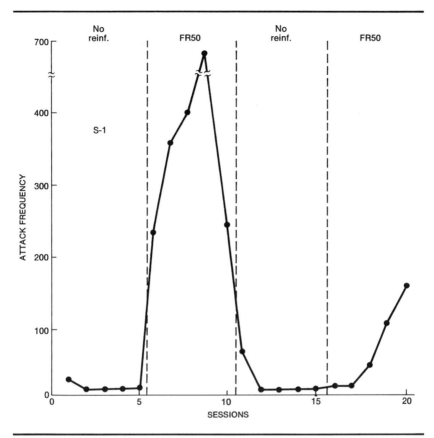

Figure 17. *Frequency of aggressive responses made against a target pigeon by pigeon number 1 in alternated nonreinforcement and FR-50 sessions. Under nonreinforcement, the reinforcement mechanism was inoperative. Under FR-50, the pigeon received food reinforcement on an FR-50 schedule. (From Gentry, 1968)*

ratus, he would receive marbles, which could be exchanged for the items in the other room.

Each subject was then progressively shaped to respond for reinforcement delivered after every fiftieth response (FR-50). After twenty reinforcements had been delivered on this schedule, the reinforcement system was made inoperable for three minutes.

Six of the children displayed peak aggressive behavior during the FR-50 segment of the experiment, and an additional two during the final extinction segment. Thus, Peterson's study offers some reason to believe that human aggression may be at least partially influenced by schedule variables.

Comment. In an assessment of these findings, perhaps the most important observation to be made is the striking similarity in aggressive behavior generated by several different antecedent circumstances. Also, however, similar antecedents (such as reinforcement schedules) may produce a variety of pathological outcomes. Thus, we might compare the above studies with the review of the Kelleher and Morse studies.

Regardless of their implications for the study of aggression at the human level, the results discussed here strongly suggest that we must exercise caution in advancing any unitary theory of aggression. On the other hand, if it seems reasonable to assume that human aggression is the consequence of a combination of aversive experiences (pain, the schedule of reinforcement, punishment, extinction arrangements, etc.), it might be instructive to conduct research that incorporates several of the independently identified relevant variables.

Weiner: Conditioning History and
Maladaptive Human Operant Behavior

The manner in which response history influences pathological behavior in the natural environment is, of course, much more complex (and probably more obscure) than is revealed in the previous studies. Only further extensions of the relevant variables will provide insight into the more subtle determinants of conventional psychopathological events. What is seriously lacking in our perspective is a body of literature analyzing such processes in humans. A good start, however, has been made by Harold Weiner. This investigator has devised an ingenious method for analyzing the manner in which response history in humans results in effects analogous to naturally occurring forms of pathological behavior.

The critical notion in Weiner's analysis is the effect of reinforcement schedules on the persistence of behavior, despite the fact that such behavior produces unnecessary (preventable) loss of positive reinforcement (Weiner, 1970). Such behavior "may be viewed as maladaptive relative to the responding of another individual when it fails to produce as much reinforcement under the same schedule of reinforcement" (Weiner, 1965, p. 935). The question that interested Weiner was: "If two individuals are operating under similar environmental circumstances and one functions effectively (produces optimal reinforcement) and another functions ineffectively (produces minimal reinforcement for a maximum of effort) how do their response histories contribute to such differential effects?" (p. 935).

In one study (Weiner, 1965) subjects were given points for button pressing under different reinforcement schedules. The points could be exchanged for money, the amount being contingent upon their total point count. In one condition every fortieth response produced one hundred points (FR-40). In another condition the first response after ten seconds produced one hundred points (fixed-interval 10 sec., or FI-10 sec.). In a third condition one hundred point reinforcements were obtained if the subject allowed at least twenty

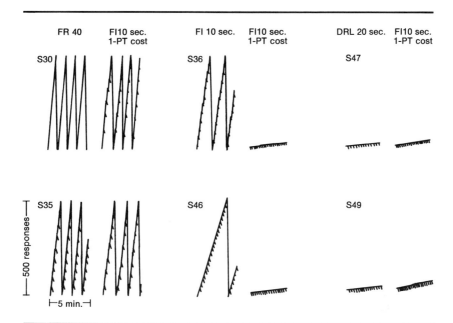

Figure 18. *FI 10 sec. 1-point (1-pt) cost responding following FR 40, FI 10 sec., and DRL 20 sec. conditioning histories. Vertical marks on the record indicate the occurrence of 100-point reinforcements. (From Weiner, 1965)*

seconds to elapse between two successive responses (Differential reinforcement of low rate-20 sec.). Responses that occurred before twenty seconds elapsed delayed the next reinforcement for at least another twenty seconds. Obviously, the pattern of responding required under each of these conditions was quite different. Under the FR schedule, for example, the subject could maximize reinforcement by responding at a rapid rate; in the DRL condition, on the other hand, a subject could maximize reinforcement by responding no more than once every twenty seconds; under FI requirements the subject could maximize reinforcements by responding frequently at the end of the interval.

These conditions obtained for ten hours and represented the subjects' differential reinforcement histories. In the next stage all subjects were shifted to an FI-10 sec. reinforcement schedule with the additional provision that each response also resulted in the loss of a point from the total score. Optimal reinforcement was thus obtained when the subject responded once immediately after each ten-second interval. The performance of the subjects under these conditions differed markedly. (See Figure 18.)

Following an FR-40 history subjects obtained relatively low point scores by emitting maladaptive high rates of constant responding between FI reinforcements despite one-point cost punishments. Subjects with FI-10 sec. histories and DRL-20 sec. histories, on the other hand, obtained higher point scores (were more adaptive) by emitting relatively low FI-10 sec. one-point cost response rates.

Weiner rightfully suggests that the maladaptive effects observed in the subjects with the FR-40 response history may be more a function of the type of schedule change required, rather than the amount of response change required. Thus, these subjects were required to switch from a response-based schedule to a time-based schedule, which was not true in the case of the other subjects. "Given erroneous 'ratio' responding, the constant responding of the FR-40 subjects between FI-10 second reinforcements despite one-point cost is not surprising. It appears that such responding may have resulted from the 'ratio' nature of a response-reinforcement relationship during a conditioning history" (Weiner, 1965).

Comment. Weiner's work represents an important elaboration of the previous studies cited. For one thing, it extends the operant analysis to humans. For another, it provides for a possible analysis of the interaction between current determinants (or stimulus change) and prior response history, as these processes interact in the natural environment. Thus, one possible source of difficulty contributing to maladjustment may be the "incompatibility" between two or more reinforcement schedules. Perhaps certain schedules in the natural environment are more common than others, resulting in certain specifiable characteristics (for example, high, stable rates). These response characteristics may be maintained in the face of the demands of a suddenly introduced, new reinforcement schedule, resulting in inefficient, maladaptive behavior. In fact, Weiner has indeed reported that most of his subjects respond at high (often maximal) rates when placed on a fixed-interval reinforcement schedule, which requires only one response per appropriate time interval in order to maximize the response-reinforcement ratio. Perhaps such schedule interactions also offer an alternative explanation of the earlier Pavlov "delay" procedure. (See Chapter 4.) Thus, rather than a clash between excitation and inhibition, the effects may occur as a consequence of the incompatibility between behavior acquired under one schedule and the responding required as a function of schedule change.

In any event, it would seem to be a matter of considerable importance to begin to isolate schedule effects in the natural environment. There is now good reason to believe that many perplexing questions relative to complex human behavior might be answered by such an endeavor.

Haughton and Ayllon: Sweeping Clean
Pathological behavior is often characterized by bizarre rituals and useless repetitive acts. Psychotics, for example, may continually pace the floor, count objects, or display other apparently compulsive acts. Although there has been much psychodynamic speculation about the etiology of such phenomena, there are virtually no experi-

mental studies isolating the relevant variables responsible for such behavior. An exception is provided by a study by E. Haughton and T. Ayllon (1965).

As part of a general program in the application of operant principles to the analysis and modification of disturbed behavior, Haughton and Ayllon demonstrated the manner in which a bizarre ritual could be acquired and eliminated in a fifty-four-year-old female patient diagnosed as schizophrenic.

Regular daily observations of the patient revealed that she spent 60 percent of her waking time lying in bed, approximately 20 percent of her time sitting and walking, and the remainder in a variety of other activities. In short, she simply refused to do anything on the ward except smoke. A new response, holding a broom in an upright position, was arbitrarily decided upon as the behavior to be conditioned, with cigarettes as the reinforcing agent.

The procedure initially involved giving the patient a broom, followed immediately by a cigarette while she held the broom. Subsequently, reinforcement was delivered on a variable-interval basis when the patient exhibited the selected response. "In a matter of a few days, the patient developed a stereotyped behavior of pacing while holding the broom" (Haughton & Ayllon, 1965, p. 96).

Several further manipulations were conducted to establish a stable pattern of response frequency. "Once the response was well established, it was possible to maintain it through the use of a conditioned reinforcer or token" (Haughton & Ayllon, 1965, p. 96).

Finally, the reinforcement contingency was withdrawn to ensure the elimination of the behavior. This was duly accomplished with no further evidence of broom holding in a two-year follow-up.

In order to independently assess the relationship between this patient's behavior and clinical examples of compulsive rituals, the experimenters had two psychiatrists who were unaware of the conditioning procedure evaluate the patient's behavior. In each case the analysis emphasized the "psychodynamic" importance of broom holding as representative of the regression process commonly observed in schizophrenics who display such "ritualistic" behavior.

As Haughton and Ayllon conclude, "the apparent uselessness of the patient's behavior is indeed the hallmark of behavior often clinically described as 'compulsive' or 'psychotic.' " Yet, examination of some of the environmental conditions under which the response was developed may make it easier to understand how similar cases of behavior are developed and maintained by environmental contingencies (Haughton & Ayllon, 1965, p. 96).

Comment. In some quarters the Haughton and Ayllon study is regarded as providing "critical" support for the operant interpretation of pathological behavior. There is little question that the bizarre ritual was regarded as a genuine pathological manifestation by the examining psychiatrists. It is equally clear that their interpretation of the behavior was erroneous, in that the ritual was acquired completely as a function of operant principles. Thus, the response was acquired by means of a reinforcing contingency, and extinguished when the contingency was disrupted. Little more remains to be said, except that further efforts of this kind might shed light on other types of pathological conditions.

Pathological Verbal Behavior:
The Operant Conditioning Paradigm

Beginning with J. Greenspoon's now classical demonstration of the modification of speech as a function of reinforcing consequences (Greenspoon, 1955), the past fifteen years have witnessed an increasing interest in the application of learning principles to the study of language and verbal behavior. The thesis underlying this line of inquiry is that psychologists can obtain much knowledge by isolating the behavioral variables that determine the acquisition, maintenance, and modification of verbal behavior, in the same way that they analyze the learning process of any response system. The verbal conditioning literature provides some support for this thesis, although many writers (especially cognitively oriented linguists) strongly disagree (Chomsky, 1965), and even behaviorally oriented psychologists take exception. Hence the argument that the verbal-reinforcement effect occurs only if the individual is aware of the reinforcing circumstances, that is, can verbalize the contingencies (Spielberger & DeNike, 1966).

Regardless of the outcome of these arguments, at the very least the verbal conditioning paradigm offers some important clues to some of the variables that may influence pathological verbal behavior. In a study by K. Salzinger and S. Pisoni (1960), for example, reinforcement in the form of verbal agreement resulted in an increase in the subjects' affect statements. Although this is a dimension of verbal behavior that is not clearly pathological (under some circumstances, as in psychotherapy, it is highly desirable), exaggerated and excessive use of affect statements may be considered an important component of neurotic and psychotic behavior, when, for example, one's verbal repertoire is dominated by physical complaints or depressed statements. The Salzinger and Pisoni study has important implications for the analysis of such verbal processes.

The procedure involved thirty-minute interviews with normal patients who had been admitted to a general medical hospital. The interview was divided into three segments: a base-line period in which the operant rate of affect statements prior to conditioning was measured, a reinforcement condition, and an extinction condition. Affect was defined as any verbal response employing affect references ("I'm satisfied," "I like it," "I was upset"). Reinforcement was defined as verbal agreement ("Mmm-mmm," "I see," "yes").

The results indicated that affect statements increased significantly during conditioning and declined during extinction, whereas other verbal dimensions remained relatively constant throughout the interview. Clearly, then, the experimenter's use of verbal reinforcement contingent upon affect statements influenced the subjects' verbal behavior. Although there are no studies in the verbal conditioning literature specifically designed to generate pathological rates of affect-related verbal behavior, the implications of the Salzinger and Pisoni findings for such attempts seem clear.

Just as excessive rates of verbal behavior may reflect pathological conditions, certain verbal deficits may also represent a pathological state of affairs. At least one dimension of autism and schizophrenia is frequently characterized by a sparse or reduced verbal repertoire. Similarly, repression in neurosis may be operationally defined as the absence of verbal statements related to alleged traumatic events, this absence preventing insight. An example of how such a condition may arise is provided in a study by C. W. Eriksen and J. L. Kuethe (1956).

The subjects in this study were required to form an association to each of fifteen words, five of which were randomly selected as critical stimuli. The subjects' associations to these five words were punished by strong shocks to the ankle.

Trials were repeated and the original associations punished until the subject substituted a different association on two successive trials or until a maximum of ten trials had been presented.

In a second stage of the study, the same stimulus words were presented for fifteen seconds, and the subjects were required to produce a chain of associations for each word during that time. They were also told that no shock would be administered during this stage of the investigation.

After the above procedure was completed, each subject was interviewed to determine if he had discovered the "true" nature of the experiment and could verbalize the changes in his behavior. On the basis of these interviews, the subjects were divided into a high-awareness group, and a low-awareness group.

Both groups showed a similar rate of decline in punished associations, while maintaining nonpunished associations at a stable level. Also both groups reached criterion in an average of about four trials; however, the two groups differed in their reactions to critical stimuli. Although both the trend and the magnitude of the high-awareness group on this measure suggested a "deliberate" attempt to withhold punished associations and substitute alternative responses, this process occurred more rapidly and more efficiently in the low-awareness group. These differences are revealed in Figure 19.

Eriksen and Kuethe argue that these results represent a paradigm for repression, since anxiety-provoking thoughts (that is, those associated with punishment) were prevented from occurring "automatically," that is, without the subjects' awareness of having deliberately and intentionally changed thoughts. In fact, insight was correlated with slower avoidance.

As previously indicated, one should be cautious when relating such efforts to psychoanalytic concepts; however, regardless of the

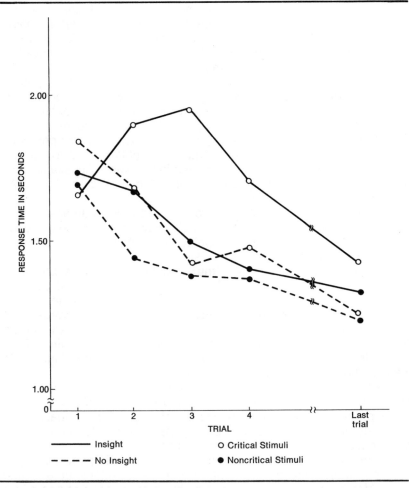

Figure 19. *Reaction times to critical and noncritical stimuli as a function of trials. (From Eriksen & Kuethe, 1956)*

analogy between this experimental form of repression and the psychoanalytic concept, it seems clear that verbal deficiencies may occur as a function of aversive response consequences. Sandler (1964) demonstrated that a similar effect (reduced speech) may occur even when the aversive events are social cues, rather than primary punishers.

A further experimental example of the etiology of abnormal verbal behavior is provided in a study by B. Flanagan, I. Goldiamond, and N. Azrin (1959). A normally fluent subject was required to read aloud from printed material and to press a microswitch with each nonfluency (defined as hesitation, stoppage, repetitions, or prolongation of the rhythmic flow of verbal behavior). The subject was

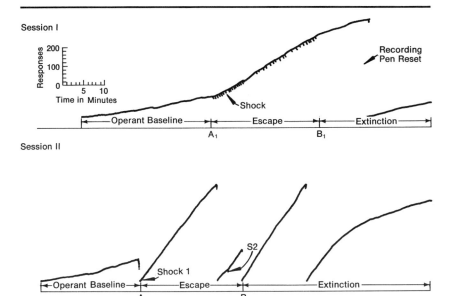

Figure 20. *Instatement and elimination of stuttering responses in a normally fluent individual through control of response-contingent consequences. (From Flanagan, Goldiamond, & Azrin, 1959)*

informed only that there might be occasional shock and that he could terminate the experiment at any time.

After a stable base-line reading rate was observed (and the validity of the measure verified), the conditions were changed. A pulsed shock was administered, accompanied by flickering of the room lights. Each microswitch press turned off the shock and eliminated the light flicker for ten seconds (escape procedure). The subject could thus eliminate both aversive events by responding at ten-second or shorter intervals.

Figure 20 presents the changes in the subject's behavior. Note the increase in nonfluencies leading to less frequent shock (indicated by the downward marks on the cumulative curve). When the aversive contingency was withdrawn, the nonfluency rate returned to the previous level. Reintroduction of the experimental event in Session II resulted in an immediate and extremely high nonfluency rate and a corresponding reduction in shock frequency. Removal of the aversive condition once again resulted in a reduction of the nonfluency rate, although the reduction was somewhat delayed.

In a third test, one week later, stuttering occurred in the presence of the flickering light alone, and for obvious reasons, although the subject's speech in the natural environment was normal, the sessions were discontinued. It is of interest to note that, when questioned, the subject attributed his stuttering to anxiety over his inability to read simple passages.

With some minor variations in procedure, similar effects were observed with two other subjects.

Comment. There is much that remains to be done in the operant analysis of pathological verbal conditions, although a good start has been made by these and other studies. O. R. Lindsley (1960), for example, has described a method for analyzing hallucinatory behavior and shown how its "pathological" characteristics interact with other, more normal dimensions of operant behavior. A. H. Buss and A. Durkee (1958) reported an increase in hostile verbalizations as a function of verbal conditioning in an interview situation.

Additional efforts might focus upon the analysis of other forms of pathological verbal behavior (many of which are often *assumed* to be symbolic of a psychodynamic process) as determined by learning variables. Thus, excessively high rates (sometimes termed *pressure of speech*) may be influenced by reinforcement schedules; extremely low rates (as in depression, withdrawal, catatonia, autism, etc.) may be the result of aversive events, the positive reinforcement of response systems incompatible with speech, or some combination. "Paranoid" statements, "clang associations" etc., may also be investigated as extensions of operant behavior.

What is required is the recognition that verbal characteristics, which represent the most critical dimension of social behavior, are, implicitly if not explicitly, inextricably involved in the assessment of psychopathology, and that they are as amenable to investigation as any other dimension of human behavior. Once this is realized, these response dimensions can be operationally defined and exposed to a learning-theory analysis. There are many questions still unanswered regarding the acquisition of language, speech, verbal behavior, etc. (Skinner, 1957), and a functional analysis of such important phenomena is long overdue. The experimental model is available—only its application remains to be undertaken.

Brady: Ulcers in Monkeys

We have seen how a respondent analysis provides insight into the etiology of certain "psychosomatic" conditions. It seems possible, on the basis of such research, to consider such phenomena as learned behavior, according to the classical conditioning principle. Operant investigators have also turned their attention to psychosomatic conditions.

A good start in this direction was provided by J. V. Brady (1958) and his associates in a series of studies on the etiology of ulcers in monkeys. Although the correlation between emotional stress and ulcers has long been suspected, prior to Brady's efforts it was not clear which kinds of stress conditions produced ulcers, and why the same kind of stress resulted in ulcers in one person and not in another. The typical explanation for these differences was in terms of personality or subject variables. Brady's research, however, revealed that such effects could occur independent of any explanation based upon trait or personality differences.

The ulcer studies evolved out of prior investigations of the effects of stress on gastrointestinal functions in which a high percentage of the monkeys serving as subjects in avoidance conditioning procedures died unexpectedly. Postmortems revealed that many of the animals had developed ulcers as well as other extensive gastrointestinal damage. One procedure that correlated highly with the production of ulcers required the subjects to press a lever at least once every twenty seconds in order to avoid shock. To determine the relative influence of the psychological stress (avoidance responding) and the physical stress (electric shock) on the development of ulcers, a "yoked" procedure was implemented. Two monkeys were paired, and both received shocks every twenty seconds in the absence of responding. The "executive" monkey, however, could postpone the shocks both to himself and to his partner by pressing the lever at least once every twenty seconds. Thus, both animals experienced the same physical stress, but only one experienced the added dimension of psychological stress—the option to make the avoidance response. Six hours of stress were alternated with six hours of rest. In short order, the executive monkey learned to respond about once every twenty seconds during the stress period, which was signaled by a red light, and to stop pressing during the rest period (absence of the red light). His mate, after initial sporadic responding, stopped responding completely.

Some twenty-three days into the experiment, the executive monkey suddenly died, although it had functioned well up to and for two hours during the last session. "Autopsy revealed a large perforation in the wall of the duodenum and the upper part of the small intestine near its junction with the stomach, and a common site of ulcers in man" (Brady, 1958, p. 97). The control monkey revealed no abnormalities. A second experiment yielded similar results.

Efforts to induce ulcers more rapidly (by increasing stress through longer sessions, for example, eighteen hours of continuous avoidance followed by six hours of rest, or through more rapid shocks) were unsuccessful, suggesting that the critical factor was the relationship between the stress and rest periods. "The six-hours-on, six-hours-off schedule had produced ulcers (and occasionally other somatic disorders) despite individual differences in monkeys, variations in diet, and maintenance routines and gross alterations in preliminary physiological tests. No other schedule we had tried produced ulcers at all" (Brady, 1958, p. 100).

Physiological monitoring of the executive monkey's stomach during this time revealed some rather interesting observations. Little change in acidity level occurred during the avoidance period. A significant increase began, however, at the end of the avoidance session and reached a peak several hours later during the rest period with the greatest increase in stomach acidity after a six-hour session, a reduction of stomach acidity after a three-hour session, and little or no stomach acidity after a one-hour session. "Periodic emotional stress apparently causes ulcers only if its period coincides with some natural rhythm of the gastrointestinal system" (Brady, 1958, p. 100).

In what was essentially an attempt to replicate the Brady study in humans, R. C. Davis and F. Berry (1963) conducted an experiment in which one member of a pair of college students could avoid a noxious white noise, while his yoked partner served as the control. Although there was no measure of changes in acid concentration, the "executive" students displayed a greater gastric muscle reaction during the avoidance task than did their partners.

Comment. It now seems clear that many physiological processes are amenable to operant analysis. Thus, there is evidence that heart rate (Lang, Stroufe, & Hastings, 1967), the galvanic skin response (Kimmel, 1967), and a variety of other autonomic functions (Miller, 1969) may be influenced by response consequences.

Given these facts, it is simply a matter of time before further analysis will reveal the manner in which such determinants are involved in psychosomatic conditions. Although this question is now receiving considerable attention, primarily as a result of N. E. Miller's publications, it should be remembered that there is an extensive history of similar efforts. Various practices have long been employed for the control of physiological processes. Furthermore, extensive research, especially in Russia, has demonstrated the manner in which physiological processes are conditioned to environmental events. What is not clear is the exact influence of operant variables in these phenomena. More precise delineation of this issue should provide answers to this question.

Addiction Paradigms: Further
Extensions of the Operant Model

Traditional analyses of drug and alcohol addiction have provided little knowledge of the etiology of such conditions. One popular approach emphasizes the interaction between personality variables and traumatic events. Thus, the drug addict or the compulsive drinker are seen as individuals who are prone to escape rather than to cope with stressing situations.

More recently, operant procedures have been used in studies of addiction demonstrating their relevancy for an understanding of the manner in which such behavior is acquired and maintained. A study by S. R. Goldberg *et al.* (1969) is representative.

The investigation initially involved the establishment of morphine dependency in rhesus monkeys. This was accomplished by implementing an instrumental procedure in which lever pressing delivered 0.1 milligram/kilogram of morphine sulphate per self-injection, through chronically implanted jugular catheters. This procedure is an interesting one, in itself, and suggests that intravenous narcotic

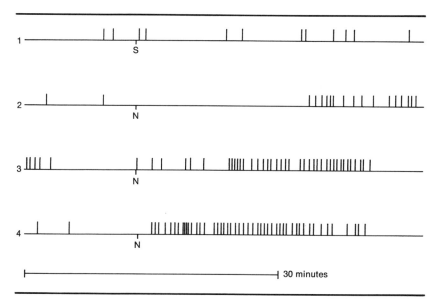

Figuge 21. *Self-administration of morphine in a rhesus monkey. Each up-ward deflection represents a self-administration of morphine. Days 1 to 4 indicate the frequency of morphine self-administration responses before and after intravenous injections of saline (S) or nalorphine (N) (0.1 mg/kg). (From Goldberg et al., 1969)*

self-administration injections in primates is readily established and requires no special behavioral consequences other than the rein-forcement obtained from the narcotic itself. Thus, it contradicts the popular belief that escape and avoidance contingencies are neces-sary conditions for such behavior.

Subsequent to the establishment of morphine dependency, a substance (nalorphine) that induces a severe withdrawal reaction in morphine users (restlessness, piloerection, vomiting, salivation, body tremors, and general irritability) was administered intrave-nously once each successive day.

Figure 21 compares the morphine response rates on those days when nalorphine was injected with those days when saline (an inert substance) was injected. Each upward deflection represents a self-administration of morphine. Note the increase in response rate in the first nalorphine session (day 2), which occurred some twenty-five minutes after nalorphine administration. On successive days the rate increased, and the delay decreased. "By day 4, the in-creased rate of morphine responding appeared within 2 minutes of the nalorphine injection. . . . If we assume that the administration of nalorphine to morphine-dependent monkeys produces aversive stimulation which can be reduced by administration of morphine then the decreased self-administration response latencies after re-peated nalorphine injections may reflect the development of condi-

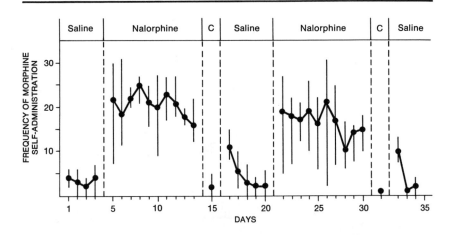

Figure 22. *Frequency of self-administration of morphine in the thirty-minute period following the intravenous injection of saline or morphine (0.1 mg/kg) during conditioning in three morphine-dependent rhesus monkeys. Each point represents the average frequency of self-administration in the three monkeys, and the vertical bars represent the range. Injections of saline or nalorphine were omitted on the control days (C). (From Goldberg et al., 1969)*

tioned escape or avoidance responding" (p. 1307), that is, negative reinforcement.

In the final stage of the study, the investigators presented a neutral stimulus (flashing red light) once each day, at the same time each day for ten minutes before and thirty minutes after the intravenous injections of saline or nalorphine and, for control purposes, on two days when no intravenous injections were administered.

Figure 22 reveals the average frequency and range of morphine responses during the thirty-minute period following the intravenous procedures and under the control conditions. The changes in response rates (an increase in the nalorphine and stimulus conditions) "indicates that the stimulus associated with injections had acquired the property of increasing self-administration of morphine" (p. 1307), that is, conditioned negative reinforcement of responding to avoid the withdrawal reaction.

It seems appropriate to consider some of the implications of this important study. First, a pathological condition (morphine dependency) acquired under *non*aversive conditions was influenced initially by subsequent exposure to an aversive event (nalorphine), which increased drug intake, and finally by a previously neutral stimulus associated with the aversive event. These changes are readily explained by the laws of learning, which also suggest that similar processes may operate in drug addiction at the human level.

Thus, aversive events, which exist in the natural environment in a variety of forms and circumstances (including social and legal prohibitions), may have the effect of *increasing* drug intake, rather than the putative effect of reducing drug intake. Furthermore, *any* stimulus associated with the escape and avoidance of these aversive events "can acquire conditioned properties which result in their playing an important role in the control of self-administration of drugs" (Goldberg *et al.,* 1969, p. 1307).

Comment. The literature relating to drug addiction as a function of learning variables is surprisingly extensive. A number of investigators have shown how self-administration of morphine, ethyl alcohol, and other drugs may be acquired and maintained. D. Lester (1961) introduced a procedure demonstrating the manner in which alcohol consumption may be produced as an adjunct to reinforcement by food delivered to hungry rats contingent upon the appropriate response. J. D. Keehn (1969, 1970) has explored further parameters of this basic procedure, and J. J. Perensky *et al.* (1968) studied some of the circumstances in which such behavior was maintained after the initial positively reinforcing conditions were withdrawn.

In still another relevant investigation, P. B. Everett and R. A. King (1970) first established high rates of collateral Kool-Aid drinking in rats who were bar pressing to obtain food delivered on an interval schedule. Subsequently, increasingly higher concentrations of ethyl alcohol were added to the Kool-Aid, with the result that the animals displayed many of the behavioral patterns associated with intoxication. The authors suggest that such schedule-controlled examples of alcoholism may be analogous to human alcohol consumption, since the drinking behavior is "voluntary"—there are no arbitrary experimenter-controlled contingencies.

Nevertheless, the relevance of this line of inquiry for understanding addiction in humans, of course, remains to be determined. Keehn (1969) and others argue that the question of drug addiction or "dependence" as a behavioral phenomenon can best be understood through the study of the acquisition and maintenance of drug-taking behavior. If we accept this assumption, of course, the above studies are clearly relevant. Let us further consider how the Goldberg study might serve as a particularly important model for understanding some of the issues. For one, it relates to one of the recurrent themes presented in this section. Thus, the final product, a high rate of self-administration of morphine, emerged out of the interaction of learning variables. Initial acquisition was accomplished through positive reinforcement provided by the drug. Subsequently, responding increased as a function of negative reinforcement. Finally, the behavior was brought under the control of a previously neutral stimulus associated with negative reinforcement.

Such "behavioral dependence," then, might be considered to be caused by a combination of behavioral determinants in which the final response produces frequent and immediate reinforcement (both positive and negative) and the aversive consequences of the drug are relatively long delayed. Under such circumstances, where the behavior produces a highly reinforcing outcome and the aversive outcome is long delayed, and where the behavior has generalized, one might predict that the behavior would be extremely resistant to change. A similar analysis may be made to many other forms of pathological behavior, such as overeating, smoking, satyriasis, and psychopathy (extreme form of manipulation of people to one's selfish benefit).

Let us extend this argument to human circumstances. Initial acquisition might occur in the context of peer-group approval (positive reinforcement), escape from peer-group disapproval (negative reinforcement), or some combination (modeling?) of the two. The highly reinforcing consequences of the behavior may be sufficient to maintain the behavior and generate even higher rates.

Finally, the punitive events that the drug user typically encounters in the form of social prohibition may serve to *increase* drug taking generating still further negatively reinforcing properties. Of course, to complete the analysis, we would have to examine the differential influences of social events on different individuals. As we have seen, this would require a determination of how such factors as censure are more aversive and approval more reinforcing for some individuals than others. This, in turn, would require an analysis of individual reinforcement histories, which brings the wheel full circle once again.

Conclusion

As this review suggests, in a little more than twenty years operant investigators have elaborated the study of response consequences, so that it includes a wide variety of areas, touching, indirectly as well as directly, on many topics relevant to the causes of pathological effects. The skeleton of the research model (Skinner, 1938) and the applied model (Skinner, 1953) have now been fleshed out and reflect the characteristics of a vital, sentient program. Furthermore, this progress has been made in the face of heavy criticism from many different quarters. Most important, from the standpoint of psychopathology, the study of complex interactions between response consequences seems to offer some insight into the manner in which ostensibly similar antecedent events may have a wide variety of effects, as well as the manner in which similar pathological conditions may be attributed to different causes.

Much remains to be done, of course, in advancing the model to maturity. Several suggestions along these lines have already been offered in this chapter. Reliance upon the model as a viable one will increase to the extent that such interest bears further experimental fruit.

Chapter 6 / Other Behavioral Analogs: Operant-Respondent Combinations

In this chapter we will review a number of studies in the experimental psychopathology literature that, for one reason or another, do not fall clearly into the confines of strictly operant or respondent processes. In one respect, these studies may be considered examples in which operant and respondent processes are both involved. In some instances, this interaction was inadvertent, as in the case of those studies ostensibly formulated within the Pavlovian framework, while empirically involving instrumental behavior. In others, there is an explicit acknowledgment of such an interaction, and the work reflects the investigator's bias in favor of two-process learning theory. In still others, the experiments were formulated within the context of general behavioral theory, rather than in terms of any specific learning model.

Many of the studies reviewed in this chapter have long been considered prototypes of the experimental analysis of pathological phenomena. Some are clearly attempts to grapple with psychoanalytic concepts; others offer a more general approach to the analysis of psychopathology, especially in terms of conflict processes; and still others are less concerned with the implications for understanding the etiology of psychopathology, but are nevertheless relevant to such a line of inquiry.

EXPERIMENTAL NEUROSIS IN HUMANS: TWO ANALOGS

Watson and Rayner: Little Albert's Phobia

The first explicit attempt in America to investigate pathological reactions in humans was conducted by the crusty father of "behaviorism," John B. Watson (Watson & Rayner, 1920). This endeavor
was part of Watson's program to apply the Pavlovian model to all
facets of human behavior, normal as well as pathological. However,
the precision of his methodology leaves much to be desired, thereby
making it difficult to evaluate his findings. It seems clear that, although Pavlovian operations were employed, the study is also subject to interpretation within the operant framework.

The subject chosen for study was little Albert, nine months of
age at the start of the experiment. Prior testing revealed no fear response when Albert was confronted with a variety of visual stimuli
(animals, inanimate objects, etc.) and the loss of physical support.
In addition, no one had ever seen him display fear or rage under
ordinary conditions. However, when presented with a sudden loud
sound (the striking of a hammer upon a steel bar), Albert displayed
the typical unconditioned startle reaction, trembled, and started to
cry. Some two months later, this information was employed to condition fear to a previously nonfear-arousing stimulus.

The actual procedure is somewhat vague but, among other
things, involved the striking of the bar when Albert reached for a
white rat (punishment procedure), the pairing of the sound with
the white rat independent of Albert's behavior (classical conditioning), and noncontingent, as well as contingent, pairing of the sound
with other "ratlike" stimuli, on different occasions and under differing circumstances. The results suggested to Watson that Albert had
acquired a conditioned fear response. For example, after the sound
had been presented with the rat present, the rat alone would produce Albert's crying response and avoidance behavior. Furthermore,
Albert showed the same reactions, to a lesser degree, in the presence of a dog and a rabbit (as well as other stimuli), although Watson's claim of a generalized fear must be accepted with reservation,
in view of the subsequent pairing (contingently and noncontingently)
of the sound with the other stimuli.

Despite the obvious shortcomings of this experiment, Watson
was quick to recognize its implications for psychopathology at the
human level. Thus, he states "that many of the phobias in psychopathology are true conditioned emotional reactions either of the
direct or the transferred type" (Watson & Rayner, 1920, p. 14).

Comment. Although frequently cited by behaviorists as an experimental prototype of phobias in humans, Watson's effort is of more
importance from a historical perspective than from the standpoint of
isolating functional relationships or its contribution to theory. The
resemblance to clinical phobias is, of course, striking, especially the

generalization of the fear response to other stimuli. In retrospect, however, it seems clear that Watson did not isolate the necessary and sufficient conditions for this effect, let alone provide support for his argument that the conditioned response was the building block of behavior. Although common sense and natural observation support the principle of acquired fears as Watson conceived it, his own study reveals that the process is far more complex than his theoretical model suggests. It could be argued, for example, that Watson's procedure involved a punishment effect, and it was this component that constituted the critical variable.

Nevertheless, this early effort provided good evidence in support of a learning-theory approach to the analysis of phobias. Despite this evidence, however, there were virtually no experimental attempts to replicate and systematize Watson's work, with humans, until some fifteen to twenty years later. Since the majority of the experimental efforts during that time were conducted with infrahuman subjects, the fundamental relationship between Watson's study and this continuing line of research remained obscure; thus, little was contributed to the clinical literature.

Freeman: Difficult Discriminations in Humans
The discrimination procedure first used by Pavlov to induce experimental neurosis has also been employed by others in research with humans. We have already reviewed Krasnogorski's efforts with children. A somewhat different example is provided by G. L. Freeman's (1940) study with adult subjects.

Student volunteers were required to discriminate between two stimuli with different levels of brightness. If the difference was detected within ten seconds, the appropriate response (a finger reaction) enabled shock avoidance. Errors and failure to respond within ten seconds after the second stimulus was presented resulted in shock.

The experimental series began with easily differentiated pairs of stimuli, which were made increasingly similar until they were alike. Thus, the subject was forced to discriminate between two nearly equivalent stimuli or receive shock. After thirty pairs of stimuli were presented or three consecutive shocks administered, the original easy discrimination task was reintroduced. This procedure enabled Freeman to compare the subject's first discrimination performance with subsequent efficiency. In addition, changes in palmar skin resistance during the experimental conditions were also recorded.

Table 3 reveals that the average number of discriminations diminished in each successive series, that is, "S breaks more quickly on each discrimination following failure with difficult ones. This disorientation is accompanied by an increase in general bodily excitement (decreased skin resistance) especially significant because increased practice in the later series should favor decrease in excitement" (Freeman, 1940, p. 118).

TABLE 3. Number of Discrimination Problems Completed by Every S Before Failing, Together with the Average Reaction Time (RT) and Palmar Skin Resistance (PSR)[a]

(Reaction times in sec.; resistance in 1000 ohms)

S	SERIES A			SERIES B			SERIES C		
	Prob.	RT	PSR	Prob.	RT	PSR	Prob.	RT	PSR
1	17	1.72	39	15	.97	38	17	.64	39
2	12	1.23	9	9	.57	8	10	1.50	12
3	11	2.09	18	6	1.81	15	8	.75	14.5
4	17	1.77	—	5	1.17	—	11	1.12	—
5	9	1.78	39	15	1.59	36	19	1.98	33
6	6	.65	—	5	.44	—	6	.46	—
7	14	1.18	75	10	1.34	77	16	1.17	72
8	5	7.64	—	10	6.35	—	14	3.71	
9	16	2.68	73	11	1.16	73	13	2.05	73
10	20	1.77	49	9	1.29	45	10	1.61	44
11	20	1.08	34	19	1.44	31	10	1.47	25
12	5	2.55	17	7	1.79	17	2	2.07	17
13	20	1.38	15	6	1.42	15	10	1.61	15
14	21	2.52	120	6	2.82	120	9	2.22	113
15	9	4.30	55	6	5.33	55	9	2.13	55
16	5	1.60	—	10	2.45	—	9	2.81	—
17	10	1.50	76	14	4.10	80	9	2.91	74
18	19	1.30	20	11	.98	19	7	.76	20
19	9	4.04	19	10	3.54	17	7	3.18	17
20	17	2.63	43	10	3.63	38	7	3.38	30
21	15	2.00	88	6	1.40	85	6	1.20	85
22	12	1.86	66	6	1.23	62	6	1.25	61
23	20	.42	15	9	.24	11	6	.16	11
24	14	1.46	123	11	1.20	130	6	1.27	124
25	9	2.39	20	3	3.01	20	4	2.88	20
26	9	3.57	109	5	4.96	118	4	4.34	108
27	9	2.59	27	8	2.69	20	4	3.31	20
28	14	2.51	127	6	2.12	125	7	2.24	115
29	15	1.67	87	12	1.84	78	10	1.91	84
30	20	1.94	28	11	3.46	24	6	2.50	26
Av.	18.5	3.28	85	14.5	3.32	84	13.2	2.88	77

[a] From Freeman (1940).

Comment. As in Watson's case, the Freeman study reflects only a superficial resemblance to Pavlov's procedure in its use of increasingly difficult discriminations. Thus, it is relevant to ask to what degree the results were influenced by the negative reinforcement contingency (the avoidance response) as well as by the inclusion of a punishment arrangement (shock for incorrect responses). Freeman's findings are of interest, however, in that they extend the use of the "difficult discrimination" paradigm to humans and reveal the effects of prior aversive experiences on subsequent efficiency. This finding bears upon the issue of the effects of historical determinants on pathological behavior.

Masserman: Feline Phobias

As indicated in Chapter 3, J. H. Masserman was one of the first investigators to provide an experimental analysis of abnormal phenomena. Although much of his work has methodological and theoretical limitations, he was extremely imaginative in generating conflict situations resulting in effects that bore a dramatic resemblance to human abnormal behavior. Although the rather informal nature of his experimental procedures hampers analysis of cause-and-effect relationships, it also enabled Masserman to pursue each pathological effect as it occurred. Thus, he contributed a great deal of anecdotal information about a variety of clinical phenomena.

The basic conflict procedure (Masserman, 1943) involved placing an animal (usually a cat) in an enclosed chamber and training it to lift the lid of a food box at one end of the chamber. Conflict was induced by delivering shock through a grid floor or delivering an air blast as the animals were opening the box or starting to eat. Variations of this arrangement involved stimulus discrimination (training the animal to eat only in the presence of certain stimuli), chaining responses (training cats to step on a pedal that produced the discriminatory stimuli), and manipulating the aversive events (gradually increasing the shock intensity).

Generally, after a few experiences in the conflict situation, the cats uniformly displayed a strong avoidance reaction to all facets of the experimental environment. In addition,

> *these neurotic animals exhibited a rapid heart, full pulse, catchy breathing, raised blood pressure, sweating, trembling, erection of hair and other evidence of pervasive physiological tension. They showed extreme startle reactions to minor stimuli and became irrationally fearful not only of physically harmless light or sounds, but also of closed spaces, air currents, vibrations, caged mice and food itself. The animals developed gastro-intestinal disorders, recurrent asthma, persistent salivation or diuresis, sexual impotence, epilepti-form seizures or muscular rigidities resembling those in human hysteria or catatonia. Peculiar "compulsions" emerged, such as restless elliptical pacing or repetitive gestures and mannerisms. (Masserman, 1943, p. 41)*

Changes in behavior were also observed outside the experimental environment. Some cats refused to eat in their home cages; some became aggressive, others inactive. Furthermore, these effects were maintained indefinitely, even when the aversive stimuli were no longer presented, leading Masserman to compare such effects to phobias in humans.

Control observations established the fact that these effects were induced by the competing demands (hunger and fear) of the situation. Thus, no durable effects were observed when the shock was delivered independent of the eating response, in contrast to the phobias produced by the conflict situation.

With this information as a foundation, Masserman proceeded to explore a number of other clinically relevant possibilities. For example, one extension of these efforts provided information regarding the study of alcoholism. Phobic animals were drugged with alcohol and returned to the chamber. This resulted in a reduction in neurotic behavior and the reinstatement of normal behavior. When these animals were subsequently given an opportunity to choose between alcoholic and nonalcoholic drinks, "about half the neurotic animals in these experiments began to develop a quite unfeline preference for alcohol; moreover in most cases the preference was sufficiently insistent and prolonged to warrant the term 'addiction' " (Masserman, 1950, p. 50). In another variation, after training animals

> to depress a disc-switch to obtain food, the switch was so rearranged that its manipulation produced little or no reward. The animal would then develop a marked tendency to push down upon other objects in its environment, such as saucers, loops, boxes, or other cats. This obsessive manipulative activity took many forms: sitting on the switch or on similar platforms rather than in more comfortable places, prying into the experimenter's clothes instead of into the food-box, and so on. (Masserman, 1943, p. 40)

In still other experiments Masserman modified the manner in which the shock condition was manipulated. For example, when the aversive event was introduced in mild form and only gradually increased in intensity, many of the animals would continue to work under these conditions, even after food withdrawal, which would ordinarily result in extinction. Thus, the shock, clearly aversive under *most* circumstances, displayed positively reinforcing properties under these circumstances, resulting in resistance to extinction, and suggesting an analog of masochistic behavior in the clinical environment.

Comment. As previously indicated, an adequate analysis of Masserman's efforts is hampered by the informal nature of his research. Although other investigators have replicated and confirmed some of his findings (Lichtenstein, 1950), an operant interpretation might help to clarify further some of the processes. Many of Masserman's operations might be considered examples of the punishment of appetitive behavior, thus representing situations involving multiple response consequences, that is, punishment superimposed over behavior with a positive-reinforcement history. We have already seen how such an arrangement provides important implications for the study of human pathological events.

Before this information can be applied, however, a more systematic analysis than Masserman's is required. Some of the questions to be considered are the stage of learning in which punishment is introduced and the intensity of the punishment. Several examples from the relevant research literature are available. N. E. Miller (1960) confirmed Masserman's finding that the suppressive effects of punishment can be reduced by gradually increasing the intensity of the punishment, although R. H. Walters and J. V. Rogers (1963) found that prior exposure to punishment enhanced its later suppressive effect. The resolution of this difference is perhaps provided in a study by E. B. Karsh (1963) in which prior exposure to *weak* shock reduced the effect of subsequent punishment, and prior exposure to *strong* shock enhanced the effects of later punishment.

Such an analysis bears upon the question of individual differences in responding to the same contemporary stimuli. Why, for example, do some individuals "resist" stress and others "break down"? Questions of this kind can perhaps best be answered through an analysis of the relationships between response consequences (especially those of a punishing nature) in the individual's prior history.

Wolpe: A Replication and an Extension of Masserman's Work

Wolpe's research on experimental neurosis was designed to support his contentions regarding the etiology of neuroses. As we have seen, Wolpe rejected Pavlov's explanation of nervous system impairment in favor of the argument that neurotic behavior can be understood completely in terms of learning principles (Wolpe, 1958, p. 37). He postulated two basic learning situations: (1) exposure to ambivalent stimuli in which equal and opposing responses are elicited and (2) mere exposure to noxious stimuli. Wolpe believed the second category of events had been overlooked by the classical experiments on neurosis, and his own research was designed to investigate this type of situation. Evidence that could be marshaled in support of such a position would contradict Masserman's argument in favor of interpreting neurosis as a consequence of motivational conflict.

Consequently, Wolpe repeated Masserman's procedure in which food-deprived cats were first trained to make a food-approach response (lifting the lid of a food box or orienting themselves toward the food box) at the sound of a buzzer (discriminative stimulus). After the cats had acquired this behavior, Wolpe shocked the cats just prior to the end of the response chain. His procedure was repeated until the food-approach response was completely suppressed. In addition, however, Wolpe also employed a classical conditioning procedure (exposure to a noxious event); a second group of cats was placed in a similar experimental chamber and then exposed to a conditioned stimulus, which was followed several seconds later by a shock.

No differences between the animals in the two groups were observed in terms of either the immediate shock-elicited reactions, the long-range effects (for example, refusal to eat in the experimental chamber even after prolonged deprivation), or the generalized effects outside the experimental situation.

Thus, Wolpe argued that in addition to the conventional conflict model, neurosis could occur as the result of noxious experiences.

Comment. As in the case of Masserman, Wolpe's procedure lacks the rigor necessary for isolating functional relationships. Despite the general finding that two ostensibly different procedures resulted in similar effects, there is much that remains to be determined. Suffice it to say that both situations probably involved respondent and operant processes, although this is obscured by Wolpe's procedure. Thus, although there is considerable evidence that noxious events suppress behavior, thereby providing support for Wolpe's thesis, there are numerous reports in the literature that serve to qualify this general conclusion. An answer to this question can be obtained, however, by a systematic analysis of relevant variables, for example, the magnitude of the noxious stimulus, the frequency of the noxious stimulus, and the subject's prior history.

Miller: The Conflict Model and Neurosis

In some quarters N. E. Miller's conflict model (1944) has long been regarded as a highly productive approach to the general analysis of pathological behavior. Most investigators would also acknowledge that Miller has provided an extensive series of studies relevant to the experimental analysis of specific phenomena.

Miller's line of inquiry evolved out of the study of runway learning and represents an elaboration of such efforts; thus, for example, his experiments frequently involved two or more runway response alternatives. When these alternatives competed with one another, conflict was engendered. Miller and others consider such a situation to be the critical determinant underlying many forms of neurotic behavior. It takes little stretch of the imagination to recognize the fundamental relationship between this interpretation and other theories. The Oedipus complex may be regarded as an example of conflict in which the mother may represent both an object of sexual gratification and the threat of the withdrawal of love in the presence of overt libidinal expressions.

Aside from the basic assumption that neuroses are caused by such conflict, the behavior that emerges during the conflict experiments appears "to be typical of conflict behavior in a wide variety of other situations: squirrels in conflict about taking a nut from a child's hand, children in conflict about petting strange animals, bashful boys in love with a girl but afraid to ask for a date, and various phenomena observed in the clinic" (N. E. Miller, 1959, p. 204).

Although Miller was impressed with the clinical implications of such a model, he also considered it to be the prototype for conflict in all areas of human endeavor. In fact, Miller was concerned primarily with analyzing "the *laws* of conflict behavior instead of at-

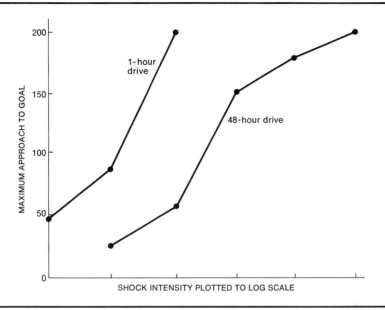

Figure 23. *Effect of strength of shock and of hunger on farthest run toward goal in an approach-avoidance conflict. (From N. E. Miller, 1959)*

tempting to produce allegedly neurotic behavior" (N. E. Miller, 1959, p. 205).

Of the various conflict arrangements that may be specified (see the discussion in Chapter 3), the most pertinent for behavior pathology is the simultaneous presentation of approach and avoidance alternatives that are equal in strength, that is, the presentation of an object or situation that is equally attractive and repelling. It is characteristic of such situations that they involve fear as one of the response tendencies. Under these circumstances the typical conflict signs emerge: vacillation, equivocation, disruption of prior learning behavior, etc.

An unpublished study (cited by N. E. Miller, 1959, p. 212) is representative. Rats were trained to run down an alley to obtain food while wearing a harness that enabled the investigators to measure nearness to the goal. After training, the rats were shocked at the goal, with different groups of rats receiving different shock intensities. In addition, the rats were divided into two groups, one experiencing one hour of food deprivation, the other forty-eight hours of food deprivation. Figure 23 shows that decreasing the strength of hunger or increasing the strength of electric shock caused the rats to stop farther from the goal (N. E. Miller, 1959). Obviously, at some parameter values approach and avoidance tendencies are equal, and conflict will ensue.

Of the numerous experimental contributions that Miller has

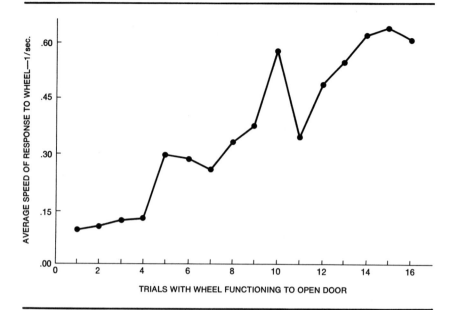

Figure 24. *Learning the first new habit, turning the wheel, during trials without primary drive. With mild pain produced by an electric shock as a primary drive, the animals learned to run from the white compartment, through the open door, into the black compartment. Then they were given trials without any electric shock during which the door was closed but could be opened by turning a little wheel. Under these conditions the thirteen of the twenty-five animals that turned the wheel enough to drop the door on four or more of the first eight trials learned to turn it. This figure shows the progressive increase in the average speed with which these thirteen animals ran up to the wheel and turned it enough to drop the door during the sixteen nonshock trials. (From N. E. Miller, 1948a)*

made to the psychopathology literature, the following two are frequently considered to be among the most significant.

The first involved the study of fear as an acquired drive, thus paralleling "clinical observations which indicate that fear (or anxiety, as it is called when its source is vague or obscured by repression) plays a leading role in the production of neurotic behavior" (N. E. Miller, 1948a, p. 89).

A shuttle box type of apparatus was employed in which the subject was required to run from an electrified area into a safe compartment in order to escape shock. Once the subjects had acquired this response, Miller attempted to determine whether or not they would turn a "wheel" that removed the barrier between the shock compartment and the safe area, even when the shock was withdrawn (during extinction). About half the animals acquired this instrumental response. The average wheel-turning speed displayed over sixteen trials is shown in Figure 24. "It can be seen that there is a definite

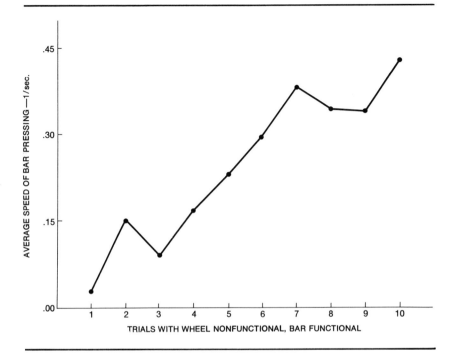

Figure 25. *Learning a second new habit, bar pressing, under acquired drive. Conditions were changed so that only pressing the bar would cause the door to drop and allow the animals to run from the white compartment, where they had been previously shocked, into the black one, where they had escaped shock. During nonshock trials under these conditions, the animals learned a second new habit, pressing the bar. Each point is based on the average speed of thirteen animals. (From N. E. Miller, 1948a)*

tendency for the animals to learn to turn the wheel more rapidly on successive trials" (N. E. Miller, 1948a, p. 94).

Subsequently, the wheel was made inoperable, but a new response, depressing a lever, was instrumental in removing the barrier. As shown in Figure 25, "the speed of bar pressing increased throughout the ten non-shock trials during which that response caused the door to drop" (N. E. Miller, 1948a, p. 96).

These findings suggested to Miller that the cues in the shock compartment acquired the functional properties of a drive, and that escape into the safe compartment acquired the functional properties of a reward, as demonstrated by the learning of new behavior. These effects could be enhanced or diminished, depending upon the degree of shock intensity and the length of the extinction procedure.

Miller explained this behavior in terms of an acquired drive that enables the organism to be more adaptive in complex variable situations, but also results in behavior that appears to be "baffling and apparently lawless to any investigator who has not had the opportunity to observe the conditions under which the acquired drives are established" (N. E. Miller, 1948a, p. 99). In terms of clinical phenomena, "one hypothesis is that neurotic symptoms, such as compulsions, are habits which are motivated by fear (or anxiety . . .) or by a reduction in fear" (N. E. Miller, 1948a, p. 99).

The second of Miller's significant paradigms involves the concept of displacement. Clinical theory argues that when the direct expression of an impulse is inhibited (as in aggression against an employer), the impulse will be indirectly expressed in other ways or in the same way but under different circumstances. Freud considered such "displacement" of threatening impulses (or id energies) to be responsible for a multitude of responses from slips of the tongue to the creation of complex works of art. Similarly, seemingly "inappropriate" behavior may also be considered within a drive-reduction context.

Miller offered an explanation of such processes in terms of the approach-avoidance conflict model. Consider, for example, the consequences of parental discipline. When a child is punished for misbehavior, this generates counteraggressive impulses directed toward the parent. However, since the punishing agent is also feared, the aggressive impulse is displaced elsewhere, and the child, seemingly without provocation, perhaps attacks a younger sibling. Thus, it might be assumed that the aggression generalized from the parent to the sibling, as in stimulus generalization.

Miller recognized, however, that the displacement process is a complex one; that is, although aggression may generalize, the inhibitory influence may also generalize. Thus, in order to predict the manner in which displacement will be manifested, it is necessary to determine, for example, the gradients of generalization of both aggression and inhibition or of both approach and avoidance. If the gradient of generalization of the inhibiting response is steeper than that of the displaced response, then as stimulus similarity decreases, the strength of the inhibiting response diminishes in relation to the displaced response, and the probability increases that the displaced response (aggression) will occur.

To test this interpretation, Miller and D. Kraeling (1952) trained hungry rats to run down a wide, white alley to obtain food placed behind a hinged shield. Subsequently, increasingly stronger shocks were applied to the shield until the response was completely suppressed. Finally, in order to test the generalization of the approach-avoidance conflict thus engendered, the shock was withdrawn, and the rats were divided into three groups. One group was tested in the original alley; another group, in an alley that was slightly different from the first; and the third group, in an alley that was very different.

Figure 26 shows the percentage of animals in each group that reached the goal during four test trials. Only 23 percent of the animals tested in the original alley went to the goal, as compared with

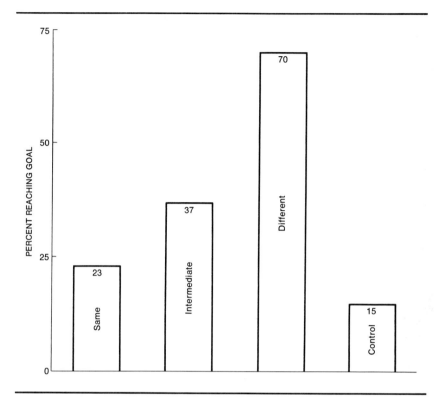

Figure 26. *The percentage of Ss in each group reaching the goal during the four test trials.* (*From Miller & Kraeling, 1952*)

70 percent of the animals tested in the very different alley. In other words, the greater the stimulus difference, the greater the probability that the previously punished response would occur, or, in Miller's terms, the approach tendency generalized more strongly to the new stimulus situations than did the avoidance tendency.

Comment. The conflict model represented a major advance in the experimental analysis of behavioral situations that seemed to bear a resemblance to pathological events. Thus, where common sense suggested that conflict may be engendered in many childhood experiences, resulting in neurotic behavior, investigators were now provided with a method for systematically manipulating two or more incompatible determinants (reward and punishment, for example) and observing the related effects.

Unfortunately, the correspondence between the behavior generated in the Miller model and pathological behavior in the natural environment was more apparent than real. As B. Maher (1966) has indicated, in the Miller model the data are obtained from animals moving in space (down a runway, for example), whereas most of the clinical applications of the model are to human beings behaving over *time*. This is a subtle but highly important distinction. In other words, "many human behavior chains occur in relation to goals which may be reached after some temporal period has elapsed, but which do not necessarily have any particular or fixed relation to the person in space" (Maher, 1966, p. 140). Moreover, the correspondence between the conflict studies and the more complex phenomena encompassed by the Dollard and Miller theory may be called into question.

In any event, we might consider an operant analysis as an alternative for assessing conflict situations. Thus, a conflict arrangement might be interpreted as one in which concurrent operants are operating or one in which multiple response consequences are present. Such an arrangement enables the effects of variables to be separately evaluated and manipulated over time and space, thereby enhancing the model's applicability. Furthermore, determinants can be programmed to "produce" any effect desired. For example, conflict might be engendered when a positively reinforced response also results in shock of sufficient intensity to produce oscillation and the usual conflict signs.

Similarly, Miller's analysis of displacement continues the Freudian assumption that changes in behavior are a function of changes of energy in drive outlets. Perhaps an equally plausible approach would be to analyze such situations in terms of stimulus control, in which the behavior that is emitted depends upon the relationship between the stimulus antecedents and their response-consequence associations.

This brief review scarcely gives justice to the many contributions Miller has made to the field. More recently, for example, Miller and his associates have published the results of a series of studies confirming the operant conditioning of a variety of visceral responses, thus demonstrating that physiological processes, previously considered immune to such influences, can indeed be modified by response consequences (N. E. Miller, 1970). Thus, increases and decreases of the salivary response in thirsty dogs were conditioned by a positive reinforcement contingency; the heart rate in curarized rats increased or decreased as a function of positive reinforcement in the form of brain stimulation (furthermore, these changes came under the control of a discriminative stimulus associated with the reinforcement contingency); contraction of the smooth muscle of the large intestine increased or decreased as a function of similar reinforcement; and other visceral responses were modified as a function of escape and avoidance contingencies.

It is perhaps too early to assess the importance of these recent efforts for the study of pathological behavior, but the implications seem clear. At the theoretical level, there is a strong suggestion that some of the traditional views regarding the dichotomy between classical and instrumental conditioning require reassessment. At the applied level, Miller's work has implications for analyzing the origin of psychosomatic conditions "allowing them the more flexible possibilities of instrumental reinforcement by rewards which do not have to be limited to those stimuli eliciting the particular symptom as a specific conditioned response. . . . It remains for further work to demonstrate the degree to which the appropriate social conditions for rewarding such learning actually occur in various societies" (N. E. Miller, 1970, p. 159).

Mowrer: The Neurotic
Paradox and the Vicious Circle

We have already described Mowrers' theoretical contributions to the study of pathological behavior. In addition, Mowrer has offered a definition of certain forms of psychopathology which has the advantage of being amenable to empirical analysis. He states that the core characteristic of neuroses is the persistence of behavior that results in a high degree of punishing consequences and a minimal degree of reward. The normal individual, in contrast, attempts to maximize reward and minimize punishment. This "neurotic paradox" circumscribes the many examples of self-defeating behavior so characteristic of maladjustment (Mowrer, 1948).

Mowrer's first experimental report (Mowrer, 1950) of such an analog was provided by an observation of "vicious circle" behavior reported by Judson Brown: A rat that had been trained to run a runway in an escape-extinction procedure left a "safe" segment of the apparatus to cross an electrified portion. This response *enhanced* resistance to extinction and resulted in repeated and durable exposure to the punishing event, as contrasted with unpunished rats who stopped running in a shorter period of time.

Subsequently, Brown and his colleagues explored the further possibilities of such vicious circle, self-punitive behavior. In one study (Brown *et al.*, 1964) rats were trained to escape from an electrified start box with a straight six-foot runway into a safe goal box. Following escape training, a modified extinction procedure was introduced. After five additional escape trials, the shock intensity was gradually reduced over the next five trials. In addition, on the first extinction trial the shock was restricted to the last two feet of the runway for one group, and to the entire six feet of the runway for a second group. Thus, no shock was presented in the start box itself. A third group was extinguished in the conventional manner.

Figure 27 shows the mean speed in feet per second exhibited by the groups over six extinction sessions.

> *It is apparent that the long-shock group proved to be most resistant to extinction, followed sequentially by the short-shock group and no-shock groups. . . . The persisting behavior involved repeated approaches toward and toleration of stimuli, which, if defined in terms of Ss' original escape reactions*

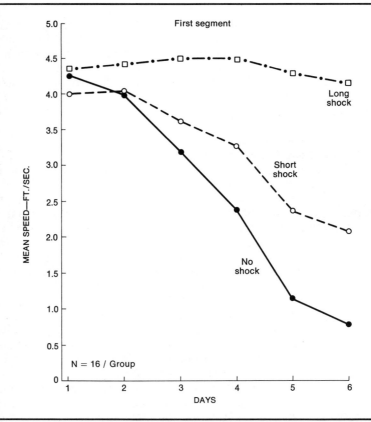

Figure 27. *These extinction curves exhibited by the three groups were derived from measurements of running speed in the first two-foot segment of the alley. (From Brown et al., 1964)*

> *would have to be labeled obnoxious. It seems justified, therefore, to describe such behavior as "masochistic-like." (Brown et al., 1964, p. 132)*

Mowrer has also focused upon the concept of regression and has provided an experimental analog of this Freudian mechanism (Mowrer, 1940), which he considered to be of fundamental importance in neurosis.

Mowrer argues that habits are acquired at each successive stage of development and endure with varying degrees of strength. If, subsequently, the established habit system meets with frustration, the specific nature and extent of these "relative fixations" determine the pattern of regression. Thus, when the individual is prevented from attaining gratification, there may be a reversion to an earlier stage of development in which gratification was obtained. It is this process that is assumed to be the basis of all neurosis. "In thus retrogressively resorting to earlier modes of gratification, the individual reencounters *old* anxieties; and it is the coexistence of both pain- and pleasure-giving functions in the symptomatic acts of the psychoneurosis that gives them much of their apparent mystery, unintelligibility, and tenacity" (Mowrer, 1940, p. 60).

Although Mowrer recognizes that regression, as encountered by the clinician, is a more complex phenomenon than this conceptual analysis would suggest, such an interpretation is amenable to experimental investigation, as in the following study (Mowrer, 1940).

Two groups of rats with different training histories were employed. One group (control) was administered ten shock trials in which the shock was maintained until the rat terminated it by a lever-press response (habit B, escape training). This condition was maintained for three days. Animals in the second group were administered one inescapable fifteen-minute shock each day for six days. Under these circumstances all of the subjects learned to "sit up" on their hind legs (habit A), thereby reducing the aversive properties of the shock (partial escape). The bar-press escape contingency was then made available to the experimental animals, with the result that all of these animals also learned to press the lever within thirty trials. That is, after equal amounts of training in habit B, the animals in the two groups behaved in an indistinguishable manner. On the next day the escape response was punished in both groups by a slight brief shock. Under these conditions the control subjects continued to display habit B, but four of the five subjects in the experimental group "regressed" to habit A. "This type of change seems to possess all the essential attributes needed to qualify as regression in the traditional psychoanalytic sense," thus confirming Mowrer's argument that "regression is historically conditioned (by the presence or absence of prior fixations) and that it is primarily in the *genetic* sense that this concept has greatest usefulness and meaning" (Mowrer, 1940, p. 79).

Comment. Like Miller's, Mowrer's contributions to the experimental analysis of pathological behavior are so wide ranging as to defy any unitary analysis. Aside from his formulation of two-factor theory, perhaps more than any other psychologist, he has attempted to provide an experimental foundation for a variety of clinical concepts, including anxiety, phobia, and reaction-formation, in addition to the two reviewed above. Although his explanations are often couched in psychoanalytic terminology, the empirical content of his efforts can rest on its own value.

Furthermore, Mowrer's methodology does allow a direct interpretation by the operant conditioning model. For example, both studies described above enable a historical analysis of the events responsible for the production of maladaptive behavior. Thus, the Brown *et al.* study may be interpreted within the two-stage model (punishing a response acquired via negative reinforcement). The study of regression represents an example of the three-step model:

escape responding (habit A) followed by acquisition of a second, more adaptive response (habit B), and finally, when habit B was mildly punished, regression to previously learned response. Mowrer's focus upon the historical determinants, or "past experience," and the explication of these antecedent events in learning-theory terms is thus completely compatible with the operant model. In some respects, his work falls in the category of those studies that have analyzed the effects of prior, inescapable shock on subsequent behavior. Thus, such procedures may be interpreted in the light of two- and three-stage behavioral models.

Solomon, Kamin, and Wynne: Traumatic-Avoidance Learning and the Vicious Circle Effect

Investigating avoidance learning and avoidance extinction in dogs, R. L. Solomon and his colleagues (1953) obtained effects that were highly suggestive of clinical phenomena at the human level. In a prior study (Solomon & Wynne, 1953) dogs were trained to jump from a shocked compartment to a nonshocked compartment in order to avoid a very intense shock. (We have already discussed the implications of avoidance learning for understanding various pathological conditions.)

The first interesting observation was the persistence of the behavior during extinction. The latencies of the response to the pre-shock stimulus gradually decreased, and the behavior of the animals became more and more stereotyped. Figure 28 shows, for example, a reduction in mean latency from 2.7 seconds during the criterion trials to 1.6 seconds after twenty days (two hundred trials) of extinction. Here again, we have evidence that bears upon the experimental analysis of the acquisition of phobic reactions.

Subsequently, Solomon and his associates subjected the animals to a variety of extinction procedures, some of which produced further examples of vicious circle behavior. In one case, for example, an animal, after receiving only three avoidable shocks during the acquisition condition continued to respond after the shock contingency was withdrawn (as in extinction) for 490 trials. In an attempt to reduce this resistance to extinction, the previously "safe" compartment was electrified, so that the dog was now, in effect, leaving a safe compartment to jump *into* shock. Far from displaying a reduced resistance to extinction, the animal continued to jump on each trial, even when, on the hundredth trial, the shock duration was increased to ten seconds. Only after a glass barrier prevented the dog from responding in three of the ten session trials was there subsequent extinction.

Several experiments were then conducted in order to determine the efficacy of these various procedures for establishing resistance to extinction. For example, in one study (Solomon *et al.,* 1953) the shock procedure was introduced with seven animals after two hundred extinction trials, and after ten extinction trials with six others.

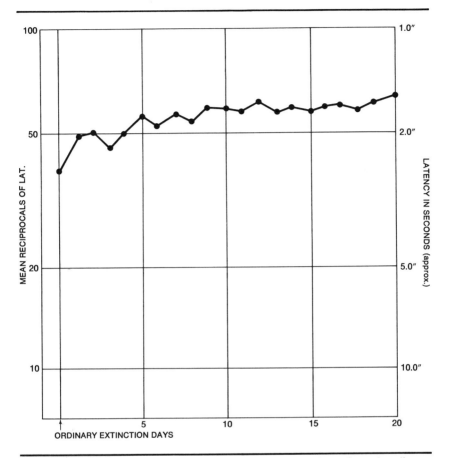

Figure 28. *Mean reciprocals of latency as a function of number of ordinary extinction days. Each point is the mean reciprocal of response latency for thirteen dogs for the ten trials of a given day. (From Solomon et al., 1953)*

Over the course of the next one hundred trials, in which the animals were not shocked if they did not jump and *were* shocked if they did, only three of the subjects extinguished (one in the two-hundred-trial group and two in the ten-trial group). Thus, ten animals continued to display a response that resulted in a highly aversive consequence, despite the fact that refraining from such behavior would have resulted in no aversive consequences. Furthermore, these animals "jumped *faster* and *more vigorously* into shock than they had jumped previously under the ordinary extinction procedure" (Solomon *et al.,* 1953, p. 295). One dog stopped jumping into shock in the second extinction session and then started again. If anything, then, the punishment of the avoidance response in extinction seemed to increase the strength of the jumping response in most dogs and resulted in the persistence of behavior that was more than

merely nonadaptive, since it resulted in highly painful consequences.

Comment. The Solomon *et al.* studies had important implications at
the theoretical and applied levels and were responsible for generating an extensive series of investigations on the phenomenon of
"learned helplessness." For one, the results were interpreted as
providing support for a "two-process" theory. Thus, a conditioned
emotional reaction to the preshock stimulus was established via
classical conditioning, and that reaction served as a drive until the
instrumentally reinforced response enabled avoidance of the painful
event. Furthermore, the persistence of the response in the face of
highly punishing circumstances revealed the durability of the behavior and reflected some of the characteristics of self-punitive
behavior. (One difference between Solomon and Mowrer exists in
that the former maintains that skeletal responses [voluntary] as well
as autonomic responses may be classically conditioned.)

If we apply this reasoning to such human events as anxiety
conditions and phobias, the argument would assume that a fear
drive has been conditioned under traumatic circumstances and that
this drive sustains anxiety-avoiding behavior. In fact, L. Turner and
Solomon (1962) delineated the role of several variables in such fear
conditioning in humans. Thus, the most effective arrangement is one
that initially employs a brief CS-UCS interval and introduces the
UCS at a high intensity. These variables can then be subsequently
modulated, and conditioning will be maintained.

Of the many investigations that have extended these findings, a
study by D. Campbell *et al.* (1964) is of particular interest. Although
it exemplifies the classical conditioning paradigm in that no instrumental avoidance response was involved, it is included here because the findings, that is, the striking durability of fear conditioning,
are congruent with the Solomon results.

The experimenters used the Scoline-paralysis reflex in the conditioning procedure. Scoline (succinylcholine chloride dihydrate)
produces nearly complete paralysis of the skeletal musculature and
interrupts respiration for about two minutes. Although no pain is
involved, the situation is usually described as a terrifying one because of the subject's inability to control breathing. Only one trial
was administered, during which time the galvanic skin response,
respiration, heart rate, and muscle tension were monitored. For one
group of subjects (the experimental group) a tone was presented
before and during the paralysis. A second group received just the
Scoline, and a third received just the tone.

Three thirty-trial extinction sessions were presented to test the
durability of any conditioning. The first was presented five minutes
after the test trial; the second, one week later; and the third, three
weeks later. In contrast to the control subjects, the experimental
subjects failed to extinguish on any of the responses monitored. Of
particular interest was the finding that the "voluntary" responses

(respiratory and muscular) failed to extinguish along with the autonomic measures. "Traumatic" experiences, then, can be established under laboratory conditions and can be seen to exert a variety of durable effects in humans as well as infrahumans, although ethical considerations suggest that we proceed with extreme caution.

One final word about the traumatic-avoidance procedure warrants repeating. One major distinction between a two-process interpretation and an operant interpretation of such events is based upon the concept of drive. The assumption that anxiety, associated with certain aversive stimuli, generates a drive that maintains avoidance behavior is rejected by operant theorists. Instead, avoidance behavior is accounted for in reinforcement probability terms; that is, the response that maximizes (negative) reinforcement will recur. Operant theorists are uncomfortable with the term "anxiety" (Estes & Skinner, 1941; Schoenfeld, 1950) and would restrict its use to an empirical demonstration of the manner in which conditioned emotional reactions influence ongoing behavior. An analysis of the relevant variables governing the interaction between these reactions and ongoing behavior should ultimately provide us with general functional relationships. Thus, specific changes resulting from such an interaction may be a function of the compatibility or incompatibility between the ongoing operant and the responses to the conditioned aversive stimuli. When the variables generate incompatible reactions, as in the classical Estes and Skinner study, operant responding will be suppressed during the anxiety condition. In other cases, however, the variables governing ongoing behavior and anxiety reactions may be compatible, in which case operant behavior would *increase* upon exposure to threatening stimuli. For example, F. H. Kanfer (1958) and Davidson (1970b) report increases in verbal responding as a function of the presence of stimuli that have been associated with aversive events. Such information may be relevant to those conditions generally characterized by excessive response rates (pressure of speech, hypomania) as well as to the manner in which such conditions are maintained by events in the natural environment.

FIXATION: SEVERAL EXPERIMENTAL ANALOGS

Another of the more prominent characteristics of psychopathology is the persistence of behavior that was appropriate to one time and place in other relatively less appropriate circumstances. Freud considered such "immature" modes of behavior a function of fixation in which personality development was halted at a relatively primitive stage. We have previously discussed some of the relevant theoretical considerations with regard to this concept. Let us now turn to several examples from the experimental literature.

Such phenomena, although not necessarily considered within the context of fixation, have long been of interest to experimentalists. For example, the persistence of behavior under apparently nonreinforcing circumstances may be related to the study of resistance to extinction, which is frequently a function of the reinforcement schedule (Ferster & Skinner, 1957). Perhaps the most commonplace example is "compulsive" gambling, and tantrumlike behavior, especially in adults, may be considered in the same context. The most relevant investigations, however, are those that reveal the persistence of unproductive behavior in the face of more adaptive alternatives.

An elaborate series of investigations in this area was undertaken by N. R. F. Maier and his associates. Essentially, Maier argued that perseverative behavior, that is, the persistence of inefficient response patterns, was a function of strong frustration or anxiety (Maier, 1949) caused by exposure to an insoluble problem.

His procedure (Maier *et al.,* 1940) involved the presentation of an ambiguous situation to rats. The rats were placed on a jumping stand, and two cards were placed in front of the stand, each with its own distinctive visual pattern. When the animal leaped off the stand in the direction of a stimulus card, the card either fell back (correct card), making food accessible, or it was latched (incorrect response), resulting in food loss and punishment (the animal bumped its body against the card and fell into a net).

In the typical discrimination learning procedure, one card is always designated as correct. This card is randomly alternated from right to left, and the animal is required to discriminate between the correct stimulus and the alternative. Maier, however, selected both the "correct" card and the position at random, so that regardless of response pattern the rat succeeded on half the trials and failed on the other half. Under these circumstances the majority of the rats established a stereotyped habit, always jumping either to the right or the left.

After this pattern emerged, the animals rarely succeeded when presented with the standard discrimination problem, as contrasted with rats that had not experienced the frustrating condition. This, according to Maier, was responsible for the fixation.

Subsequently, however, other investigators have shown that the complex nature of the Maier procedure introduced methodological difficulties. It has been demonstrated further that the insoluble nature of the problem is *not* the critical factor in producing such fixations (Wilcoxon, 1952; Lauer & Estes, 1955), thus disputing Maier's basic assumption.

More recently, a study by Karsh (1970) has provided further information relevant to the concept of fixation. Although this study is representative of the operant methodology, we have chosen to include it here because of its obvious relationship to this concept.

Deprived rats were first trained to press one of two levers (presented one at a time) to receive continuous food reinforcement. They were then presented with both bars simultaneously, only one of which was associated with reinforcement. Ordinarily, when these circumstances obtain, rats not only learn to reverse their choice

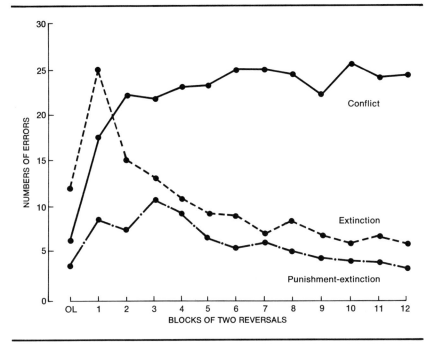

Figure 29. *Mean number of errors per problem during original learning (OL) and twenty-four reversals (averaged for pairs of reversals) for three experimental groups. (From Karsh, 1970)*

when appropriate, but actually improve in later reversals. After 110 trials, during which the animals learned to select the positive lever when presented with both bars, Karsh introduced the following reversal procedure. In one group of rats the incorrect response was simply extinguished in the usual manner. In a second group of rats the incorrect response resulted in shock punishment as well as the failure to produce positive reinforcement. In a third group (the conflict group) the incorrect response produced both punishment and food reinforcement. In all cases the shock was of brief duration (0.15 seconds) and moderate (85 volts) intensity. In all, there were twenty-five such reversals. Under these conditions the rats always had a more adaptive alternative available, and responding on the negative bar (analyzed as errors) represented fixation. Figure 29 shows the mean number of errors for the three groups.

> *The most striking feature was that the conflict animals did not reverse their choice at all, although both other groups reversed. Instead, they fixated on one bar and continued to choose it, regardless of whether it was the positive or negative in a particular condition. Most conflict animals maintained a preference for the bar that was positive in original learning. (Karsh, 1970, p. 874)*

Comment. Investigations of this nature provide us with a direct analysis of at least some of the conditions under which organisms display rigid, stereotyped, maladaptive behavior patterns. Note that the outcomes can be explained completely on the basis of learning variables. Thus, this procedure falls into the general model that analyzes interactions between historical variables and current determinants. In the conflict group a response was initially acquired under positive reinforcing circumstances. During the test condition the same response resulted in multiple consequences (one of which was shock) and was maintained despite the availability of a more adaptive (nonshock) alternative. Within this model a host of variables may be tested (shock intensity, shock duration, shock schedule, plus those dimensions related to the similarity of response alternatives) against the ongoing behavior. Such testing should enable a general description of the circumstances under which fixation will or will not occur.

In the Karsh study, for example, it seems reasonable to assume that if the shock were more intense, introduced earlier in training, and the two bars placed immediately adjacent to one another, the probability of a reversal would be increased. On the other hand, if shock occurred on an intermittent basis and the positive reinforcement schedule was gradually increased, the probability of a fixation effect might be enhanced. In general, such efforts should help to fill the gaps in the three-stage model described earlier.

THE DEPRIVATION MODEL: EXPERIMENTAL ANALYSES

As we have indicated, there is an extensive body of literature relating the effects of "deprivation" to pathological behavior. We have selected for review an array of procedures stemming from a number of different experimental models, including research on early restriction, critical periods of development, and sensory isolation in humans. The variables most often manipulated include biological deprivation, sensory restriction, physical restraint, confinement, and reduced social contact. Thus, we impart to the term "deprivation" a wider meaning than is ordinarily employed.

In general, the evidence suggests that any one of a number of such experiences may result in one or more behavioral deficits and other anomalies, including impaired pain reactions, reduced avoidance efficiency, deficient problem-solving ability, and deficient social functioning, as well as such representative forms of inappropriate behavior as hoarding, mutism, catatonia, compulsions, and ritualistic behavior. Furthermore, the earlier the age at which deprivation is experienced, the longer the deprivation period, and the more varied the forms of deprivation, the greater the range and durability of the pathological outcome.

In view of the consistency of the findings and the comprehensiveness of the endeavor, one is tempted to argue that the deprivation paradigm represents the most impressive experimental approach to the study of psychopathology currently available. As we shall see, however, this is probably an overstatement of the case.

The studies we have included by no means exhaust the available literature. They have been selected for one or more of the following reasons: (1) They are prototypes of a particular line of study. (2) They reflect a highly refined methodology. (3) They are relevant to examples of pathological behavior in the natural environment.

Sensory Restriction in Infrahumans

Some of the most interesting work in this area was undertaken at McGill by R. Melzack and his associates. Representative of their efforts is a study (Melzack & Thompson, 1956) in which three groups of Scotch terriers were raised under several different deprivation conditions. In one condition a group of dogs was maintained in individual cages with unrestricted vision. A second group of dogs was housed by twos and threes with vision restricted. A third group of dogs was housed in individual cages and had restricted vision. These events were introduced at the age of four weeks (just after weaning) and maintained until the animals were seven to nineteen months old, after which they were released into the "normal" environment.

Tests of the effects of the deprivation were initiated about three weeks after termination of the experimental conditions by comparing the behavior of the experimental animals with normally raised dogs in terms of dominance, social curiosity, and canine-human interactions.

In general, the behavior of the deprived dogs was deviant from the behavior of the normally raised animals in almost every respect. For example, ordinarily when two hungry dogs are fed simultaneously, a competitive struggle ensues characterized by growling or barking, with the dominant dog remaining in control of the food. Rarely is there evidence of "sharing." Deprived animals, however, almost never displayed such organized, competitive behavior, as reflected by the number of "wins" scored by the normal dogs over the deprived dogs, and the high frequency of sharing behavior displayed by deprived dogs when pitted against each other. Similar results were obtained even when deprived dogs were tested against younger normal dogs.

Similarly, when a normal dog is introduced to an unfamiliar dog, he will typically show sustained, socially organized curiosity, characterized by a high initial frequency of sniffing, looking, growling, etc., in close proximity to the other animal, which diminishes upon repeated exposure. Deprived dogs, however, displayed a diffuse, disorganized form of excitement under such circumstances, which increased rather than decreased upon repeated testing.

Finally, with regard to human-dog interactions, the normally reared dogs reacted appropriately to each of the different behavioral roles portrayed by the experimenter, for example, approaching the "friendly man," stalking the "fearful man," and avoiding the "bold man." The deprived dogs, however, displayed little or no consistent, organized adient social response to the friendly man. "Any attempt by *E* to pat or touch the dogs produced only jerky withdrawal movements with a marked concomitant increase in excitement" (Melzack & Thompson, 1956, p. 88). In addition, few of the deprived dogs displayed the efficient forms of escape and avoidance reactions revealed by the normal animals in the presence of the bold man. The only dimension in which no difference was obtained between the two groups was the stalking of the timid man, possibly because this is a more primitive form of behavior and therefore less dependent upon advanced learning.

Although there was no attempt to examine the relationships between the different forms of deprivation and specific pathological effects, it seems fairly evident "that restriction of early social and perceptual experiences has a definite retarding effect on the emergence of normal, adult social behavior in dogs, whether toward members of their own or other species" (Melzack & Thompson, 1956, p. 89).

Maternal Deprivation in Infrahumans

There is considerable evidence regarding the profound effects of social isolation on deviant behavior in infrahuman primates. Representative of these efforts is a study reported by R. E. Miller *et al.* (1969). These investigators compared the appetitive behavior of three rhesus monkey reared in isolation with similar measures in normally raised monkeys. On every measure the isolated monkeys displayed abnormal patterns. For example, they drank more fluid than the controls did (a difference that was maintained even when a bitter solution was added to the water) and "clearly over-ate in comparison with their normal controls" (hyperphagia).

Probably the most extensive analysis of the effects of early social deprivation on subsequent psychopathology in lower organisms, however, is provided by the work of Harlow and his associates. Their line of inquiry emerged out of attempts to establish a disease-free colony. Monkeys separated from their mothers at birth were observed to exhibit abnormalities rarely seen in feral animals.

> [*These*] *laboratory monkeys sit in their cages and stare fixedly into space, circle their cages in a repetitive stereotyped manner and clasp their heads in their hands or arms and rock for long periods of time. They often develop compulsive habits, such as pinching precisely the same patch of skin on the chest between the same fingers hundreds of times a day; occasionally, such behavior may become punitive and the animal may chew and tear at its body until it bleeds. Often the approach of a human being becomes the stimulus for self-aggression. This behavior constitutes a complete breakdown and reversal of the normal defensive response.* (Harlow & Harlow, 1962, p. 138)

EXPERIMENTAL CONDITION	PRESENT AGE	BEHAVIOR				
		None	Low	Almost normal	Probably normal	Normal
RAISED IN ISOLATION						
TOTAL — Cage-raised for 2 years	4 years	■□▨				
TOTAL — Cage-raised for 6 months	14 months	□▨				
TOTAL — Cage-raised for 80 days	10½ months			■□▨		
PARTIAL — Cage-raised for 6 months	5 to 8 years	■ ▨	□			
PARTIAL — Surrogate-raised for 6 months	3 to 5 years	■ ▨	□			
RAISED WITH MOTHER						
Normal mother; no play with peers	1 year	▨■				□
Motherless mother; play in playpen	14 months			□	▨	■
Normal mother; play in playpen	2 years					■□▨
RAISED WITH PEERS						
Four raised in one cage; play in playroom	1 year				■	□▨
Surrogate-raised; play in playpen	2 years				▨	■□
Surrogate-raised; play in playroom	21 months					■□▨

■ Play
□ Defense
▨ Sex

Figure 30. *Results of experiments are summarized. The monkey's capacity to develop normally appears to be determined by the seventh month of life. Animals isolated for six months are aberrant in every respect. Play with peers seems even more necessary than mothering to the development of effective social relations. (From Harlow & Harlow, 1962)*

Animals separated from their mothers also displayed deviations in a number of other dimensions, including impaired sexual behavior, reduced curiosity, and inadequate dominance patterns. A catalog of these observations and the related deprivation circumstances is presented in Figure 30.

Subsequently, a series of studies were undertaken for the purpose of isolating the variables responsible for such effects. In one such study, for example (Harlow & Zimmerman, 1959), monkeys were separated from the mother shortly after birth and raised in cages with "surrogate" mothers for five to six months. The inanimate surrogate mothers were constructed of either hardware cloth (wire) or wood covered with terry cloth. In addition, only the wire surrogate lactated for some monkeys, and only the cloth mother lactated for the other subjects. Thus, the four experimental conditions were as follows: (1) cloth fed—cloth reared; (2) wire fed—cloth reared; (3) cloth fed—wire reared; (4) wire fed—wire reared. Various tests were conducted to isolate the effects of these differing conditions. In almost every measure deprivation of contact comfort (provided by the cloth) resulted in abnormal behavior. For example, when cloth-reared monkeys were initially confronted with a fear stimulus, they characteristically took refuge behind their mother and then began to explore the unfamiliar object. Wire-raised monkeys, on the other hand, also ran to the wire surrogate on such occasions, but then were observed to "either clutch themselves and rock and vocalize for the remainder of the test or rub against the side of the cubicle" (Harlow & Zimmerman, 1959, p. 424).

Differences were also obtained when the differentially raised animals were placed in an open field test. When the "mothers" were present, the cloth-reared monkeys displayed the typical patterns of oscillation—moving back and forth from mother to object. Emotional indices (vocalization, crouching, rocking, and sucking) increased sharply when they were tested in the absence of the mothers. On the other hand, "the infants raised with wire mothers are highly emotional under both conditions," revealing the patterns described above, "similar to the autistic behavior of deprived and institutionalized human children" (Harlow & Zimmerman, 1959). Concomitantly, there was a lack of normal exploratory behavior and aggressive play behavior on the part of the wire-raised subjects. In addition, differences in affectional retention were also investigated long after the mother was withdrawn from the cage. Once again, the cloth-raised monkeys continued to display appropriate social behavior when the surrogate was reintroduced during test conditions, whereas wire-raised monkeys developed no durable affectional attachments to their surrogates.

Emphasis has also been placed upon the effects of social deprivation on normal maternal behavior. In one such study (Seay *et al.,* 1964) the maternal behavior of four socially deprived, artificially inseminated female monkeys was compared with the maternal behavior of feral monkeys. In general, all four experimental animals were totally inadequate mothers, and constant intervention by the laboratory staff was required in order to protect the offspring. "Two mothers were violent and abusive and the other two were primarily indifferent and withdrawn" (Seay *et al.,* 1964, p. 347), although the aggressive behavior diminished within three to four months. Interestingly enough, the offspring appeared to be normal in every respect, probably because of exposure to normal peer experiences. Nevertheless, it is obvious that early social deprivation or inadequate social bearing disrupts the maternal behavior pattern in the rhesus monkey.

Finally, L. A. Rosenblum and Harlow (1963) conducted an interesting experiment which combined a conflict model with the deprivation model and produced some highly provocative effects. Under the assumption that contact with the mother was highly reinforcing to infant rhesus monkeys, the investigators raised six monkeys with a cloth surrogate until 160 days of age. Two of the animals (the experimental subjects) also received highly noxious air blasts of forty-five seconds in duration, during varying periods of contact with the surrogate. Contrary to expectation, the experimental subjects spent a significantly greater period of time in contact with the surrogate than did the control monkeys. Thus, it would appear that the aversive stimulus augmented responsiveness to the surrogate, even though the aversive stimulus was coincident spatially and temporally with the surrogate (Rosenblum & Harlow, 1963, p. 84).

Social Isolation in Humans

With further extensions of the deprivation model, a number of investigators have analyzed the effects of reduced environmental stimulation on intact, normal humans. These efforts have ranged from the elimination of a single sensory experience for relatively brief durations to almost complete isolation for as long as several months.

Perhaps the most influential of these studies was one reported by W. H. Bexton *et al.* (1954) in which twenty-two male college students were paid to live under "isolated" conditions. The subjects were placed in a sound-attenuating cubicle; they wore special goggles, which permitted only translucent light, and white gloves and cardboard cuffs, which reduced tactual stimulation. The subjects were required simply to rest, and could only take time out from the experimental environment for eating and toilet activities.

There were several interesting observations, which served as the impetus for a host of subsequent investigations (Schultz, 1965). First, few subjects continued in the experiment for more than two or three days, suggesting that the experience was an unpleasant one. Second, there was some tentative evidence of impairment in various learning skills. Third, and perhaps most provocative, many subjects reported that they had experienced special sensations, which the investigators described as hallucinations. The importance of this last finding for students of psychopathology is self-evident, and a good deal of further research was stimulated. In all of these studies, however, the investigators relied upon verbal reports to obtain their information regarding "hallucinations," which casts doubt upon the validity of their results (Zuckerman & Cohen, 1964).

Comment. The deprivation literature suffers from the problems common to the entire field of psychopathology. Rossi (1969) has reviewed this area and indicated that even the term itself has an ambiguous status. Furthermore, many of the inconsistencies in the findings require clarification. For example, the typical focus of many early-experience studies is upon the manner in which early deprivation results in behavioral deficiencies, such as impaired avoidance efficiency. But other investigators have reported findings that, at first glance, appear to be incompatible with the basic assumption. N. O'Connor (1968) and L. Casler (1968), for example, cite studies that report no observable differences in intellectual impairment between children raised under normal conditions and children raised under deprived circumstances (in institutions). Other investigators (LaBarba & White, 1971) have even shown an inverse relationship between maternal deprivation in mice and mortality on exposure to pathogenic substances. The point is that the effects of early deprivation on adult patterns of behavior is complex, with the relevant variables still remaining to be identified. Thus, except for the general conclusion that relatively severe forms of deprivation in humans produce anomalies, no evidence has been provided to support the recurrent theme regarding the importance of such early experiences as mothering, for example (Ribble, 1943; Spitz, 1945; Bowlby, 1952), which enjoys considerable face validity. The necessary and sufficient conditions have yet to be specified.

On the other hand, with an operant approach one might attempt such an analysis by distinguishing between early experiences in terms of extinction arrangements (absence or withdrawal of positive reinforcement), punishment conditions, or negatively reinforcing contingencies and move from that into an analysis of more complex arrangements.

For example, many of the relevant investigations in the deprivation literature involve the absence of reinforcing events, either as defined by the organism's own history or as defined by knowledge of the general species. In this sense, a deprivation experience may be regarded as a variation of the extinction paradigm, if earlier reinforcement is subsequently removed. When a *massive* extinction program is introduced very early in the organism's history (as seems to be the case in the Harlow procedures), there is virtually no opportunity for the reinforcement of appropriate behavior, and the effects are often profound and durable. When a limited extinction program is introduced after normal maturity has been maintained (as in the case of the human studies in sensory restriction), the effects are usually transitory and ambiguous. Within these two extremes we may postulate an infinite gradation of "deprivation" experiences, which may then be translated into an experimental design. For example, one question that would seem to be particularly relevant to the study of pathological behavior involves the differing effects of deprivation introduced before and after positive reinforcement has been established. Thus, L. J. Yarrow (1964) summarizes a series of observations of children's reactions to maternal separation as follows:

> There is a sequence of responses following separation, beginning with crying and strong protest, and followed by progressive withdrawal from the environment and from relationships with people. The immediate reaction of active protest (*crying or motor expressions of unhappiness*) is thought to represent an active effort to regain the lost mother. After this period of active protest, despair and resignation are reflected in increasingly withdrawn and apathetic behavior. This passivity is often interpreted by hospital and institutional personnel as evidence of the child's having settled down and adapted to the situation. If a substitute mother-figure is available, some children may develop a possessive, anxious attachment to the substitute mother. However, if as is usually the case, there is a series of

changing mother-figures; the child does not form an attach-
ment to anyone in the hospital or institution, and shows little
feeling toward his parents when they visit. Although on the
surface the children seem happy and well adapted to the situ-
ation, they act as if neither mothering nor any contact with
humans has much significance for them. . . . This pattern of
"detachment" Robertson and Bowlby consider a precursor of
the development of the psychopathic personality or affection-
less character. (p. 96)

An operant interpretation of these events might analyze the
"active protest" as a result of the withdrawal of reinforcement. Such
a consequence is frequently observed as an immediate effect in
extinction. As extinction continues, response frequency declines,
often resulting in "despair and resignation." If, on the other hand,
reinforcement is made available under sparse, but highly articulated
circumstances, a powerful stimulus-response chain may emerge,
characterized by a "possessive attachment" to the discriminative
stimulus. If, however, discriminative cues are not available (that is,
there are few and random reinforcements), the individual may appear to be "detached' or neutral with regard to generally arousing
stimuli.

Thus, the sequence of reactions outlined by Yarrow appears to
be compatible with observations that have been made in circumstances where response-consequence arrangements have been
systematically analyzed. Perhaps a similar analysis of clinical phenomena might offer some assistance in resolving the inconsistencies
in the deprivation literature.

THE SOCIAL-LEARNING MODEL:
BANDURA AND AGGRESSION IN CHILDREN

Of the many attempts to analyze the causes of aggression in humans, one of the most refined experimental models has been
provided by Bandura and his associates. The popular notion of
aggression as a generalized trait or characteristic is specifically rejected by Bandura in favor of a position that emphasizes *discriminative* patterns of aggression as a function of particular but relevant
events in the person's environment. "The likelihood that a given
pattern of behavior will be rewarded, ignored, or punished is dependent upon, among other factors, the characteristics of the per-
former, the specific form and intensity of the behavior, the objects
toward whom the actions are directed, the social situations in which
they occur, and various temporal factors" (Bandura, 1969, p. 14).

To study this process, Bandura has employed an experimental
paradigm that analyzes the effects of a social model on the expression of aggressive behavior. In one such study (Bandura *et al.*,
1961) nursery school children were independently rated by an experimenter and by a nursery school teacher for the extent to which
they displayed several different forms of aggression. After being

rated, they were randomly distributed to one of three conditions. In one condition the children were individually exposed to either a male or female adult model who displayed aggression toward a five-foot inflated Bobo doll. In the second condition the male and female models did not display any aggressive behavior. In the third condition (control) the children had no experience with a model but were tested in the same fashion as the children in the experimental conditions.

Immediately after the model experience, the children in the first two conditions (as well as the controls) were taken to a second room that contained several attractive toys, but after about two minutes of play time, they were told they could not play with them. Instead they were taken to a third room (the experimental room), which also contained a variety of toys, including some that could be used in imitative or nonimitative aggression, as well as others that tended to elicit nonaggressive forms of behavior.

The results revealed a highly significant difference between the aggressive behavior of the children exposed to the aggressive model and that of the children in the other two groups. "Thus, subjects given an opportunity to observe aggressive models later reproduced a good deal of physical and verbal aggression as well as nonaggressive responses substantially identical with that of the model" (Bandura *et al.,* 1961, p. 580). This imitation effect was most pronounced in the case of boys who observed the male aggressive model.

Comment. One learning-theory explanation for the acquisition of aggressive behavior in children has been formulated in terms of the relationship between discriminative stimuli and reinforcing consequences (Skinner, 1953). Thus, children match the reinforced behavior of adults for which they are similarly reinforced, and the adult behavior serves as a discriminative stimulus for the child's behavior (Miller & Dollard, 1941).

Bandura distinguishes his efforts from this interpretation on the grounds that imitation may occur even though there is no opportunity for the subject to perform the model's behavior in the exposure setting and without any explicit reinforcement delivered to either the model or the observer.

Regardless of whether a reinforcement or an observational model is employed, both positions are incompatible with conventional "dynamic" interpretations in which aggression is considered a function of frustration or anxiety and hostility is regarded as a "release" or "safety valve" for bottled-up tension.

CONCLUDING REMARKS

It would seem appropriate, at this time, to briefly review the previous material in order to gain a perspective of the current status of inquiry into the causes of pathological behavior.

If we consider Freud's theory as a landmark on the route to

establishing a behaviorally based system regarding cause-and-effect relationships, the ensuing seventy years can be characterized as a period during which many notions were promulgated, a variety of principles were proposed, and conclusions and recommendations were formulated and popularized, but little research was generated to support these statements. The particular inadequacies of psycho-analysis in this connection were recognized very early in the game, whereupon psychologists began to search for other explanatory models. Some of these merely translated the unconscious conflict principle into a quasi-behavioral system; others substituted other dispositional constructs; and still others focused more or less exclusively upon establishing functional relationships.

As the "personality-theory based" approach began to give way to an empirically based aproach, the field was plagued with inconsistent findings, contradictory evidence, and a bewildering maze of conflicting statements by authorities. Thus, while popular sentiment argued that a depriving and rejecting parent caused emotional disturbance, evidence from other quarters indicated that too much attention might produce the same outcome. The position that punishment would cause psychic damage was incompatible with the equally popular view that facing stress was a good way to build character and become better adjusted to life's exigencies. One could indeed invoke evidence from the research literature to support either position (Levine, 1960).

The growing recognition of this unhappy state of affairs reinforced dissatisfaction with traditional theories, which had provided little assistance in resolving the contradictions in the literature.

More recently, even some of our most cherished clinical notions and practices have been called into question. Szasz (1960) rejected the concept of mental illness with its attendant pejorative connotations on the grounds that it has contributed little to our understanding of deviant behavior and impaired the treatment process. W. N. Schoenfeld (1950) described the many shortcomings inherent in the popular concept of anxiety, and T. R. Sarbin (1968) clearly described how the term "anxiety" has come to mean "all things to all men" as a pseudoexplanatory mechanism. (Consider, in a similar vein, the concept of insecurity, which is frequently invoked to "explain" immature behavior.) Stuart (1970) drew a convincing picture of the deleterious effects of dispositional diagnosis, a practice that only a short time ago was the clinical psychologist's chief stock-in-trade. Zigler and Phillips (1961) rejected the traditional classification model.

What we see in these recent developments are several independent but related streams of thought converging into a river of general disenchantment regarding the status of knowledge in this area. It reflects, we believe, the beginnings of a profound change in our approach to the analysis of pathological behavior.

Far from being chagrined, we believe this controversy to be a healthy state of affairs: the precursor to an ultimately more viable and effective approach to the analysis of the causes of deviancy. We see emerging from this winter of discontent the answer to many of the questions that have plagued the field, especially the resolution of the host of inconsistencies in the literature. It is our further opinion that reinforcement theory will play an important role in this change, especially in terms of reformulating traditional approaches into a more viable system.

As we have seen, a number of investigators have already formulated theoretically relevant positions in this connection. On the basis of such analyses, the traditional focus upon studying the "cause" of deviancy can be reconceptualized in terms of (1) initial or eliciting circumstances, (2) maintenance circumstances, and (3) current determinants. In such a model investigations can be implemented at any of these stages and ultimately proceed to an analysis of the relationship between the stages. Studies initiated at stage 1, for example, would be roughly analogous to the traditional emphasis placed upon childhood experiences. (Obviously, a deleterious experience may occur at any stage of development, although the effects of such experiences might differ as a function of different reinforcement histories.) Investigations at the second stage would attempt to analyze the effects of relevant variables (punishment, extinction, negative or positive reinforcement) on behavior that has a relatively limited history and is determined by relatively unitary variables. Investigations at the third stage, of course, would represent the most complex development of the experimental analysis of pathological conditions, and would focus upon the effects of current determinants as they relate to different but extensive reinforcement histories. For example, when the failure of reinforcement generally leads to extinction (reduction in the frequency of responding), a *functional* analysis would determine the *specific* effects of an extinction process on behavior with varying reinforcement histories. Thus, it is the analysis of the relationships between these stages that will ultimately provide answers to the questions that have plagued the field.

It is apparent from the literature that such analyses are already being formulated. Patterson and Reid (1970), for example, are satisfied that modeling theory may explain the *initial* circumstances that may be responsible for deviant behavior, but they further assert that it is what happens *afterward* that is of critical importance in the further development of the behavior. Thus, many typical childhood experiences may result in deviant behavior; for example, the birth of a sibling or hospitalization might represent varying durations of deprivation (that is, the withdrawal of social reinforcement). Modeling effects may produce the first occasion on which a sibling hits his younger brother or the first occasion on which he reacts with fear to being left alone, but it is the kind of reinforcement schedules that the child is subsequently exposed to that determines the final outcome. Moreover, evidence from other quarters provides additional information related to these questions. In subsequent chapters, for example, we shall review many examples of behavior modification. In most of these studies, evidence regarding the circumstances *immediately* responsible (reasons for) for the maintenance of these conditions is provided. In terms of our previous analysis, these variables constitute *current* determinants. Perhaps the most representative finding that emerges from these endeavors is the importance of inadvertent social reinforcement in the maintenance of many pathological conditions. Although early determinants can rarely be specified, there is now overwhelming evidence to support the notion that social contingencies frequently conspire to foster and maintain the very forms of behavior that are most objectionable by social standards. A study by Lovaas *et al.* (1965a) is representative. In this case, an attempt was made to determine the effects of social reinforcement on head banging in an autistic child. The evidence clearly indicated that comments made in a sympathetic and reassuring manner contingent on head banging resulted in an increase in the frequency of the undesirable response.

Through such a focus and the research models that it generates, many of the current inconsistencies may be resolved. True, our present status still suggests that the same or similar antecedent conditions often result in differing outcomes, and conversely, the same outcome may be traced to different antecedent circumstances. With the proper specification of the variables, however, we can discover why the withdrawal of positive reinforcement leads to aggressive behavior on one occasion and to a reduction in the frequency of problem solving on another.

Within such a framework the concept of cause can be recast. If we can draw no other conclusions at present, at least we can assert with some degree of assurance that the search for unitary, simplistic determinants is doomed to failure. On the contrary, the evidence that we have at hand serves to reinforce the often repeated warning that abnormal behavior is complex and multifarious. Answers to the question "Why?" can be determined, but only after we make a genuine commitment to a scientifically based strategy grounded upon experimental methods.

SUMMARY

In line with our emphasis upon scientific methodology and experimental support, we have attempted to provide an overview of several prominent theories as well as an in-depth review of the major experimental models that they have generated.

In addition, where possible, an operant analysis of the various events has been offered. A brief summary of the preceding material might help clarify some of the issues that have been raised and amplify the reasons for such an analysis.

Let us evaluate the theories from the standpoint of experimental support. We have already found psychoanalysis seriously deficient in this respect, especially with regard to the fundamental principles of unconscious motivation and psychic determinism. Although these propositions have had a powerful appeal for students of psychopathology, there has been an unresolved conflict between the belief in their validity and an accommodation to scientific practices. Furthermore, the purported relationship between critical early experiences and adult neuroses, although capable of verification, has also been called into serious question.

It is primarily for these reasons that psychologists have looked to other systems and models for an understanding of the causes of psychopathology. While these positions may not suffer as seriously as does psychoanalysis from lack of experimental evidence or contradictory evidence, their value can be assessed from the standpoint of correspondence between formal theoretical statements and events in the clinical environment.

Thus, although classical conditioning theory continues to experience some difficulty with the concept of innate temperament, a more serious limitation is revealed by the attempt to stretch the principle of classical conditioning over the entire range of clinical events, thereby resulting in extrapolations beyond the data. It still remains to be determined whether the alleged examples of experimental neurosis by classical conditioners might not be interpreted by other systems. Thus, perhaps, the growing enchantment with two-factor theory.

In a similar vein, Dollard and Miller and Masserman and Wolpe, on the basis of studies of conflict analogs in infrahuman organisms, explain psychopathology as a function of concurrent, incompatible drives. However, again the degree of correspondence between the experimental models and the natural clinical environment surely leaves a great deal to be desired.

On the other hand, the deprivation model, which at least in terms of face validity appears to reflect a satisfactory correspondence between experimental events and clinical phenomena, continues to be plagued with inconsistent findings and a consensually acceptable methodology.

The remaining systems, two-factor theory, operant theory, and social learning theory have only recently come to the fore and their ability to withstand the above criticisms remains to be determined. There is obviously adequate experimental support for the limited range of phenomena that they have analyzed. Whether these models can be elaborated is a matter of future experimentation. If, however, an analysis of pathological events is restricted to the empirical level, there is some reason to believe that operant theorists are already on the brink of generalizing the principle of response consequences to a much wider range of events than had been the case previously. Thus, if by deviant behavior we mean the presence of undesirable behavior or the absence of desirable behavior as defined by community standards, it is quite clear that operant theory already has the power to investigate many forms of such phenomena.

PART THREE / THE MODIFICATION OF PATHOLOGICAL BEHAVIOR
A. Deceleration Methods
B. Acceleration Methods

In this section the emphasis will be upon experimental and clinical techniques that have been shown to be effective in modifying behavior from a previously pathological rate to a normally acceptable rate of occurrence. This, of course, is the primary function of the practicing clinician, whose major concern is the rehabilitation of patients. Consistent with the emphasis of the rest of the book, an empirical approach is offered, so that treatment techniques are not automatically accepted without some data, and hopefully, experimental tests demonstrating their effectiveness.

Also, consistent with the general philosophy expressed throughout this volume, pathological behaviors will continue to be examined from the point of view that these are primarily learned responses that in some way are out of phase or inconsistent with the reinforcing contingencies in the community from which the individual came. One corollary to this principle is that treatment programs should be individually tailored with these community contingencies in mind, since they are ultimately responsible for maintaining any changes effected in the clinical setting. Thus, the goals of a behavior modification program with a slum-dwelling individual might be expected to be quite different from the goals set for work with an urbane urbanite or a member of a hippie commune.

The contents of this section may be most closely identified with the current trends in clinical psychology and the related fields that, grouped together, are labeled behavior modification. This identification represents a good fit as long as it refers to learning- and research-oriented modification of pathological behavior. Very little distinction will be made here between the broad base of laboratory-oriented research and treatment known as behavior modification and the group of techniques popularly termed behavior therapy, which a growing number of clinicians report they are practicing. The point will continue to be stressed that much of what goes on in the laboratory may have clinical utility, and that proper growth in either area will stimulate expanded frontiers in the other. Consistent with this viewpoint will be the presentation of several studies or techniques that have not yet had clinical application, but that seem to be relevant to the problem of modification or at least have clinical implications for the functional analysis of behavior.

A short note on the history and development of behavior modification, followed by a description of some of the important elements in its current practice will help to elucidate the nature of behavior modification. Differences between the practice of behavior modification and more standard psychotherapeutic strategies will occasionally be revealed.

HISTORICAL NOTE

Behavior modification and behavior therapy both have short histories, especially when compared with medicine or even clinical psychology. While medicine was launched with the Renaissance and the practice of clinical psychology is frequently dated to the foundation of Lightner Witmer's clinic in 1896, popularized behavioral forms of therapy are singularly a product of the mid-twentieth century. Some of the first forms of conditioning to be applied to abnormal or pathological behaviors were V. M. Bekhterev's (1932) attempts to apply classical conditioning techniques to sexual perversions, Watson and R. Rayner's (1920) study of the acquisition of a phobic response, and Mary Cover Jones' (1924a, b) studies of the treatment of children's fears. Intriguing and creative as these beginnings were, however, they did not inspire further systematic clinical work, which had to wait for some rapprochement between a well-developed behavioral science and a mature clinical practice.

The first major historical stream to contribute to the development of behavior modification and therapy, then, was the whole body of work within the Pavlovian tradition. Pavlov's own (1927, 1928) work with animals, reviewed in Part Two, suggested that many forms of pathological behavior may be acquired according to the principles of conditioning, and his work contained the germinal notion that other learning techniques might be useful in modifying or eliminating pathological forms of behavior. Both Pavlov (1927, 1941) and Bekhterev (1932) speculated on ways in which classical conditioning principles might be used to explain and potentially modify pathological behaviors. The actual applications that Pavlov (1927) used most frequently, however, were rest and drugs, which gave rise to whole schools of psychiatry based upon principles and techniques other than those of conditioning and learning.

In the meantime the Russian work was influencing learning theory investigators in America, as indicated in the earlier review of the work on experimental neurosis. Again, the main thrust of this work was directed toward etiological, rather than therapeutic, investigation. And, again, the influence was primarily upon American research investigators, rather than upon practicing clinicians.

A great deal of pioneering work was done in the 1930s by American investigators, but with little or no clinical impact. K. Dunlap (1932), for example, originated negative practice, which was later applied to the treatment of tics, stuttering, and nail biting. H. L. Hollingworth's (1930) redintegration theory suggested rehearsal in the presence of original stimuli. L. W. Max (1935) reported one of the first aversion treatments of homosexuality, and Jersild and Holmes (1935) reported early treatments of childrens' fears.

Some of the major reasons for the limited clinical impact of these studies were lack of psychologists trained in any kind of scientific technology, lack of funds to establish experimentally oriented programs at the few clinics that existed, and nonscientific orientation of the practicing clinicians, resulting in impaired communication and contact with the journals.

The growth of the Hullian school in the 1930s and 1940s provided the impetus for a new wave of clinicians, who attempted to translate traditional psychotherapy into Hullian terms (Miller & Dollard, 1941; Shoben, 1949; Shaw, 1946). This influence is still felt in England, where Eysenck (1947, 1959, 1961b) applies Hullian and Pavlovian conditioning models and techniques in diagnosis and treatment. As will be revealed later, European clinicians still largely share this orientation.

It was not until the 1950s that conditions were ripe for the large-scale extension of conditioning and learning principles and techniques into routine clinical practice. Several factors contributed to this readiness, including the proliferation of psychologists involved in treatment efforts after World War II, the maturation of technological developments within both classical and operant conditioning areas, and the evident failure of traditional treatment techniques to help in mental hospitals, institutions for the retarded, and penal institutions or with extreme forms of pathological behavior, such as sexual deviation, alcoholism, drug addiction, and psychosis.

In the early 1950s Wolpe (1954) applied his notion of reciprocal inhibition to psychotherapy, reviewed his animal model of experimental neurosis, and applied the modification techniques developed there to the treatment of human phobic behaviors. The current status of this historical strand will be reviewed under the Wolpean topic systematic desensitization.

Later in the 1950s Ogden Lindsley (1956) used an operant conditioning analysis of schizophrenic behavior, an application for which he coined the term "behavior therapy." This pioneering work made very clear the direct relevance of the operant technology, which Skinner had begun to develop in 1938, to clinical diagnosis and treatment. For the first time, base rates of response of schizophrenic patients were measured over days and months and found to vary with schedules and types of reinforcers, as well as with competing pathological behaviors, such as hallucinatory episodes.

The next ground-breaking event was the direct application of conditioning principles to the treatment of pathological behaviors observed on psychiatric wards, first to one patient at a time (Ayllon & Michael, 1959; Ayllon & Haughton, 1964), then to whole wards of patients, in token economy and contingency management programs. (See Chapter 10.) Much of the rest of this historical development will be described in the chapters to come.

THE CURRENT STATUS OF BEHAVIOR MODIFICATION
The current practice of behavior therapy is significantly different from more standard psychotherapy, along several important dimensions. In the first place, most traditional therapists are primarily clinically oriented; that is, they most often see their primary goal as helping people. Behavior therapists usually share this goal, but more often than not will operate within a research framework in order to allow a more precise assessment of therapy outcome and individual responses to treatment.

It must be recognized that there may be almost as much variation within either of these two general kinds of orientation as between them. However, there are clear differences between the majority of the subscribers to the two kinds of models, and the current discussion will attempt to point out modal, rather than extreme, differences.

Some of these differences are clearly philosophical. The basic tenets, assumptions, and philosophical systems are most clearly different between psychoanalytic and operant conditioning orientations, for example. Some of these differences were alluded to earlier (see Chapter 3) and will not be elaborated at great length here. Suffice it to say that the more traditional practitioners are usually more cognitively oriented and make more assumptions about the nature of man and his perfectability through self-actualization (Rogers, 1942, 1951), insight (Freud, 1920; Wolberg, 1954), or interpretation (Freud, 1920; Wolberg, 1954). As was revealed in Chapter 3, the psychoanalytic model is the most complex, focussing upon the interaction between genetic factors, a psychosexual model of development, and personal experiences, which together produce pathological states such as neuroses and psychoses, and defenses such as regression, fixation, and repression, projection, reaction formation, and displacement. Translated into clinical practice, this orientation has given rise to a set of techniques that depend almost exclusively upon verbal and gestural interchange in a one-to-one or group setting. Some of these techniques include psychodynamic interpretation and diagnosis, free association, interpretation of defenses, interpretation of resistances, interpretation of dream content, forming and working through of transference, and supportive and reeducative techniques within the psychoanalytic model (Alexander, 1948; Alexander & French, 1946; Freud, 1920; Wolberg, 1954). Most of these techniques are still conducted by the psychoanalyst sitting erect and taking notes or otherwise recording the patient's verbalizations (or his interpretations of the patient's verbalizations) out of sight of the patient, who reclines on a couch. From the patients' free associations (and resistances thereto), the analyst may construct past history, previous traumatic experiences, defensive structure, repressed areas, impulses and impulse control, diagnosis, and prognosis and motivation for therapy. Most patients who are accepted for therapy are "neurotic." (Freud's classic patients were obsessive-compulsive or hysteric.) Once a patient is accepted for psychoanalysis, he is usually seen for a standard fifty-minute hour once each weekday over periods ranging from three to ten or more years at a cost of fifty to one hundred dollars per hour.

Nondirective, or client-centered, therapy (Rogers, 1951), also a traditional form of treatment, subscribes to the philosophy of self-actualization; the basic tenet is that everyone has the capacity for self-growth, and the task of the therapist is to remove barriers to this personal growth. Thus, the therapist plays the role of nondirective catalyst to this growth or self-actualization. The techniques most frequently used by the Rogerian therapist include accepting and reflecting the patient's feelings, attempting to adopt the client's frame of reference or point of view, and supporting exploration and the expansion of awareness, while providing empathy, warmth, and genuineness. Some of the characteristic changes observed as a function of successful client-centered therapy are increase in behavioral planning, increase in mature and decrease in immature behaviors, decrease in psychological tension (as reflected in verbalizations), decrease in defensive behaviors and increase in awareness of such behaviors, increased tolerance, and improved adjustment. Although Rogers (1951) and others have suggested that client-centered counseling might be universally applicable to all kinds of people and problems, probably most clinical psychologists would agree with Thorne (1944) that this method is perhaps most successful with middle and upper class individuals experiencing situational or emotional crises. Nondirective therapy is most often conducted with individuals or groups in a face-to-face position, often at the rate of one to three interviews per week, over a total number of sessions that may range from five to one hundred (Rogers, 1951). Typical private therapy charges may range from ten to thirty-five dollars per hour.

Almost from its inception, traditional verbal psychotherapy has faced severe criticism. The body of literature questioning the method is perhaps as extensive as the literature extolling its virtues. A number of excellent critiques are available to the interested reader (Eysenck, 1952b, 1961a; Levitt, 1957; London, 1964; Rubinstein & Parloff, 1959). Suffice it to say that the criticisms range from the allegation that psychotherapy is no more effective than doing nothing, through to the claim that psychotherapy is restricted by its very nature to the verbally facile, thereby excluding many patient populations, to the argument that the only changes occurring in psychotherapy are changes in verbal behavior (that is, all that is learned is the therapist's language system).

More recently, an even sterner indictment has been expressed in some quarters. In essence, these critics suggest that traditional psychotherapy has not only failed to confirm its original claims, but has, in fact, damaged some individuals in subtle and diverse ways, especially where patients have been labeled and treated on the basis of traditional diagnostic categories. Stuart (1970) has provided an excellent and concise treatment of this issue.

The problem of precise evaluation and comparison of traditional and other treatment methods is made more difficult by the lack of appropriate experimental designs and controlled clinical trials in most previous work. Rogers (1951) must be congratulated in this regard for establishing research technologies specifically for this purpose and collecting a mass of data from a systematic clinical viewpoint.

Behavior therapy, by contrast, subscribes to the philosophy of determinism reviewed and discussed in Chapter 1. From this point of view, it is assumed that most behaviors, pathological and normal, are learned according to the general principles of classical and operant conditioning and general learning theory. Once learned, most behaviors, it is assumed, can be modified by general sets of techniques, variables, and procedures that may have wide applicability.

Typically, the course of behavior therapy may correspond roughly to the single-subject research design with reversals (ABA) discussed in Chapters 1 and 2. In the first, or A, condition some assessment and measurement of the target behavior or behaviors normally takes place. The assessment may range from simple, direct measurement of the behavior to intake interviews, gathering of reinforcement history of perhaps several behaviors, and multivariate measurement, perhaps of many covarying response systems (for example, concurrent measures of phobic avoidance, physiological responses, and self-reports of attitudes or feelings). Often treatment does not commence until a stable rate or frequency of behavior is observed in the A condition. In the second, or B, condition behavior therapy per se takes place. Following an observed change in the behavior, therapy may be terminated, but measurement may be continued to determine whether or not the observed improvement will last. If it does not, the therapist may choose to reinstate the same or another therapeutic technique.

As we will see, the techniques available to the behavior therapist may vary from extinction, massing and flooding, implosion, fading, aversive conditioning, and desensitization within the classical conditioning area to extinction, satiation, fading, feedback, counterconditioning, imitation training, time-out, aversive conditioning, reinforcement, instructions, self-control programs, token economies, or contingency management within the operant conditioning model.

Any of the behavior therapist's techniques may be used alone, in combination, or as part of a treatment program incorporating many of the procedures in concert. Frequently, the behavior therapist interacts with the patient directly, administering a predesigned program during the treatment phase. In this one-to-one, face-to-face treatment, the behavior therapist may appear to be similar to a standard psychotherapist. However, the philosophical system, analytic model, and content of the therapist's verbalizations would most likely differ, with the behavior therapist often applying a conditioning technique through verbal means.

In some treatment situations the behavior therapist may do little more than teach the person with problems how to measure and treat them himself, as Lindsley (1971) does in his "precision teaching." This model may be applicable to many private practice and academic settings.

In some cases there may be very little direct interaction between the behavior therapist and the patient. In some research-oriented treatment programs, for example, technicians may escort the patients to isolation booths, where their treatment is conducted automatically by electronic or recording apparatus. In some cases the patients may be given an opportunity to engage in the pathological behavior in the treatment situation so that the behavior can be treated directly. Such treatment may be conducted individually or in groups (Davidson, 1972a, 1972b). Lindsley (1970) has demonstrated the possibility of conducting therapy with the therapist in one such chamber dispensing auditory and video contact in order to reinforce appropriate responses on the part of the patient.

In behavior therapy with children, the therapist may spend the majority of the therapy time teaching the parents treatment procedures that they can use at home to modify problem behaviors, instead of attempting to treat the behavior directly (Patterson & Gullion, 1968; Wahler, 1968).

In the most massive behavior modification programs, staffs may administer, dispense, and regulate contingency management or token economy programs for entire groups of people. As will be discussed later, this model greatly increases the number of patients or clients the behavior therapist can treat, while still retaining high-quality service. To date, programs of this size and scope have been established on psychiatric wards with schizophrenic patients, with mentally retarded adults and children, with juvenile delinquents, alcoholics, and the hard-core unemployed, in remedial classrooms, and with geriatric patients (see section on token economies in Chapter 10), as well as with nursery school children, slum-dwelling and Indian children, and high-school dropouts (see section on contingency management in Chapter 10).

Perhaps because of its radical departure from traditional philosophy and psychotherapy, the behavior modification movement has also been the target of criticism from a variety of quarters. Among the arguments that have been formulated, the most frequently mentioned are that behavioral approaches ignore the whole person, overlook the importance of symptom substitution, are ahistorical, and are restricted in their applicability to certain problem conditions.

The first three issues are interrelated and require some elaboration. The assumption underlying these arguments is that problem behaviors do not operate as independent entities, and any attempt to treat them as such is simplistic and possibly harmful. Thus, the behavior therapist who removes a phobia, stops an autistic child from banging his head, or increases the social behavior of a catatonic schizophrenic has not, in any real sense, "cured" the patient, but has simply changed one component of his behavior. Thus, the basic underlying cause has not been attacked, and until such resolution is accomplished, the individual will continue to manifest problem behavior, perhaps in another and more serious form.

The whole man argument appears to represent a variation of the molar versus molecular controversy, which caused a great deal of debate in psychology over twenty years ago. The resolution of this argument, at least in terms of theoretical biases, came about when it was recognized that the distinction was arbitrary and relative, rather than absolute, and of little further utility in psychology (Littman & Rosen, 1950). Whether one chooses to analyze a discrete response or a more "complex" form of behavior, the analysis must still be conducted in terms of functional relationships between independent variables and dependent variables. At the clinical level, the therapist may elect to focus upon whichever behavioral dimension is relevant in terms of the problem condition that is present and the state of scientific knowledge. In any event, there is no sacred dichotomy between those efforts which focus upon several response systems simultaneously and those which focus upon one or two response systems.

Consider a situation in which the problem consists of a child's misbehavior. Since it is generally assumed that such difficulties are a product of the home environment, specifically, parental influences, a case may be advanced that any attempt to modify the child's behavior without regard to parental change is doomed to failure. In fact, it is customary to initiate child therapy only if the parents also participate in a counseling or therapy program. The rationale is often that behavior is under the control of environmental contingencies, many of which are arranged by the parents.

A more appropriate position might be, however, that the actual form and breadth of the therapist's intervention should depend upon the circumstances. Thus, in some cases a behavior change program might focus exclusively upon a change in parent-child practices with little or no emphasis upon parent-parent relationships. In others, a formal marital-counseling procedure might be the major part of the program, with the goal being the creation of an atmosphere that is also conducive to a positive change in the child. In still others, child therapy and marital counseling might be instituted simultaneously. In any event, the decision would be made on the basis of a behavioral analysis and practical considerations.

The symptom-substitution controversy appears to be an outgrowth of the implicit clinical assumption that all problems are the outward manifestation of an inner hypothetical process. This process is assumed to have a source of energy that will express itself in a variety of ways, and therefore, when one symptom is removed, another will crop up. The argument is most clearly identified with psychoanalysis but appears to have been accepted by many clinicians of various theoretical orientations. This view is based upon the disease-symptom, medical model, which, when applied to problematic human behavior, is difficult to support on logical grounds. The behavioral model clearly recognizes the possibility that one form of maladaptive behavior may, under certain conditions, be "substituted" for another. What it does not accept, however, is the notion that this must *necessarily* occur, and that when such evidence is present, that it therefore serves as proof of the underlying assumption. On the contrary, learning theory provides an alternative explanation, which enables a prediction of when such events might occur and how they can be controlled (Yates, 1958; Krasner and Ullmann, 1965). Thus, Bandura (1969) suggests that in the course of social development a person acquires a response hierarchy for coping with the environment. That hierarchy is ordered in terms of favorable reinforcement history, and when the order is changed (as, perhaps, in therapy), other responses (some of which may also be maladaptive) may occur. This suggests, however, not that one symptom has been substituted for another, but that the treatment effort has failed to provide for a more effective change. Thus, "a poorly designed program of therapy aimed solely at eliminating maladaptive behavior patterns does not in itself quarantee that desired modes of behavior will ensue" (Bandura, 1969, p. 50). Obviously, then, an effective therapy program is designed to increase the probability that only desirable behavior will emerge.

Because behavior modification procedures have resulted in numerous successes in clinical areas, questions have arisen on occasion regarding the importance of etiology. That is, because many of these techniques have been effective in modifying behaviors of widely divergent or unspecified etiology, some people have asked whether it is important or even necessary to know the background of a particular behavior before designing a modification program. As indicated in Chapters 1 and 2, the current preference is for a functional analysis of pathological behaviors, including the study of etiological, or acquisition, as well as modification, or treatment, variables. In addition, it would seem to be not only important but sometimes crucial to know in particular the reinforcement history of a specific pathological response in order to tailor the maximally efficient modification program for that behavior. Such historical information has special relevance regarding the advisability of aversive conditioning programs. Generally, aversive conditioning procedures should be considered only as a court of last resort and appetitive, extinction, or counterconditioning techniques tried first. For example, with negatively reinforced or maintained behaviors such as phobias or withdrawal reactions, treatment with aversive techniques may well exacerbate the problem condition by increasing, rather than decreasing, the rate of the behavior in question (see Chapters 5 and 9). Similarly, the knowledge that an autistic child's lack of verbal behavior can be traced largely to a thinning of positive reinforcement might lead to a program in which the proper vocal and, later, verbal responses are elicited via instructions, prompts, and commands, and then systematically reinforced. On the other hand, should the child's lack of verbal behavior be due to an extensive punishment history, an elicitation model might be less appropriate than the reinforcing of spontaneous behavior as it occurs, perhaps beginning with nonverbal behavior until regular imitation can be secured. This is similar to the program used and reported by D. M. Baer *et al.* (1967).

Even though many behavioral techniques may be powerful enough to affect behaviors of diverse histories in similar ways, it will frequently be helpful if not of vital importance to know and properly use the etiology (reinforcement history) when selecting and prescribing treatment procedures. Thus, a clinical history and fact-gathering procedure may be very helpful in treatment planning.

In summary, it would appear that many of the objections leveled against behavior modification can be resolved on logical grounds. In the last analysis, however, all of these issues, together with the question of limited applicability, must be put to the empirical test. The following section reviews at least a portion of the literature relevant to these issues. Once again, the emphasis will be on a laboratory-based rationale. Preference will be given to those techniques, programs, and procedures which have developed as a result of laboratory research. In many cases animal studies will be presented and suggestions made for analogous techniques that might be effective in modifying human behavior. It is fortunate that, within the general areas of conditioning and learning, many principles and behavioral phenomena have been observed to generalize from animal to human models. Thus, it seems appropriate that more animal models come into popular play within the behavior modification movement, in keeping with our medical and pharmacological colleagues, who use animal models to screen new drugs and surgical procedures. For similar reasons, it would seem expeditious to screen behavior modification procedures with animals, particularly when they might be dangerous or of questionable help to humans. Animal models also offer the advantages of laboratory control, particularly in terms of specified reinforcement histories, which cannot usually be obtained with humans. As N. E. Miller (1959) has stated,

> *the assumption is that all the psychological processes found in other mammals are also present in man. It should be noted that this assumption does not deny the possibility that man may have additional capacities which are much less well developed or absent in the lower animals. All that is assumed is that what is found in lower mammals will probably be found in man. (p. 204)*

This section of the book has been set up to correspond roughly to Part Two. Thus, the first chapter will deal with methods of modification developed within the classical conditioning paradigm, and the remaining two chapters will review many of the operant conditioning procedures that have been used for treatment purposes. Most of the latter are concerned with the reduction or elimination of pathological behavior, although studies will be discussed later that are relevant to shaping or increasing the probability of normal or appropriate behaviors.

As in the studies reviewed in Part Two, conditioning concepts and procedures have not always been employed in a consistent manner in the following studies. Thus, there is considerable overlap between the studies reported in the operant and the respondent chapters, particularly when aversive procedures have been employed. In the current context the distinction between operant and the respondent studies has been made in terms of procedural differences. Classical conditioning arrangements are defined as those in which the experimenter's focus is upon the contingency of stimulus events with little or no specific programming of response consequences. All other arrangements are regarded as operant or combined operant-respondent arrangements. We shall attempt to clarify this distinction further in the relevant chapters.

Since these chapters focus upon methods and techniques of behavior modification, an area that is rapidly coming to have a vast literature, each chapter surveys only some of the representative trends or reports within each category. The chapters, therefore, are not exhaustive or comprehensive.

A / DECELERATION METHODS
Chapter 7 / Classical Conditioning Treatment Techniques

A VARIETY OF EARLY PAVLOVIAN STRATAGEMS

The results Pavlov and his colleagues reported in the area of experimental neuroses were also accompanied by numerous attempts to modify or eliminate these maladaptive outcomes. These efforts were made for at least two reasons. First, the core of the experimental neurosis was the disruption of the conditioned response. Thus, some ameliorative effort was necessary in order to reinstate the learned reaction. Second, Pavlov was quick to recognize the clinical implications of these investigations.

Although Pavlov and his associates did not employ adequate controls to isolate the necessary and sufficient conditions responsible for the pathological outcomes, many unexpected and unusual behaviors did occur, as the reader may recall. Some, such as the absence of responding to the conditioning stimulus and the "ultra-paradoxical phenomenon" (response to only previously negative conditioned stimuli), were directly related to the actual conditioning procedures. Other pathological behaviors took the form of responses that competed with the conditioning procedures, such as resistance to entering the experimental areas, vocalizations, drowsiness, and general excitation. Still other behaviors involved changes which occurred outside the experimental environment, for example, restlessness, refusal to eat, and other allegedly "symptomatic" behavior.

When such problem behaviors occurred, a variety of procedures were employed in attempts to "cure" the animal. Since these were frequently used in combination and in an unsystematic manner, it is impossible to isolate the key variables that might have been responsible for any improvement in the neurotic condition. The procedure most often mentioned in Pavlov's reports was rest and removal from the experimental procedure, that is, a "vacation" from conditioning. Thus, in M. N. Yerofeeva's experiment (1916) the dogs were allowed three months' rest, and N. R. Shenger-Krestovnikova (1921) allowed them one and one-half months' rest. (It is interesting to note that a similar practice is frequently employed to overcome the rigors of military combat.) In reviewing this work, Pavlov stated that such rest appeared to be the only cure for the experimental neuroses, especially for dogs of the inhibitable type, when conditioned discriminations had been disrupted.

Although this conclusion must be treated with caution, such "rest" does at least seem to have been followed by improvement in the subject's performance in subsequent conditioning procedures. It is difficult to explain how simple removal from the experimental situation might have been responsible for this improvement, if we assume that neurotic behaviors were truly generated by the experimental procedures, since the usual mode of extinction of such responses consists of presentation of the conditioned stimulus unpaired with the unconditioned stimulus.

The therapeutic utility of Pavlov's approach is called into further question by its failure to eliminate neurotic behavior in animals observed by Gantt (1944), Liddell (1956), and Masserman (1946). Liddell, for example, noted the persistence of neurotic reactions even after eight or nine years of rest.

Perhaps these differences can be resolved by examining the opportunity for new learning that may have occurred in the Pavlovian situation but not in the others. For example, the animals' entire response hierarchies may have shifted a great deal while they were living outside the laboratory, where social, play, and sexual behaviors, once denied the animals, became available. New responses acquired in this context may have successfully competed with the neurotic responses when Pavlov returned his animals to the laboratory. Experimental analysis would be required, of course, to give this speculative line of reasoning any formal status.

Perhaps the most extensive treatment method, other than rest, involved the administration of bromide drugs (as discussed shortly), especially with dogs of the excitable type, although once again a systematic analysis is lacking.

In addition to using rest and bromides, however, Pavlov and his associates also modified the actual experimental procedures themselves in order to retrain those animals displaying neurotic responses. Some of the techniques that were employed included introduction of the experimenter into the experimental room in order to pacify the animal; reintroduction of stimuli used earlier in conditioning, including the simpler or more discriminable stimuli; and retraining the animal in another room. Each of these techniques involved more or less extensive modification of the basic conditioning procedure, since, for Pavlov, the core of the experimental neurosis was the disappearance or disturbance of the conditioned response. For this reason most of the attempts to modify the neurotic behavior involved retraining procedures of one kind or another. Thus, one should not expect to find experimental trials of classical extinction among Pavlov's "cures" of experimental neurosis.

The technique of retraining can be very useful and effective as a "cure," although the single-subject studies done in Pavlov's time gave only anecdotal support to this position. A more modern investigation of the effects of retraining procedures after the disruption of performance was conducted by N. E. Schneiderman et al. (1971). In this study the investigators used differential classical conditioning of the nictitating membrane response in rabbits to different intensities of intracranial stimulation. Each animal was trained over a period of many months. At most intensities the conditioned discriminations were quite pronounced. After training, the animals typically responded at above 90 percent CRs to the positive conditioned stimulus (CS+) with less than 20 percent response to the negative conditioned stimulus (CS−). However, when the CS+ and CS− were brought sufficiently close together in intensity, performance broke down, and the rabbits did not respond to either stimulus. Reintroducing the initial physical dimensions of CS+ and CS− resulted in an immediate resumption of high levels of differential conditioning.

Of even greater interest, however, were the correlated changes in extra-experimental behavior that were also observed. Schneiderman (1971) reported that the animals were maintained in holding cages before and after each experimental session. During these waiting periods the animals frequently left their cages and explored the waiting room, as well as other animals' cages. Pronounced differences were noted in exploratory and social behavior as a function of performance in the differential conditioning situation. Following good discriminative performance, animals nearly always explored the waiting room. After exposure to differential discrimination (and resultant poor performance in the experimental situation), however, the rabbits moved about much less, did not attend to movement within the waiting room, and never voluntarily left the holding cage. This difference in behavior was most dramatically demonstrated in the performance of one male animal. This animal explored and copulated at almost every opportunity following successful discrimination performance, but never left the holding cage either to explore or to copulate following breakdowns in discriminative performance. Exploratory and copulatory behavior commenced, however, following improved performance in the discrimination situation. Similar reversals were completed three times with the same animal, so that the correlation between discrimination breakdown and related abnormalities was more than anecdotal. Thus, this experiment is a model of more scientific rigor than was brought to bear in Pavlov's day upon the study of pathological behavior using the technique of classical conditioning. Incorporating the advantages of a functional design with single subjects, the experiment included several reversals, showing that it was the narrowing of the gap between CS+ and CS⁻ and the difficulty in discrimination that gave rise to the experimental neurosis and not fortuitous circumstance.

In summary, it appears that Pavlov's rest and bromide cures were not as effective as they seemed initially, although experimental retraining in a simplified, nonconflictful task has often proved successful in reducing or eliminating classically conditioned forms of pathological behavior.

As mentioned earlier, Pavlov (1927) stated that rest seemed to be the only cure for experimental neuroses in dogs of the inhibitable type, but that administration of bromides was found most effective in restoring conditioned inhibitions which had been lost during experimental neuroses in dogs of the excitable type.

Similarly, Masserman (1943, 1946) tried rest and drugs in an effort to modify experimentally produced neurotic behavior. Unlike Pavlov, he found rest to be largely ineffective, but found some measure of success with the administration of alcohol as a therapeutic agent (Masserman, *et al.,* 1944, 1945). With these findings Masserman initiated a number of studies dealing with the effects of alcohol on appetitive (positively reinforced) and avoidance behaviors.

A great deal of research has been conducted, with both human and animal subjects, in an effort to identify those drugs which are effective in reducing or eliminating pathological behaviors. A number of the available reviews suggest the rapidly growing sophistication in behavioral pharmacology (Boren, 1966; Brady, 1956, 1957; Dews, 1956). However, because most drugs only affect behavior while they are present within the biological system or shortly after withdrawal, and only indirectly affect conditioning and learning, these efforts will not be reviewed more extensively here.

PAVLOVIAN EXTINCTION

The extinction procedure (that is, the presentation of only the CS in the absence of the UCS) has often been used with classically conditioned responses of many kinds, but rarely have these responses been analyzed as pathological behaviors. Several reviews of the classical conditioning literature (Kimble, 1961; Gormezano, 1966) have indicated the rapidity with which classically conditioned responses may be reduced in frequency or eliminated by extinction procedures.

Reviews of classical conditioning in animals (Kimble, 1961) have supported the general principles that extinction shows a much more rapid course following continuous rather than intermittent reinforcement, that it may be hastened by variations that clearly mark the transition from acquisition to extinction trials, and that the longer the course of acquisition is (the greater the number of reinforcements), the longer extinction will be retarded. Similar relationships have been found with human subjects, but more variability is some-times reported also. D. D. Wickens (1939) and R. H. Lindley & K. E. Moyer (1961), for example, in studies of classically conditioned finger withdrawal, found that subjects did not always stop respond-ing as quickly as predicted when instructed that shock would no longer be delivered.

At present, straight extinction does not appear to be popularly used as a treatment for classically conditioned clinical behaviors, possibly because other modification programs, such as counter-conditioning or desensitization, may be preferred. As will be dis-cussed, the latter techniques offer the advantage of conditioning new, more constructive behaviors while programming extinction for pathological responses. Extinction has been used successfully with at least one pathological behavior, which was both conditioned and eliminated. This was shown in Rachman's (1966a) interesting func-tional analysis of fetishist behavior in normal subjects reported earlier. Rachman exposed subjects to slides of black, knee-length women's boots (CS) for fifteen seconds followed by a thirty-second exposure to colored slides of female nudes (UCS). Plethysmo-graphic measures of penile volume indicated that the three unmar-ried male volunteer subjects showed conditioned erection to the slides of the boots (defined as analogous to fetishistic behavior). Similar responses to shoes of different colors and appearance in-dicated stimulus generalization. Extinction was then programmed (unpaired presentations of the boots) until no sexual responses oc-curred. One week later, spontaneous recovery of the response occurred, and further extinction trials were administered until the response again disappeared. A later replication (Rachman & Hodg-son, 1968) confirmed these findings. It is important to recognize that the antecedent conditions underlying the pathological behavior were well articulated, a situation which rarely obtains in the natural en-vironment.

There are other suggestions which possibly limit the efficacy of extinction. Thus, extinction may be greatly retarded following trau-matic classical or avoidance conditioning. R. L. Solomon and L. C. Wynne (1953) demonstrated this early with barrier jumping in dogs (which may be more akin to operant conditioning). Following condi-tioning with high-intensity shock, some dogs continued to emit the avoidance response for hundreds of trials with little or no sign of extinction. Figure 31, for example, reveals the reduction in response latency over some thirty extinction trials for one subject. These authors suggested that partial irreversibility may occur following such traumatic conditioning.

Similarly, Campbell *et al.* (1964), in a study mentioned earlier, conditioned galvanic skin response, respiration, cardiac, and mus-cle tension responses to the injection of succinylcholine, which pro-duced muscular paralysis and temporary cessation of respiration for up to two minutes. Subjects who endured the procedure said they

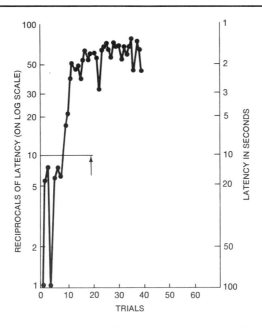

Figure 31. *Performance of a single, typical dog in avoidance conditioning with traumatic shock as the UCS. The horizontal line is drawn at the level of the CS-UCS interval. Thus, responses below this line were escape trials; responses above it were avoidance trials. Shock was turned off permanently at the point indicated by the arrow. (From Solomon and Wynne, 1953)*

experienced terror at the inability to breathe or regain control of skeletal musculature. Following a five-minute recovery period, thirty extinction trials were programmed. Extinction sessions were conducted again one week and three weeks later. In contrast to control subjects, who were exposed to either the UCS or the CS (a tone) alone, none of the experimental subjects showed behavioral extinction. (See Figure 32.) Galvanic skin and cardiac responses increased and occurred at shorter latencies, while the muscular and respiratory responses tended to decline slightly. Thus, this study also suggested some partial irreversibility of conditioning following exposure to a traumatic UCS.

In summary, extinction would seem to be a feasible program for modification or elimination of a classically conditioned pathological behavior, particularly if the behavior were known to be based upon a history of continuous reinforcement (or some approximation to that schedule) and the history did not include traumatic conditioning. If schedules other than continuous reinforcement were known to exist, some variation on extinction, such as massing or flooding, might be recommended.

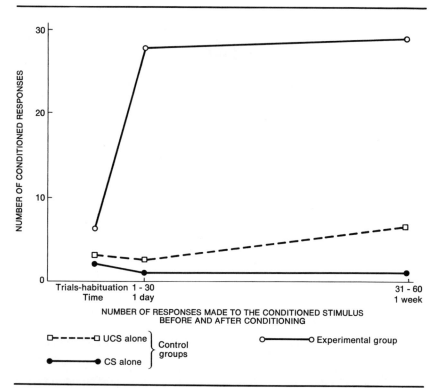

Figure 32. *Mean number of UCR and CR for experimental and control subjects during the habituation period and sixty extinction trials.* (*From Campbell* et al., *1964*)

MASSING AND FLOODING

Several investigators have devised variations upon the classical extinction model (removal of the UCS as the only change) and put them to the experimental test. The variations to be reviewed here are known as massing, flooding, and implosion. They consist largely of systematically changing the mode of presentation of the CS in addition to UCS removal. These techniques rely largely upon the empirical constructs of generalization decrement (Kimble, 1961) and the discrimination hypothesis (Mowrer & Jones, 1945) which have indicated that extinction occurs more rapidly when the difference between the acquisition and the extinction conditions is clearly discriminable. Thus, with most of these techniques there is an attempt to provide a clearly discernible contrast between prior conditioning circumstances and extinction, under the assumption that responding will decrease more rapidly.

One variation of the conventional extinction procedure involves the massing of extinction trials. This technique can be programmed experimentally in at least two different ways. The usual method is to decrease the intertrial interval, so that many more extinction than acquisition trials occur within the same period of time. The logical extreme of the massing technique, flooding, involves the continuous presentation of the CS, thus providing constant exposure of the subject to the CS.

M. Baum and I. D. Oler (1968) compared the efficacy of these two procedures in producing extinction of a classically conditioned avoidance response in rats. The animals were trained to avoid shock by running from one area of the apparatus to another. The authors found that the frequent presentation of trials (massing) produced extinction of the running response more rapidly than did flooding. Flooding in this case consisted of response prevention, or the use of a physical barrier to restrict the animal to the area where shock had been delivered. In a second experiment the authors found again that flooding was not as effective as the massing of trials in producing rapid extinction when the avoidance behavior had been trained, extinguished, and then retrained.

The major difference between the two techniques used in these experiments, besides the amount of exposure to the conditioned stimulus (or stimulus complex), was the fact that the conditioned response was prevented from occurring in the flooding, but not in the massing procedure. On the basis of the difference between the training and extinction conditions alone, one might expect the reverse—that the flooding technique would prove to be superior in reducing resistance to extinction. The authors report, however, that only a long period of response prevention was effective in producing extinction.

In a later study Baum (1969) found that extinction by flooding was enhanced by two other variables: less intense shock (the UCS) during acquisition and the presence of another, naïve animal during extinction. Baum took great pains to posit that learned fear is less intense under both conditions, but other explanations are also possible. For example, stronger shock may result in more rapid acquisition of the response and increased resistance to extinction, with the result that more flooding would be required to extinguish the response. Similarly, generalization decrement or imitation may explain what Baum called the social facilitation of flooding with the naïve animal present.

In a much earlier study A. T. Polin (1959) found that extended exposure of the subject to the conditioned stimulus with free opportunity to engage in the conditioned response produced more rapid extinction than a standard number of trials with the response being physically prevented. Once again, although the procedures differed, extinction by the massing of trials with free opportunity to respond was more effective than response prevention.

Although further research is needed, the suggestion seems to be that patients undergoing extinction of classically conditioned responses should be allowed to make the conditioned response in the absence of the unconditioned stimulus. On the other hand, the research of I. M. Marks (1969), Boulougouris *et al.* (1971), and S. Rachman (1966b, 1969) on phobias seems to contradict this suggestion. These investigators reported the rapid treatment of specific phobias, such as claustrophobia or snake phobia, by flooding. In this procedure the patient was exposed to the feared object (enclosed room or a snake) for extended periods of time. When possible, flooding was continued for one or two extended sessions until the phobic behavior was eliminated. Multiple measures of physiological and attitudinal behaviors, in addition to exposure to the phobic object, supported the wide range as well as the predictability of treatment effects.

These investigators did not report any experimental comparisons of massing and flooding, although they did report that to the extent that subjects are allowed to terminate sessions prior to extinction of the phobia, the phobia may be exacerbated. This was explained as escape conditioning based upon negative reinforcement of the response. More will be said about this form of operant conditioning in Chapter 9, although a few comments seem warranted at this point.

Many of the studies investigating the process of extinction in classical conditioning also appear to involve instrumental processes, especially when an aversive paradigm has been employed (see McAllister & McAllister, 1971). Thus, although investigators have used discrete trial procedures with a preaversive stimulus (the CS) and demonstrated a fear response in the presence of the previously neutral stimulus, if escape or avoidance of the UCS was allowed, the procedure could not be regarded as pure classical conditioning, as revealed in Chapter 4. This is clearly the case in the Baum studies but is probably also true of most of the similar procedures. We have included these studies in this section because of the investigators' theoretical bias and their interpretation of the results within the framework of the classical conditioning model, but we will continue to reanalyze such procedures by alternative systems.

IMPLOSIVE THERAPY

A technique developed for clinical use by T. G. Stampfl and D. J. Levis (1967) shows some similarity to the massing procedure. Stampfl calls his technique "implosive" therapy and appeals to psychoanalytic interpretations and clinical intuitions as well as classical conditioning principles for theoretical support.

Stampfl begins with the initial assumption that neurotic symptoms, phobic responses in particular, are classically conditioned fear responses maintained by anxiety reduction and that extinction can be accomplished by massing of the CS at high intensity. Thus, the subject is instructed to imagine the most fear-producing situation that can be associated to the phobia. The scene to be imagined may be designed by the therapist on the basis of a psychoanalytic interpretation of the problem condition. These scenes, then, are repeatedly described to the patient until the patient reports a reduction of the fear.

In R. A. Hogan's (1966) description there is some grading of scenes to be imagined, but the process he describes appears to be designed to create the most intense reaction possible. For example:

A person afraid of a snake would be requested to view himself picking up and handling a snake. Attempts would be made to have him become aware of his reactions to the animal. He would be instructed to feel how slimy the snake was. Next, he would be asked to experience the snake crawling over his body and biting and ripping his flesh. Scenes of snakes crushing or swallowing him, or perhaps his falling into a pit of snakes would be appropriate implosions. (p. 26)

Ostensibly, the continued presentation of such stimuli should produce extinction of a classically conditioned fear response. Several implosive therapists have produced some evidence to support the efficacy of this approach.

Hogan (1966) compared twenty-six hospitalized psychotic patients who were treated with implosion therapy with control subjects and found that the experimental subjects showed greater rate of discharge and improvement on the MMPI (a diagnostic test used frequently by psychologists). However, direct behavioral measures of change were missing.

Hogan and J. H. Kirchner (1967) compared implosion therapy and mild relaxation training in female college students who showed fear of rats. The experimental subjects received individually tailored instructions and were asked to imagine different scenes depending upon the therapist's evaluation of those scenes that would evoke the maximal anxiety. After one short session fourteen of the twenty-one experimental subjects picked up a white rat, whereas only two of the twenty-two controls would do so. An appropriate behavioral test was used in this case, but unfortunately, the independent variable (treatment) was not well controlled.

Stampfl states that his technique is based on the Pavlovian extinction model, in which the CS is presented in the absence of the UCS. As has been discussed, the extinction of a classically conditioned emotional response should proceed most rapidly when the extinction trials are clearly and discriminably different from the acquisition trials. There is ample data to support this point of view, but with human patients information about acquisition trials is very rare. It is often difficult to determine the exact conditions under which human subjects have learned *any* response, let alone one that is very disturbing to them. Thus, as in the case of the massing and flooding experiments, it seems reasonable to assume that instrumental processes may also be involved.

In any event, until implosion techniques can be more readily specified and replicated, it will be difficult to develop research tools for their proper evaluation. In addition, several therapists of other persuasions (Wolpe & Lazarus, 1966) state that in some cases use

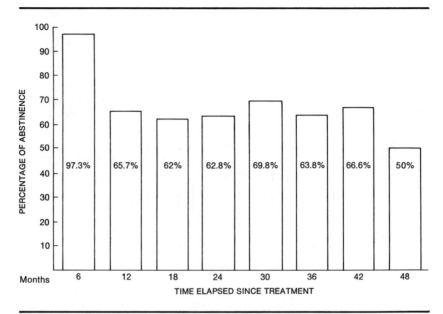

Figure 33. *Showing the percentage of abstinence at the present time among patients treated during each six-month period during the past four years. (From Voegtlin, 1940)*

of the technique has exacerbated, rather than alleviated, anxiety symptoms and phobic responses. Others (Bandura, 1969) have warned against the use of such techniques until their proper evaluation has indicated more positive results.

CLASSICAL AVERSIVE CONDITIONING

Classical conditioning procedures with aversive unconditioned stimuli are frequently used to teach a person a conditioned fear to a formerly attractive stimulus. The procedure usually involves pairing the attractive stimulus with an aversive stimulus that ordinarily elicits pain, nausea, muscular retraction, etc.

For example, W. L. Voegtlin and F. Lemere (1942) and Lemere and Voegtlin (1950) have reported results from a long-term treatment program with alcoholic patients at Shadel Sanitarium in Seattle. In their conditioning program patients are given injections of emetine or apomorphine, which frequently elicit nausea and/or vomiting within thirty minutes. A drink of the patient's preferred alcoholic beverage, sometimes mixed with salt water, is given just before vomiting occurs. This procedure is repeated four to seven times during the ten days of initial inpatient treatment. Each patient is then instructed to return at several intervals for booster treatments. The authors have reported 40 to 50 percent abstention from drinking over a two-year follow-up and 50 to 60 percent over one year, as shown in Figure 33.

Rachman (1965), Rachman and J. Teasdale (1969), and C. M. Franks (1963) have already presented a succinct criticism of such drug-aversive conditioning paradigms. One of their major points is that if alcohol is viewed as the conditioned stimulus and the emetic drug as the unconditioned stimulus in these studies, then, the procedure being employed is backward conditioning, since the UCS is presented prior to the CS. As Franks (1963) comments, backward conditioning is a very tenuous form of conditioning, if it occurs at all. In addition, these critics have pointed out that the reaction to the drug is difficult to predict and control, the latency of the vomiting response sometimes varying from five to thirty minutes. This is contrasted to most unconditioned stimuli, which elicit their characteristic reflexive responses in less than one second. Many other difficulties are encountered with the drug-aversive procedure, including aversive and avoidant reactions to the whole procedure on the part of both patients and staff, aggressive and hostile patient reactions (Bandura, 1969), impossibility of precise measurement of stimuli and responses, and the need for an attending staff to protect against potentially undesirable reactions (heart slowing, aggressive outbursts, etc.).

On the other hand, because some of the drug-aversive procedures are frequently effective in modifying pathological behavior, it could be that some form of conditioning more powerful than backward classical conditioning is actually involved. Thus, it might be more fruitful to regard procedures such as that of Voegtlin and Lemere (1942) as punishment, since the pathological response (drinking liquor) is followed by a potential noxious event (nausea and vomiting) and the probability of the response is allegedly reduced (Azrin & Holz, 1966).

In view of these questions a number of experimenters have proposed the use of electric shock instead of drugs in aversive conditioning models. As Azrin and Holz (1966) point out, electric shock offers several advantages over the use of other stimuli: It makes constant contact with the subject; the stimulus can be varied over a wide range of values to produce differential effects; the effects are usually immediate; and it can be easily administered, does not require medical supervision, has few physical contraindications and produces similar effects (though perhaps at different intensities) in all subjects. In response to the methodological difficulties described above, many of the investigators who have used electric shock in the aversive control of behavior pathology have designed their procedures and analyzed their results within the context of operant rather than classical conditioning. These studies will be reviewed, therefore, in the section on operant procedures.

COUNTERCONDITIONING
One of the most popular and effective of the classical conditioning procedures used in behavior modification is counterconditioning. As previously suggested, counterconditioning involves the extinction of

a previously conditioned response while at the same time programming the conditioning of a new response. One frequently used classical counterconditioning procedure is to present the previously learned conditioned stimulus paired with an unconditioned stimulus that elicits a new response (a response unlike the previously learned conditioned response).

A laboratory model with some similarity to standard Pavlovian counterconditioning was used by B. Klein (1969) with rats previously trained to escape shock in a two-compartment chamber. During extinction three groups of animals were either: (1) confined in the side of the chamber where shock had been delivered with food present (counterconditioning group); (2) confined without food (flooding); or (3) not confined at all (standard extinction). The results suggested that counterconditioning was more effective in reducing fear than the other techniques. However, postconditioning preference tests showed no differential effectiveness between counterconditioning and flooding procedures.

Several varieties of aversive counterconditioning have been used with alcoholic patients, a few of which have already been reviewed. N. V. Kantorovich (1928) presented cards with names of drinks, odors, tastes, and pictures of bottles and kinds of alcoholic beverages to twenty alcoholic patients. Each of these stimuli was paired with an electric shock. Ten more alcoholics in a control group received only medication and hypnotic suggestions that they stop drinking. Following this treatment all but one member of the control group returned to drinking a few days after the completion of the program. By contrast, seventeen of the twenty experimental subjects developed stable aversions to alcohol, and fourteen remained abstinent over follow-up periods ranging from three weeks to twenty months.

The Voegtlin studies (Lemere and Voegtlin, 1950; Lemere *et al.,* 1942a, b; Voegtlin, 1940) may also be regarded as a variety of counterconditioning, since alcohol (the appetitive CS) is paired with injections of an emetic drug (UCS). The emetic drug then elicits nausea and vomiting, hopefully leading to future aversive and avoidant reactions to alcohol. The difficulties involved in this procedure have already been indicated. Kant (1944), in an interesting variation, has attempted to reduce responding to the CS (alcohol) by instructing the patient to spit it out after tasting it.

Although Lemere and Voegtlin (1950) have reported high rates of abstinence following their procedure, they have also observed some specificity and lack of response generalization. (Some patients would drink alcoholic beverages that were not used as CS in conditioning.)

In order to increase the probability of response generalization, some therapists, particularly in Europe, have used a counterconditioning procedure proposed by G. DeMorsier and H. Feldmann (1950), in which apomorphine is used as the unconditioned stimulus and treatment sessions are scheduled every two to four hours until the patient shows aversive reactions to all common alcoholic beverages.

In addition, there are several forms of verbal counterconditioning that approximate the classical conditioning model. M. M. Miller (1959), for example, has given hypnotic instructions to alcoholic patients to visualize and reexperience the worst hangover they can remember, including all the unpleasant physiological reactions and nausea. When the patient begins to grow nauseous and to vomit, he is asked to smell and taste various alcoholic beverages. The suggestion is also made to the patient that the taste or smell of alcohol will evoke nausea in the future. Up to 80 percent abstinence over a period of eight or nine months has been reported using such techniques.

S. S. Anant (1967a, 1968) and B. Ashem and L. Donner (1968) have similarly induced aversion to alcohol through verbal means. Anant's procedure involves inducing deep relaxation in each patient, then presenting a hierarchy of scenes involving drinking behaviors associated with vomiting. Anant believes relaxation training renders the patient more suggestible to the aversive effects of the scenes in the hierarchy. He has reported up to 96 percent abstinence in twenty-six cases over periods of eight to fifteen months.

Similar counterconditioning techniques have been used with other problem conditions in addition to alcoholism. One of the first of these was the well-known example reported by Jones (1924a) with a fifteen-month-old boy named Peter, who was afraid of rabbits. As evidence of the severity of this fear, Peter would cry and attempt to escape whenever a rabbit was brought in his presence.

The therapists decided that if they could condition a response incompatible with fear to the sight of the rabbit, Peter would no longer display the irrational fear. Thus, the child was given ice cream, which he thoroughly enjoyed. While he was eating, a rabbit was brought into the room but was placed as far away from Peter as the walls would allow. Gradually, over several sessions the rabbit was brought closer to the child until it was sitting on the same tray as the ice cream. Eventually, Peter reached out and touched the rabbit, while eating ice cream. Then he stroked it, after which he showed no more signs of fear of rabbits.

The experimental methodology used in this case was a variation of counterconditioning, or reciprocal inhibition, as Wolpe (1958) calls it (described in the next section). Thus, we might regard the case of Peter as an early example of desensitization of a phobic behavior. The example illustrates several important principles. First, extinction of the phobic or escape-avoidant behavior occurred as long as it was replaced by an incompatible behavior in the presence of the previously feared stimulus (phobic object). Second, the experimenters used a "fading" procedure in presenting the rabbit to Peter. That is, the rabbit was first introduced across the room, where it would not elicit the phobic response. Then the distance between the rabbit and Peter was gradually decreased until Peter could touch the rabbit. Third, fading continued steadily except when the incompatible behavior (eating) was disrupted and the phobic behavior was observed. Fourth, as in many clinical cases, the type of conditioning that occurred was complex. Thus, the rabbit initially elicited phobic behavior yet following conditioning, approach responses (touching and stroking the rabbit) were observed, although they were never specifically trained. It appears that the rabbit, by virtue of its association with the ice cream, became a positive stimulus (possibly a conditioned reinforcer) for approach responses. Thus, some variety of operant, in addition to classical conditioning, may have been involved in this case.

DESENSITIZATION

Perhaps the most widely used and studied behavior modification technique was developed by Wolpe (1952) as the result of laboratory research dealing with the experimental neuroses. As mentioned in Chapters 3 and 4, Wolpe set out to replicate and improve upon Masserman's (1946) procedures for studying experimental neurosis in cats. In addition to producing persistent food aversion, avoidance, and fearful behavior in cats, however, Wolpe was also interested in isolating techniques for "treating" his experimental subjects. The solution that was found to be most effective in reinstating appropriate behavior was to reintroduce the subject to the experimental task (eating) in a totally different environment from the one in which he was originally conditioned. As the subject regained the formerly suppressed behavior, the experimental environment was gradually changed to reflect more of the characteristics of the original experimental space. Wolpe found this procedure was successful as long as the subject's eating behavior was recaptured each time and it did not show "fear."

From these observations Wolpe argued that the most successful way to teach his subjects to eat again was to gradually expose them to a hierarchy of stimuli graduated from least to most like those in the original situation, where the neurotic behavior was initially acquired. This is a counterconditioning procedure, since 1) the presence of the conditioned stimuli and the absence of shock defined the extinction procedure, and 2) the delivery of food allowed the learning of a new response (actually the relearning of the old, normal eating pattern).

Consequently, Wolpe (1954) designed his behavior modification program on the basis of this research. For him successful therapy depends upon the inhibition of anxiety, which he sees as similar to the fearful behavior exhibited by the cats with an experimental neurosis. Wolpe further feels that reciprocal inhibition may be involved in most counterconditioning, and is the essential ingredient in all successful therapies. Consequently, the recommended treatment for a strong phobic or avoidant response in a human would be "desensitization," a variation of counterconditioning in which the patient is taught to relax, and anxious phobic responses are extinguished. To accomplish this, the therapist first trains the patient to relax, by using instructions and techniques of muscular relaxation similar to those proposed by E. Jacobson (1938). Next, by inquiry, the therapist constructs an "anxiety hierarchy," or list of stimulus objects or events arranged from least to most anxiety-provoking. Then, while the patient is relaxed, he is instructed to imagine items from this list. The therapist begins with the least threatening and works in the direction of the most threatening as long as the patient is able to maintain the relaxed state. Whenever the patient shows any signs of muscular tension, fear, or anxiety, the therapist stops presenting the item responsible for the anxiety and returns to a less threatening item, one that the patient can handle without obvious disturbance. This "adjusting" procedure is repeated until the patient can voluntarily expose himself to all the items on the list without emotional arousal. Frequently, the patient is instructed to practice the procedure at home by himself. When the patient can successfully maintain relaxation in the presence of all the items in the hierarchy, he may also be able to approach and interact with the actual stimulus objects, events, or situations outside the confines of therapy, as several studies have demonstrated (Wolpe, 1954, 1958).

More research has been done with the desensitization technique than with any other single technique or form of therapy. For the interested student, the major reviews of this literature are Wolpe (1954, 1958, 1969), Bandura (1969), F. H. Kanfer and S. S. Phillips (1970); Paul (1969a, 1969b), and Wilkins (1972). Perhaps the most definitive evidence of the efficacy of Wolpe's technique was provided by Paul (1966). Phobic patients were randomly assigned to one of four conditions in which desensitization was compared with three other conditions. As Figure 34 reveals, the desensitization procedure was the most effective in reducing anxiety.

In spite of the large body of literature, which has, on the whole, supported the therapeutic utility of desensitization, there still remain several unresolved issues regarding the effectiveness of desensitization. There is contrary evidence, for example, regarding the necessity of relaxation for the production of the appropriate behavioral changes. There is also some question as to whether it is necessary to proceed in graduated order from the least threatening to the most threatening items in the hierarchy or whether the reverse order (as in some implosive procedures) might not provide therapeutic changes also. Finally, there is some suggestion that mere exposure (without relaxation) to the items on the hierarchy might be sufficient to produce reduction or elimination of phobic responses.

Several experimenters have found that relaxation is not strictly necessary to reduce anxiety or phobic responding. Paul (1969b) has shown progressive improvement in a variety of anxiety measures even in the absence of complete relaxation (Figure 35). Rachman (1968), further states that training in muscle relaxation is probably unnecessary, since fear reduction has been demonstrated with novitiate experimenters and with subjects who are only minimally

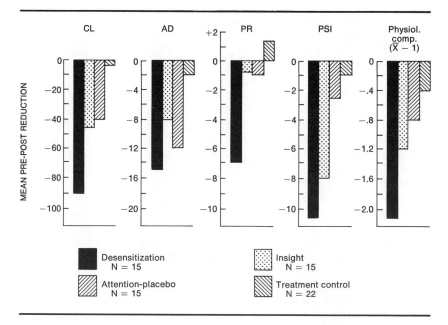

Figure 34. *Mean reduction in observable manifestations of anxiety (CL), cognitive experience of anxiety (AD), and physiological arousal (PR, PSI), and standardized composite of PR and PSI from pretreatment to posttreatment stress conditions. (From Paul, 1966)*

exposed to relaxation training. A. A. Lazarus (1965) has reported cases in which subjects were instructed to increase, rather than decrease, muscle tension, but have nevertheless shown fear reduction. Z. H. Garfield *et al.* (1967), G. Cooke (1966), and B. J. Ritter (1968) have reported successful desensitization with subjects who were physically active during in vivo training. G. C. Davison (1966) reported that subjects undergoing chemically induced muscle relaxation experienced anxiety, suggesting that the two may not be behaviorally incompatible at all. Thus, it would appear that the necessity for relaxation in desensitization remains to be established.

Similarly, it does not appear to be necessary to organize the stimulus materials into a fear hierarchy, as advised by Wolpe, in order to produce fear reduction. Supporting this view, Wilson and Smith (1968) found that anxiety reduction could be obtained in severely anxious subjects by relaxation training and the presentation of freely associated scenes that were not necessarily related to the problem behavior and were not organized hierarchically. M. Wolpin and W. Raines (1966) reported success when subjects imagined fear-provoking scenes in the absence of both relaxation training and hierarchical organization. Thus, hierarchical organization does not appear to be necessary or of central importance.

Finally, studies by M. K. Wagner and N. R. Cauthen (1968) and

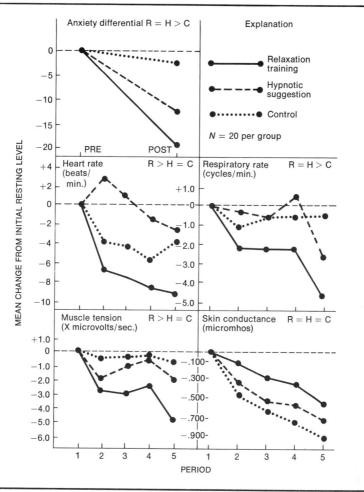

Figure 35. *Mean change from initial resting level on all measures during session I. (From Paul, 1969b)*

H. Leitenberg, W. S. Agras, D. H. Barlow, and D. C. Oliveau (1969) indicate that direct positive reinforcement, such as the therapist's verbal approval for the subject's approaching a snake or praise for agoraphobic subjects who increase the number of steps they take into open areas, may be sufficient for therapeutic gain and reduction in fearful behavior. Perhaps, then, repeated exposure to the primary stimulus events that were present during training is all that is necessary for the extinction of learned fear or avoidance responses. As we have seen, according to the generalization decrement hypothesis (Kimble, 1961), presentation of the CS with a markedly different order, scheduling, pattern, etc., may hasten extinction. The studies just reviewed suggest that direct reinforcement of incompatible behaviors may be all that is necessary to reduce or eliminate phobic or avoidance behavior and, at the same time, provide the subject with a more constructive, useful response to the same stimulus configuration.

FADING PROCEDURES

Fading is a very important technique, which is widely used in operant as well as in classical conditioning. As we have seen, the fading procedure involves gradually changing some aspect of the conditioning situation (usually a stimulus) along one of its relevant dimensions. In the Jones (1924a) study, for example, a fading technique was used in treating Peter's phobia for rabbits. Jones presented the rabbit at a great distance initially, then gradually decreased the distance of the rabbit from Peter, who was busy eating. Fading was continued until Peter's eating behavior was disrupted, at which time the steps were retraced and the rabbit returned to a greater distance from Peter.

Other investigators have used or suggested similar techniques. Pavlov (1927) recommended that some of the dogs that had developed experimental neuroses be retrained in a room different from the one in which the pathological behavior had developed.

As we have seen, Wolpe (1952) used this suggestion with his experimentally neurotic cats, who would not eat following application of electric shock. To retrain these animals, Wolpe reintroduced them to the conditioning situation in a distinctly different room; then, after the eating responses were restored, he moved them through successively more similar rooms until they were returned to the original room in which conditioning had begun. Wolpe was so impressed with this technique that he incorporated it as an important element in his desensitization practice, the therapy he proposed for human phobic patients.

The gradual introduction, in desensitization, of items ever higher on the hierarchy of anxiety-arousing events represents an application of the fading technique. It is similar to other behavioral applications in that stimulus control procedures are used so that each new stimulus will evoke, not anxiety or phobic responses as in the past, but a new response for the person, usually relaxation.

Obviously, fading is an invaluable technique imbedded in, or used as an adjunct to, many forms of behavioral therapy. It has been used even more popularly and widely in operant conditioning than in classical approaches, and its use in this connection will be reviewed in the next chapter.

CONCLUSION: EFFICACY OF
CLASSICAL TREATMENT TECHNIQUES

As has been revealed in this chapter, most of the treatment techniques that have been developed within the classical conditioning framework have been complex combinations of traditional classical conditioning procedures and, sometimes, treatment techniques borrowed from other areas. Thus, systematic desensitization, one of the most widely used of all behavior therapy techniques, involves many stimuli and responses more or less distantly related to the pathological behavior in question and, perhaps, even more distantly related to classical conditioning as traditionally conducted in the laboratory. The difference between the well-defined overt stimuli of the laboratory and the ambiguous covert imagery of desensitization seems clear.

The level of complexity and eclectic orientation (particularly apparent in the writings of the implosive therapists) make the functional analysis of these techniques extremely difficult. As reported in the sections on classical aversive conditioning and desensitization, positive results have been found with many variations of these techniques, but, as indicated earlier, these successful outcomes do not necessarily support the theoretical rationale that inspired the treatment. Thus, for example, Voegtlin's (1940; Lemere and Voegtlin, 1950) far-reaching program with alcoholic patients may have achieved its effects largely as a function of punishment, rather than classical aversive conditioning, which may be only minimally responsible for the outcome.

Just as desensitization appears to be a complex combination of classical and other clinical and conditioning techniques, so, too, the largely effective outcomes reported in the literature (Kanfer & Phillips, 1970) have been explained by variations of classical desensitization procedures, as well as by alternative explanations of the mechanism of action of systematic desensitization.

The diversity observed in contemporary classical conditioning treatment techniques may have been inherited from previous investigators. As indicated at the beginning of the chapter, Pavlov tried a great number of techniques in the attempt to alleviate or cure his animals' experimental neuroses. Those that were reputedly the most effective (rest from conditioning and administration of bromide drugs) were either not directly related to the conditioning problem or tended to generate complex results from the conditioning point of view.

There are, however, at least two outstanding examples of functional analyses of pathological behavior that were executed in the laboratory with normal, rather than clinical, samples and that represent prototypes of experimental rigor. One, a successful application of retraining and reversal techniques (Schneiderman *et al.,* 1971), focused upon the nictitating membrane reflex and correlated social-sexual behaviors in rabbits, and the other (Rachman, 1966a) conditioned and then extinguished a behavior analogous to foot fetishism. Programmatic endeavors such as these greatly extend our knowledge of the power of the classical conditioning technology, as well as support its clinical efficacy, at least when the acquisition conditions can be specified.

Chapter 8 / Operant Behavior Modification Procedures: Deceleration Techniques

As indicated in Chapter 5, in an operant analysis environmental consequences are considered to be primarily responsible for the acquisition and maintenance of pathological behavior. Response consequences will again receive major attention in this chapter, as we review operant techniques for decelerating behaviors. The argument presented here may be considered a logical extension of the principles previously discussed. That is, theoretically, those variables that are responsible for problem conditions may also be invoked in the treatment of these conditions. For example, in cases where an adventitious reinforcement arrangement may be responsible for tantrum behavior or delusional speech, simple removal of the reinforcing arrangement (extinction) should result in the modification of these behaviors (that is, a reduction in their frequency). Similarly, when "inadequate" stimulus control may have resulted in a behavioral deficit, such as lack of speech in an autistic child, acquisition processes including successive approximations, discrimination, training, etc., should result in speech acquisition.

The actual application of variables in the modification of behavior in the natural environment, however, is often more complex than this simplistic model would suggest. In fact, many failures in treatment may be attributed to the lack of sophistication on the part of the clinician, who may have analyzed a problem condition (either implicitly or explicitly) as an example of simple positive reinforcement or negative reinforcement.

Thus, although the general focus of a treatment program may involve the use of procedures designed to either reduce or increase response frequency, the effectiveness of the techniques will depend upon their interactions with present and past determinants.

Perhaps a brief review and an elaboration of operant terminology might be useful at this point. The similarities and differences between respondent and operant concepts, procedures, and applications have already been described. Definitions of operant terms will now be advanced in the context of a commonplace mother-child interaction.

A reinforcer is any environmental change following a behavior that serves to increase the frequency of the response. Thus, if a mother picked up her child each time he cried, this might result in an increase in the frequency of crying behavior. The term "reinforcement" refers to the operation in which a reinforcer is delivered (in this case, picking up the child). The schedule of reinforcement denotes the number of responses or the temporal sequence of behaviors necessary for the delivery of reinforcement. For example, if the child were picked up on each crying occasion, this would constitute a continuous schedule of reinforcement; reinforcement for every third crying response would represent a fixed-ratio three schedule; reinforcement on the average of every third time (ranging perhaps from one to five) would be considered a variable-ratio three reinforcement schedule. Paralleling these response-based schedules are the time-based schedules: fixed-interval schedules, in which reinforcement follows the first response after some given period of time has elapsed (such as three minutes), and variable-interval schedules, which provide for reinforcement for the first response after a variable temporal period (for example, an average of three minutes with a range of anywhere from one to five minutes). Although reinforcement schedules are often difficult to specify precisely in the natural environment, their importance in terms of both acquisition and modification cannot be minimized. Since many behavioral characteristics are a function of the schedule, any modification effort must include an attempt to analyze the schedule's effect on the problem condition.

The term "contingency" denotes the temporal and qualitative relationship between a response and a reinforcer. Immediate reinforcement is always more effective than delayed reinforcement. Adventitious reinforcement refers to reinforcers that accidentally follow a response, thereby exerting control over the behavior. For example, if our hypothetical mother should inadvertently enter a room in which the child was already crying, this accidental contingency might reinforce crying behavior. Punishment is the response-contingent application of any stimulus that results in a decrease in response frequency. With the crying child, for example, a loud noise (mother shouting, vacuum cleaner suddenly being turned on) might result in cessation of crying. If an aversive agent acquires functional control over escape and or avoidance behavior, it qualifies as a negative reinforcer. Thus, turning off the vacuum cleaner contingent upon crying cessation, would demonstrate an escape conditioning arrangement. Similarly, if the child stopped crying in response to the mother's threats, an avoidance contingency would be defined.

Extinction represents the termination of reinforcement (either positive or negative). Thus, if the mother stopped picking up her child, this might result in a reduction of crying behavior. Conversely, if the avoidance contingency (mother's threats) stopped operating, crying frequency should increase. Variations of these procedures, such as time-out from positive reinforcement and response cost, may be functionally equivalent to punishment and may also exert control over response frequency. For example, taking a toy from the child, removing the child from the mother, or putting the child into a "time-out" room might all function to reduce the frequency of crying.

Stimulus control typically refers to discrimination training that produces responding in the presence of one stimulus but not another, for example, responding in the presence of a stimulus correlated with positive and/or negative reinforcement, and response cessation in the presence of a stimulus associated with extinction or punishment. Thus, our by now familiar child may cry in the mother's presence, as a consequence of previous "babying" experiences, but not in the fathers' presence, due to previous punishment contingent upon crying behavior. To the extent that other people may have treated such behavior in a similar manner, these reactions may also occur in their presence, thus demonstrating stimulus generalization. If the child also displays responses other than crying, such as screaming and whining, in the mother's presence without specific reinforcement, we might suggest that response generalization has occurred.

Again, it must be emphasized that although a theoretical analysis might offer the above explanations, only a functional analysis would enable us to specify their actual application to any given situation. Furthermore, it is important to bear in mind that the concepts are defined by their effects. Thus, food is reinforcing to the hungry organism, but not to the satiated one. Paddling may have a punishing effect on one child and a reinforcing effect on another.

STRAIGHT EXTINCTION:
WITHDRAWAL OF MAINTENANCE CONTINGENCIES

As with classical conditioning techniques, operant extinction is most often used in combination with other techniques. C. D. Williams (1959), however, reported the successful modification of tantrum behavior in a twenty-one-month-old infant by extinction alone. The child had been seriously ill during the first year and a half of his life, with the result that one of his parents routinely spent one-half to two hours in his bedroom each night waiting for him to fall asleep. On the few occasions when this was not done, the child cried and had

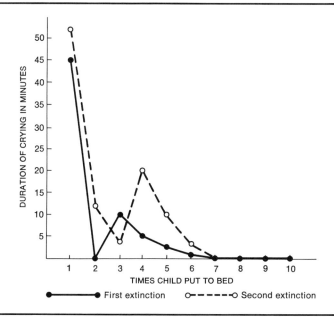

Figure 36. *Length of crying in two extinction series as a function of successive occasions of being put to bed. (From Williams, 1959)*

a tantrum. Once the child was medically cleared and declared in good health, social reinforcement (in the form of remaining with the child until he fell asleep) was terminated (extinction); that is, the parents now tucked the child into bed and then left the room. Although the child screamed and cried for forty-five minutes the first night of treatment, the parents did not reenter the room. By the tenth night of this procedure, the child no longer screamed or cried and was observed to smile as the parents left the room. About a week later an aunt visited and spent extra time putting the child to bed, which reinstated the tantrum behavior and confirmed the function of social reinforcement. A second extinction series was programmed, and no tantrums were observed after the eighth night. These results are plotted in Figure 36. No further tantrums at bedtime were reported during the next two years.

This study supports the views of Skinner (1938, 1953), Ferster (1958, 1961) and others who have observed that extinction can be a very effective deceleration technique for modifying behavior with long-lasting results. In this case, a troublesome behavior was apparently eliminated for at least two years by a rather simple technique. Since it is often difficult for parents to understand the relationship between their own behaviors and the problem behaviors of their children, the use of such techniques may help them learn effective methods in the resolution of problem behaviors.

Ayllon and his colleagues (Ayllon & Michael, 1959; Ayllon &

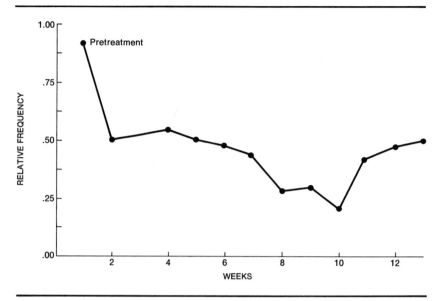

Figure 37. *Extinction of psychotic talk. (From Ayllon & Michael, 1959. Additional information and related research can be found in Ayllon & Azrin, 1968.)*

Haughton, 1964) have reported several dynamic and creative applications of extinction procedures to reduce pathological behaviors of hospitalized chronic psychotic patients. In the earlier report, for example, a female psychotic patient had been the target of verbal abuse and even beatings from other patients for her persistent delusional verbalizations. In addition, nurses reported they occasionally listened to her bizarre talk or expressed sympathy and understanding in an effort to determine what was bothering her and thus to help her. Despite these experiences (and perhaps because of them), the patient's verbalizations remained at a high rate during the three years in which they were observed. After the nurses were instructed to ignore her psychotic talk, the percentage of such responses fell from a base rate of 91 to 25 percent. An "unprogrammed reversal" in the contingency occurred when a social worker interviewed the patient several times and inadvertently reinforced her delusional statements. (See Figure 37.)

In another study Ayllon & Haughton (1962) similarly treated chronic mealtime problems in psychotic patients. Previously, the patients had not responded to announcements of mealtime, and had been individually escorted to the dining room by members of the staff and spoon-fed their meals. The experimenters assumed that this treatment reinforced and maintained the problem behaviors, so extinction in this case involved simply announcing mealtime and closing the dining room thirty minutes later. No one was assisted as

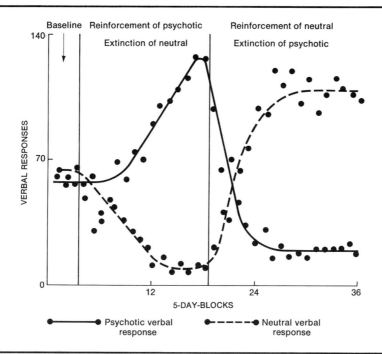

Figure 38. *Reversals in the incidence of psychotic and neutral verbal behavior as a result of variations in social reinforcement of these two classes of verbalizations. (From Ayllon & Haughton, 1964. Additional information and related research can be found in Ayllon & Azrin, 1968.)*

in the past, and no wheedling or cajoling was allowed. Under the new regime a few meals were missed initially, but very soon all the patients went unassisted to the dining room and ate their meals by themselves.

Extinction procedures were also used to modify the delusional verbalizations or psychosomatic complaints of three chronic schizophrenic women. In the first case the patient's delusional references to herself as the queen were measured, as well as her neutral (nonpsychotic) statements. Initially, social reinforcement was made contingent upon psychotic verbalizations, which increased to high frequencies. Then the same reinforcement was made contingent upon nonpsychotic verbalizations, and extinction was programmed for the psychotic verbalizations. Consequently, delusional statements declined to near zero, and neutral statements increased. (See Figure 38.) Although not strictly limited to an extinction procedure, this example is included here because it is a powerful demonstration of the effectiveness of extinction and demonstrates, as well, the multiple base-line technique (Baer *et al.,* 1968). In the multiple base-line procedure, a contingency that has been demonstrated effective with one behavior is later introduced contingent upon another behavior. This is one of the replication techniques that supports the statements of generality and reliability that can be made about a contingency.

With the other two women who showed high frequencies of somatic complaints during base-line measurement, social attention, consoling, and sympathy were withdrawn as reinforcers for these responses, reducing them to near-zero rates. A reversal was later done, with attention and sympathy again following each of the patients' complaints. After somatic complaints had increased to high frequencies, extinction was again programmed, and the behaviors finally decreased to near-zero occurrence.

Chronic headbanging and other forms of self-injurious behavior have been observed to occur with some frequency at institutions where patient-staff ratios are low. This observation supports Ferster's (1961) notion that when positive reinforcement is rarely forthcoming, the child may show an increase in aversive means of controlling the environment. Self-injurious behaviors are usually very effective in bringing rapid human physical contact or attention of some kind. O. I. Lovaas *et al.* (1965a) and B. G. Tate and G. S. Baroff (1966) have both found that withdrawal of reinforcement in the form of attention, or the physical contact of another person, will lead to a diminution or cessation of the response. In the Lovaas case, however, extinction was slow, and the child continued to bang her head about 10,000 times before stopping altogether. This may have occurred because the child had a clear-cut discriminative stimulus (S^D) marking her extinction sessions. (She was locked in a padded cell for the daily half-hour extinction sessions.) Parenthetically, Lovaas commented in connection with this case that it might be more humanitarian in the long run to apply response-contingent punishment, which he demonstrated could reduce the frequency of the response much more quickly.

Tate and Baroff (1966), on the other hand, produced much more rapid reduction of self-injurious behavior by programming response-contingent withdrawal of human contact. They also found, however, that response-contingent electric shock was superior in rapid suppression of the same behavior.

Earlier than the above developments, A. J. Yates (1958a) suggested an extinction technique for the treatment of stammering and tics. He theorized that such responses were drive-reducing conditioned avoidance responses, originally evoked in a traumatic situation. Yates further predicted, via the Hullian model of conditioned inhibition, that voluntary massed practice of the response would increase inhibition and result in a decrease in response rate. At the same time a "negative habit of not doing the tic" should increase. Yates felt that this procedure would not only produce extinction of the tic or stammering, but also generalize beyond treatment.

Data from several patients supported Yates' predictions. The findings, according to Yates, showed that prolonged massed practice followed by lengthy rest periods produced the best results. Patients also reported significant improvement outside the test situation.

In examining Yates' position, however, several comments may be relevant. Positing a drive reduction process (avoidance conditioning) without either reconstructing the acquisition circumstances or manipulating the aversive events that control the behavior seems to be a questionable practice. "Negative practice" may result in the reduction of a facial tic, but its success may be due to the extinction of a socially reinforced response. Other explanations may also be possible.

The general functional utility of extinction programs, when made contingent upon a wide variety of behaviors, has been noted. In addition, it should perhaps be commented that straight extinction programs seem particularly appropriate when: (1) rapid reduction of the response is not critical, in contrast to such self-injurious behaviors as head banging and self-mutilation, and (2) other constructive behaviors already exist which can be substituted for the extinguished response. More specifically, extinction arrangements might be useful when the termination of current contingencies will *naturally* result in an increase in the frequency of more constructive behaviors.

Thus, many patient- and child-care practices may inadvertently reinforce inappropriate behaviors (Gelfand *et al.,* 1967) which can be reversed through extinction. In the case of the eating problems reported by Ayllon and Haughton, the patients ate, but not without assistance until after treatment. Similarly, in Williams' case the child slept, but not in the absence of the parents until after treatment by extinction.

On the other hand, rather than use extinction alone with patients who show general behavioral deficits, it might be more effective to use extinction in combination with other techniques that explicitly program consequences for new, more constructive behaviors than might occur "naturally." Some of these techniques will be reviewed in the sections on counterconditioning and shaping normal behaviors.

(Some similarity will be noticed between Yates' technique of negative practice and the next technique to be considered: satiation. Both techniques bring the rate of the pathological behavior to an increased level prior to its diminution or disappearance.)

SATIATION

Satiation is an experimental operation somewhat analogous to giving a hungry person all he wants to eat. The technique operates on the basic assumption underlying any reinforcement process; that a particular stimulus will more likely function as a reinforcer if it has been associated with a history of deprivation in the organism. Experimental satiation might be programmed in the laboratory by allowing an organism to work for a particular reinforcer until that reinforcer no longer controlled the behavior. For example, if a rat is allowed a small pellet of food contingent upon each press of a bar, his rate after several hundred of these responses will be observed to fall to new low levels, with successively longer pauses between responses. Thus, a reduction in response rate resulted from a decrease in deprivation (hunger) and an increase in body weight (Ferster & Skinner, 1957). This effect can often be demonstrated to be independent of inanition, exhaustion, or other response inhibitors by exchanging the reinforcer for another (perhaps liquid) reinforcer, which will reinstate responding at a high rate.

Ayllon (1963) applied satiation in an interesting way to hoarding behavior. In one case a female chronic schizophrenic patient had hoarded towels in her room for most of the nine years she had spent in the institution. At any one time, 20 to 30 towels could usually be found in her room, even though the nursing staff removed the towels twice a week. Treatment consisted of merely giving the patient an additional towel without comment whenever she was in her room. In addition, no towels were removed from her room during this time. The patient initially expressed her pleasure at this change in staff practice. During the first week an average of 7 towels a day were given to the patient; by the third week the number had increased to about 60 per day. When the total number of towels in her room reached 625, the patient asked to have them removed, and then began taking them out herself, since no one helped her do so. Follow-up was continued over a twelve-month period, during which an average of 1.5 towels were found in the patient's room per week, despite the prior feeling of some staff members, who regarded her hoarding as an expression of a basic need for love. (See Figure 39.)

With three male, mentally defective patients who hoarded magazines, paper, and rubbish in their clothes, Ayllon and Michael (1959) used a combination of satiation and extinction. Hoarding was apparently maintained by the attention involved in the routine inspection of these patients by the nursing staff and by "dejunking" routine (removal of the hoarded trash). The authors also suspected that partial deprivation of magazines and papers played some role in the maintenance of hoarding (there were few available on the ward). Treatment consisted of flooding the ward with magazines and the cessation of dejunking inspections. The patients' clothing was checked after they went to bed, but no items were removed. Soon after this program was initiated, one patient (the worst offender, who had developed skin rashes as a result of continued hoarding) no longer carried magazines and rubbish in his clothes, but kept a stack of magazines on his lap while in the dayroom. These were counted, and there was a decline from thirty-five to forty-five initially to ten or fifteen near the end of the program. Treatment was terminated after nine weeks, since the· hoarding had decreased to near zero for all three patients.

J. H. Resnick (1968) also applied a satiation technique in order to decelerate cigarette smoking. Three groups of male and female smokers were assigned to (1) smoke at their normal rate for a week,

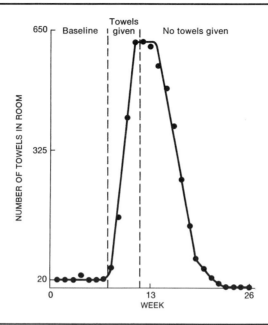

Figure 39. *A response, towel hoarding, is eliminated when the patient is given towels in excess. When the number of towels reaches 625 the patient starts to discard them. She continues to do so until the number found in her room averages 1.5 compared to the previous 20 towels per week. (From Ayllon, 1963. Additional information and related research can be found in Ayllon & Azrin, 1968.)*

(2) double their normal rate for a week, or (3) triple their normal rate for a week. At two weeks and again at four months after treatment, the experimental groups showed significant reduction in their smoking rates (but rare cessation and some increase during follow-up) compared to the controls, whose rates did not change. More durable results might have been obtained if the experimental groups had a longer exposure to the satiation schedule, for example, or if they had been given instructions to smoke at the assigned rate until they felt ready to renounce cigarettes for life. It might be of further aid if the subjects could be informed that they would reach that point after a minimal amount of time (such as two to three weeks). This might help guarantee sufficient contact with the satiation schedule to efficiently change (or eliminate) the behavior.

Satiation would appear to be a very useful technique with certain behaviors. Like giving candy to a baby, too much of a good thing may become aversive. As was mentioned in the last section, there may be very little difference between satiation and negative practice procedures, especially when motor behaviors are the target. In both cases, the frequency of the behavior is first raised to a very high rate. This increase may be sufficient to reduce or eliminate the behavior altogether. In the case of motor behaviors, the possible mechanisms of action may involve fatigue, extinction of prior reinforcement (such as social reinforcement), or the additional self-control that may result from emitting a response following instructions.

On the other hand, the satiation technique would probably not be prescribed for other kinds of problem behaviors, particularly those that can be dangerous to the treated person or others. For example, it would not be the treatment of choice for destructive head banging, suicidal rumination, alcoholism, overeating, or drug addiction.

However, satiation may work very well, under the conditions recommended above, for smoking and other similar behaviors, especially if they do not occur at extremely high rates. Institution of a satiation program with a person who already smokes three or four packs of cigarettes per day might have little effect, partly because it might not be physically possible to smoke at much higher rates. Thus, satiation may be maximally effective with behaviors that occur at low to moderate rates.

FADING TECHNIQUES

As described in the last chapter, fading procedures usually involve gradual changes in some aspect of the conditioning situation (usually a stimulus) along one of its dimensions. The examples given previously contained operant as well as classical conditioning components and thus will be mentioned again in passing. The classical example was the case of Peter and his phobia of rabbits, which Jones (1924a) treated by introducing a rabbit, first at long range, then gradually closer and closer, while Peter ate in a high chair.

Similarly, fading is also a standard part of desensitization. After a hierarchy of phobic stimuli has been constructed, the patient is presented with the least anxiety-producing stimuli, and then the more disturbing stimuli are gradually faded in. As with many applications of the fading procedure, the patient's limits of tolerance control the rate of stimulus fading. For example, when the patient who is properly trained in desensitization can no longer maintain relaxation in the presence of a particular item, the therapist usually returns to earlier items from the hierarchy with which the patient can cope.

Unfortunately, clinical applications of the fading procedure, although widely used, have rarely been systematically analyzed. However, the experimental literature can provide a useful model. In a classic demonstration with animals, in contrast with the usual discrimination procedure, H. S. Terrace (1963) presented reinforcement to pigeons only in the presence of a stimulus that was available most of the time, and then faded the availability of the stimulus temporally while the probability of responding during the stimulus remained high. With careful adjustment of this technique, subjects continued to respond only in the presence of the stimulus, developing what Terrace called errorless discrimination.

Subsequently, Sidman and L. T. Stoddard (1967) adapted the Terrace technique for discrimination training in retarded children. Using this method, they demonstrated that the children could discriminate between different forms with fewer errors than was accomplished by training without fading. With fading, for example, the children were able to overcome responses incompatible with successful discrimination, such as position preferences, that occurred in the absence of fading. Thus, half of the children who did not acquire successful discrimination on the basis of reinforcement and extinction alone did so once fading was introduced.

Fading techniques have also been used frequently and successfully in various speech-training programs. For example, in teaching tacts or "naming" responses to autistic children, Lovaas (1967), T. R. Risley and M. Wolf (1967), and Davidson (1971) have all successfully used tacting probes, such as "What is this? . . . Nose." Such probes may initially elicit imitative responses, but they can then be faded along continua such as intensity of the tacted word or the temporal interval between the interrogative portion of the probe and the tacted word. In either case, the child may eventually respond with the correct tact ("nose") following presentation of the interrogative prompt alone.

Fading has also been widely applied to the "thinning" of reinforcement schedules in an attempt to maintain a response over longer posttreatment intervals. For example, K. Allen *et al.* (1964) increased social interaction in formerly isolated children by making teacher attention contingent upon interaction. Once social interaction was established, reinforcement was delivered on an increasingly intermittent schedule, with the result that social play was maintained through the rest of the school year.

Similarly, when an individual is being prepared to leave a token economy program (see pp. 292 ff.), he is often exposed to a gradual fading out of token schedules, while contingencies operating in the outside world are gradually faded in. Ayllon and Azrin (1968) and Schaefer and Martin (1969) have explicated the principles of such procedures.

In summary, fading techniques are being used increasingly in many diverse applications in behavior modification programs. Fading may be central to modifications ranging from systematic desensitization to errorless discrimination. The technique seems to be a very powerful way to train an organism in new discriminations. When combined with a counterconditioning method, as in desensitization or in Sidman and Stoddard's (1967) study, a maximally effective treatment may result, which substitutes a constructive response for a pathological one.

FEEDBACK

Various kinds of feedback procedures have been used in behavior modification, essentially to signal the subject that a response of a particular class has been made. Usually feedback is in the form of discriminative stimulation and is contingent upon a response. Feedback conditions have been noted to have varying effects, ranging from apparent functional equivalence to positive reinforcement, through little or no consistent effect, to apparent functional equivalence to punishment. Perhaps a review of some of the previous uses and outcomes of feedback procedures will enable some generalization regarding expected outcomes.

Lindsley (1971), in his precision-teaching programs, often trains a person to record and chart the frequency of behaviors he wishes to decelerate or eliminate. According to Lindsley and others who have used this system, this minimal instruction and the self-charting technique alone may be followed by a decrease in the frequency of the behavior. Similarly, some behaviors that the person wishes to increase have shown acceleration following self-charting. For example, an underweight anorexic patient at the Miami Veterans Administration Hospital showed a fourfold increase in the number of bites consumed at meals when he plotted the rates himself. Another patient who complained of obsessive sexual thoughts showed frequencies decreasing to zero when asked to record and plot the number of these thoughts per day. Apparently, then, feedback, defined in this way, can function to increase or decrease behaviors, perhaps depending upon other important controlling conditions.

In addition, H. Leitenberg, W. S. Agras, L. E. Thompson, and D. Wright (1968) found that feedback assisted in the reduction of two forms of phobic behavior. A program of increasing exposure to two kinds of phobic objects (a small room for a claustrophobic person and a knife for a patient afraid of knives) was expedited when feedback of the time of exposure to each object was provided. Moreover, progress was slower when feedback was removed, and was again expedited when feedback was reintroduced, demonstrating that extraneous stimuli could not have been responsible for the observed change. The authors also found that adding and removing verbal praise did not alter the rate of change provided by feedback.

Several experimenters, including Flanagan *et al.* (1958), Goldiamond (1965b), and G. A. Soderberg (1968), have found that feedback, in the form of white noise-delayed auditory feedback of speech, was effective in suppressing the rate of stuttering (punishment effect) in subjects with such problems.

Finally, a number of investigators in the "biofeedback" movement have found that response-contingent feedback (a light or similar stimulus) can be effective in modifying physiological responses such as galvanic skin response, electroencephalogram frequencies, and heart rate. J. Brenner, R. Kleinman, and W. Goesling (1969), D. Shapiro *et al.* (1970), B. Tursky *et al.* (1970), and several others, who have worked with physiological responses, found that contingent feedback analogous to the rate of the response desired seems to function better than digital or discrete feedback. This is plausible, since analog feedback provides more information and reports on smaller and usually more immediate changes than digital (all or none) feedback.

Issues that do not seem clearly resolved as yet include whether feedback functions as S^D or reinforcement, whether feedback (depending upon whether it is associated with an appetitive or aversive schedule) can be expected to accelerate or decelerate particular behaviors, and whether any programmed reinforcer is needed in addition to feedback. Similarly, feedback has not been subjected to as much controlled comparison as other, more established techniques of modification. For example, it does not seem clear whether feedback, desensitization, or counterconditioning might be more effective in eliminating phobic behavior, tachycardia, etc.

COUNTERCONDITIONING

Counterconditioning, in operant as in classical conditioning, is procedurally defined as deceleration or extinction of a previously learned response and simultaneous conditioning of a new one. In operant programs this usually denotes removal of reinforcement (or punishment) of the previously learned pathological response and reinforcement of the new one. This procedure is frequently the preferred technique, since it may be maximally effective in eliminating a pathological behavior while simultaneously replacing it with a more adaptive, constructive behavior, and it may be particularly effective when the two responses are mutually incompatible. The technique has the added advantage of a wide range of applicability, as revealed by the following review.

In a psychotherapeutic situation, H. C. Rickard *et al.* (1960) applied verbal reinforcement to the rational statements of a delusional psychiatric patient, and programmed extinction (by looking out the window or at the floor) whenever the patient emitted delusional verbalizations. The frequency of the reinforced class of responses was observed to increase concurrent with a decrease in delusional material. Furthermore, a two-year follow-up with this patient (Rickard & Dinoff, 1962) indicated the retention of reinforcement control of rational behaviors. In addition, these authors report that less delusional speech was observed in other hospital situations, indicating possible generalization of the effects.

B. Hart *et al.* (1964) applied a counterconditioning methodology to operant crying in two preschool boys. Approving attention was administered to the boys' appropriate noncrying responses to distressful situations, and attention was removed from crying unless the boys were hurt. Under these conditions inappropriate crying decreased to low levels, and more appropriate responses increased. Two reversals of this procedure reinstated operant crying to a high frequency (until it suddenly dropped off in one child during a reinforcement condition). With this one exception, these data give strong support to counterconditioning technology, as well as to the author's contention that operant crying may be largely a function of adult attention.

In a more experimental context, S. W. Bijou and R. Orlando (1961) make the excellent suggestion that when a response persists despite the removal of all apparent consequences, extinction should be continued until the subject shows pauses, perhaps of increasing duration, between responses, and then reinforcement should be provided again. In other words, noncontingent rotation of extinction and reinforcement components of a schedule may lead to an adventitious contingency, which can be eliminated by requiring a pause (change-over delay) before reentry into the reinforcement component.

In order to facilitate counterconditioning, several investigators have used programs that applied aversive contingencies to a pathological behavior, while delivering positive reinforcement contingent upon more constructive responses. For example, J. G. Thorpe *et al.* (1964) used shock-escape conditioning (described again in Chapter 9) with homosexual subjects. The individual received shock contingent upon verbalizations describing homosexual behaviors, and statements describing heterosexual behaviors terminated shock. The subjects were also instructed to masturbate in the presence of pictures of attractive females and to use these images in masturbatory fantasies. The authors reported that this counterconditioning technique was much more effective than an earlier attempt (Thorpe *et al.,* 1963) using masturbatory conditioning alone.

A similar counterconditioning approach with homosexual clients (Solyom & Miller, 1965) delivered punishment shock while the person was looking at pictures of nude males, and the reviewing of pictures of nude females was reinforced by termination of continuous shock. The authors reported that plethysmographic measures of sexual responses to female stimuli increased in magnitude, but little or no change occurred in response to male pictures. Should this outcome correlate with overt bisexual responses, it would seem to fall short of the goal of therapy.

M. P. Feldman (1966) applied similar methods to conditioning of homosexuals and also to alcoholic patients. His procedure differs from the previous two in the addition of an escape-avoidance response, which the subject could use to terminate or avoid shock. With the homosexuals the escape-avoidance response also changed the picture of a nude male to one of a nude female. With alcoholics the sipping of alcoholic beverages led to the onset of shock; spitting the beverage out terminated shock. All of these studies will be mentioned again later.

In a different approach to the treatment of pathological sexual behavior, Davison (1968) applied a counterconditioning technique to a student who masturbated to sadistic fantasies of injuring women. The student was allowed to use his own fantasy to initiate sexual arousal, but was then instructed to masturbate while looking at *Playboy* nudes. Later, the sadistic stimuli were followed by imagined nauseous scenes and feelings. This technique enabled the client to eliminate the sadistic fantasies on his own.

H. L. Mees (1966) has reported a similar counterconditioning technique which a patient also learned to bring under self-control. Again, the patient entertained sadistic fantasies, which were found, in this case, to vary independently of normal fantasies and normal heterosexual behavior. Aversive conditioning of the sadistic fantasies alone was ineffective until combined with explicit reinforcement of normal heterosexual fantasy. Once the client learned this response, he was able to continue conditioning under self-control.

In a study also to be considered under the aegis of aversive techniques, Barrett (1962) found that several counterconditioning devices could be used to control tics in a neurological patient with whom pharmacological and psychological treatments had failed. Self-control techniques and tic-produced white noise both reduced the rate of the response to some extent, but a procedure in which continuous music was interrupted after each occurrence of a tic was the most extensive and reliable. In this case use was made of a natural reinforcer, the patient's love for jazz music.

Finally, Gambrill (1967) has suggested, on the basis of animal studies aimed at elimination of avoidance responses, that counterconditioning of a response competitive with the avoidance response may bring rapid response suppression, but that if the competing response is only tenuously acquired or is removed, the avoidance response may increase in rate again.

This review has suggested the range of current studies of counterconditioning in clinical settings. On the basis of the evidence it appears that these procedures are among the more powerful techniques available to the clinician for the modification of behavior. By explicitly programming extinction or aversive consequences contingent upon pathological behaviors and positive reinforcement contingent upon more constructive, useful responses, the probability of durable modification may be maximized. When programs of this sort are combined with shaping of new behaviors and fading of reinforcement through progressively intermittent schedules, it might be possible to obtain results that would last indefinitely, since natural contingencies might then maintain the changes.

It should be emphasized that the efficacy of complex counterconditioning programs is dependent upon a thorough analysis of the variables influencing the pathological behavior, as well as those variables necessary to shape and maintain new, more constructive responses. Beyond this, the coordination of therapeutic variables with community-maintaining contingencies may become a principal focus. Thus, this kind of design may involve as great a level of complexity (and required level of sophistication) as any of the previously discussed procedures, but the apparent power and value of such a program may warrant the extra effort. Variations on the counterconditioning model that deliver reinforcement contingent upon incompatible behaviors or that focus upon acceleration, rather than deceleration goals, will be considered in Chapter 10.

MODELING

Modeling has also been analyzed by experimentalists and therapists alike for the purpose of determining the manner in which such processes may influence behavior. As noted in Part Two, the concept of modeling, or imitation learning, is the cornerstone of a number of theories of human behavior. In the typical procedure an individual is exposed to the display of a particular response by another member of the same species. After this exposure the influence of the model's response on the observer's behavior is studied. In this chapter the focus will be upon the use of modeling to decelerate pathological behavior.

Perhaps the most obvious use of modeling, or social imitation, is found in procedures that take advantage of the commonplace experiences that prevail in childhood. One of the first therapeutic reports of such a procedure was Jones' (1924b) observation that children who were afraid of rabbits would approach and touch the animals more frequently after observing other children do so. A. Jersild and F. B. Holmes (1935) described a systematic treatment program based upon this observation. Perhaps the most systematic and extensive use of modeling procedures, however, is reported by Bandura and his colleagues. For example, Bandura *et al.* (1967) exposed dog-phobic nursery school children to a fearless peer model, who petted and fed a cocker spaniel while the other children enjoyed a festive party atmosphere. Children thus treated showed greater subsequent reduction of dog-avoidance behavior than control groups exposed to the party alone or to the dog and the party, but without a model. Fear reduction in the experimental group was maintained through a follow-up a month later. A later study (Bandura & Menlove, 1968) demonstrated that the same effects could be obtained using a symbolic filmed presentation of the model's interaction with the dog. This experiment also showed that a child's interacting with many dogs produced greater approach responding in the observing children than a film of a child approaching and petting one dog.

Modeling and desensitization procedures have also been compared. Bandura, E. B. Blanchard, and B. J. Ritter (1968) exposed four groups of snake-phobic subjects to (1) a film of a model interacting progressively with a snake, (2) a live model doing the same, after which each subject could try each step as tolerated, (3) a standard desensitization procedure, and (4) no treatment (control condition). All three experimental groups increased in approach responses, but the live modeling group showed the most gains, with the phobic response eliminated in 92 percent of the members. The latter group's responses also indicated the greatest anxiety reduction on rating and semantic differential scales. Finally, when the film-modeled and desensitization groups were exposed to live models, they, like the modeling group, also approached and held the snake and showed anxiety reduction on rating scales. A systematic replication by Ritter (1968) showed extinction of snake phobia in 53 percent of a group exposed to a live model alone and in 80 percent of a group exposed to a model plus the same kind of guided experience.

Modeling has also been used to treat more complex forms of fear conditions, as well as other behavior problems. Thus, symbolic modeling was used to modify social withdrawal in preschool isolates by R. D. O'Conner (1969). In this experiment one group of nursery school isolates watched a film in which more and more active social interactions between children occurred with positive consequences. They also listened to a sound track that emphasized how appropriately the models were behaving. Control children did not have the benefit of the film and sound track, but watched a film showing social interaction. They showed no change in their withdrawal behaviors. Experimental children, on the other hand, increased their rates of interaction to such an extent that they equaled the rate of such behavior in nonisolated nursery school children.

In an area which has traditionally been resistant to treatment, I. J. Janis and L. Mann (1965) found significant reduction in cigarette smoking in a group trained to engage in "emotional role playing" of patients being told that they had developed lung cancer and could expect only pain, hospitalization, and early death. Even at an eighteen-month follow-up, the experimental group continued to smoke less than the control group, which had heard one of the sessions on tape but had never engaged in the role playing.

Thus, a variety of problem conditions have been decelerated by means of several modeling procedures. In addition, however, the social imitation model has also been adapted for use with other problem conditions, especially when conventional modes of communication are not available. Although the experimenter's focus often was upon increasing response frequency, the extensive nature of the problem conditions involved a concurrent deceleration of other behavioral dimensions. For this reason we have chosen to include these cases in the present review.

Lovaas (1967), Risley (Risley & Wolf, 1967), and others have used imitation training in teaching speech and other operant responses to autistic and retarded children. For example, Lovaas *et al.* (1967) used imitation training of nonverbal responses with food reinforcement. Successive approximations to the behaviors modeled by an adult were reinforced in order to train schizophrenic children in generalized imitation, which was indicated by the child's appropriate matching on the first trial of a novel behavior. Lovaas (1967) has also found that in speech training with autistic children, initial training with food can later be supplemented by social and perhaps even self-generated reinforcers for imitative speech responses. Lovaas (1967) has often observed that as imitative responses are learned, the frequency of pathological responses such as tantrums and self-stimulatory responses decreases. More will be said about this in Chapter 11.

Obviously, modeling or some variant thereof has been used

pragmatically to achieve many forms of behavior modification. As with most of the techniques considered in this chapter, however, the procedure is not univariate. That is, it does not consist of only one dimension or variable, but overlaps several. Thus, for example, Bandura (1969) seems to believe that social imitation can occur on the basis of pure contiguity between stimuli and responses in the presence of a model (which would not require any specific behavior on the part of the observer-learner), whereas J. L. Gewirtz and K. G. Stingle (1968) believe that generalized imitation depends upon reinforcement of a functionally related class of behaviors. (The behaviors, therefore, can be learned only on the basis of performance and reinforcement of the responses.) This issue will be discussed again in Chapter 10. Other important issues include whether or not it is important (or necessary) for the observer to perform guided and perhaps graded imitative responses in order for modification to occur, whether or not learning can occur in one trial, and whether modeling, psychodrama, or desensitization is superior in achieving modification of pathological behaviors. So far the data do not provide clear-cut answers to these questions. The use of imitation learning to accelerate desirable behaviors will be discussed in Chapter 10.

CONCLUSION: EFFICACY OF
OPERANT DECELERATION TREATMENT
The primary objective of the techniques reviewed in this chapter has been response deceleration. That is, each of the treatment procedures has been used to produce a decrease in the frequency of some form of pathological behavior. Though some arbitrary distinctions were made, most of the techniques are primarily employed for this purpose, with the possible exception of modeling, which is more complex than the other procedures and was included in this chapter because of its similarity in emphasis to counterconditioning. Thus, modeling has frequently been used simultaneously to decelerate a pathological behavior (for example, phobic behaviors) as well as to accelerate a constructive behavior.

It is impossible to indicate directly and experimentally the comparative clinical efficacies of the techniques just reviewed. Only a very general outline and the most suggestive kinds of general conclusions can be offered at this time.

Extinction, for example, has not been systematically compared as a clinical prescription to the other deceleration techniques. It has, in several cases, been directly compared with punishment, however, as we shall see in more detail in Chapter 9. Holz and Azrin (1963), for example, in comparing extinction, satiation, punishment, and stimulus change, found that punishment led to a more immediate, complete, and long-lasting reduction of key pecking in pigeons than the other techniques. Tate and Baroff (1966) and Lovaas *et al.* (1965a) found punishment to be more immediate and complete than extinction or time-out from positive reinforcement in the treatment of self-injurious behavior.

On the other hand, extinction would appear to be the treatment of choice for delusional verbalizations, eating problems, and similar behaviors successfully treated by Ayllon and Haughton (1962). In addition Yates (1958a) has had some success in treating tics with his "negative practice" variation of extinction.

Satiation, one of the techniques used unsuccessfully by Holz *et al.* (1963a), has been applied to certain behaviors that have been traditionally difficult to deal with, such as hoarding (Ayllon, 1963) and smoking (Resnick, 1968), although in the latter case it has not yet yielded striking success. Satiation may be particularly appropriate with behaviors that occur at intermediate operant rates, since, under these conditions, large increments in response rates can be realized. This type of treatment may, then, (1) reduce the rate of a response by virtue of the aversive characteristics associated with the high rates, (2) reduce a state of deprivation for whatever reinforcers may have controlled the behavior, or (3) break the ties between the response and previous environmental stimulus control, and bring the response under self-control, with resultant reduction.

Fading, which has been found to be a very important technique, is used in desensitization and in many stimulus control programs, but it is rarely used to the exclusion of other conditioning strategies. For this reason it may be viewed as an adjunctive, rather than as a principal behavior modification technique.

Feedback techniques are most frequently used in combination with self-control, contingency management, or other more programmatic approaches, some of which will be reviewed in Chapter 10. However, Lindsley (1971) and Leitenberg *et al.* (1968) have recently obtained behavior deceleration with independently programmed feedback systems. In addition, the extension of feedback systems into the area of physiological responses (Brenner *et al.,* 1969) has demonstrated some interesting and important possibilities. More research needs to be done with feedback systems, particularly to substantiate or refute the earlier proposed S^D function of feedback. Thus, it would be interesting to determine whether or not the feedback process could function independently to accelerate some behaviors (perhaps positive ones that the subject wishes to increase) as well as to decelerate others (that the subject wishes to eliminate).

Since it combines extinction with positive or negative reinforcement, counterconditioning reaps the advantages of both conditioning procedures. Only a few of the many studies using this popular technique were reviewed here, but properly applied, counterconditioning seems to be one of the most powerful modes of treatment. Its clinical utility probably extends beyond the reduction or elimination of pathological behavior to the shaping of more constructive or normal behaviors. More will be said about counterconditioning from this point of view in Chapter 10.

Imitation training has been a popular clinical practice in one form or another throughout the entire history of behavioral psychotherapy. Similarly, modeling is probably an important aspect of most forms of therapy, since the patient seems to acquire many of the therapist's responses in one way or another. The rapid systematic development of the modeling technique, with the elaboration of a related theoretical structure, is largely due to the efforts of Bandura, who has also provided one of the major studies comparing the efficacy of modeling with that of desensitization. In this study Bandura *et al.* (1968) found that modeling was superior in several ways to desensitization in the treatment of snake phobias.

Chapter 9 / Operant Behavior Modification Procedures: Aversive Techniques

Despite the precautionary note sounded by many writers regarding the use of aversive techniques in clinical practice (Franks, 1966; Rachman & Teasdale, 1969), the popularity of these techniques appears to be increasing. Scientists and practitioners alike have noted the methodological and pragmatic, as well as the moral and ethical, issues involved in the prescription of such techniques. An excellent summary of the issues involved is provided by Baer (1970), and a few comments in addition to his summary will be given in the present orientation.

If aversive techniques are to be successful (that is, permanently reduce or suppress undesirable behavior), the individual must be exposed to stimuli he would otherwise escape or avoid. The ethical question involved in such treatment practices cannot be circumvented by suggesting that the behavior therapist "knows what's best for the patient," as does the surgeon who recommends a painful operation in order to remove an infected organ or other tissue. Aversive techniques, on the whole, probably have not been used clinically or researched thoroughly enough to recommend their use as standard modification techniques.

With most forms of pathological behavior, milder, less aversive techniques, such as extinction, desensitization, counterconditioning, satiation, or fading are usually recommended first, and more extreme aversive techniques are used only as a last resort, when other techniques fail. This would seem to be a good, conservative rule of general clinical practice. Like most rules, however, there are exceptions.

In the case of those few conditions which can cause identifiable physical as well as psychological damage to the individual, an aversive technique might be recommended in order to prevent further injury. Of course, it always helps to have experimental support before making such a recommendation. With self-destructive behaviors such as head banging, the reports of Lovaas *et al.* (1965a) and Tate and Baroff (1966) support the position that an aversive technique such as punishment can produce more rapid response deceleration than extinction. Although more research of this nature is required, in such extreme cases it would seem that immediate application of an aversive technique might be most effective in rapidly eliminating a physically harmful behavior, and would, therefore, be most ethical.

On the other hand, with many behaviors, such as those that might have been acquired or maintained by aversive stimuli, the use of aversive techniques may be contraindicated. For example, the literature dealing with the application of punishment to avoidance behaviors (Brown *et al.,* 1964; Sandler, *et al.,* 1966a; Solomon *et al.,* 1953) has repeatedly demonstrated that such procedures may result in increasing, rather than decreasing, response rates. Perhaps because of such findings, aversive techniques might not be recommended for such clinical behaviors as phobias, which may have been acquired or maintained by aversive stimuli.

Similarly, with cardiac ailments or other physiological states (often subsumed under the clinical rubric of anxiety), aversive techniques may be contraindicated simply because of the possibility of eliciting higher rates or of exacerbating these states. For these reasons the nature of the behavior to be modified, its etiology, or the presence of other conditions may militate against the use of an aversive technique. In brief, much more needs to be accomplished in terms of defining where and when *not* to use aversion therapy.

For the behavior therapist interested in such techniques, a thorough reading of the experimental literature on punishment, beginning with the major reviews (Solomon, 1964; Church, 1963; Azrin & Holtz, 1966) is highly recommended, as well as the several reviews of aversion therapy (Franks, 1966; Rachman & Teasdale, 1969; Kushner & Sandler, 1966; Feldman, 1966). Taken together, this literature indicates the complexity of these techniques, the number of variables requiring control, and the ease of producing perhaps the opposite of the anticipated outcome (for example, an increase rather than a decrease in response rate) as a function of the simple manipulation of one or two variables.

Since this chapter is concerned only with operant techniques, the focus will be upon those procedures in which the consequences rather than the antecedents of a response class are manipulated. (Aversive techniques which manipulate antecedents are an outgrowth of classical conditioning, reviewed in Chapter 7.) Operant aversive techniques are so named because of the functional relationship between a response and a stimulus that the organism would ordinarily avoid or escape. In the punishment procedure the stimulus is typically delivered contingent upon a response. In the same way that positive reinforcement is best defined functionally as the delivery of any stimulus following a response that produces an increase in the future probability of that response, punishment is best defined as the contingent delivery of any stimulus that results in a decrement in the future probability of a response (Azrin & Holz, 1966). Although this definition may appear to be circular, it is actually very helpful, since it (1) focuses upon the function of a stimulus in a particular context, (2) allows the possibility that a given stimulus (for example, a particular intensity of electric shock) may be a punisher on one occasion (for example, contingent upon a positively reinforced response) and not on another (for example, contingent upon a negatively reinforced response), (3) is consistent with general reinforcement theory (for example, is the opposite of the definition of positive reinforcement) and, (4) allows the development of transsituational punishers (for example, a particular intensity of electric shock, which may meet the definitional criteria across many positively reinforced responses).

One class of punishing events that may meet all of the requirements of the above definition is time-out from positive reinforcement (TO). This technique is defined procedurally as the removal of positive reinforcement contingent upon a response. Thus, following the occurrence of an undesirable response, positive reinforcement may be withdrawn from the organism for a preset period of time. Some discussion of both laboratory and clinical use of this technique will follow.

Escape and avoidance procedures are the other traditional aversive techniques. In escape conditioning the occurrence of a response removes an aversive stimulus, and in avoidance conditioning a response postpones the occurrence of the aversive stimulus. Since both of these techniques produce an increase in the probability or frequency of a response, they are regarded as examples of negative reinforcement. That is, they serve the same function as positive reinforcement (producing an increase in response rate), but they do so through the removal or postponement of a stimulus, rather than by producing a stimulus as in positive reinforcement.

Thus, time-out and punishment have in common a predominant focus upon the deceleration of behaviors. Escape and avoidance conditioning, on the other hand, may also increase the frequency of some behaviors through negative reinforcement.

TIME-OUT FROM POSITIVE REINFORCEMENT
Perhaps the mildest form of punishment is the response-contingent removal of reinforcement (Leitenberg, 1965). In a typical time-out (TO) experimental procedure, the subject first acquires a bar-press

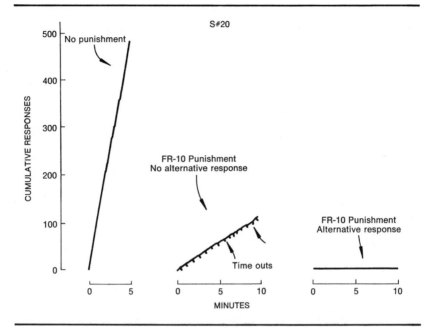

Figure 40. *Comparison of the effectiveness of time-out from reinforcement as punishment with and without the availability of an alternative response for securing reinforcement. Left curve shows responding maintained by a 5-minute variable interval schedule of cigarette reinforcement (reinforcements not indicated). Center curve shows the moderate level of responses which ultimately resulted when thirty-second time-outs were scheduled as punishment for every tenth response. The same variable interval reinforcement schedule remained in effect. Right curve shows the absence of punished responses during the same time-out punishment schedule when an unpunished alternative response was made available. (From Holz et al., 1963)*

response by means of positive reinforcement; then during the time-out period the behavior is no longer reinforced. The time-out period may or may not be accompanied by an exteroceptive stimulus.

A commonplace example of time-out is provided by the parent who sends a child to his room for fighting at the dinner table, thereby denying him dessert.

Holz *et al.* (1963) demonstrated the effectiveness of time-out with hospitalized mental patients, who were trained to press a button at a high rate for points, which could be exchanged for privileges. When responses were followed by preset periods of time-out from this reinforcement, the rate of button pressing declined, but it did not reach zero. When an alternative response also provided reinforcement, time-out from reinforcement of the original response was effective in completely eliminating the response. These differences are revealed in Figure 40. This led the investigators to conclude

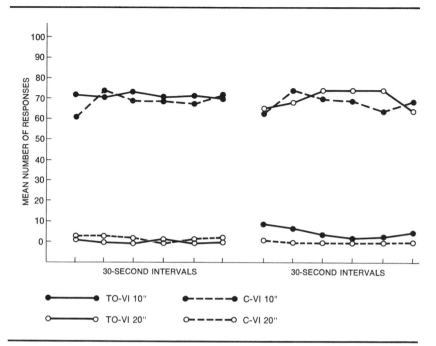

Figure 41. *Mean response rate on variable-interval, ten-second and variable-interval, twenty-second manipulanda by TO and control groups before and after exposure of TO groups (solid lines) to TO. (From Willoughby, 1969)*

that TO may be even more effective in eliminating behavior if the overall frequency of reinforcement can be maintained by means of an alternative unpunished response.

R. H. Willoughby (1969) performed a systematic replication of the Holz study, again comparing the effects of punishing a single response with the effects of TO when an unpunished response was also available. The subjects were sixty preschool children, who were trained to press a lever on a variable-interval schedule of reinforcement. TO was then administered for ten seconds following every seventh response, which reduced the response rate for a short period by about 25 percent. In a second experiment responses on one of two levers were reinforced more frequently, which produced a preference for that lever. When TO was delivered contingent upon presses on the preferred bar, the subjects switched to the formerly unpreferred lever, even though the frequency of reinforcement on the two levers was the same, as can be seen in Figure 41.

Taken together, these two experiments demonstrate rather clearly that even a brief time-out from positive reinforcement may suppress or eliminate a response in humans, particularly when an alternative unpunished response produces reinforcement. Although

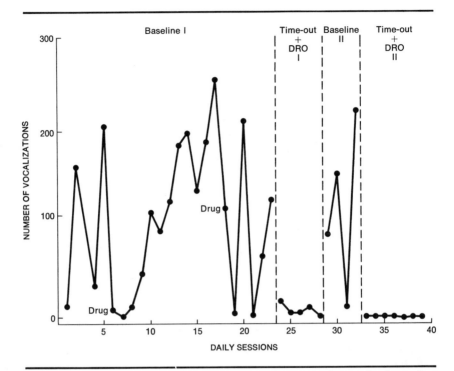

Figure 42. *Number of vocalizations per one-hour session under base-line and time-out plus DRO (differential reinforcement of other behavior) conditions. (From Bostow & Bailey, 1969)*

the responses in these two experiments were simple motor behaviors rather than clinical behaviors, the implication is clear that time-out might similarly affect any well-maintained and controlled behavior.

In a test of clinical effectiveness, D. E. Bostow and J. B. Bailey (1969) employed a variation of the TO procedure in order to modify severe and chronic disruptive and aggressive behaviors in two retarded patients in a state hospital. Positive reinforcement was delivered following appropriate behaviors, and brief TO (physical removal to an isolated booth or a corner of the room) was applied contingent upon loud vocalizations in one patient and aggressive behavior in another. This procedure reduced the two pathological behaviors, which had been chronic and severe, to near-zero rates. These changes are revealed in Figure 42. One reversal demonstrated even more conclusively that TO was responsible for the change, when the pathological responses increased again following removal of the contingencies. This effect, in turn, was followed by a second reduction to low rates when TO and reinforcement for appropriate behavior were reintroduced. This study, then, clearly indicates that TO can be very effective with pathological behaviors, even when they are of rather severe intensity and lengthy history. The authors also commented that TO procedures were instituted without undue disturbance of normal ward routine.

C. Keutzer (1967) and Davidson (1969) have both used therapy time as a reinforcer and time-out from therapy as a punisher for treatment purposes. Keutzer modified a standard psychotherapeutic procedure to use time allowed in therapy as a reinforcer to help a neurotic woman increase or accelerate desirable study habits. Similarly, Davidson reported the effective use of time-out from therapy to suppress reports of psychosomatic-like complaints. In this study the patient was a chronic, male veteran schizophrenic who had been seen for several successive years by several therapists in an outpatient VA facility. Over the years the patient's highest frequency of verbalizations centered on physical complaints, for example, that he had contracted cancer, despite repeated physical examinations testifying to his good health. Since he was punctual for his therapy appointments and seemed to have good rapport with his therapist, it was decided to use therapy time as a reinforcer for talk about topics other than his physical complaints. Thus, he was instructed that in the future his therapy session would end as soon as he verbalized a physical complaint. In the next session following these instructions, he mentioned a physical complaint ten minutes after the hour began, and the therapy session was immediately terminated in accord with the earlier instructions. In the following session conversation centered on more constructive topics for a half hour, and in the next session, for forty-five minutes. Thereafter, there were virtually no references to physical symptoms. Again, time-out seemed to have been an effective punisher of pathological behavior, with TO duration contingent upon patient behavior, rather than being preset, as in the standard procedure.

In another interesting study V. O. Tyler and G. D. Brown (1967) used a TO procedure that has been employed with increasing frequency in institutional settings. This technique involves physically removing a subject (frequently a child) to a TO room, which is used only for this form of punishment. Typically this condition is maintained for a preset duration or until the undesirable behavior has ended. In this study the TO room was an unfurnished four-by-eight-foot room, and a subject was placed there for fifteen minutes immediately following an undesirable response. The subjects were fifteen male residents, thirteen to fifteen years old, in a treatment center for delinquents. Undesirable responses included breaking the rules during a pool game, throwing balls, and other aggressive behaviors. These behaviors had previously been followed by warnings, suspension from play, or termination of the activity. During a seven-week test period, the misbehaving individual was simply escorted to the TO room and left there for fifteen minutes, which markedly reduced the frequency of misbehaving. To test for any lasting effects, the TO contingency was removed, with only verbal reprimands following misbehavior. During thirteen weeks of this control condition (actually a reinstatement of the earlier ineffective conditions), the rate of misbehaviors showed a rapid increase. In a final twenty-week period TO was reintroduced, and misbehavior again rapidly decreased to a very low rate.

Thus, this study demonstrated that a TO procedure consisting of physical isolation and time-out from the ordinarily available reinforcers, none of which were specifically programmed or controlled, may be very effective in reducing the rate of several undesirable behaviors in a group setting.

For those interested in using time-out clinically or experimentally, recommended readings include Leitenberg (1965), T. Verhave (1962), and Ferster (1958, 1960). It should be kept in mind that the effectiveness of TO in modifying behavior is derived from denying the subject access to a particular schedule of positive reinforcement. Thus, time-out from negative or otherwise aversive schedules might be expected generally to *facilitate* behavior (Verhave, 1962, 1966), while time-out from positive reinforcement may often reveal suppressive effects akin to other punishers. In school settings, for example, sending a child from an aversive classroom to the principal's office contingent upon inappropriate talking might increase the frequency of such talking, while sending the same child out of a favorite class might be expected to decrease the frequency of the same response. Thus, the effects of TO cannot be assessed independent of the type of reinforcement schedule with which it is associated.

PUNISHMENT

Perhaps the most common approach to the modification of undesirable behavior in society generally involves the response-contingent application of a noxious stimulus designed to reduce response frequency. As described earlier, there is an extensive body of experimental literature which may be relevant to the clinical use of punishment techniques. An excellent review of the literature regarding the punishment of human behavior has recently been provided by Johnston (1972). Many of the issues raised in this section are thoroughly explored in this paper, and it would appear to be of invaluable assistance to the clinical investigator. Unfortunately, this information has had little impact on clinical practice because of its recency and/or its focus upon basic operations. Nevertheless, there is good reason to believe that it is of considerable import to behavior modification. This chapter will briefly acquaint the reader with some of this material and review more extensively the use of punishment procedures in clinical contexts. Throughout this discussion the major distinction between the basic literature and the applied efforts will be in terms of the kinds of responses (that is, pathological or otherwise) modified, although the greater complexity of the behavior in most clinical and applied cases is acknowledged.

With regard to basic processes, punishment represents one of the more thoroughly analyzed topics in experimental psychology. As we saw earlier, a number of excellent reviews are available, and the interested reader is directed to these major sources of information. Some of the most important basic work regarding the analysis of the effects of punishment on operant behavior that also has clinical implications has been provided by Azrin and his associates (for example, Azrin & Holz, 1966). Suffice it to say that the effects of punishment on positively reinforced operant behavior depend upon reinforcement and punishment schedules, contingency with behavior, temporal delay, duration, intensity and frequency, etc. This knowledge provides a foundation for the application of punishment in the treatment of at least some pathological conditions. On the other hand, the effects of punishment on negatively reinforced behavior are not nearly as well identified. In fact, the data from such investigations have caused considerable difficulty at the theoretical level (see the introduction to this chapter) and provide good reason for exercising caution at the treatment level. Nevertheless, the use of punishment for therapeutic purposes continues, and a number of studies are available that report successful outcomes.

A series of investigations designed to modify stuttering serves as an overview of the manner in which basic procedures have been variously employed.

Flanagan *et al.* (1958, 1959), for example, have indicated how stuttering can be controlled by aversive response-contingent consequences. In the first experiment three adult male stutterers read assigned passages, while the experimenters manually recorded each dysfluency. After stuttering stabilized, punishment (a one-second blast of a 6,000 hertz tone at 105 decibels) was delivered contingent upon each stuttering response. This resulted in a markedly decreased rate of stuttering, which increased again once the punishment contingency was removed, as shown in Figure 43. Flanagan *et al.* (1959) also found an increase in stuttering with escape from shock as the controlling contingency, suggesting that at least some kinds of stuttering may be motivated by this form of stress, and that removal of the aversive contingency may, in some cases, alleviate the condition.

In a more comprehensive program developed later, Goldiamond (1965b) instructed stutterers to read assigned passages aloud for fifty-minute periods. This provided a measure of the base rate of stuttering, as well as a measure of the overall rate of reading. During the treatment phase the rate of reading was reduced by a slower mechanical presentation of the material, and punishment was delivered by the subject himself, who pressed a microswitch each time he stuttered. In this case punishment was a 250-millisecond delayed auditory feedback through earphones of the subject's own voice. This procedure established slow, stutterless reading in thirty subjects in ten to fifty sessions. (See Figure 44.) Once this dysfluency-free behavior was established, the duration of delayed auditory feedback (DFB in Figure 44) was gradually faded, and the rate of presentation of material was increased (T/C).

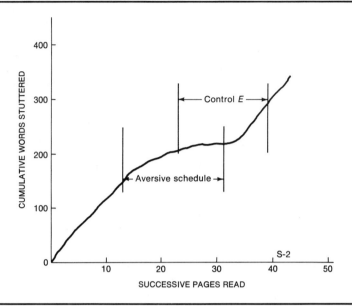

Figure 43. *Cumulative record of words stuttered in aversive and non-aversive (control) periods, with two different experimenters. (From Flanagan et al., 1958)*

In this manner fluent and rapid reading was maintained under laboratory conditions, although no report is available as to whether these improvements persisted outside the laboratory. This is another apparently effective method using response-contingent punishment to suppress and maintain the rate of pathological behavior at near zero, at least within the conditions of the laboratory.

Soderberg (1968) has systematically replicated and extended the work of Goldiamond. Thus, Soderberg found that delayed auditory feedback slowed the speech rate of eleven student stutterers and suppressed their rate of stuttering. He also reported that the suppressive effects of delayed auditory feedback persisted after removal of the contingency, allowing shaping of dysfluency-free reading rate to higher levels. Soderberg also reported that delayed auditory feedback was more effective in reducing stuttering than was auditory masking.

As mentioned earlier, one of the more extensive clinical uses of punishment has been with self-injurious behaviors, probably because such problems have been resistant to treatment and require immediate intervention. Tate and Baroff (1966), for example, worked with a partially blind nine-year-old psychotic boy who banged his head, slapped his face, and kicked himself at the rate of five to eight times per minute, thereby endangering himself to permanent visual impairment. The first phase of treatment consisted of contingent re-

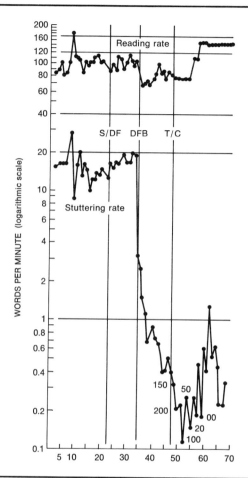

Figure 44. *Reduction in stuttering rate and establishment of fluent reading in a chronic stutterer. (From Goldiamond, 1965b)*

moval of physical contact and conversation with the boy for three seconds after each self-striking response. This contingency reduced self-striking responses to less than one per minute. Return to the control condition indicated rates that were still lower than initial base rates (now one to three responses per minute in four periods, nine responses per minute in one period). Reintroduction of the extinction condition led to another decrease, but not as great a one as the initial reduction (a rate ranging from .75 to 1.5 responses per minute). In the last treatment phase response-contingent electric shock, combined with verbal praise for desirable behavior, reduced self-injurious responding to zero. These gains were apparently maintained for a long period thereafter. Furthermore, whereas the boy had previously been physically restrained in bed, following the treatment program he participated in daily activities and showed an increase in other constructive behaviors.

In a similar case Risley (1968) attempted counterconditioning of dangerous climbing in a six-year-old girl, who had injured herself as a result of frequent falls. When climbing behavior was ignored and incompatible responses reinforced, little change resulted. Similarly, brief confinement in a TO room also proved ineffective. Administration of several shocks combined with verbal reprimands, soon eliminated the climbing in the presence of the experimenter. The effect did not generalize to the home, however, and the mother was also trained to punish the behavior with shock, with the result that frequency of climbing in the home was reduced from twenty to two responses per day. In addition, several improvements in social functioning were observed. Thus, the girl became more attentive and responsive, which allowed the learning of many new constructive behaviors. (Other similar reports of generalized effects of aversive as well as other forms of behavior therapy will be reviewed in Chapter 11.)

Lovaas has also reported several cases of rapid suppression of self-destructive behaviors such as head banging by punishment contingencies. For example, B. Bucher and Lovaas (1968) report the cases of two schizophrenic children who had engaged in self-mutilating behavior for five or six years. One, a boy who was usually kept physically restrained, beat himself 3,000 times in ninety minutes after removal of the restraints. This behavior was virtually eliminated in four sessions by applying twelve response-contingent shocks. The second subject, a girl, had banged her head with high frequency for six years, and only fifteen intense shocks combined with verbal reprimands ("no") suppressed the behavior to near zero in one session. Figure 45 shows constructive changes in three measures observed by the investigators. Again, in these cases punishment seemed not only to reduce the pathological behavior quickly, but also resulted in increased attentiveness to the therapists and an increased probability of newer, more constructive learning.

Considerable interest has also been expressed in the use of aversion therapy with sexual deviations, probably, again, because they have been resistant to conventional treatment and because of the strong legal and social prohibitions against such behavior (Kushner & Sandler, 1966). The literature in this area is rapidly expanding (Feldman, 1966), and a number of innovative techniques have been reported. The focus here will be limited to several of the more promising recent trends.

I. M. Marks and M. G. Gelder (1967) have reported an interesting study of shock punishment of sexual deviations (transvestism and fetishism) with five patients, who revealed few other pathological forms of behavior, were cooperative, and were motivated to change. A variable ratio of shock was presented contingent upon performance of the pathological response, in vivo, and in fantasy, at the subject's signal. A transducer was used to measure penile erection,

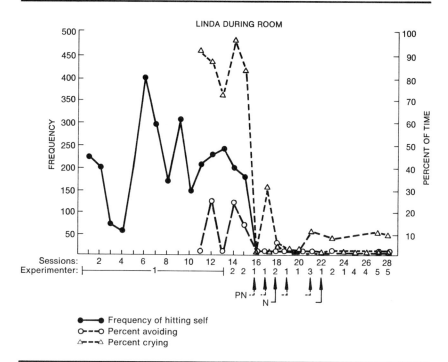

Figure 45. *The frequency of Linda's self-destructive behavior and the percentage of avoiding and crying, in the living room, as a function of shock. The ordinate gives sessions and the particular experimenter present during these sessions. Shock (P) and/or "no" (N) was administered by experimenter 1 during sessions 16, 17, 19 and 22, by experimenter 2 in session 18, and experimenter 3 in session 21. (From Bucher & Lovaas, 1968)*

which occurred regularly during instructed performance prior to treatment, but was suppressed by shock punishment. Fantasy images of these pathological behaviors were also suppressed by shock, became indistinct, lost their "pleasurable" sensations, and were no longer accompanied by erections. On the other hand, unpunished images did not show suppression and similar changes. Associated attitudes, autonomic changes, and closely related symptoms also decreased. The target behaviors (transvestism and fetishism) showed marked improvement during treatment, but were not followed up long enough to warrant reports of stable changes. As in the reports of Lovaas *et al.* (1965b), Bucher and Lovaas (1968), and Risley (1968), many changes representing improvement were noted, although, in this case, since no reversals or other controls were used, it is impossible to pinpoint the exact reason for the change.

The Marks and Gelder study is similar to J. R. Cautela's (1967) technique of "covert sensitization." In this form of treatment neither the undesirable stimuli (or behaviors) nor the aversive stimulus is actually presented to the subject. Instead, the subject is instructed to rehearse the pathological behavior in fantasy and then to imagine some punishment. Frequently a natural aversive consequence may be selected as the instructed punishment image. Alcoholic subjects, for example, might be instructed to imagine walking into a bar and ordering a drink, which then causes the experience of nausea and, finally, vomiting. Embarrassment and other unpleasant social reactions may also be described to the subject.

Although it is still too early to judge the experimental and/or clinical efficacy of covert sensitization, several studies have been reported with somewhat varied results. Cautela (1967), for example, has applied this technique to a variety of clinical problems, including homosexuality, delinquency, and such compulsive behaviors as smoking, alcoholism, and overeating. Ashem and Donner (1968) report that of a group of fifteen alcoholic patients treated by covert sensitization, six were still abstinent after a period of six months. Anant (1966, 1967a, 1967b) has also done a great deal of work with covert sensitization, or verbal aversion, as he calls it. In this variation the patient is instructed to imagine various responses associated with drinking and, as consequences, to imagine situations involving social shame or degradation. Unfortunately, Anant's reports show decreasing success over time. For example, in one early report twenty-five alcoholics who were treated by verbal aversion in either a group or an individual situation, were reported abstinent over follow-up periods ranging from eight to fifteen months. In a later report, however, only three of fifteen patients, who were treated on a group basis, were still sober on follow-up, six to twenty-three months later.

Obviously, it is important, both theoretically and clinically, to determine whether a method such as covert sensitization is as effective as other more standard punishment techniques, since it does not require any special apparatus or perhaps as much retraining of the clinician in special techniques.

Cautela's attempt with alcoholics is one of a long series of punishment procedures designed to treat this chronic problem condition. Although many such techniques have been developed and discarded and no one effective treatment has been devised, the effort is very much a continuing one.

One approach to the modification of alcoholic behavior resulting from an analysis of basic punishment effects has recently been initiated by Davidson (1972a, b, c). In an earlier study Davidson (1970a) found that shock, paired with reinforcement and increased from low to high intensity, revealed several effects as a result of changes in intensity alone. At low intensities the shock had no effect on behavior; at intermediate intensities response rate increased and at high intensities the shock resulted in behavioral suppression. After demonstrating these effects with rats, Davidson showed that a similar schedule and procedure produced the same effects in alcoholic patients.

In the clinical application subjects were first administered a questionnaire designed to determine alcoholic preferences and daily quantities consumed. In the first few conditioning sessions upper and lower shock thresholds were subjectively determined. Once these were established, each patient was instructed to work at his own rate on a console that automatically delivered a small shot (two cubic centimeters) of the preferred alcoholic beverage diluted 50 percent with water after the subject completed thirty responses (FR 30) on a candy vendor plunger. Once the subject stabilized on this schedule, thus providing a base line, shock was introduced contingent upon the reinforced response (each thirtieth response), and gradually increased in intensity.

Subjects consistently showed no change in response rate at low intensities; responses were facilitated in some cases at slightly higher intensities and then suppressed to zero (response cessation) at the terminal intensities, as revealed in Figure 46. Once the criterion of cessation was reached, the shock electrodes were removed, and the subject was allowed to respond in the absence of shock. Eighty to 90 percent of the subjects did not respond under these conditions, and similarly did not respond upon return to the hospital later for follow-up observations. Forty percent of these subjects remained abstinent outside the hospital; another 25 percent drank at low rates, after showing preferences for new (untreated) beverages, over follow-up periods of one to four years. Three subjects out of fifteen drank for a few days to a few weeks, then stopped, reporting they became nauseous and vomited.

In addition, most of the patients who stopped drinking reported that they found employment and remained employed for longer than they had worked for up to ten years previously. Thus, this study seems to demonstrate possible generalized effects produced by an aversive schedule similar to the studies of Lovaas *et al.* (1965b) and Bucher and Lovaas (1968).

Finally, punishment procedures are being applied in a number of atypical situations, frequently with surprising success. For example, an interesting application of punishment contingencies to writer's cramp has been reported by L. A. Liversedge and J. D. Sylvester (1955). This form of motor impairment is usually attributed to fatigue, nervous and emotional problems, etc., and evidently occurs with relatively high frequency in Great Britain, where the Liversedge and Sylvester work was done.

Liversedge and Sylvester defined writer's cramp as hand tremors and muscular spasms in writing tasks. Of the thirty-nine cases treated, although few of the subjects showed similar psychological or personality characteristics, all were ordinarily able to use the hand muscles in nonwriting tasks without evidence of tremor or spasm. It would seem, therefore, that reinforcement contingencies specific to the writing situation (such as escape or avoidance conditioning) may have been involved in these pathological conditions.

Two pieces of apparatus were used to treat muscular spasms.

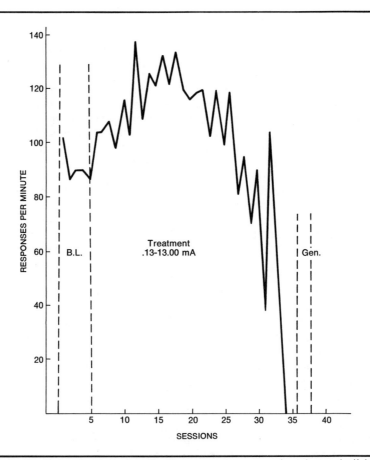

Figure 46. *Rate of plunger pulls (in responses per minute) per half-hour treatment session on FR 30 (thirty pulls delivered two cubic centimeter alcohol reinforcement), through base line (no shock), treatment with reinforced response-contingent shock of .13 to 13 milliamperes intensity and generalization (no shock). (From Davidson, 1972a)*

One delivered shock whenever excessive thumb pressure, which was measured with a pressure guage, was applied to a pen, and the other delivered shock whenever the subject deviated from a path cut through a metal maze. In the treatment of tremors the subject was required to insert a metal stylus into a series of progressively smaller holes in a metal chassis, which was electrified so that shock punishment resulted when the stylus made contact with the sides of the holes.

According to the authors, normal writing was regained and maintained in twenty-four of the thirty-nine subjects for up to 4½ years after three to six weeks' treatment. Of the remaining fifteen subjects, ten showed no improvement, and five improved but later relapsed. The ten failures had a longer history (six to twenty-one years) of writer's cramp than the other subjects, which might partially explain the failure.

Although punishment is probably the oldest and most frequently used technique for modifying behavior, it is also the most controversial, especially in regard to its clinical use. Even if the practitioner can resolve the ethical problems to his own satisfaction, there still remains the question of practical efficacy. In this connection, it is important to remember that many variables contribute to the optimal punishment arrangement. In terms of our earlier discussion, the two major components of punishment technology are the variables governing response history and the variables governing the punishment event. Most of the studies to date have focused upon the latter component, and although much important information has been provided, the former area has been seriously neglected. Two important exceptions, as we have seen, are Azrin's work leading to important information regarding the interaction between behavior with a positive-reinforcement history and relevant parameters of the punishment condition, and the work on punishment of negatively reinforced behaviors.

Much more needs to be done before a satisfactory foundation of information has been established for the implementation of punishment techniques in treatment. For this reason alone, as we have continuously emphasized, a conservative rule of thumb would, in general, restrict the use of punishment as a last-order form of treatment to be used under highly circumscribed conditions.

By the same token, however, information is rapidly accumulating, so that some tentative conclusions can be made regarding a systematic approach to the clinical use of punishment. First, with regard to historical variables, it seems clear that a distinction should be made between those conditions in which negative reinforcement is a prominent feature and those characterized predominantly by positive reinforcement. Punishment in the former circumstances may lead to an increase in the behavior, rather than suppression. Even in the latter case, however, caution should be exercised, since the punishing stimulus may acquire positive-reinforcement properties, and stimuli associated with the punisher may acquire conditioned punishment properties, thereby impairing other components of the treatment interaction.

With regard to punishment variables, the situation at present is much more definitive. A considerable body of literature has been amassed regarding the optimal conditions for demonstrating the punishment effect. In this connection Azrin and Holz (1966) have pointed out several advantages of shock over other stimuli: (1) Shock can be precisely specified and measured in physical units, (2) it makes constant contact with the subject; (3) the ability of the subject to make unauthorized escape or avoidance responses can be limited; (4) shock may be varied over a wide range of values to produce different effects, and it elicits few strong and enduring skeletal reactions, and (5) shock does not require medical supervision. Therefore, as Rachman and Teasdale (1969) have also indicated, shock has both clinical and experimental advantages over the use of many other stimuli. This may explain the recent proliferation of studies using clinical applications of punishment paradigms with electric shock.

On the other hand, the traditional reluctance to employ shock on the part of both the patient and the therapist suggests that alternative aversive events should be made available. As we have seen, considerable ingenuity has been exercised in this regard. Thus, investigators have used a wide variety of stimuli from delayed auditory feedback to imagined scenes, as in covert sensitization. The search for other alternatives continues. Lazarus (1968), for example, has offered a challenging argument based upon clinical observations which suggest that punishment may be enhanced by matching the modality of the aversive stimulus to the modality of the behavior to be modified. Thus, he posits that white noise may be most effective in suppressing auditory hallucinations, tactile stimuli such as electric shock might be of benefit in suppressing motor compulsions, and an aversive olfactory stimulus (a foul mixture of smelling salts) might be the best suppressor of compulsive eating. Not enough research has yet been conducted to determine the validity of these hypotheses.

Aside from these considerations a number of other important questions remain to be resolved. Among these questions are: How effective are punishment paradigms compared to other aversive techniques and to appetitive approaches? How durable are the effects of punishment procedures? How often do punishment techniques produce generalized beneficial effects, as reported by Lovaas, et al. (1965b), Bucher and Lovaas (1968), and Davidson (1972b), as well as undesirable side effects?

ESCAPE CONDITIONING

Operant escape conditioning can be defined procedurally as the presentation of an aversive stimulus, the termination of which is contingent upon some operant behavior. The usual effect of such conditioning is an increase in the future probability of the operant response. J. A. Dinsmoor (1968) has found, for example, that learning under such contingencies follows the general principles governing other similar behaviors. Furthermore, escape conditioning is possible under variable ratio, variable interval, and fixed ratio schedules of negative reinforcement (Dinsmoor, 1962, 1968).

Escape conditioning has not been used as widely, either in the laboratory or clinic, as have other aversive techniques, perhaps because, by the very nature of the technique, the aversive stimulus is usually delivered at higher frequencies and/or longer durations than in any other technique. Thus, in most clinical applications this technique is combined with an avoidance procedure in order to enable the reduction or elimination of the aversive stimulus through "efficient" behavior.

For example, in a study that involved punishment as well as escape and avoidance conditioning (Baer, 1962), cartoon viewing by children was interrupted whenever they sucked their thumbs. In addition, the cartoons were reinstated contingent upon thumb removal, which constituted the escape paradigm. It was also possible for the children to avoid the cartoon interruption by refraining from thumb-sucking. Such treatment was effective in controlling this behavior in three five-year-old boys.

As another example of combined escape and avoidance conditioning, Feldman (1966) and his colleagues (Feldman & MacCulloch, 1965; MacCulloch, Feldman, & Pinshoff, 1965) have developed one of the most successful techniques yet reported for treatment of homosexuality. In this procedure each patient viewed a projected slide of a nude male. After eight seconds of viewing, a painful electric shock was delivered and maintained until the patient responded by closing a switch that automatically terminated shock, removed the male slide, and projected a female nude slide. Responses that occurred in less than eight seconds resulted in shock avoidance. Although homosexual behavior is usually resistant to modification, ten out of sixteen patients showed complete cessation of homosexual fantasy and behavior and some increase in heterosexual behavior or fantasy (Feldman & MacCulloch, 1965). Feldman (1966) later found a similar modification in eighteen of twenty-six patients three to twenty-four months after therapy.

In a study previously reviewed, Lovaas, *et al.* (1965b) used escape-avoidance training to teach two autistic children to approach adults. Prior to conditioning the children showed no evidence of social responsivity, speech, or play appropriate to their age (five). Instead, they engaged in self-stimulatory and bizarre behaviors, which had not responded to traditional therapy. In Lovaas' procedure the command "Come here" was followed by shock presented through a grid floor until the child moved in the direction of the therapist (escape conditioning). Eventually, both children learned to approach the therapist soon after the verbal conditioned stimulus (avoidance) as shown in Figure 47. In addition, these changes were again accompanied by a reduction in pathological behaviors as well as an increase in constructive behaviors, such as paying attention to adults, displaying affection, and other social behaviors. (See Figure 48.) In this case an apparently simple and straightforward aversive conditioning procedure seemed to result in several important constructive changes, most of which were maintained over many months.

J. G. Thorpe, *et al.* (1964) designed a combination punishment-escape arrangement which has been used recently by a number of clinicians. In this procedure termed aversion relief therapy, the patient is instructed to say a symptom-related word (for example, "homosexual"), after which shock is presented and maintained until

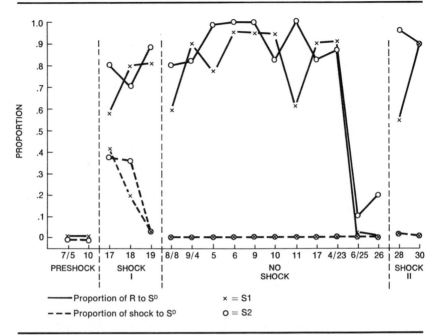

Figure 47. *Proportion of time the twins responded to the experimenter's commands* (*proportion of R to S^D*) *in relation to shock administration, and proportion of shock to S^D* (*commands*). (*From Lovaas, et al., 1965*)

the patient says a symptom-incompatible word (for example, "heterosexual"). Variations of this technique have employed masturbation and nude slides instead of verbalizations. This procedure has reportedly been effective in reducing anxiety and phobic, homosexual, transvestite, and overeating behaviors. The technique also has implications for self-control, since the subject may perform the escape response (for example, the symptom-incompatible word) whenever necessary.

P. E. Gendreau and P. C. Dodwell (1968) report the effective reduction of cigarette smoking via a shock-escape procedure. In their program shock was administered until the subject extinguished his cigarette. In addition, the shock intensity was increased so that it became more and more painful. Differences between experimental and control groups were detected both at the end of treatment and two years later.

In a recent application of escape conditioning, R. E. Vogler *et al.* (1970) served liquor to alcoholic patients in a simulated bar. Upon drinking, the patients received a shock, which was maintained until they spat the drink into a spittoon. In this study, one of the first carefully controlled conditioning approaches to alcoholism, one group of alcoholics was treated only during hospitalization, and a second group received booster treatments in addition to hospital

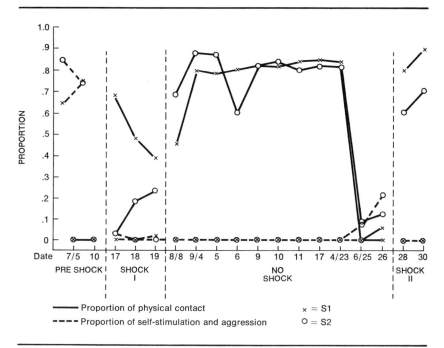

Figure 48. *Proportion of self-stimulation and tantrums (pathological behaviors) and physical contact (social behaviors) in twins, as a function of shock administration. (From Lovaas, et al., 1965)*

treatment following discharge. Control observations included pseudoconditioning (random shock), sham conditioning (no shock), and routine ward treatment. Follow-up data revealed no differences between the three control groups, which were then pooled and compared with the experimental groups. The findings demonstrated a significant increase in time before there was a relapse in the experimental subjects. The authors further commented that booster treatment sessions were helpful and that several patients showed long-term effects of treatment.

In summary, although several variations on escape conditioning have been experimentally tested, none of them seems to have become very popular. As suggested previously, part of the reason is probably inherent in the kind of stimulus control that emerges under these circumstances. That is, the procedure requires that a given response be produced in the presence of an aversive stimulus. As a consequence, responding may ultimately occur only in the presence of the aversive stimulus once good schedule control has been established. Clinicians (and perhaps experimentalists, too) seem to have preferred arrangements in which emitted responses remove or eliminate an aversive stimulus even before it occurs, as in avoidance.

Nevertheless, Thorpe, Lovaas, and Vogler have reported escape conditioning techniques with potential long-range treatment effects. More research in this area would help isolate clinically relevant variables.

AVOIDANCE CONDITIONING

As already indicated, avoidance conditioning is a procedure in which responding postpones an aversive stimulus prior to its occurrence. When the same response terminates an ongoing aversive stimulus as well as postponing it, the procedure is usually defined as escape-avoidance conditioning. In comparison to other learning paradigms, even simple avoidance conditioning is a highly complex phenomenon. As a result there has been a long and heated debate regarding the explanation of avoidance responding. A brief review may aid in clarifying the issues at hand.

On a purely empirical level, the mystery centers on an explanation of the maintenance of avoidance responses, which, by definition, occur in the absence of the aversive stimulus. Most two-factor theorists seem to agree that avoidance conditioning is characterized by a cyclic process in which each new encounter with the aversive stimulus reconditions fear, the fear then motivating a fresh cycle of avoidance responding, which then, more or less slowly, extinguishes and brings the organism in contact with the aversive stimulus again. The data, however, do not always support such predictions. As mentioned previously, particularly in traumatic avoidance (Solomon *et al.*, 1953, see Figure 31; Campbell *et al.*, 1964) initial contact with a highly noxious stimulus may apparently result in avoidance responding that may endure indefinitely. In some cases responses learned in this fashion have persisted for long periods of time despite the complete removal of all aversive consequences.

A competing explanatory system, which is more parsimonious and empirical (Herrnstein, 1969), proposes that organisms respond on avoidance schedules to reduce the frequency or density of aversive stimulation. By logical extension this system might explain the short-term maintenance of avoidance responding in the absence of aversive stimulation, but like other explanatory systems, it does not adequately explain long-term avoidance behavior. It is apparently, then, the long-term maintenance phenomenon that has attracted many clinicians to the avoidance model, as an analog of the etiology of phobic learning (Wolpe, 1952, 1962) as well as for its treatment possibilities.

Combinations of treatment-oriented escape and avoidance conditioning reviewed in the last section will again be mentioned in passing. The work of Feldman (1966) and his colleagues (Feldman & MacCulloch, 1965; MacCulloch *et al.*, 1965) has stimulated the wide use of the anticipatory avoidance conditioning model for the treatment of homosexuality and, with less success, of alcoholism (MacCulloch *et al.,* 1966.)

In the typical procedure with homosexuals, the patient establishes hierarchies of attractiveness of clothed and unclothed male and female images on projected slides. The patient then reports the intensity of shock that is very unpleasant. Next, the patient is told he will see a male picture and that several seconds later he might receive a shock. He is also instructed that he can turn off the slide by pressing a switch whenever he wishes to do so, but that he should leave it on as long as he finds the slide sexually attractive. Shock is terminated or postponed contingent upon each switch press. The patient is also instructed to say "no" when he wishes the slide to be removed, in addition to pressing the switch. The authors report that the usual course of treatment progresses through several escape trials, then several trials of mixed escape and avoidance, and ends in a series of trials during which the patient avoids shock on each trial. After three consecutive avoidance trials, an intermittent shock schedule is introduced. Occasionally, female nudes are projected contingent upon switch presses, in addition to male nude removal and shock termination.

As noted in the last section, ten out of sixteen patients treated by this method showed complete cessation of homosexual fantasy and behavior during therapy and reported occurrence of heterosexual fantasy or behavior outside of therapy. A later report (Feldman, 1966) showed similar modification in eighteen of twenty-six patients, which was maintained through three to twenty-four months of follow-up therapy.

Feldman and MacCulloch (1965), in agreement with the two-process theory of avoidance, report that only those patients who showed conditioned cardiac responses to the male slides also showed consistent shock avoidance and improvement from treatment. Interestingly, these authors failed in their attempt to apply the same type of procedure to the treatment of alcoholism (MacCulloch *et al.,* 1966). The authors suggest that the reason for the failure may have been the lack of development of conditioned cardiac responses, which may have resulted in inconsistent avoidance.

One of the more promising variations of avoidance conditioning technology has been termed productive avoidance by J. Zimmerman (1969). In this type of treatment the patient or client enters into a contractual agreement with the therapist. The patient agrees to deposit a sum of money in a bank that is regulated by the therapist. This money is refunded to the patient contingent on meeting certain prescribed criteria, which may range from nonoccurrence of the treated pathological behavior, through reduction in the frequency of the target behavior, to following prescribed steps in the shaping of more constructive behaviors.

T. J. Tighe and R. Elliott (1968) and Elliot and Tighe (1968) have applied the same technology to various behaviors with some degree of success. In the second study (Elliot & Tighe, 1968) for example, subjects who volunteered for a program designed to reduce their cigarette-smoking behavior posted money for a twelve- or sixteen-week period, and the money was refunded to those who refrained from smoking during this time. Of twenty-five subjects who participated in the program twenty-one abstained from smoking through the duration of the study. Rates of continued abstinence at follow-up periods between three and twelve months were 36 to 38 percent.

As in most aversive arrangements, the escape and avoidance paradigms are still plagued by a number of unresolved issues, ranging all the way from basic issues over the essential motivation underlying avoidance behavior to the clinical utility of such techniques. In general, the avoidance paradigm appears to be of greater clinical value than the escape procedure, since it provides the opportunity for the complete elimination of aversive stimulation, although its clinical value is still in question. The major problem in this area is the relative lack of precision in most clinical efforts. Many techniques that allege to be pure examples of avoidance conditioning, in fact, combine escape and avoidance processes in an unrefined manner. (Some of these combinations will be reported later.) Where properly implemented, clinical studies may contribute information at the basic level as well as at the applied level. As just reviewed, Feldman and MacCullough (1965) report data that seem to support the two-process theory of avoidance conditioning. It would obviously be helpful to have more data relevant to this question. It would also be of considerable value to determine the relationships between basic processes and applied efforts, as in the confirmation of traumatic avoidance learning in humans by Turner and Solomon (1962) and Campbell *et al.* (1964).

In addition, there needs to be more work, in general, with avoidance schedules of various sorts in order to compare their clinical efficacy with other techniques. Some of the reports of such comparisons will be reviewed subsequently.

COMBINATIONS OF AVERSIVE
AND OTHER FORMS OF CONDITIONING

Some therapists have devised techniques that defy simple classification within the categories previously proposed. Some of these reports will be separately reviewed here.

J. Hsu (1965) reported a technique that combines classical conditioning or punishment with avoidance conditioning. In his procedure alcoholic patients were presented with an array of three alcoholic beverages (beer, wine, and whiskey) and three nonalcoholic beverages. The patient was instructed to drink each of the six drinks in any order, after which thirty-second pulses of electric shock were delivered to the patient's head .5 to 5 seconds after he swallowed the alcoholic beverages. This procedure was followed for three days, then the patient was allowed to select five drinks on the fourth day and four on the fifth. The patient was then released from the hospital and requested to return for booster sessions four weeks and six months later.

According to Hsu's report, the procedure was upsetting and threatening to most patients, as reflected by the high dropout rate (only sixteen of forty completed the initial treatment and first booster). Follow-up data are not provided, making it impossible to properly evaluate this form of treatment. With the high dropout rate and the reported aversiveness of the treatment in general, modifications of the procedure itself may be in order, for public relations, if not in the interest of more humane and successful treatment.

Several programs have been launched that combine aversive techniques and other forms of behavior modification. For example, a punishment contingency may be applied to a pathological behavior, while a concurrent positive reinforcement program is introduced to increase the probability of constructive behavior (a form of counterconditioning). Several of these programs have been applied to pathological levels of alcoholic drinking.

Blake (1967), for example, found greater abstinence from drinking over a one-year period with a combination of aversive conditioning and relaxation training than with aversive conditioning alone. The combined procedure produced 43 percent abstinence over one year, while aversive conditioning alone produced only 23 percent abstinence. Had the relaxation training been response- and stimulus-contingent, as in desensitization, the results might have been enhanced. In addition, J. Thimann (1949) and Voegtlin and Broz (1949) found that aversive conditioning alone was most successful with alcoholic patients who had developed their pathological drinking behavior as a result of prolonged heavy social drinking and who had enough other constructive behaviors to improve significantly as a function of maintained sobriety. This suggests that the history of the alcoholic behavior should be analyzed in planning therapy or modification.

D. A. Pemberton (1967) compared the effect of what he called intensive treatment, which consisted of either instrumental escape conditioning, uncovering psychotherapy combined with drug-assisted abreaction, or a combination of both, with supportive psychotherapy, sometimes assisted by drug therapy or Antabuse. Although the confounding of variables in this study allows only suggestive conclusions, twenty out of forty-seven alcoholic patients (half male, half female) profited from "intensive treatment," and only eight of forty-two patients given "routine" treatment were classed as successful outcomes. Follow-up periods ranged from eight to twenty-four months after discharge.

Although the work of Lemere and Voegtlin (Lemere, *et al.* 1942a, b; Lemere & Voegtlin, 1950; Voegtlin & Lemere, 1942; Voegtlin 1940, 1947) was reviewed in the section on classical aversive conditioning, their work is not unadulterated by other variables and must be considered as a package which includes, in addition to aversive conditioning, group and individual psychotherapy and various kinds of adjunctive therapies that are a part of the standard treatment regime at Shadel Sanitarium.

E. C. Miller *et al.* (1960) have reported a variation of the Lemere and Voegtlin technique that involves classical aversive conditioning in a group setting. In another variation on the same basic theme, M. J. Raymond (1964) has introduced an operant counterconditioning procedure. In this procedure aversive conditioning is first established in standard classical fashion via emetic drugs, after which an inert substance (a placebo) is substituted for the emetine. Following this placebo injection, the patient is allowed to choose from a variety of beverages including both alcohol and soft drinks. If the subject chooses a soft drink rather than alcohol (which, the author reports, regularly occurs at this point), the response is followed by the absence of nausea or vomiting, and thus is, perhaps, negatively reinforced.

The general outcome of the punishment of an operant response when reinforcement of an alternative response is available (counterconditioning) has been compared to straight punishment by Herman and Azrin (1964), who used noise as punishment with mental patients. In both cases aversive conditioning was much more effective in producing response suppression when an alternative response was available. Willoughby (1969) and D. E. Bostow and J. B. Bailey (1969) found similar results with time-out in a counterconditioning paradigm.

The previously reviewed report of Risley (1968) indicated that in the treatment of self-injurious climbing behavior extinction combined with reinforcement of incompatible responses (staying down off the furniture) and even response-contingent TO were not as effective as response-contingent shock.

The technique used by Baer (1962) to control thumb-sucking could be described as a combination of escape-avoidance and punishment training. As mentioned in an earlier section, Baer presented cartoons to three five-year-old boys, but withdrew them contingent on thumb-sucking, reinstated them upon thumb removal, and continued them contingent upon long delays in thumb-sucking (avoidance). This technique was effective in controlling the behavior.

Several of the techniques reported earlier that were applied to homosexuality combined escape and avoidance procedures, as well as appetitive training. For example, it may be recalled that Feldman and MacCulloch (1965) used shock escape-avoidance conditioning signaled by a slide of a male nude. The patient's escape or avoidance response, which removed the male nude often also projected a slide of a female nude. This pairing of the male nude with shock termination would constitute negative reinforcement and may well have been responsible for the increase in heterosexual fantasy and behavior reported by the authors.

Although there has been some proliferation of studies combining various laboratory procedures, and some therapists (Lazarus, 1972; McBrearty *et al.*, 1968) have called for broad-spectrum behavior therapy using multiple techniques to simultaneously treat multiple behaviors, such a recommendation would seem premature at this point. It would be more parsimonious and possibly more informative in the long run, to investigate the effectiveness of separate techniques in separate groups initially. Clinical trials comparing the effects of no treatment or nonspecific treatment versus one or two specific treatment conditions would seem to offer more potential for screening of new techniques at this point. The law of parsimony would seem to call for investigation of single variables before more complex, multivariate studies are attempted. More will be said about studies comparing aversive and other forms of therapy in the next section.

CONCLUSION: EFFICACY OF AVERSIVE BEHAVIOR THERAPY

Because of ethical and humanitarian as well as scientific reasons, it is very important to carefully compare the efficacy and outcome of aversive therapy with other forms of behavior therapy. Therefore, we will review the studies of the effects of aversive procedures compared with other forms of modification of the same pathological behavior.

Holz and Azrin (1963) compared the effectiveness of several possible procedures designed to eliminate behavior that was previously shaped to a stable rate under laboratory control. The response was key pecking by pigeons on a schedule of reinforcement that required a pause of minimal duration between responses (DRL). Shock punishment of each response was found most effective along several dimensions, including immediacy, completeness, and duration, or longevity, of the effect (response reduction). Since the pigeons often did not pause long enough to meet criterion and obtain reinforcement on the DRL schedule, punishment, by reducing response rate and, consequently, short inter-response pauses, often increased the efficiency of their performance. Thus, the more shock the subjects received, the more food they got. This experiment represents all the refinement of a laboratory model for the comparison of behavior modification procedures. A next logical step might be the comparison of the same procedure in humans, especially when dealing with a condition that is characterized by "inappropriate" response rates.

In clinical applications comparing aversive techniques with other treatments, Thorpe *et al.* (1963) compared positive with negative, or aversive, conditioning in a male homosexual patient. Although insufficient control was exercised to report this as more than an interesting and sophisticated case study, the authors did find that aversive techniques were more effective than nonaversive methods in modifying homosexuality.

Similarly, R. J. McGuire and M. Vallance (1964) reported that extended conventional treatment did not reduce the frequency of a graduate student's masturbation to fetishistic fantasy, nor did it reduce his resultant guilt feelings. A punishment procedure was then used. The client was instructed to produce his usual fantasies and then raise his hand, at which point a shock was delivered. Later, when he could no longer summon the fantasy stimuli, he was presented with slides of persons dressed in the fetishistic stimuli and then shocked. He was also instructed to similarly treat himself with the conditioning apparatus at home. Following this treatment, he reported elimination of fetishistic fantasies and reduction of masturbation. In addition, when masturbation did occur, he reported successful masturbation in the presence of normal heterosexual fantasy for the first time in his life. The authors also reported favorable results in treating obsessional ruminations, obesity, smoking, and alcoholism with similar techniques.

In the treatment of cigarette smoking, shock punishment (McGuire & Vallance, 1964), shock escape conditioning (Gendreau & Dodwell, 1968), drug-induced nausea, and an aversive blast of smoke and hot air (Wilde, 1964; Lublin and Joslyn, 1968) have been shown to be at least minimally effective, while few other forms of potential treatment have been very productive. In one of the few studies in which aversive conditioning, desensitization, and supportive counseling were compared directly, Koenig and Masters (1965) found little difference in the treatment outcomes and very little modification by any of these procedures.

Aversive varieties of conditioning seem to have been more successful with alcoholism than other forms of treatment. Kantorovich (1928), for example, found that pairing the sight, smell, and taste of various alcoholic beverages with shock produced total abstinence in fourteen of twenty alcoholics over a three-week to twenty-month follow-up period. By contrast, hypnotic suggestion and medication ended in the patients' return to drinking within a few days. Blake (1967), however, produced greater abstinence over a one-year period by combining aversive conditioning with relaxation training (43 percent abstinence) than by aversive conditioning alone (23 percent).

Aversive paradigms have frequently produced modification of self-destructive or self-injurious behavior when other techniques have failed. Tate and Baroff (1966), for example, found that time-out from reinforcement reduced but did not eliminate self-injurious behaviors. Contingent electric shock, however, virtually eliminated the behavior. Lovaas and his colleagues (Lovaas, *et al.,* 1965a; Bucher & Lovaas, 1968) have also demonstrated that extinction or even brief withdrawal of social reinforcement may be sufficient to reduce self-destructive behavior, but shock punishment may be quicker and more permanent.

Goldiamond (1965b) and others have demonstrated that punishment contingencies are highly effective in reducing or eliminating the rate of speech dysfluencies such as stuttering or stammering. However, not enough definitive work has been done to reveal whether aversive contingencies result in longer-term modification outside the treatment setting than nonaversive techniques.

Aversive forms of behavior therapy have also been successfully applied to several other behaviors, including transvestism (Blakemore *et al.,* 1963a, b; Cooper, 1963; Glynn & Harper, 1961; Lavin *et al.,* 1961; Marks & Gelder, 1967), exhibitionism (Evans, 1967; Kushner & Sandler, 1966), compulsive behaviors (Cautela, 1966, 1967), obsessive thoughts (Walton, 1960; Walton & Mather, 1963; Kushner & Sandler, 1966), fetishism (Kushner & Sandler, 1966; Marks & Gelder, 1967; Raymond, 1956; Thorpe *et al.,* 1964), compulsive over-eating (Cautela, 1966; Ferster *et al.,* 1962; Stuart, 1967), and compulsive gambling (Barker & Miller, 1966a, 1966b, 1968). Most of these studies did not involve direct experimental comparisons of aversive and other forms of treatment, but these behaviors have frequently been refractory to more traditional means of treatment.

In keeping with the ethical philosophy expressed earlier, aversive techniques have been used primarily with behaviors that have been resistive to most other forms of treatment. As technology develops and more powerful techniques of appetitive training (such as stimulus-control techniques, fading, modeling, counterconditioning, and reinforcement of incompatible behaviors) advance, aversive techniques may one day be unnecessary. With that goal in mind, it would be helpful to continue the present trend toward proliferation of studies comparing the clinical utility of aversive and nonaversive behavior modification strategies.

In this section both appetitive and aversive techniques that aim primarily at reduction or elimination of a pathological target behavior have been reviewed. Differences between operant and classical conditioning tchniques have been indicated, as well as the behaviors they may be best suited to treat, when that information was available. Various kinds of stimulus-control techniques have been reviewed, within both classical and operant areas.

It would be well if, at this point, the recommendation of one specific technique could be made on the basis of the target behavior to be treated. Unfortunately, behavioral technology has not progressed to that point, and it may be some time yet before such a cookbook becomes available. Until that happy day more research is clearly in order, particularly the comparative programmatic variety of clinical research that will illuminate and reveal those techniques that are most effective and efficient in treating particular classes of pathological behaviors. The major difficulty here is the complex nature of the events at hand. As we have seen, aversive procedures are far more complex than would appear at first. Indeed, Dinsmoor (1954) calls into question the practice of distinguishing between a negative reinforcement procedure and a punishment procedure. Thus, he argues that both processes are involved in any aversive arrangement (that is, punishment processes are evoked in avoidance arrangements and vice versa), but that this is frequently obscured by the experimenter's focus upon one or the other. The implications of this argument for aversion therapy are quite clear. When an ostensible avoidance arrangement is in effect, the therapist must also be aware of possible punishment effects. Once again, answers to such questions can only be obtained through basic research and then extended to the world of human events.

B / ACCELERATION METHODS
Chapter 10 / Shaping
Normal Behavior

The emphasis in the preceding section was on behavior modification techniques designed primarily to reduce or eliminate pathological behaviors by direct treatment. Both classical and operant conditioning techniques, such as extinction, satiation or negative practice, fading, massing, flooding, and aversive methods, were reviewed and their applications discussed. In addition, some combined techniques, such as extinction programmed for the pathological behavior combined with reinforcement delivered contingent upon other, more constructive behavior, were discussed. These combined techniques were presented under the rubric of counterconditioning, which offers the additional advantages of a deceleration program for the pathological behavior and an acceleration program that is explicitly planned for a new, incompatible, and usually more constructive behavior.

There are other procedures that do not focus directly upon modifying pathological behaviors. Instead, these methods are aimed at increasing the frequency of normal behaviors. Consistent with the definition of normal behavior proposed earlier, the term, as used here, refers to behaviors or frequencies of behavior consistent with the reinforcing practices of a particular community. Thus, the term is relative and refers to those behaviors that are supported and reinforced by a particular group. Reinforcing practices are assumed to vary with the cultural, subcultural, and socioeconomic class of the individual.

The collections of techniques to be considered in this chapter might be expected to function particularly well where deficient normal behavior exists because of insufficient socialization or lack of exposure to the proper cultural contingencies, as well as other possible etiological factors. On the other hand, when many behaviors that are incompatible with those reinforced in the cultural group are habitual, another ·approach might be more appropriate. Thus, for example, with compulsive, habitual pathological responses of long standing, such as chronic alcoholism, smoking, drug addiction, or overeating, the measured frequency of these behaviors may not decrease as a function of a program designed to shape or increase the frequency of normal behaviors. Instead, this technique might work very well with those behaviors that consist in the main of deficits, such as in childhood autism, depression, cultural deprivation, and retardation, where the patient's main tasks may be to learn habits of personal hygiene, speech, and academic and social behaviors.

Some of the programs to be reviewed have been extended to normal populations as well as specifically identified clinical groups. For example, programmed instruction is now a part of many of the better school systems; self-control programs have been used to expedite creative behaviors; and contingency management systems have been installed to speed and make more precise the process of education.

With its heavy emphasis on positive reinforcement as a controlling principle, the behavior modification movement has created a new view of human nature, which assumes that man has a broad capacity to change and develop within a rapidly changing environment. This view is vastly different from the traditional clinical model of man, which tends to focus upon pathology. Little is known as yet of man's ultimate creative capacity, but the programs to be reviewed now have opened the door to new possibilities.

Since the breadth and number of programmatic applications of the techniques and principles to be reviewed have proliferated at an extremely rapid rate, only a general survey is presented here.

REINFORCEMENT OF BEHAVIORS INCOMPATIBLE WITH PATHOLOGY

Several studies have demonstrated that one of the most effective ways to deal with pathological behavior is to reinforce a constructive behavior that is incompatible with the pathological behavior. For example, one of the productive methods of treating enuretic, or nocturnal bedwetting, behavior is to present an effective reinforcer following successively longer continent periods during the day. Eventually, this increased control during the day may result in nocturnal bladder control as well (Kimmel & Kimmel, 1970).

Similarly, H. Lal and Lindsley (1968) report the successful elimination of constipation by delivering reinforcement (playtime in the bathtub for a three-year-old boy) only after a bowel movement.

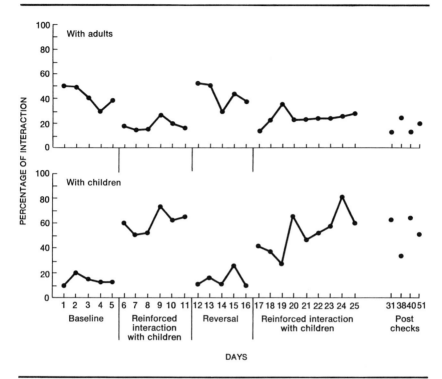

Figure 49. *Amount of social behavior displayed by a child as a result of variations in social reinforcement of adult and peer interactions. (From Allen et al., 1964)*

In another similar procedure Allen *et al.* (1964) increased the rate of social interaction with a group of peers in a withdrawn nursery-school girl by presenting teacher attention contingent upon social interaction with other children. Reversal of the contingency resulted in a decrease in social interaction with peers, and reintroduction increased it again, demonstrating the functional relationship between interaction and teacher attention. As social behavior increased again, the schedule of teacher attention was faded out to an intermittent schedule, which resulted in maintenance of the behavior through the rest of the school year. Figure 49 shows the changes in social interaction during the course of therapy.

M. K. Wagner (1968) reduced the frequency of masturbation in an eleven-year-old girl from seven times per hour to zero by delivering positive reinforcement contingent upon responses incompatible with masturbation. The schedule of reinforcement was again faded out through continuous, fixed-interval, and intermittent deliveries. Eventually, masturbation was completely eliminated by this procedure and was not observed again during the rest of the school year. These studies provide strong evidence that the reinforcement of incompatible behaviors is an effective approach to the modification of pathological conditions.

In most of the speech-training programs with autistic children (Lovaas, 1967; Risley & Wolf, 1967), self-stimulatory and other pathological behaviors have decreased as speech training progressed. Lovaas has stated that self-stimulatory behaviors (such as bizarre arm flapping and rocking movements) may be inversely related to many other behaviors. He notes that an organism may find ways to stimulate itself when external stimulation has been reduced to low levels. At any rate, an increase of more desirable behaviors in autistic children may be accompanied by reductions in such pathological behaviors.

As mentioned in Chapter 8, Ferster and DeMyer (1962) used a programmatic operant conditioning approach to manipulate the behavior of autistic children. The subjects were initially severely disturbed and showed infrequent speech and very frequent self-stimulatory behaviors. The children were exposed to an experimental room in which they were trained to make simple operant responses, such as pressing a lever that initially delivered unconditioned reinforcement, then later token reinforcers, sometimes on complex schedules of reinforcement. As the children learned these responses, self-stimulatory, tantrumlike, and other atavistic behaviors decreased noticeably in frequency. This finding may again support Lovaas' assumption that self-stimulatory and other pathological behaviors that occur at high frequency in autistic children are inversely related to other, more constructive behaviors. Thus, direct reinforcement for lever pressing on increasingly complex schedules led to a decrease in pathological behaviors, even though the pathological behaviors were not systematically treated in any way, and despite the fact that the two classes of responses may not have been physically incompatible.

In many classroom situations problem behaviors are unwittingly maintained by teachers who pay more attention to such behavior than to constructive work and study behaviors. In some of these settings the teachers may rationalize their own behaviors on the basis of maintaining discipline or not allowing children to interrupt the quiet study of others. Functional analyses often reveal however that the teacher's mild aversive treatment of the problem behaviors has some small temporary effect (enough to maintain the teacher's continued use of the same technique), but the problem behaviors may accelerate in the long run. Sometimes all that is needed to combat this state of affairs is for the teacher to reinforce only appropriate study behaviors (which are usually incompatible with such problem behaviors as speaking out, jumping up, and running around). W. C. Becker *et al.* (1967) found, for example, that reinforcement for study and work behaviors was more effective in increasing these desirable behaviors and extinguishing problem behaviors than several other techniques, including extinction of problem behaviors alone. The authors observed that this technique was effective even when reinforcement was presented to a child who was behaving appropriately in the presence of another who was misbehaving. Thus, some modeling of the correct behaviors as well as some reduction in peer reinforcement for misbehavior may have played a part in these results.

In several of the imitation-training programs (see Chapter 8), behaviors incompatible with pathology have been learned and reinforced via modeling. Thus, Baer *et al.* (1967) produced imitation learning of motor and verbal behaviors that had initially occurred at very low rates in three retarded children. These authors went on to state that learning to imitate the verbal behaviors was facilitated by prior learning of the imitated motor behaviors. Similar procedures with filmed models have been used in teaching language to autistic children (Humphrey, 1966), in language training (Sherman, 1965; Wilson & Walters, 1966), in the modification of hyperaggressive behaviors in children (Chittenden, 1942), in treating social withdrawal in children (R. D. O'Connor, 1969), and in modifying phobic responding in children (Bandura, Grusec, & Menlove, 1967; Bandura & Menlove, 1968; Bandura, Blanchard, & Ritter, 1968).

Using direct reinforcement for behaviors incompatible with pathological responses, G. R. Levin and J. J. Simmons (1962) increased the persistence of hyperaggressive boys in performing academic tasks; G. L. Martin and R. B. Powers (1967) increased the attention span in brain-damaged and retarded children; G. King *et al.* (1960) increased interpersonal responsiveness and speech in severely withdrawn schizophrenic patients; Isaacs *et al.* (1960) increased speech in a mute catatonic; H. L. Cohen (1968) improved academic performances in delinquents; and R. G. Wahler (1968) increased cooperative behaviors in oppositional children.

As later sections of this chapter will reveal, complex motivational systems, such as token economies and contingency management programs, use the principle of reinforcement of incompatible behaviors to accelerate an even wider range of constructive, normal behaviors.

Maximal clinical utility of this principle is gained, of course, when the behavior which is incompatible with a particular form of pathology is desirable in itself. Ayllon and Michael (1959), for example, illustrated the negative case when they found they could decrease violent episodes in a psychotic woman by reinforcing the incompatible response of sitting quietly on the floor. The latter response, however, was found to be physically incompatible with social approach behaviors, which were among the goals of treatment. Unfortunately, when reinforcement of floor sitting was discontinued and attempts made to shape social approach behaviors, the patient again became violent.

The studies reviewed here indicate that direct reinforcement of normal behaviors incompatible with pathological responses can be a very powerful therapeutic technique. Later sections will indicate that sometimes only a subtle variation (the explicit programming of extinction or punishment for the response to be decelerated) differentiates this technique from counterconditioning.

REINFORCEMENT OF DESIRABLE BEHAVIOR

Positive reinforcement is at the core of most of the programmatic approaches to behavior modification reviewed in this chapter. So many of the programs already in existence use positive reinforcement, singly or in combination with other techniques and treatments, that it will be possible here to survey only the main thrust of some of these programs. In most of these efforts the concern with pathology is minimal or nonexistent, which often sets them apart from other approaches.

In an early laboratory demonstration Azrin and Lindsley (1956) found that reinforcement served to increase the rate of a cooperative response between pairs of children. They reported that presentation of reinforcement contingent upon cooperative behavior (dropping a marble into two separate holes at the same time) increased the rate of the behavior, and extinction (removal of reinforcement) reduced it. Several reversals demonstrated that contingent presentation of the reinforcer maintained control over the behavior.

Several applications of positive reinforcement to physiological responses (Kimmel & Hill, 1960; Grings & Carlin, 1966; Kimmel, 1967; Ascough & Sipprelle, 1968; Black, 1968; Shapiro *et al.*, 1970) have demonstrated that even these behaviors, once thought to be beyond the pale of operant control, may be accelerated or decelerated by appropriate positive reinforcement or other stimulus control. Figure 50, for example, reveals the manner in which heart rate and blood pressure changes in human subjects occurred as a function of contingent reinforcement. The recent pioneering work of N. E. Miller and his colleagues (Miller & DiCara, 1967; DiCara & Miller, 1969; Miller, 1969) clearly indicates the number of physiological systems that may be susceptible to such control, as well as the possibilities of clinical treatment of such pathological states as tachycardia and hypertension. Benson *et al.* (1971) provide striking evidence of changes in blood pressure in hypertensive patients as a function of differential reinforcement. These efforts, although largely experimental, clearly demonstrate the role that reinforcement may occupy in treatment programs of the future.

As indicated in previous passages, reinforcement plays a primary role in most of the speech-training and verbal conditioning studies. Lovaas (1967; Bucher & Lovaas, 1968), for example, frequently uses unconditioned reinforcers such as food in initial speech training with autistic children. By pairing conditioned social reinforcers such as verbal praise with the unconditioned reinforcer on an increasingly intermittent basis, the latter can frequently be faded out. This teaches the child the elements of social reinforcement, which is where control by the natural reinforcers of the environment is expected to begin. Risley and Wolf (1967) report findings similar to Lovaas'.

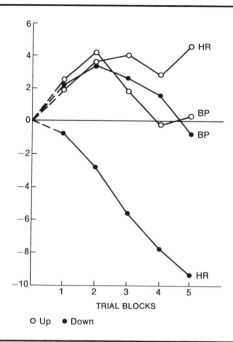

Figure 50. *Average heart rate and systolic blood pressure in subjects reinforced for increasing (up) and for decreasing (down) heart rate. Curves are
based on five best heart rate conditioners in each group. Each point is
mean of five subjects, five trials each. Ordinate is both beats per minute
and minHg. All values were adjusted for initial levels. (From Shapiro* et al.,
1970)*

In related areas, reinforcement operations have been used to
reinstate speech in deficient or mute patients (Isaacs *et al.,* 1960;
Salzinger *et al.,* 1965; Sherman, 1965) as well as to control the content of conversation (Verplanck, 1955; Azrin *et al.,* 1961), or the content reported by subjects in experiments (Kanfer, 1968; Krasner,
1965; Salzinger, 1959), and the content reported by patients in traditional psychotherapeutic treatment (Bandura *et al.,* 1960; Murray,
1956; Truax, 1966). The application of reinforcement systems to the
shaping of desirable behaviors has proceeded directly from many of
the early studies of verbal conditioning in laboratories to various
clinical settings and problems, such as the modification of delusional and hallucinatory verbalizations (Ayllon & Haughton, 1964;
Ayllon and Michael, 1959; Lindsley, 1956; Rickard & Dinoff, 1962)
and the recovery of speech in aphasic patients (Goodkin, 1969) and
psychotics (Isaacs *et al.,* 1960; Sherman, 1965).

Many of these developments have been in line with Krasner's
early (1962b) analysis of the therapist as a "social reinforcement machine." In one application of precise behavioral technology the pa-

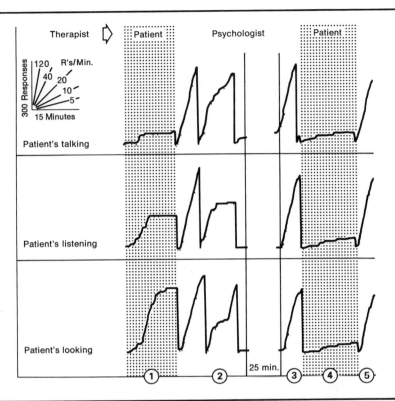

Figure 51. *A psychologist can elicit and maintain the talking, listening, and looking behavior of a chronic psychotic adult for at least ten to fifteen minutes (panels 2, 3, and 5). However, another psychotic patient serving as a therapist cannot hold the patient's attention (panels 1 and 4). (From Lindsley, 1969)*

tient responds continuously in order to gain verbal and visual access to the therapist through closed-circuit television (Nathan *et al.,* 1964; Lindsley, 1970). The therapist, in addition, may respond to control verbal and visual communication contingent upon the patients' verbalizations. This reinforcement operation, labeled conjugate reinforcement by Lindsley (1963b, 1969) has enabled acceleration of desirable and deceleration of undesirable verbalizations in psychotherapeutic interchanges (see Figure 51). The sophistication and precision of such control procedures would seem worthy of much more extensive investigation.

Reinforcement principles have seen wide application in educational settings. The entire development of programmed instruction (Brown & L'Abate, 1969; Morrill, 1961; Lumsdaine and Glaser, 1960; Skinner, 1968) has shown increasing application to diverse subject matter as well as increasing sophistication of technology, with teaching machines and computer-assisted courses the most recent development (Atkinson, 1968; Coulson, 1962). Thus, functional analysis of the educational process has progressed to the point where programmed-learning instructional units are available in standard academic areas ranging from reading, writing, and arithmetic to entire courses on graduate and undergraduate levels (Woody, 1969; Ferster & Perrott, 1968; Skinner, 1968). In many of these courses self-instructional skills are taught to the student, who can then use these skills to progress independently, at his own rate, through assigned units, demonstrating his mastery of the content of each unit verbally (Keller, 1968; Ferster & Perrott, 1968). This approach requires much more active involvement in the educational process on the part of the student, but it also guarantees a much greater density of reinforcement for mastery of material than is found in traditional classrooms. As a result, students successfully completing such programs usually show a much higher level of proficiency (Keller, 1968; Silberman, 1962; Skinner, 1968). In addition, the same technology has been applied to areas as diverse as teaching parents and teachers functional analysis in dealing with children (Patterson & Gullion, 1968), teaching psychology students basic principles of conditioning and learning (Holland & Skinner, 1961), and teaching engineering students the principles of electrical theory applied to the programming of electromechanical control equipment (Hetzel & Hetzel, 1969).

Another burgeoning area involves the use of reinforcement systems in rehabilitation. Contemporary programs in many institutions for retarded individuals now use reinforcement systems to teach basic self-care, personal hygiene, and elementary social skills to children and adults once thought ineducable. Retarded children have been taught, via these systems, to feed themselves, engage in personal grooming, dress and undress themselves, engage in elementary social interactions, and engage in elementary vocations (Giles & Wolf, 1966; Bensberg, 1965; Girardeau & Spradlin, 1964; Lent *et al.,* 1970; Minge & Ball, 1967).

Several programs have been designed to apply reinforcement principles to the rehabilitation of delinquents. In many of these programs socially, rather than antisocially, oriented behaviors have been taught to delinquents, frequently as an outgrowth of their acquisition of educational or vocational skills. For example, in a large-scale program designed by Cohen (1968; Cohen *et al.,* 1968) contingencies similar to those in the community were applied in an effort to teach educational and vocational skills. With a point system that was similar to the token economies to be reviewed later in this chapter, the program placed special emphasis on positive incentives, self-management of study behaviors, and individual initiative. With points earned through study and work behaviors, the boys, all former school dropouts, could earn the use of private rooms, recreational activities, extra courses, and added freedoms. As a result, the boys studied diligently and showed scholastic achievement of more than two grade levels on achievement tests after an eight-month period.

Another program for delinquent rehabilitation demonstrated that reinforcement may be delivered for entire sequences of behavior and thus produce more controlled acceleration than reinforcement for specific, isolated behaviors (Martin *et al.*, 1968). Initially the group was stratified at several levels, which led to confusion and bickering, since different levels of accomplishment were reinforced with similar payoffs. When the system was changed, however, so that entire phases of behavior, clear goals, and behavioral prerequisites for promotion from one level to the next were specified, both progress and morale were accelerated.

Burchard and Tyler (1965) implemented a similar system with delinquents, combining positive reinforcement for social and academic performances with social isolation and token loss for antisocial behaviors.

Rehabilitation of chronic, psychotic, institutionalized patients has progressed from programs applying contingencies to individual patients (Lindsley, 1956a; Ayllon, 1963; Ayllon & Michael, 1959) to token economies for an entire ward (reviewed later). On the individual level contingent reinforcement has been effective in modifying extreme withdrawal and passivity (Schaefer & Martin, 1966) and social and verbal behaviors (King *et al.*, 1960; Lindsley, 1963a, 1963b; Isaacs *et al.*, 1960; Sherman, 1965).

One example of a model rehabilitation program for chronic schizophrenic patients (Fairweather, 1967) extended the concept of a halfway house. The program began with reinforcement delivered contingent on social, personal hygiene, cooperative, and vocational behaviors at various graded levels. Following the inpatient program the patients moved as a group to a house in the community, where they managed the house and their own business (such as a janitorial service). In this program individual independence and responsibility were specifically programmed, along with development of social and vocational skills. A comparison of groups in this program with a traditional ward revealed less pathological behavior, more social behavior, more verbal interaction, and much more participation in weekly ward discussions in Fairweather's (1964) rehabilitation group.

Reinforcement procedures have also been used to increase the efficiency of rehabilitation workshops. For example, R. F. Johnson *et al.* (1965) worked with three female chronic mental patients, who were slower than the average workshop member. When the delay-of-reinforcement interval was decreased and the contingencies programmed more precisely, all three subjects significantly increased their rates of productivity. Similarly, J. G. Hunt and J. Zimmerman (1969) increased group productivity and maintained higher productivity during reinforcement than nonreinforcement periods (multiple schedule) in a sheltered workshop. Coupons exchangeable for canteen items were used as reinforcers in this program.

Several programs have compared the efficacy of individual and group contingencies. Wolf and Risley (1967) found better control of disruptive classroom behavior when a problem child and her classmates each received a point for desirable behavior than when the child alone earned five points. In this case the group contingency may have brought into play peer reinforcements more powerful than the extra points. There are probably subtle group pressures brought to bear when everyone's reinforcement is at stake.

Finally, reinforcement systems have been analyzed as to their arbitrary or natural character (Ferster, 1967a). In Ferster's analysis arbitrary reinforcers are reinforcing to the administrator for a long duration, but to the reinforced person for only a short period. Natural reinforcement, on the other hand, is in keeping with the current repertoire of the reinforced person. A natural reinforcer may also be one frequently used by the reinforcing community in which the individual lives. Ferster (1967b) also went on to apply a thorough operant analysis of the natural reinforcers used by a clinician in treatment of autistic children (Ferster & Simons, 1966). This analysis seems very much in keeping with the goal of most therapeutic programs—to return the individual to his place in society, where the natural reinforcers take over.

In summary, the use of reinforcement principles has permeated most of the operant-oriented behavior modification programs. In this section only a few of these were reviewed. Emphasis was placed on reinforcement programs in physiological, speech training, educational, and rehabilitative settings. The number and variety of these applications illustrate the advances and current level of sophistication in this area. Other applications of reinforcement in more complex or varied technologies will be considered in later sections of this chapter.

SCHEDULES OF REINFORCEMENT
Since the publication of Ferster and Skinner's monumental *Schedules of Reinforcement* (1957), the number of laboratory investigations demonstrating schedule control over behavior have proliferated. However, this has not been accompanied by a similar application of schedule variables to clinical problems. Many writers have commented, for example, on the basic principle that intermittent schedules of reinforcement tend to increase resistance to extinction far beyond that revealed by schedules of continuous reinforcement. Yet the vast majority of published clinical reports still involve continuous schedules. One of the exceptions is a study by Allen *et al.* (1964) in which teacher attention was delivered contingent upon social interaction in a normally isolated nursery school child. One reversal indicated that social interaction increased with reinforcement and decreased when it was withdrawn. Up to this point only continuous reinforcement was programmed. As the experiment ended, reinforcement was being delivered on an increasingly intermittent schedule. A follow-up indicated that social interaction was maintained, perhaps by other "normal" contingencies, through the rest of the school year.

Training of this sort may be functionally equivalent to the suc-

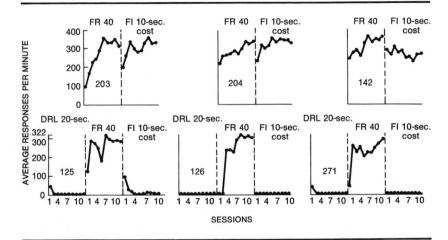

Figure 52. *Session-to-session response rates during the FR 40 or DRL 20-sec, to FR 40-histories and under the FI 10-sec. cost schedule. (From Weiner, 1970)*

cessful training of a salesman or a gambler. In either case the gambler or salesman may have initial heavy or frequent reinforcement, followed by progressive fading or "leaning" of the schedule through increasing intermittency. If the initial training schedule has been appropriately heavy or frequent enough, behaviors acquired thus may persist despite very infrequent "payoffs."

H. Weiner (1965, 1970) has certainly given clear demonstration of the effects of schedule determinants upon human operant responding. (See Chapter 5.) Examining the differences between time- and response-dependent schedules, Weiner demonstrated that the individual trained on one may respond pathologically, in accord with his past history, following a schedule change. Frequently, this perseverative behavior may persist even in the face of clearly programmed punishment (Weiner, 1962, 1964). Sometimes all that is needed to teach the subject behaviors that are appropriate to the schedule change is to train him on the appropriate kind of schedule. Weiner (1962, 1970), for example, found that subjects frequently work at maximal rates on fixed-interval schedules. This may be defined as pathological behavior, since the subject is making many more responses than are minimally required by the schedule. Exposing the subject to DRL (differential reinforcement of low rates) schedules, anywhere in his programmed history, however, was sufficient to teach him behavior appropriate to the FI schedules, apparently because the DRL requires pausing for reinforcement (Weiner, 1964, 1970). Postreinforcement pausing is a constructive behavior, of course, on FI schedules. Figures 52 and 53 show the differential effects of reinforcement history on schedule performance.

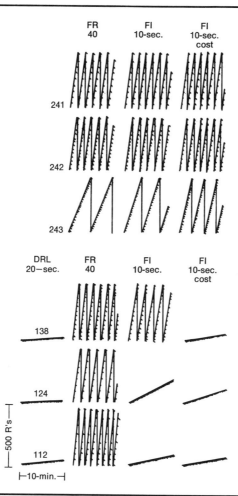

Figure 53. *Final performances under FR 40 history or DRL 20-sec. to FR 40 history schedule sequence and under FI 10-sec. and FI 10-sec. cost. (From Weiner, 1970)*

Such schedule interactive effects may occur much more frequently than was previously suspected. These interactive effects sometimes reach a level of complexity and intricacy not found in simple schedule work. This is the thesis of papers by Sandler and Davidson (1971) and Morse and Kelleher (1966, 1970). From this point of view, schedules of reinforcement are seen as fundamental determinants of the rate, topography, pattern, and probability of behavior. When schedules are intermixed, either simultaneously or consecutively, interesting new patterns of behavior, sometimes unpredictable a priori, may emerge. For example, using both avoidance and appetitive training histories, Morse and Kelleher (1966),

Stretch *et al.* (1968), and McKearny (1968) have reported maintenance of accelerating patterns of behavior by extremely strong electric shocks following deletion of the training schedule (reviewed in Chapter 5). In this case shocks as strong as twelve milliamperes functioned in a manner equivalent to positive reinforcement when delivered on FI schedules. The pattern of behavior persisted for many months and was not essentially modifiable by time-out following shock delivery or continuous punishment of responses immediately following shock delivery. The clinical implications of these findings, both for etiology and modification, should be obvious, yet precise human parallels have not yet been revealed.

Sandler and Davidson (1971) have analyzed two- and three-stage schedule interactions from a clinical point of view (Chapter 5). They looked, for example, at the work that has been done on the possible combinations and permutations of the following schedules: positive reinforcement, negative reinforcement, punishment, and extinction. The two-and three-stage models were cast in terms of schedules of acquisition, maintenance, and modification. Thus, for example, a response may have been acquired on a schedule of continuous reinforcement and then shifted to extinction (two-stage). In this case cessation of responding would be expected to occur quickly. However, had the response been shifted from continuous to variable ratio reinforcement prior to entering extinction (three-stage), the response rate would be predicted to decrease much less rapidly (Ferster & Skinner, 1957; Lovibond, 1963a). Use of the same model (and research reviewed previously) enables the prediction that "punishment" of a response maintained on a schedule of negative reinforcement may lead to an increase, rather than a decrease, in the rate of response.

Similarly, persistent, resistive behavior may be acquired on a schedule of adventitious reinforcement. Such a schedule occurs when the contingency between responding and reinforcement is accidental, as in many time-dependent schedules. As indicated earlier, organisms have acquired interesting and unusual behaviors as a function of such schedules (Skinner, 1953, 1959; Herrnstein, 1966).

The power and precision of schedule control is reflected in another way by the studies that have been done of immediacy versus delay of reinforcement (Renner, 1964). On the basis of these studies many contemporary clinical investigators use a time-contingent schedule of reinforcement as a control for the experimental analysis of the response-contingent schedule of interest (Lovaas *et al.,* 1966; Baer *et al.,* 1967). These and other studies have shown that response-contingent schedules maintain behavior at high rates, while reinforcement delivered on temporal schedules independent of behavior regularly produces decreases. Another schedule variation that also interrupts the contingency between behavior and reinforcement consists of delivering several reinforcements in advance of any behavior. This procedure also produces regular decreases in response rate (Ayllon & Azrin, 1965; Bandura & Perloff, 1967).

Experimentalists are currently examining schedules of much greater complexity than reviewed thus far. Some of these schedules involve the presence or absence of discriminative stimuli, which may signal different schedule components (multiple and mixed schedules). Other, even more complex schedules may use the presence or absence of S^{D}s to signal several different schedule or behavioral requirements, all of which may have to be completed to reach terminal reinforcement (chained and tandem schedules). Some idea of the rigor of control over a long chain of diverse behaviors can be gathered from the work of R. Pierrel and J. G. Sherman (1963). These investigators taught Barnabus, a lowly rat, to climb a spiral staircase, cross a bridge, climb a ladder, pull a chain that would bring a toy car, climb aboard the car, pedal it through a tunnel to another stair, go down the stairs, squeeze through a small tube, enter an elevator, descend by pulling a chain (which also raised a Columbia University flag), and press a lever, which automatically delivered a food pellet. These behaviors were taught to Barnabus, one at a time, beginning with the terminal component (pressing the bar) and working backwards. Such techniques might be very useful in shaping normal behaviors in people, although few systematic applications have been reported.

Another laboratory model for working with complex behaviors around the clock has been developed by J. D. Findley, who worked with both monkeys (1962) and human volunteers (1966). This complex multioperant program makes possible the programming and measurement of many and varied behaviors on a twenty-four-hour-a-day basis. On these schedules subjects may engage in any of several different behaviors under the control of differing schedules of reinforcement at any time. In some cases stimuli may inform the subject that a more limited range of behaviors (say, recreational or academic) are available. Sometimes the subject need make only one or several responses to gain access to a variety of behavioral components, any one of which may terminate in reinforcement. Findley (1962) calls such schedules branching chains, or trees, and claims that behavior under the control of such schedules may be more easily maintained and brought under very complex stimulus control than is true in the case of long serial chains (such as the one performed by Barnabus). It is unfortunate that such information, which is directly relevant to the level of complexity that is preferred by many clinicians, has had little or no clinical impact.

In summary, the behavior modifier sees schedules of reinforcement as being among the most important determiners of human behavior, pathological or not. The impact of schedule controls has been most clearly stated by Morse (1966):

> *The experiments pertaining to schedules have additional general significance in showing the tremendous range of behaviors*

that can be produced by schedules, the power of behavioral control induced by schedules, and the intricate relations that exist among the variables controlling behavior. The range and complexity of behaviors that can be produced by intermittently reinforcing responses in time is incredible. That these scheduling procedures are the most powerful techniques known for generating behavior is, of course, of fundamental significance; it emphasizes that histories of reinforcement are the primary determinants of behavior. (pp. 57–58)

To this perhaps one should add that the challenge now is for the competent, sophisticated therapist to begin to apply his intervention techniques, in accordance with modern technology.

USES OF INSTRUCTIONS

Several experiments have demonstrated that instructions have powerful effects upon behavior. Instructions have been used in traditional modes of therapy, such as directive and reeducative therapies, as well as in hypnotherapy. In many cases patients generally behave as instructed unless there are moral or other kinds of resistances. Some experimenters have suggested that appropriate responding to instructions is the result of classical conditioning. This may be largely because the instructions are antecedents (perhaps conditioned stimuli) that have come to control behavior as a result of prior conditioning. However, instructions may also function as S^Ds for avoidance or escape contingencies. This is most clearly the case in experiments in which the subject is informed that he must regularly attend or perform in some instructed manner or suffer loss of experimental credits or pay. Instructions might also be functionally equivalent to S^Ds for positive reinforcement, as in those experiments in which the subject is informed that he will be paid or otherwise reinforced for each emission of a particular response. Thus, the functional nature of instructions probably depends in a complex way upon the nature of the current contingency, scheduling factors, and the prior conditioning history of the subject.

Ayllon and Azrin (1964) demonstrated that instructions yielded more immediate control over behaviors to be reinforced than a reinforcement contingency alone, but that a combination of reinforcement and instructions led to quicker shaping and longer-lived control than either alone, as shown in Figure 54. In addition, when discrepancies between instructions and schedules of reinforcement existed, the former gradually lost control to the latter.

Levitz and Ullmann (1969) also found that both instructions and reinforcement could be used to manipulate rates of measures of disturbed thinking, but that instructions led to a more rapid, albeit less durable, increase in such indices. This study is of interest because it was performed with undergraduate students and also because it used different training and test tasks. Thus, the effects of reinforcement and instructions were separately analyzed in one

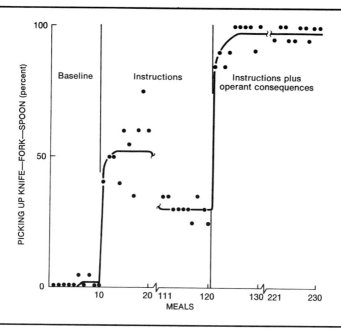

Figure 54. Percentage of patients who displayed the appropriate responses during base-line, instruction, and combined reinforcement-instruction phases of the study. (From Ayllon & Azrin, 1964. Additional information and related research can be found in Ayllon & Azrin, 1968.)

experiment where the Holtzman inkblots were used as pre- and post-test measures and a word association test was used for training, and in a second experiment where the two measures were exchanged.

Several studies of classroom behavior have demonstrated that in these settings instructions alone may yield only minimal or momentary control over behavior, perhaps because their frequent use has led to satiation and aversiveness. Some of the loss of instructional control in educational institutions may also be due to lack of relationship to any consistent contingency. Zimmerman et al. (1969) demonstrated that instructions followed by consistent praise for each appropriate response were not sufficient to maintain behavior in seven male retardates with "attentional deficits." However, when the same instructions were followed by reinforcement with tokens exchangeable for tangible reinforcers, instruction-following behavior was differentially maintained in four of the boys, and an additional two boys either responded appropriately to most instructions or showed improvement through the token-reinforcement condition.

A procedure that is similar to the use of instructions in order to bypass shaping and quickly secure behavior at high rates is *response priming* (F. O'Brien et al., 1969). This method was used to prompt reluctant, chronic mental patients into suggesting feasible

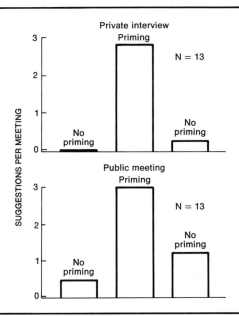

Figure 55. *Number of suggestions per meeting made by thirteen chronic mental patients when they were invited to attend the meeting (no priming) and when attendance at the meeting was required (priming). The upper graph is the data for experiment 1, during which the thirteen patients met with the meeting leader individually and in private; the lower graph is for experiment 2, during which the thirteen patients met with the meeting leader as a group. (From O'Brien et al., 1969)*

improvements in their treatment programs. Response priming consisted of requiring the patients to attend a meeting at which they were further prompted to make the appropriate suggestions. The technique vastly increased the rate of suggestion making, as revealed in Figure 55, but the authors found the rate fell to a low level when either priming or reinforcement (execution of the suggestion) were used alone.

Another variation on the prompting theme has been used in the teaching of speech (Lovaas *et al.,* 1966) and imitation (Lovaas, 1967; Bandura, 1962, 1969). In most of these studies the subject is simply instructed to "do this" or is instructed in a minor variation on this prompt, and his past conditioning history is thus used.

From the studies just reviewed, it appears that instructions may be used frequently as a substitute for the longer and more laborious shaping of new behaviors required so often in animals. Particularly, when instructions are consistent with the conditioning history of the subject new or complex behaviors might be rapidly accelerated, although some form of reinforcement may be necessary to maintain the same behaviors on a long-term basis.

SELF-CONTROL PROCEDURES

One criticism of the behavior modification movement in general, and of the conditioning therapies in particular, is that these are mechanistic forms of treatment that rob an individual of his uniqueness and dignity and tend to make automatons of people. However, many of the current trends within behavior modification clearly indicate that this need not be so. The token economies, for example, may require an individual to earn tokens in one particular way (work, for example) or any of several different ways (engage in any one of several desired behaviors), but the tokens, once earned, are exchangeable for many things, depending upon the individual's preference. Both aspects of the token economy are realistic contingencies analogous to those that prevail outside the hospital, where people are required to earn money, which can then be spent in many diverse ways.

In addition, in many of the newer therapeutic regimes patients are offered a behavioral or therapeutic menu. For example, a patient might be informed that a particular hospital can provide a desensitization program, a token economy, attitude therapy, aversion therapy, sensitivity training, or traditional psychotherapy, and the individual is allowed some choice as to which program he would like to enter. Frequently, contractual agreements are made, so that the patient is informed as to what will be expected of him in any of these therapeutic milieus, and he is expected to keep his part of the bargain.

In some of these facilities and in an increasing number of outpatient, educational, or private practice settings, programs of contingency control are placed in the hands of the patient or client seeking modification. Since the individual is himself responsible for measuring the frequency of the treated behaviors as well as for dispensing or arranging reinforcements on a particular schedule, the programs have been labeled models of self-control. Goldiamond (1965a), for example, has presented a rationale and case studies illustrating the application of self-control procedures in a counseling setting. Most of the procedures used or recommended to the individual are extensions of principles and techniques developed under the controlled conditions of the laboratory. Frequently, the subject is trained in behavioral analysis and to act as his own experimenter, counting the rates of his desired or pathological behaviors, selecting (perhaps with the help of the counselor) the appropriate modification procedures, measuring the resultant change in behavior, and changing procedures as needed.

O. R. Lindsley (1971) uses a similar strategy in his precision-teaching workshops. Here again, the emphasis is on applying the most rigorous techniques available from the laboratory to the analysis and modification of the behavior of an individual. In the workshops Lindsley presents, as an orientation to the program, a course in behavioral analysis. This course includes ways of identifying or pinpointing a behavior to be measured, techniques of recording and charting daily data (usually rates of a response), and the means of modification. Obviously, such procedures may be applied to the observer's own behavior as well as to the behavior of another person. However, there are certain advantages when the system applies to one's own behavior. Not only does it then fit the characteristics of a self-control program, but covert responses not available to public observation may be counted and recorded by the individual. For example, Lindsley (1971) has recorded and plotted the frequency of his urges or impulses to smoke concurrently with the number of cigarettes smoked and found that the two were positively rather than negatively correlated. That is, when he reduced his rate of smoking to low frequencies, his urges to smoke also decreased to low levels. With this technology it might be possible for an individual to program consequences for behaviors inaccessible to others. For example, an individual might be able to gain control over his impulses, fantasies, ruminative or obsessive thoughts, hallucinations, or delusions through the use of such techniques.

There is tentative data along with the above observations suggesting that when a person attributes a behavior change to his own doing, the change may be longer lasting than when the same results are attributed to an external agent. Thus, Davison and S. Valins (1969) used a pain threshold and shock tolerance test, followed by administration of a drug placebo, and ending with another shock tolerance test (with the shock intensities surreptitiously halved). The study used male undergraduate students. Half the subjects were told they had taken an active drug; the other half, that they had taken an inactive drug. Those who attributed the change in shock thresholds to themselves (because they had been told they had received a placebo) later perceived another series of shocks as less painful and tolerated higher intensities than those who were told they had taken an active drug. This study is complicated by the fact that several explanations of the outcome may be as acceptable as the one advanced by the authors. Nevertheless, the study clearly suggests that self-attributed behavior change may be longer lived than changes attributed to outside agents.

Several self-directed contingency programs have been developed and designed to modify specific behaviors. Ferster *et al.* (1962), for example, worked with obese women, who were taught to control their eating behavior by thinking of the ultimate aversive consequences (putting on weight, worsening appearance and health, etc.) of eating fattening foods, particularly snacks between meals. In this way ultimate aversive consequences, which might be expected to suppress eating of the wrong foods, were substituted for the normally reinforcing immediate consequences. The subjects in this study showed at first slow and then faster weight loss while they were in the program, although there was little long-lasting change. Stuart (1967) later capitalized on these suggestions, adding dietary recommendations and exercise programs, producing weight losses in obese women (see Figure 56).

M. B. Harris (1969) has devised and demonstrated a similar

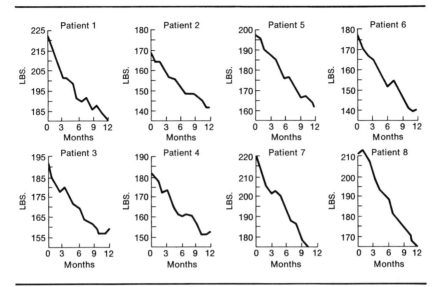

Figure 56. *Weight losses achieved by eight women using self-control procedures.* (From Stuart, 1967)

self-directed program for weight control with sixteen undergraduate students. This author stressed both self-control of stimulus conditions (eating only at meals, not eating until the stomach is overly full) and reinforcement contingencies, and found stable weight losses in the self-control group that were greater than those in a similarly motivated group of control subjects.

J. D. Nolan (1968) devised a self-control procedure to modify smoking, which emphasized stimulus control. Nolan's wife restricted herself to smoking cigarettes only when sitting in a particular chair, which also produced time-out from social and other reinforcers. (She agreed not to watch TV or talk while sitting in the chair.) This resulted in a substantial decrease in her smoking rate, which was reduced even further when the chair was gradually faded out (made less readily available). The procedure was replicated by Roberts (1969), who reported the additional advantage that undesirable emotional side effects were not observed when this procedure was used, but did occur with others.

Several experimenters have obtained commitments from subjects to participate in self-control programs using contractual agreements to carry out assigned tasks. J. T. Tooley and S. Pratt (1967), in controlling smoking, and Ferster *et al.* (1962), in treating overeating, made such agreements with clients who agreed to programs that called for gradual restrictions upon times and places in which smoking or eating was allowed.

The behavioral technology upon which various self-control programs are based has progressed to the point where precision programs are available in several different areas. Ferster (1965) has described three different types of programs, which may be separately based upon (1) reducing the ultimate aversive consequences of a behavior (for example, reducing the rates of smoking, overeating, or alcoholic intake, so that the person does not later suffer the consequences of his own behavior), (2) increasing the rates of behaviors with potentially great, if long-delayed, reinforcement (for example, educational, musical, or professional activities), and (3) altering the physical environment to produce increased stimulus control over desirable behaviors (for example, smoking or drinking in only one place, hiding cigarettes or whiskey, or removing people who might provide social reinforcement for the behavior). The preceding section has described the progress of these and other kinds of self-control programs. In later sections, the similarity and relationship between self-control systems and contingency management, for example, will be revealed.

IMITATION TRAINING

As was revealed in Chapter 8, social imitation or modeling has been used by experimentalists and therapists alike to treat pathological behaviors. While the emphasis of the earlier section was on deceleration of pathological behaviors, the focus in this chapter is on acceleration of desirable behaviors. Some of this material will be unavoidably repetitious, since many of the studies have served both purposes.

Several experiments conducted under controlled laboratory conditions (Miller and Dollard, 1941; Church, 1957; Stimbert *et al.,* 1966) have demonstrated that imitation learning is possible in rats, and that it may be superior to trial-and-error learning. For example, Stimbert *et al.* (1966) trained water-deprived "leader" rats to run an alley to one of four goal boxes. Another group of "follower" rats were run in the same alley and allowed access to water only if they followed the same path to the same goal as they had observed the leader rat select. Different follower rats were paired with different leader rats trained to approach separate goal boxes, so that simple position preferences could not be established. Follower rats learned more quickly than had leaders. Similarly, Darby and Riopelle (1959) found that monkeys that had observed the solution of discrimination problems by other monkeys learned the same discriminations more rapidly than control animals not exposed to such a model.

Other controlled laboratory studies have demonstrated that rhesus monkeys can solve puzzles and problems on the first trial following observation of successful solution by another monkey (Warden *et al.,* 1940), chimps have learned complex responses modeled by humans (Hayes and Hayes, 1952), and rats have learned discriminations (Church, 1957; Miller and Dollard, 1941), lever pressing (Corson, 1967) and operant escape behaviors (Angermeier *et al.,* 1959) more rapidly by observing the solution than by trial-and-error or response-shaping procedures. In addition, several experiments by Miller and his colleagues (Miller *et al.,* 1963; Murphy *et al.,* 1955) have shown that monkeys may subtly communicate emotions to each other that can facilitate learning, particularly of avoidance behavior. Thus, one monkey with access to a lever learned to press it to postpone shock delivered, not to himself, but to another monkey which he could only observe.

Social facilitation or imitation has also been used to restore responses previously reduced to a low rate through extinction, satiation, punishment, or conditioned suppression (Davitz and Mason, 1955; Hake and Laws, 1967; Zajonc, 1965, 1968).

Thus, it seems clear that imitation, even of unlearned responses, can occur in the controlled conditions of laboratory research with animal subjects. A great variety of responses has also been learned by human subjects in laboratory situations, including aggressive behaviors, response styles, play patterns, teaching styles, moral judgments, and self-reinforcement patterns (Bandura, 1969). McDavid (1959) found increasing accuracy of discrimination between boxes containing candy when an adult modeled the correct response for a child. Later, McDavid (1964) found that variable association of modeling and goal box color cues with the proper response led to blind imitation of the model.

As already mentioned (see Chapter 8), Lovaas (1967), Risley and Wolf (1967), and others have used imitation training in teaching speech and other operant responses to autistic and retarded children. For example, Lovaas *et al.* (1967) used imitation training of nonverbal responses with food reinforcement. Successive approximations by schizophrenic children to the behaviors modeled by an adult were reinforced. Generalized imitation was indicated by appropriate matching on the first trial of a novel behavior. Lovaas found correct imitation of modeled speech responses when reinforcement was contingent upon correct imitation, but not when reinforcement was contingent only on the passage of time. These results are shown in Figure 57. Lovaas (1967) also found that initial speech training with food can later be controlled by social and perhaps even self-generated reinforcers.

As reported in Chapter 3, Bandura (1965a, b; 1969; Bandura *et al.,* 1967, 1968) has proposed a two-factor theory of imitation learning and maintenance. Initially, according to the theory, the observational learning occurs by contiguity between the observed stimulus context of the model and the responses made by the observer. Theoretically, this increases the probability that the observer, when he finds himself in the same stimulus context, will make the same responses again. Later performance of the imitated response in test situations is maintained by direct reinforcement. Bandura, however, has not often dealt with the initial acquisition of imitative responses, since the target behavior is in most cases al-

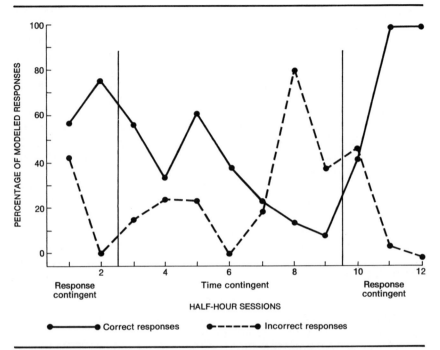

Figure 57. *Percentage of modeled responses correctly and incorrectly reproduced by an autistic child during periods when rewards were made contingent upon matching perfectly the adult's speech (response contingent) or the elapsing of a certain amount of time (time contingent). (From Lovaas, 1967)*

ready in the subject's repertoire. Thus, for example, Bandura *et al.* (1961) exposed children to films of aggressive adult models who were rewarded, punished, or given no consequence for their responses. As predicted, each group of children showed a different amount of imitated aggressive behavior. However, when the children were later offered attractive reinforcers for engaging in the aggressive responses, all the groups rose to high frequencies of behavior.

A very different interpretation and explanatory model of imitation learning has been advanced by Gewirtz and Stingle (1968), who propose that generalized imitation is a functionally related class of behaviors acquired through extrinsic reinforcement and maintained by differential, intermittent reinforcement. This represents an extension of the model suggested by Skinner (1953) in which imitation learning is based on discrimination of matching-to-sample cues. Selected imitative responses in the child are then probably supported by differential reinforcement by the parent, peer, or other social agency. This model has been extended to explain the acquisition of values, attitudes, and motives through socialization and identification of the child, but little data has been collected to confirm this programmatic extension.

Baer and Sherman (1964), however, demonstrated that imitative responses that had never received previous reinforcement could be learned in the context of reinforcement for other imitated responses. Young children in this study received social reinforcement from a puppet who specifically instructed the subjects to match his modeled behavior. When the puppet pressed a bar, several of the children imitated the response, although they never received reinforcement for doing so. Rates were higher during periods of reinforcement for other imitated responses and appeared to extinguish during reinforcement removal.

In another context, Brigham and Sherman (1968) demonstrated that preschool children would imitate nonreinforced Russian words during imitation training of English words with reinforcement for correct responses.

Generalized imitation was observed by Baer *et al.* (1967) in retarded children who showed very little imitation prior to training. After 14 sessions of reinforced imitation training, several imitation responses could be maintained without reinforcement at almost as high a rate as the reinforced responses (see Figure 58). During several sessions of time-contingent rather than response-contingent reinforcement, both classes of response decelerated, but returned to a high rate when reinforcement was again available.

These data would suggest that naive organisms or responses new to the repertoires of the experimental subjects may be needed to more thoroughly test the Bandura position that imitation may be learned in the absence of reinforcement.

On the other hand, reinforcement alone, even with additional feedback, is often not as effective as correctly modeled responses. For example, Luchins and Luchins (1966) found that trial-and-error learning of role behaviors with feedback for correctly performed component responses proceeded very slowly in college students, with sometimes thousands of errors made. Those students who were allowed to observe reinforced models, however, learned the complex role behaviors rapidly and without the frustration of the first group.

Last, Bandura and McDonald (1963) reinforced expression of objective moral judgments in children who previously expressed primarily subjective responses. Reinforcement alone produced little or no change in percent of objective moral judgments, perhaps because of the low rate, as illustrated in Figure 59. However, when another group of children were exposed to adult models who expressed objective judgments, their response rates increased quickly.

As revealed in Chapter 8, Bandura and his colleagues have extended the social imitation and modeling technique to treatment of pathological behavior, with special emphasis on phobic behaviors. For instance, Bandura *et al.* (1967) found more approaches to a dog in formerly dog-phobic nursery children who observed a fearless child pet and feed a dog during a party than children exposed to the dog or party alone. Bandura and Menlove (1968) found that a sym-

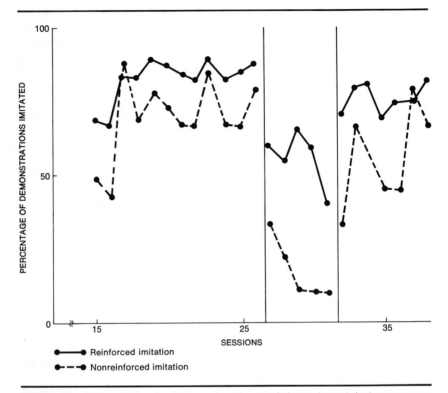

Figure 58. *Percentage of reinforced and nonreinforced modeled responses reproduced by a child during periods when rewards were made contingent upon the occurrence of matching responses or upon the passage of a given period of time (DRO). (From Baer, Peterson, & Sherman, 1967)*

bolic (filmed) presentation of a child feeding many dogs produced more approach responses than the same child feeding only one dog.

Bandura *et al.* (1968), also reviewed earlier, demonstrated that live modeling and guided participation together were more efficient in shaping snake handling and approach responses in formerly snake-phobic subjects than either modeling or desensitization alone. A later replication (Ritter, 1968) supported this finding.

O'Connor (1969) showed preschool social isolates a film of increasingly active reinforced social interaction between children. A soundtrack accompanying the film emphasized the appropriateness of the children's interactions. Children exposed to this film and soundtrack increased their interaction rates to the level of nonisolate nursery children, while control children exposed only to a film of social interaction with no reinforcement showed no change in their rates of interaction.

In a very different setting, several investigators (Duke *et al.,* 1965; Krumboltz *et al.,* 1967; and Truax *et al.,* 1966) have found that

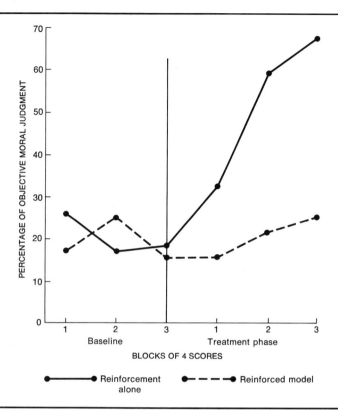

Figure 59. *Mean percentage of objective moral judgment responses produced by subjective children who were either reinforced for objective judgments or exposed to reinforced models who exemplified an objective evaluative orientation. (From Bandura & McDonald, 1967)*

modeling techniques may increase the rate of consideration or verbalization of "significant" topics in counseling or psychotherapy.

In summary, modeling techniques are now popularly found as part of the treatment delivered by therapists of many and various orientations. Modeling and imitation training may be used primarily to accelerate desirable new responses (as revealed in this section), or both to decelerate a pathological and accelerate a normal response (as found in Chapter 8). As commented earlier, the technique is neither simple or univariate. One of the unsettled controversies hinges upon whether imitation learning may occur on the basis of contiguity between the stimulus configuration of which the model is part and the responses of the observer (Bandura, 1969), or whether imitation response-contingent reinforcement is necessary at some stage of training (Gewirtz and Stingle, 1968).

Aside from this issue, it would seem important to determine whether imitation learning can occur in one trial, whether imitation combined with successive approximations or guided participation is superior as treatment to imitation alone, and whether imitation, psychodrama, reinforcement procedures, or desensitization are more efficient in the modification of pathological behaviors. As mentioned in Chapter 8, there is not sufficient data at present to answer these questions.

COUNTERCONDITIONING

Counterconditioning programs have already been considered and reviewed in Chapters 7 and 8, which emphasized decelerative modes of behavior modification. Another short discussion is appropriate within the current emphasis on models for the acceleration of normal behaviors. Since it offers the joint advantages of both accelerative and decelerative programs, counterconditioning has been favored by many therapists for the purpose of behavior modification.

As mentioned in Chapter 7, Wolpe (1958), Wolpe and Lazarus (1966), and others regard desensitization as a counterconditioning procedure in which the stimuli for former anxiety- or fear-producing responses are presented while the subject is in a relaxed state incompatible with anxiety. However, much recent research has indicated that relaxation training (as well as other components) may not be necessary in order to effect a change. The review of the desensitization literature concluded with studies of M. K. Wagner and N. R. Cauthen (1968) and Leitenberg, *et al.* (1969), which indicated that positive reinforcement of nonpathological behaviors in the presence of formerly phobic stimuli was effective in reducing phobic responding. Thus, contingencies that are programmed to follow actual behaviors, rather than their representation in the imagination, may be more effective in the modification of behavior than many of the contingencies used by Wolpe. More research needs to be done on such critical questions in order to make available more rapid and powerful conditioning treatment techniques.

In the earlier discussion of reinforcement of behaviors incompatible with pathology, several studies were reviewed which advanced the same theme: Measurement and manipulation of real clinical behaviors in vivo, rather than in the imagination, may be among the most powerful conditioning procedures.

As indicated, there is sometimes little procedural difference between counterconditioning programs and reinforcement of incompatible behaviors. At the risk of being overly repetitious, let us again review some of the studies that used counterconditioning. In speech-training programs with autistic children, counterconditioning is regularly used to increase speech and decrease disruptive behaviors of various sorts. Risley and Wolf (1967), for example, offered echolalic children reinforcement such as ice cream or other preferred foods contingent upon imitation of speech sounds or units. Disruptive behaviors such as crying, having tantrums, leaving their seats, or inappropriate imitations were followed by extinction, which in this case was a removal of reinforcement and looking away from the child. The authors report that under these conditions disruptive behaviors decreased, and appropriate imitative behaviors increased. Lovaas (1967) has varied the technique by delivering hand slaps contingent upon disruptive or inattentive behaviors. This has more similarity to the aversive counterconditioning methods reviewed in Chapter 8.

Another study reviewed previously applied counterconditioning to the treatment of a socially isolated nursery school child (Allen *et al.,* 1964). In this case teacher attention, the reinforcer, was delivered contingent on interaction with other children and withdrawn following isolated play or interaction with adults. Social interaction increased during such reinforcement periods, and fell when reinforcement was withdrawn.

Still another set of studies reviewed in earlier sections included the shaping of nondelusional speech in a psychotic patient (Rickard *et al.,* 1960). In the context of psychotherapy, these authors reinforced with attention, nods of the head, and expressions of approval normal, nondelusional verbalizations. When the patient made delusional statements, the therapist looked out the window or at the floor (extinction). As a result, delusional statements decreased, and nondelusional responses increased. Rickard and Dinoff (1962) reported that reinforcement control of the same behaviors was still in evidence in a two-year follow-up, in addition to which generalization was observed, as less delusional speech occurred in other locations within the hospital.

Among the early counterconditioning programs that aimed primarily at the acceleration of normal behaviors, we could include Jones' (1924a) treatment of Peter's phobia for furry animals and Jersild and Holmes' (1935) early report of modeling and behavioral rehearsal in the modification of children's fears.

Among the modern examples of counterconditioning with accelerative goals, Ferster and DeMyer (1962) exposed severely disturbed autistic children to an isolated experimental room containing operant manipulanda and automated reinforcement devices, which delivered a full range of reinforcers from food through music and slides to performing animals. With these reinforcers the children were taught many new behaviors, while atavistic, tantrumous, and otherwise disruptive behaviors decreased, probably because reinforcement was no longer available contingent on these behaviors.

E. H. Brawley *et al.* (1969) conducted a functional analysis of the appropriate and inappropriate behaviors in an autistic child on a hospital ward. This analysis revealed that the staff paid much more attention to the child's inappropriate behaviors (such as self-hitting, tantrums, and "junk" verbalizations) than to his appropriate behaviors. Reliability checks with independent observers reflected high levels of agreement (85 percent). Counterconditioning consisted of social and primary reinforcement for appropriate behaviors (comprehensible verbalizations, compliance to requests, use of play materials, and learning of academic skills). Reinforced responses rose from low to high levels under these conditions and dropped again during a control period. With reinstatement of the original contingencies the appropriate behaviors returned to high rates, and inappropriate behaviors disappeared. This was a powerful demonstration of the effects of counterconditioning, with well-designed controls.

Giles and Wolf (1966) used two varieties of counterconditioning in a toilet-training program for institutionalized, severely retarded males. Appropriate elimination in five such children was followed by reinforcement (food, drink, or social reinforcement such as hugs). In some cases, where positive reinforcement and extinction of inappropriate elimination produced no results, positive reinforcement was combined with aversive stimuli such as physical restraint following inappropriate elimination. Within eight weeks all five children showed consistent, appropriate elimination behavior. The reliability of changes produced by this program was supported by the replication of results across subjects, rather than by reversals as in the study by Brawley.

M. G. Harmatz and P. Lapuc (1968) applied an interesting variation on counterconditioning methodology to treat overeating in psychiatric patients. The patients were placed on a controlled diet, but other avenues to food were not restricted. One group forfeited money for failure to lose weight (aversive counterconditioning); another received social reinforcement for weight loss in a group therapy condition; and a third (control group) was assigned only the diet. Although the two experimental procedures produced weight loss during the treatment phase, only the aversive counterconditioning group continued to lose weight during the follow-up period, and the group therapy subjects regained the weight they had lost. This again was a well-controlled study within a group-statistical design. (See Figure 60.)

In an operant conditioning program for profoundly retarded adult males, T. Thompson *et al.* (1970) found half of the sixty-seven subjects unclothed, and most were incontinent and nonverbal. Treatment consisted of reinforcement (food or drink) contingent on adaptive behaviors and extinction for maladaptive behaviors. After the program had been in effect for one year, 91 percent of the patients were clothed; 82 percent were toilet trained; and almost half the patients used some words appropriately. Thus, this program was very effective in eliminating most problem behaviors and in vastly increasing the number of constructive behaviors in a patient group usually resistant to modification.

In a more natural environment G. R. Patterson and G. Brodsky (1966) used counterconditioning procedures to treat the fearful, hyperaggressive, and negativistic behaviors of a five-year-old boy. Treatment was conducted by the parents, teachers, peer group, and experimenters. Cooperative behaviors were followed by reinforcement, and assaultive behaviors were treated with time-out. Data collected throughout the program indicate that extensive changes were fairly well maintained.

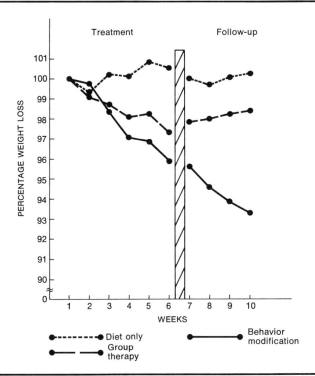

Figure 60. *Percentage of original weight for the behavior modification group, group therapy group, and the control group for each week of the six-week treatment and four-week follow-up periods.* (*From Harmatz & Lapuc, 1968*)

Counterconditioning programs have been extensively used in educational settings. S. Sibley *et al.* (1969), for example, applied teacher attention contingent on desirable classroom behaviors and withheld attention from inappropriate behaviors of a normally disruptive, assaultive, disadvantaged kindergarten boy. Social isolation following assaultive behaviors was even more effective than inattention. Inappropriate behaviors decreased and appropriate behaviors increased during the course of the program and were maintained for some time after treatment by the teacher.

McAllister *et al.* (1969) used a multiple base-line design in counterconditioning inappropriate talking and turning around in a high-school classroom. Teacher praise followed appropriate behaviors, and teacher disapproval was delivered contingent on the incompatible responses of talking and turning around. This procedure reduced the occurrence of the two target behaviors in an experimental class of twenty-five students, but observations of the same behaviors in another class of twenty-six students, taught by the same teacher, did not reveal such changes.

R. McIntire *et al.* (1970) allowed fifth and sixth graders who showed high achievement or improvement in spelling and math access to activities in a project room as reinforcement. Children who showed less improvement had less access to the room, and children who fell off in achievement were restricted to teaching machines. Reversals indicated that reinforcement was effective in improving either math or·spelling scores independently. This was another use of the multiple base-line design, which has generated interesting and useful results.

Counterconditioning has also been assigned an important or central role in psychotherapy by some commentators (Davison, 1968; Kanfer, 1966; Shoben, 1949; Wolpe, 1958). In addition, several studies have substantiated this position by offering a functional analysis of the changes observed in psychotherapies of different orientations. Truax (1966) found, for example, that several patient behaviors varied in accordance with differential response modes of the therapist, Carl Rogers. Approximations to contingencies of reinforcement were found to control several classes of client response, despite Rogers' theoretical notions of nondirective therapy. Similar analyses revealed systematic control of several classes of patient response from hostile statements to positive self-regard, in therapeutic modes ranging from nondirective counseling to Rosen's direct analysis. It might be helpful to these therapists, if they are interested in increasing their therapeutic effectiveness, to continue this type of functional analysis in an attempt to systematize their treatment process and increase their efficiency.

In summary, counterconditioning has been found to be a very powerful technique for the control of constructive, as well as pathological, behaviors. Particularly when combined with reinforcement of incompatible responses, this technique would seem to be of great value. Earlier reviews have indicated the utility of counterconditioning programs in decelerative and aversive programs, and the studies reviewed here have applied counterconditioning techniques with the therapeutic goal of accelerating constructive behaviors.

TOKEN ECONOMIES

Some of the most elaborate applications of straight reinforcement models have been termed token economies. In token economies, conditioned reinforcers (tokens such as poker chips) are delivered to patients in ward settings for desired behaviors. Extensive reports of such experimental treatment wards are available in Ayllon and Azrin's *The Token Economy* and H. H. Schaefer and P. L. Martin's *Behavioral Therapy*. In both cases, tokens were delivered contingent on constructive, desired, often work-type behaviors. Tokens were usually exchangeable for articles desired by the patients. For example, candy, cigarettes, and other items in a store or canteen, special meals, private furnishings, and room rent were often used as "back-up reinforcers" for which tokens could be exchanged, according to the needs or desires of the individual patient. Thus, the token economies exercise strict control of the contingency between the behaviors to be reinforced and delivery of the conditioned reinforcer, while allowing the patient to exchange, or "spend," the tokens as he wishes. The data reported in these two books demonstrate that this new technology, although requiring radical departures from traditional ward management routines, yields some of the most powerful behavioral control available to date.

Ayllon and Azrin's (1968) *Token Economy* offered a careful extension of principles and generalizations demonstrated in animal laboratories to a psychiatric ward of female patients, most of whom were diagnosed as schizophrenic and had lived in the hospital for many years. This report was conservatively delayed until the program had been in operation for five years to guarantee its reliability. The book lists the rules and principles that were of the most value to the program, together with prior experimental work and current data generated by the project.

The design was avowedly behavioral, concentrating only on those behaviors that could be described clearly and without subjective interpretation. In addition, each selected target behavior was a constructive one that would receive later support by the community (either inside or outside the hospital) following termination of the program. A choice of many reinforcers or potential reinforcers was made available to each individual, ranging from frequently requested events, such as a grounds pass that allowed the person to go off the ward, to high frequency behaviors such as a visit to the commissary. One patient who had earlier been denied tranquilizers for medical reasons was allowed to exchange tokens for placebos ad libitum, 648 of which were delivered over a six-month period. Several automated reinforcement mechanisms such as turnstiles, cigarette dispensers and lighters, and coin-operated televisions and radios were used, but direct supervision often functioned as well and offered more flexibility and opportunity for shaping.

Standard rules of response shaping, response and reinforcer exposure, and sampling were used, and they were combined with liberal use of instructions to prompt and shape new responses. Thus, the program combined the advantages of imitation learning and the gradual shaping of new behaviors with the aid of instructions, modeling procedures, and ample reinforcement of appropriate behaviors. The effectiveness of most of the procedures was demonstrated and often replicated via the ABA design, in which a contingency is presented, removed or changed systematically, and then reinstated. Although follow-up and more grossly clinical material is not reported, the authors state that use of their motivating environment at Anna State Hospital increased work performance of the involved patients by a factor of four. Figures 61, 62, and 63 reflect some of the constructive changes reported by Ayllon and Azrin. Note the effects of reinforcement in each case.

Schaefer and Martin, in their book, *Behavioral Therapy* (1969),

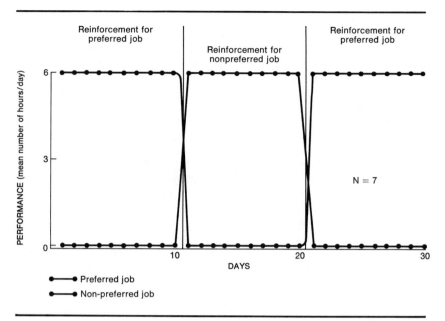

Figure 61. *Mean number of hours patients worked per day when positive reinforcement was varied between preferred and nonpreferred jobs. (From Ayllon & Azrin, 1965. Additional information and related research can be found in Ayllon & Azrin, 1968.)*

made direct efforts to cope with more distinctly clinical behaviors. This book reports on the token economy program at Patton State Hospital in California, where the ward has since been largely automated. Closed-circuit television, for example, allows observation of most space on the ward and monitoring from the nurses' station. In addition, intercommunication systems and automatic token dispensers allow nurses to reinforce behaviors from a distance with both verbal and token reinforcers. Most of the behaviors dealt with in the Schaefer and Martin text are commonly observed on psychiatric wards, so that this book may be used as a standard reference work. Because of its specificity, however, it may not be as applicable to the initiation of new programs or to work with new behaviors as the Ayllon-Azrin material.

Since these early reports the number of token economies in existence has mushroomed, so that every state seems to have at least one. California has four in the state hospital system alone. The Veterans Administration has twenty-five or more, and recent reports seem to indicate further increases. Token economies or variations thereon have been applied to at least the following by the authors indicated: adult psychotics (Ayllon & Azrin, 1968; Atthowe & Krasner, 1968; Gericke, 1965; Lloyd & Able, 1970), mentally retarded (Girardeau and Spradlin, 1964; Lachenmeyer, 1969), juvenile delinquents (Cohen, 1968; Burchard and Tyler, 1965), remedial class-

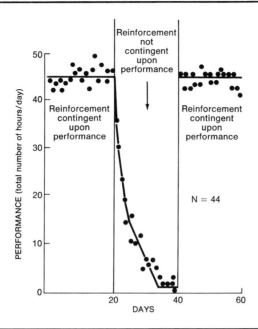

Figure 62. *Total number of hours a group of forty-four schizophrenic patients participated in rehabilitative activities when rewards were conditional upon successful completion of assignments and when the same rewards were provided regardless of whether or not the patients took part in the activities. (From Ayllon & Azrin, 1965. Additional information and related research can be found in Ayllon & Azrin, 1968.)*

rooms (O'Leary *et al.,* 1967; O'Leary, *et al.,* 1969; Wolf *et al.,* 1968), alcoholics (Narrol, 1967), hard-core unemployed (Sandler & Turner, 1973), geriatric patients (Libb & Clements, 1969), and imprisoned offenders (Clements & McKee, 1968).

From the published reports it would appear that most of the token economies recently put into operation were designed with specifically clinical goals and frequently with insufficient research design to enable adequate evaluation (see review by Kazdin & Bootzin, 1972). This poses great difficulties, since one of the redeeming values of the token economy is its research base, which, when properly integrated should allow easy evaluation of the progress made by each individual affected by the program. However, this level of evaluation is based upon regular measurement, routine troubleshooting, and readjustment of contingencies in order to maintain optimal schedules and programs for each individual involved. Many of the psychologists who have initiated such programs have found how time-demanding they can be, and have begun to opt for consultation to (rather than management of) such programs or have designed other, less ambitious projects.

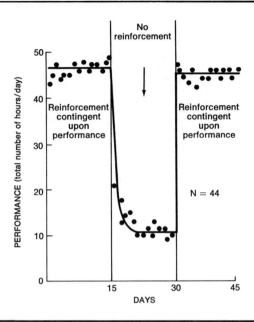

Figure 63. *Total number of hours spent each day by the group of forty-four patients performing "on-ward" activities during periods when rewards were given upon completion of work assignments, when positive incentives were not used and the various activities and privileges were freely available, and when the reinforcement contingencies were introduced into the social system. (From Ayllon & Azrin, 1965. Additional information and related research can be found in Ayllon & Azrin, 1968.)*

CONTINGENCY MANAGEMENT

Since contingency management is one of the more complex programs combining the principles of self-control and operant conditioning, it has been reserved as the last of the procedures aimed at shaping and accelerating normal behaviors. The efforts of Lloyd Homme (1965, 1966) are largely responsible for the design and development of contingency management models. The primary focus of many contingency management programs is upon the control of "coverants" (Homme's term for covert operants), which are internalized behaviors such as thinking, feeling, and imagining. Obviously, these are behaviors that are not normally accessible to the objective observer, although Homme assumes that the same learning principles and control techniques apply to these behaviors.

Similar to Lindsley's (1971) precision teaching, individuals in contingency management programs are taught to arrange consequences or specific antecedents for their own behaviors. Frequently, a pathological set of behaviors may be analyzed as a response chain, the early covert components of which are modified in the attempt to reduce the frequency of the target behavior. Thus, the patient or client may be taught very specific antecedent coverants that are incompatible with the pathological target behavior.

In the usual training procedure, the patient learns to relax and thus to discriminate between relaxed states and proprioceptive and other feedback from tense musculature. The patient is then taught to associate the word "relax" with the relaxed state. The word can then be used to reduce the frequency of tense or fearful states. Other kinds of coverants which the patient may be taught include self-mastery coverants (for example, "I am in charge of my own behavior"), statements of positive self-regard (for example, "I am a likable person"), and similar "procoverants." Once these are well learned, they can be used by the patient, since they are incompatible with thoughts and feelings of inadequacy, inferiority, and failure.

In addition, Homme has applied the Premack (1959, 1965) reinforcement model to the problem of behavior modification, so that behaviors of high frequency may be used as reinforcers for those of low probability or frequency. Thus, for example, the fearful phobic person may be trained to emit the relaxation coverant prior to making a telephone call, reading a book, or other frequently occurring normal behaviors. The high probability of the latter behaviors should increase the frequency and probability of the relaxation coverant, which, once it has been well learned, can be gradually extended to precede increasingly pathological behaviors.

Homme (1965) states that once the relaxation coverant is well learned, subjects come to feel increased mastery or control over their own behaviors. It may be very timely to teach the self-mastery coverant ("I am responsible for my being more relaxed" or "I am in charge of my own behavior") at this point. This coverant may be critical to the whole system, the success of which frequently depends upon teaching the patient self-control through coverant control.

Homme (1965) has also been responsible for the extension of contingency management to the programming of the behaviors of others. In most of these applications, behaviors of diverse kinds have been analyzed as usable reinforcers, access to which is made contingent upon the emission of desirable behaviors, a la Premack (1965). So, for example, in a nursery school class where the children most frequently ran about and screamed, the children were permitted to do this, providing they first sat quietly in their seats and watched the instructor at the blackboard for increasing intervals.

Similarly, academic programs with deprived slum-dwelling and Indian children were found very effective (Homme, 1965). A fascinating extension to "hip" high-school dropouts revealed that they would willingly do arithmetic and programmed reading assignments to obtain access to a programmed Russian course. (The author speculated that they might be able to use the Russian as a secret code the police could not break.) In addition, a blind, nontalking retardate was trained to speak more than she had during eight years of institutionalization when imitative speech allowed her to gain access to the therapist's hand (which the patient invariably seized and smelled).

Homme (1965) points out that not only does contingency management have broad application as a system, but it does not require extended training of contingency managers. Thus, technicians, who take a short course, can extend the technique to many people in need of it.

Contract management is frequently a part of contingency management programs. So, for example, the patient may be instructed that if he goes through the steps prescribed by the therapist, the therapist will make more of his services available, make a new phase of the program available, or provide more information and instruction. Programs involving contract management were described earlier in discussions of productive avoidance (Zimmerman, 1969) and of some of the token economies. In some programs motivation for treatment may be increased by allowing the patient some role or choice in treatment planning. For example, several possible contingency management systems, aversive conditioning, and standard psychotherapy may all be described to the patient, who may then either choose the treatment modality or aid the therapist in this decision. Use of techniques such as this might increase the patient's commitment to his share of the contractual agreement. It might be interesting and worthwhile to study the dropout rates of such programs to determine if this is the case.

In summary, contingency management has enjoyed wide success in dealing with behavior management problems of diverse sorts and is currently being applied to an increasing number of settings. Insofar as this system trains the subject himself in behavioral engineering and teaches him the scientific principles of self-control, it may potentially have wide-ranging effects far beyond the specific behaviors dealt with. These functions, however, will be extremely difficult to deal with experimentally, since appropriate outcome measurement models are currently lacking.

Another, perhaps even more difficult, measurement problem will arise should many clinicians accept Homme's (1966) suggestion to mix contingency management programs with standard psychotherapy. Although it is recognized that such combinations *might* be helpful to the patient, it should also be pointed out that current technology is barely equipped to measure the process, let alone the outcome results of simple, one- or two-variable treatment designs. More complex programs usually have to be evaluated globally against control groups or differently treated groups. In this sort of analysis it is impossible to determine exactly what has produced any observed improvement.

PART FOUR / BROADENING THE BASE OF BEHAVIOR MODIFICATION

Thus far in this volume the emphasis has been on the experimental analysis and treatment of pathological behavior. In this last section the focus will turn to some more general issues that have long been of concern to clinical psychologists.

The first set of issues deals in general with the long-range effects of treatment programs in environments beyond the laboratory or clinic. It is the concentration and focus on clinical follow-up that sets clinical treatment programs apart from simple administrative or management programs. In the latter cases, little more than immediate control and management of pathological behaviors may be the goal of the program, while in the former the purpose is more far-reaching. One of the hallmarks of professional treatment is the goal of teaching the patient or client something new, some constructive behavior that he can, it is hoped, use to his benefit in the future. To the extent that this goal is realized and the new behavior persists in environments other than that in which it was learned, stimulus generalization may have occurred.

As will be revealed in Chapter 11, stimulus generalization has often been experimentally analyzed in the basic laboratory, but a large gap remains between these studies and clinical applications. Much more systematic knowledge is badly needed in order properly to equip patients and clients to return to their own preferred environments and to maintain whatever benefits may have accrued from therapy.

With the currently available technology, therapists can do little more than postulate that behaviors that are well learned in treatment should persist in other environments, to the extent that these environments are similar to treatment conditions. In terms of a specific operant analysis of the stimulus configurations in both kinds of environments, however, both discriminative stimuli or setting events and reinforcement contingencies should be taken into consideration. Most of the laboratory research has concerned the former, although it should be clear that, without the proper reinforcement contingencies, behavior could not be expected to persist. Thus, it is important to prepare an individual to return to a specific extratherapeutic environment and to mimic the S^{D}s and reinforcement contingencies known to exist there, insofar as possible.

In addition, there is the question of response generalization versus response specificity of treatment. These issues have only rarely been investigated in the basic laboratory, but have been reported more frequently in clinical journals. Response generalization has been observed by several behavior therapists (Risley, 1968; Bucher and Lovaas, 1968; Tate and Baroff, 1966) who reported increases in several constructive behaviors not specifically treated in addition to decreases in pathological behaviors treated by aversive conditioning. Reports of generalized benefits beyond treated behaviors have also followed training in self-control procedures (Homme, 1965; Cautela, 1971). Thus, it appears altogether possible that some programs may generate the basis for broad improvements beyond specifically treated behaviors, but not enough systematic investigation has revealed the conditions when this might occur. Further research is needed to allow more precise predictions.

The obverse of response generalization, response specificity, has also been reported following some types of therapy. Quinn and Henbest (1967), for example, found that seven of ten alcoholic patients treated with aversive conditioning of whiskey drinking stopped drinking whiskey following treatment but continued to drink other alcoholic beverages excessively. The remaining three patients also stopped drinking whiskey following treatment, but continued to drink beer or stout, although not to excess. Thus, each of these patients showed response specificity and at least seven of the ten showed lack of response generalization. Again, not enough is known to explain very clearly why this particular aversive conditioning procedure produced such extreme response specificity, while the other aversive procedures reported earlier resulted in response generalization and no apparent specificity.

Chapter 12 will return to a consideration of some of the general philosophical background and roots of behaviorism and behavior therapy. This general discussion is designed to round out the behavioristic reorientation to clinical psychology. It is followed by a more specific discussion of methodology and how techniques developed within the laboratory have been applied in the clinic. This has become another of the identifying characteristics of behavior modification. Next will be found a summary discussion of the problems that exist in behavioral approaches to assessment, of the need for a consistent assessment model, and some preliminary proposals for solution.

The last few sections of the book will present a behaviorally oriented model of the training of behavior modification specialists, followed by a discussion of ethical problems and some prediction of future trends.

Chapter 11 / Stimulus and Response Generalization

STIMULUS GENERALIZATION

Stimulus and response generalization are both very important concepts, in the basic laboratory as well as in the clinic or applied research environment. Stimulus generalization, for example, enters into every learning task in which more than one stimulus is presented to the subject, since there are data to support the transfer of training from one learning situation to another along relevant stimulus dimensions. For instance, when a stimulus (for example, a wavelength or color of light) has been paired with a schedule of reinforcement which results in a particular response pattern, other lights of different wavelength will exercise similar control, even though they may never have been paired directly with reinforcement. The usual finding is that stimuli will show increasing amounts of control as they approach the original training stimulus in similarity. N. Guttman and H. I. Kalish (1956) have shown such functions over several wavelengths of light with pigeons and humans. (See Figure 64.) These and other investigators have also demonstrated that the generalization function is affected by the number of prior reinforcements, level of deprivation, and the number of generalization tests in extinction as well as by the stimulus dimension itself.

In clinical applications stimulus generalization is sometimes of critical importance in determining whether, for example, a therapeutic program or regime prescribed for a patient or client shows any carry-over or transfer to the extra-therapy environment. In standard

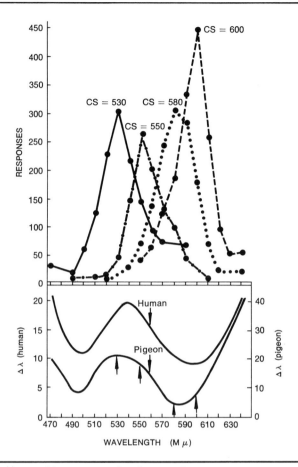

Figure 64. Upper: Mean generalization gradients, first test. Lower: Hue discrimination as a function of wavelength for pigeons and humans. (*From Guttman & Kalish, 1956*)

psychotherapy and psychoanalysis, the assumption is frequently made that insights achieved and lessons learned in the therapy hour will extend to the outside environment and change the extra-clinical life of the patient. As an experimental test of such an assumption, it might be possible to devise a measure of stimulus generalization to determine whether or not such is the case, although this has not been undertaken.

In many behavior modification programs, on the other hand, specific tests of stimulus generalization may be an integral part of the program. In desensitization, for example, one of the critical tests of the success or failure of the technique itself is the determination of whether or not the treated patient can approach and pick up a snake or other object he formerly feared and avoided. Since desensitization is conducted on the basis of a hierarchy of scenes that are visualized, a successful approach to a live snake outside therapy would be classified as stimulus generalization.

In most forms of standard psychotherapy the assumed mechanism of therapeutic effectiveness is based upon stimulus and response generalization. For example, the arguments over attitude change, cognitive dissonance, whether insight precedes behavioral change or vice versa, etc., may actually hinge on the issue of whether or not clinical treatment of a particular kind will have generalized effects outside the therapy hour. With those approaches in which the aim is to transfer control of target behaviors in treatment to extra-therapeutic environments, the issue is one of stimulus generalization. With those forms of therapy, on the other hand, in which the therapist hopes to effect changes in behaviors other than those observed during treatment, and also through change agents other than the therapist, the issue is more complex, including at least the dimensions of stimulus and response generalization and perhaps others as well.

One of the great advantages that the more explicitly programmed techniques of behavior modification offer is a kind of microcosm of the relevant dimensions of behavior change. Thus, with most of the experimental methods of modification reviewed in this volume, it would be possible to dimensionalize the relevant parameters and experimentally vary them to determine their separate contributions to treatment. In systematic desensitization, for example, Wolpe (1958, Wolpe & Lazarus, 1966) has assumed that a necessary part of this treatment is the hierarchical presentation of fear-arousing stimuli. This represents a stimulus generalization gradient with the initial response being fear. When treatment is successful, none of the stimuli on the gradient should elicit fear, nor should the initially feared object. Thus, successful treatment by desensitization involves an extension of a treatment effect beyond the imaginal series dealt with in therapy to the initially feared object. This is an extension of the stimulus generalization series to an untreated stimulus in the natural environment.

Similarly, covert sensitization (Cautela, 1966, 1967) depends upon imagined stimuli and consequences to achieve an effect not unlike the generalizing of punishment outside therapy. Thus, for example, the stimuli controlling homosexuality, alcoholism, or other compulsive behavior may be presented in imagination to the subject, who is also instructed to visualize a consequence such as nausea and vomiting. The assumption is that exposure to the actual stimulus in the environment will result in an avoidance response.

A growing number of modification projects are attempting to explicitly analyze the stimulus-control properties of the relevant stimuli in the therapeutic exchange, whether they be therapist variables, tokens, or other types of reinforcers. Isaacs *et al.* (1960), for example, in an early study used contingent reinforcement to teach two formerly mute psychotic patients to talk, then studied the generalization of this change from one therapist to another as well as outside therapy and on the ward where the patients lived. Similarly, Davison (1964) in a program designed to teach social skills to an austistic child, specifically programmed generalization tests to be conducted in the presence of experimenters other than the therapists in order to measure the maintenance of progress obtained during therapy.

In many token economy or contingency management programs, multiple schedules have been used in which one stimulus-control system or one therapist is substituted for another in order to study generalization effects. When the generalization test succeeds, the prediction of transfer to the natural environment can be made with increased confidence. Ayllon and Azrin (1968), for example, proposed reinforcer exposure and sampling techniques to achieve maximum generalization from their token economy procedures. These authors suggested that for maximum utilization of a reinforcing event, all possible stimuli should be combined with reinforcement that could be used to foster later control. (For example, visual, auditory, olfactory, and social stimuli might be combined with reinforcement practices when possible.) Consequently, they introduced several reinforcers, such as popcorn and soda, which were first available alone for purchase with tokens. Then later these items were given free with each meal. With this procedure every patient was exposed to the reinforcers, and, in addition, the patients could observe one another selecting reinforcers, eating, drinking, etc. This technique invariably increased the number of purchases of these reinforcers in exchange for tokens, and, in addition, frequently resulted in higher reinforcement consumption rates after than before the exposure.

Ayllon and Azrin (1968) have also proposed the relevancy of the "behavior rule." Under the guidance of this rule, they attempted to teach each patient only those behaviors that would continue to be reinforced following training. Thus, each patient was theoretically trained to engage only in those constructive behaviors that would continue to be reinforced, not only on the ward, but in the natural environment following discharge from the hospital. This mechanism provided new means for analyzing the behaviors that would prove maximally useful to the patient in the reinforcement communities in which he might be expected to live. Thus, the patients in the token economy, who were all females and mostly older, former housewives from lower socioeconomic classes, were taught skills such as clerical, dietary, laundry, or laboratory work. These were not only skills that the patients could master but also skills that could be expected to earn reinforcement both inside and outside the hospital. Stimulus generalization took place as the skills were transferred from the control of early dense to later intermittent schedules of token reinforcement and, following discharge, to the money economy outside the institution with those patients who were discharged.

Similarly, Schaefer and Martin (1969) effected the transition by withdrawing or fading the token schedules, while fading in the money economy and contact with the outside world. In this way it was possible to analyze the control over the behaviors modified during the program under widely differing "natural" classes of stimuli. To the extent that stimulus generalization was observed, the staff was in a position to predict that the patient was ready for discharge and might function well outside the hospital.

In short, stimulus generalization, once thought to be of great interest only to the experimentalist in the laboratory, is being increasingly used in clinical settings as an analytic tool that can enable predictions of the therapeutic effectiveness of most kinds of techniques. For example, in the frequently used ABA design, where a contingency is applied to a single behavior or a whole program of contingencies is applied to many classes of behaviors in the B condition, these contingencies being absent in the A condition, the effective control of behavior may be examined under widely different stimulus conditions. In a slightly more refined analysis of stimulus generalization in clinical settings, measurements of treated behaviors are being made in many programs outside as well as during therapy hours or treatment programs. This again may allow the therapist or program planner to predict whether or not the treated behaviors will be maintained outside treatment. Finally, in some recent programs treatment regimes have been faded out in graduated steps so that generalization could be analyzed along temporal, degree of contact, or schedule dimensions. As mentioned previously, some programs are also explicitly programming multiple schedules that assist in the analysis of stimulus generalization. For example, a treatment program may be administered by one staff (say, the day shift on a hospital ward) and the effects measured by another (say, the evening or swing shift). Such programs make use of stimulus generalization, but also allow better and more precise predictions regarding the effects of treatment programs in concurrent, but more or less dissimilar, stimulus environments.

RESPONSE GENERALIZATION
Response generalization, the counterpart of stimulus generalization, is defined as the control of different responses by a particular stimulus or stimulus complex. D. D. Wickens (1943), for example, conditioned human subjects to raise their fingers in an extensor response up from an electrode when a tone was sounded in order to avoid shock. After this procedure the subjects were instructed to turn their hands over, palms up. Under these conditions each subject made a flexor response (which again moved the finger up and off the electrode) still resulting in shock avoidance. Similar examples of response generalization have been reported in classical conditioning (Kellogg, 1939), where electrodes may be moved from limb to limb of dog subjects.

Since little is known about the mechanisms mediating response generalization, there does not yet appear to be any reliable way of predicting when the phenomenon might occur or which response classes or systems might be involved. One possibility is that correlated response classes may respond similarly to the same independent variable manipulations. Thus, for example, when desensitization is effective in reducing apparent fear of an imagined stimulus, this treatment process may also result in reduction of fear of the formerly avoided object in the natural environment. Such response generalization may depend upon a correlation or functional equivalence of the stimuli and responses involved. This might lend some support to two-process theories of fear and avoidance (Mowrer, 1947), but it may be more parsimonious to assume that fear and avoidance responses are correlated and under the control of similar contingencies, which are modified by desensitization. This sort of logic might readily extend to other data such as that of Bandura *et al.* (1968), who found that modeling and guided participation produced major changes in phobic behavior, and also generalized to affective and attitudinal changes. Further indirect support comes from experiments such as that of P. J. Lang *et al.* (1965), who found that desensitization of specific fears generalized positively to other fears as well.

Several experiments in verbal conditioning have demonstrated changes in verbal response rates that also generalized to other, sometimes nonverbal, responses, as a function of reinforcement contingencies. Lovaas, for example, has completed a series of such studies, beginning with one (1961) in which a group of children was reinforced for emitting aggressive verbal responses. In the generalization task the children were allowed to press a bar, which was followed by aggressive doll play. The children who had been reinforced for aggressive verbal responses showed higher rates of bar pressing than children reinforced for nonaggressive verbal responses. In a later experiment Lovaas (1964) reinforced use of a term denoting one of four kinds of food, then allowed the subjects (ten children) to select one of the foods for a snack. The data showed increases in the selection of the kind of food labeled by the term, another demonstration of response generalization.

Similarly, J. G. Phelan *et al.* (1967) and E. O. Timmons (1962) found transfer of responses that were conditioned verbally to correlated nonverbal behaviors. Timmons, for example, found that subjects who had been reinforced for saying words related to building activity, when asked to draw something, drew more buildings than other objects.

Brodsky (1967) went further in the analysis and questioned whether or not the controlling relation or correlation between verbal and nonverbal behaviors might not sometimes be unidirectional. This investigator worked with two adolescent, institutionalized asocial girls, recording first their base rates of social behavior in a naturalistic and an interview setting. Following reinforcement for social behavior in the interview setting, one girl showed concomitant increases in verbal behavior. However, the other girl, who received reinforcement only for verbal statements about social behavior, did not show generalization to other social behaviors. This suggests that there may occasionally be a unidirectional, or one-way, street between classes of behavior, such as verbal and nonverbal.

Risley and Hart (1968) came closer to a solution by demonstrating at least one way in which the occurrence of one behavior may show positive correlation with another. These authors found that reinforcing reports of a particular play material by preschoolers initially had little or no effect on actual use of such material (nonverbal behavior). However, once the reporting rate was high, the requiring of correspondence between the verbal and related nonverbal behaviors in order for reinforcement to occur resulted in observed increases in the use of several new kinds of materials. It is probably some such reinforcement control of two or more classes of behavior that accounts for such covariations or response generalization.

The same explanation may be extended to the issue of awareness in verbal conditioning. Historically, this question seems to have focused upon the perhaps irreconcilable views that awareness is a necessary cognitive mediator inferred from verbal conditioning (the cognitive view) and that awareness may be analyzed as any other class of response that can be separately conditioned under the control of the relevant variables (the behavioral view). In verbal conditioning experiments, then, awareness may occur as a correlated response class under the control of the same reinforcement that comes to control the response class to be learned. On the one hand, proponents such as C. D. Spielberger and L. D. DeNike (1966) have argued cogently for the cognitive point of view, with great and elaborate support from D. E. Dulany (1962), while Verplanck (1962), Greenspoon (1962), and Krasner and Ullmann (1963) have mustered support for the behavioral point of view on the other.

Since we do not have enough space to review the host of studies related to this issue, some of the efforts representing the dominant themes will be reviewed. Several researchers (Drennan & Greenspoon, 1960; Weinstein & Lawson, 1963) have told subjects of the response-reinforcement contingency, while still observing varied results, both in terms of acquisition (or lack of acquisition) of the reinforced response class and in terms of reported awareness. If their results are to be accepted as valid indicators of awareness, then awareness may be neither necessary nor sufficient for verbal conditioning.

Many more studies have sought to measure the extent of awareness during and after verbal conditioning. A number of investigators have found that awareness may occur after the fact, that is, after acquisition of a verbal response class has been observed, but almost as many have shown the reverse. In a recent study Kennedy (1970) assessed awareness after each conditioning trial, and found increases in the conditioned class in the absence of awareness and prior to awareness, but prior to an increase in reinforcement. The author concluded that performance gains and awareness are both dependent variables that are separately influenced by reinforcement. A similar conclusion was reached by Krasner and Ullmann (1963), who found that awareness was influenced by the informational cues given the subject and probably by most of the same variables that control conditioning. Therefore, these two authors suggested that a positive correlation between awareness and verbal conditioning may not be accepted as evidence that one is mediated by the other. Verplanck (1962), in an article entitled "Unaware of Where's Awareness," demonstrated how a verbal response and the awareness of whether or not that response would lead to reinforcement (statement of a rule) could be separately conditioned, so that either positive or negative or zero-order correlations between the two could be obtained by separately reinforcing the two. It would seem hard to counter such a demonstration.

Another example of response generalization is the learning of imitation. As J. L. Gewirtz and K. G. Stingle (1968) point out, imitative responses are frequently learned and controlled as a correlated response class, in the sense that the subject is reinforced initially for imitative responses of a few different types or topographies. As the number of responses that are correctly imitated and consequently reinforced increases, the probability of imitation of new responses also increases. Thus, with the typical imitation-learning background of a child, many responses may be imitated with or without reinforcement. For example, in an experiment by T. A. Brigham and J. A. Sherman (1968) three preschool children were reinforced for accurate imitation of English words. Novel Russian words were also presented, but imitation of Russian words was never reinforced. As long as reinforcement was delivered following imitation of English words, the accuracy of imitation of Russian words increased. When reinforcement was discontinued, accuracy of imitation of both English and Russian words decreased.

GENERALIZATION IN GENERAL
Some issues may involve both stimulus and response generalization. The question of symptom substitution, for example, may be relevant in this connection. In our earlier discussion (see Introduction, Part Three) we described the assumptions underlying this concept (Fenichel, 1945) and the questionable logic that supports this argument. Attempts to provide evidence in support of symptom substitution from the behavior therapy literature have also been unsuccessful. B. L. Baker (1969), for example, hypothesized that substitute symptoms would arise following conditioning treatment of enuresis in thirty children. Outcome data, however, reflected improvement in areas other than the specific behavior treated (response generalization?), including general adjustment. D. D. Cahoon (1968) suggests further research designs for the collection of data relevant to the issue of symptom substitution following behavior therapy.

With some exceptions the weight of the evidence at this point seems to suggest that patients who improve following behavior therapy frequently show improvement in other behaviors as well, contrary to the symptom substitution prediction. For example, Lovaas *et al.* (1965b) used a shock escape-avoidance procedure with two five-year-old autistic children to teach them to approach adults. These researchers found that the procedure not only resulted in approach responses in the children, but it also helped reduce or eliminate pathological behaviors, such as self-stimulation and tantrums. In addition, affection and other social responses toward adults increased following conditioning. The authors account for these increases on the basis of the association of adults with shock reduction, but this remains an excellent demonstration of response generalization following treatment.

Working with a different target problem, R. Schwitzgebel and D. A. Kolb (1964) paid adolescent delinquents to talk into a tape recorder, and reinforcement was delivered contingent on "positive" statements. A three-year follow-up revealed that the experimental group had fewer criminal charges against them, spent less time incarcerated, and suffered fewer convictions than a control group. Again, the data demonstrated improvement along several dimensions of behavior, which may have been correlated with the treated or target behavior, but which may again be interpreted as response generalization.

Similarly, Bandura (1969) has reported several instances of improvements in behaviors beyond those directly treated. One specific example is that of Bandura *et al.* (1968) in which snake-phobic subjects showed maximal change when exposed to live modeling with a snake and guided participation, as measured by frequency of snake-approach responses (look at, touch, hold the snake, etc.). Interestingly however, not only did this procedure prove more effective than symbolic desensitization or symbolic modeling, but the subjects also showed reduction of fear in other threatening situations, as well as positive affective and attitudinal changes.

Other measures such as paper-and-pencil tests have also reflected general changes representing improvement along many dimensions in addition to the behavior treated in therapy. For example, I. Al-Issa and T. Kraft (1967) reported significant changes representing improvement in such things as neuroticism, anxiety, and extroversion measures following behavior therapy. Unless these changes can be demonstrated to be *functionally* related to changes in or after therapy, however, they probably cannot be regarded as cases of response generalization.

It is entirely possible, of course, that such changes may reflect improvements which were planned but not specifically brought about during therapy. In any case, the information may be used to good effect. Thus, for example, a growing number of therapists using desensitization or covert sensitization (Wolpe & Lazarus, 1966; Cautela, 1966) are beginning to suggest to their patients or clients that they use the modification techniques at home, often with other behaviors. To the extent to which this is successful, generalized rather than specific changes can be expected to occur. It is difficult to know precisely what such changes should be labeled, although they may approach what we have defined as response generalization.

Some of the studies of self-control techniques (see Chapter 10) are also relevant to response generalization. Thus, to the extent that a therapist can teach a person a technique or techniques whereby he can treat or control his own behaviors, response generalization would be expected to occur. For example, a therapist may teach a person a technique that he can use to treat the initial target behavior and that he can similarly apply to other behaviors as well, without the help of the therapist. To the extent that this process can be promoted, many other behaviors may benefit as a result.

The previous comments regarding stimulus and response generalization serve only as an introduction to the range and complexity of changes that frequently occur following behavior modification as well as any other kind of therapeutic manipulation. In the past many of these changes have been reported and attributed to therapeutic manipulations as if they were expected consequences, although precise specification has been lacking. It is our contention that specific analyses of stimulus and response generalization will increase the predictability of some of these changes. If therapeutic programs of the future explicitly incorporate models of such generalization, this issue may resolve itself.

Future research must be directed at answering the many questions that are still unresolved. Thus, no explanation can be readily advanced for the appearance, following aversive conditioning, of constructive new behaviors that were not evident prior to treatment. Little is known regarding the change in the individual's entire behavioral repertoire following the modification of some component of that repertoire. Is there a shift in the habit family hierarchy? Once eliminated, is a formerly prepotent response class automatically replaced by the next most frequently occurring class? How can one better predict correlated response classes that might predictably change together? These are only a few of the more apparent questions to be answered.

Chapter 12 / Postlude

PHILOSOPHICAL CONSIDERATIONS

Part of the goal of this book has been to describe the relationship of behavior modification and behavior therapy to the older experimental traditions, which have been developing within psychological science in the past thirty or forty years. Much of that experimental tradition has involved the philosophical reorientation that is identified by many as behaviorism. As revealed in the opening chapters, behaviorism has provided psychology with new critical tools of analysis, at both the theoretical and practical levels, which have enabled a reorientation, a new and different point of view regarding human behavior. This is a thoroughly deterministic framework, one that lends itself well to the control and prediction of behavior. The important determiners of human (as well as subhuman) behavior are considered to be found in the internal and external elicitors and consequences of responses. Since the classes of stimuli extrinsic to the organism are most easily observed and measured, most of the emphasis has been upon these environmental determiners. Their measurement and control has become the primary job of the behavioral engineer. As a result, the prevailing experimental point of view has come to emphasize the functional relationship between changes in environmental stimuli and consequent changes in behavior.

Behaviorism is a movement with philosophical roots traceable to logical positivism, pragmatism, and radical empiricism. The source of knowledge within this system is the functional relationship between behavior and its controlling variables. Thus, one of the items involved in any behavioristic study of epistemology must be the functional analysis of the behaviors of those engaged in such a pursuit. The source of knowledge is not in the thoughts of men or in any deductions from theories that men construct, but in the relationship between man engaged in thought and its controlling variables.

When properly conducted, scientific behaviorism is self-correcting; a priori predicted relationships that are not borne out by the data fall by the wayside, and functional relationships bridge islands of isolated findings to the mainland of inductive theory construction. Without the empirical relationships at the lowest level, theoretical structures are but towers in shaky sand.

Similarly, the fact which lasts, which has pragmatic value, is the replicated functional relationship. From the clinical point of view, the treatment technique that works will persist, particularly when it is replicated across patients and therapists. From the definition of the terms of functional analysis through the entire methodology, the orientation is a practical and pragmatic one. Reinforcement and punishment, for example, the primary terms, are defined as contingent events which serve to increase or decrease the future probability of a particular response. Some critics have commented that this leaves the therapist with the necessity of making a new experimental test to determine the proper reinforcers or punishers for each new occasion, but this is clearly not the case. The entire history of the development of psychological science has marked the gradual accumulation of successful functional relationships, which offer guides and landmarks along the way. The technology has grown to the point where one can predict the potential effectiveness of a particular stimulus on the basis of deprivation and satiation, for example. Another very helpful functional analysis of reinforcement has been provided by Premack (1959; 1965). As indicated frequently in the previous pages, the clinician can now use as a reinforcer for low-rate behaviors almost any behavior in the person's repertoire that occurs at high frequency.

Behavioral analysis and assessment should be greatly aided by this entire philosophical reorientation, since the procedure is again very pragmatic, practical, and entirely individually directed. As will be discussed in more detail later, individual analysis is a part of the entire functional-analysis system and, as such, is directly correlated with treatment. Thus, this system is vastly different from the currently popular search for diagnostic labels, which alone may be psychologically damaging to an individual, and which often have little or no relationship to recommended treatment.

As revealed previously, the behavioristic reorientation has also provided a new view of man as a behaving organism. This view, which stresses the potential of the human organism to learn new behaviors, is markedly more optimistic than earlier models, such as the Freudian one, which stresses the unconscious determinism of human behavior through mechanisms, defenses, and complexes sometimes impossible to unravel. As was stressed in Chapter 10, some of the operant techniques oriented toward acceleration of constructive behaviors may not even treat pathological behaviors, whether or not they are present.

Within this volume there has been a reexamination of much of the business of clinical psychology from the point of view of a behavioral orientation. The general viewpoint was discussed first, then the methodologies and classification system to which it gave rise. This was followed by a summary of the behavior modification theories and experiments that have provided analogs, or models, of the formation of various kinds of pathological behaviors. In many areas it was suggested that the same conditioning principles and methods could give rise to human as well as subhuman pathological conditions. Later, the focus was upon behavioral modes of therapy, in which efforts to modify already existent pathological behavior or to accelerate constructive, normal behaviors held the spotlight. Perhaps it should be explicated once again that there was some redundancy because the same or similar methods were reviewed under etiological as well as therapeutic topics. Of course, this was to be expected, since, from the behavioral point of view, normal and pathological behaviors differ, not in terms of how they may be acquired or modified, but only on the basis of very arbitrary standards. The thesis of this book has now been carried almost full circle.

The remainder of this chapter will be devoted to an overall summing up and extensions into the future. Comments will be made about methodology, extensions of the laboratory model, behavioral assessment, training, and ethics. Last in the chapter will be a final summary and a prediction of some future trends.

METHODOLOGICAL EPICRISIS

It is our thesis that behavior modification has brought a new look to psychotherapy. It should also be clear that the methodology of the new wave rests upon a thorough experimental foundation and draws upon some forty years of laboratory research. It was in the laboratory, beginning as we found with the far-reaching investigations of Pavlov, that behavioral analogs for the development of pathological forms of response were executed. Thus, although the field is still very young, significant inroads have been made into the study of etiological variables that might contribute to human pathological behavior.

In our review of the various etiological models, we have seen great variation, both in terms of methodological sophistication and in terms of goodness of fit or applicability to the human problem. A few of the models, such as those of Wolpe, Ayllon and Azrin, and Bexton *et al.,* grew out of animal work and were applied directly on the human level. Thus, with these models the reader was not left to ponder the significance or applicability to human pathology. Hopefully, more of this kind of work will be done in the future. Learning theorists and empiricists alike have long suggested they could isolate the variables responsible for the formation of pathological as well as normal behaviors, and it is time more such direct bridges between animal and human behavioral events were built.

Many more such bridges have apparently already spanned the gap between animal and human labs in which modification is emphasized. In this area the push for clinical relevance plus the invasion of sophisticated technology have combined to produce far more research dealing directly with modification of already existent pathological behavior in humans than has been done with animals. There is nothing objectionable about this state of affairs, as long as the requisite amount of control to produce reliable results is available. However, as the techniques grow more complex and multivariate, as in some token economies or other combined forms of treatment, it is often preferable to do the single variable type of research first, either in humans or animals.

It would seem that the entire methodological innovation is one of the greatest contributions of the behavior modification movement. The overall picture currently demonstrates the availability of imaginative, comprehensive research programs directed toward a thoroughgoing experimental analysis of pathological behaviors. Wolpe (1952), for example, produced a pathological state in cats and investigated several possible models of modification before he ever tried systematic desensitization in humans. Similarly, Azrin maintained and operated an animal lab before he ever joined Ayllon to produce *The Token Economy.*

In our own work we have found several advantages in the joint operation of animal and human labs. For example, in the animal labs we can do the basic experimental work, attempt to shape pathological behaviors, which might not be ethically feasible in humans (for example, the shaping of self-destructive, self-punitive, or alcoholic behaviors through the use of frequent strong shock, deprivation, or round-the-clock experiments), and possibly pretest potential modification programs at a faster rate and under more control than might be available with human patients. Once the basic work is done, it is sometimes only a matter of cross-species replication to find an effective modification procedure for humans. On the other hand, when the procedure is not as effective with humans as with animals, one can return to the animal lab and sometimes explore the variables suspected to be responsible for the differences at a faster rate than could normally be done with humans.

Obviously, such a combination of basic and applied research in one program requires a breadth of orientation and the interdependence, interstimulation, and interinspiration of all factions concerned. Such a comprehensive orientation might provide a more challenging niche for research-oriented clinicians and a partial answer to questions, such as those raised by George Albee (1969, 1970), regarding the uncertain future of clinical psychology.

There are other methodological advantages inherent in the experimental analysis of pathological behavior, many of which have been alluded to previously. For example, the tools are now available to provide a rigorous experimental approach to modification within single human patients, which is the way the clinician usually prefers to work. Thus, if the data and environmental variables coalesce to permit experimental reversals, multiple schedules, or multiple base lines, frequently high-level probability statements can be made about a single case.

In addition, the experimental analysis allows a closer correlation between assessment and intervention techniques than has usually been available before. Thus, for example, the diagnostic battery of the future may consist primarily in the measurement of the rates of several responses under the control of several different stimuli. Reliability of measurement and stability of responding are usually easily obtained as a joint function of repeated measurement. Modification then usually consists of testing potential independent variables for their clinical efficacy against continued measurement. Such a technology allows the measurement of current effects of treatment variables during the process of therapy, as well as after the termination of intervention. Validity for the clinician may inhere in correlations of changes obtained in therapy with those in the patient's more natural environment. Some clinicians have reduced this to a moot point by programming intervention directly in the natural environment or by training the patient to do so himself.

Many of the studies of behavior modification reviewed in previous pages have dealt with process or maintenance variables and have not specifically programmed long-term studies of outcome. In any logical progression through the screening of new therapeutic techniques, it would seem important to study the process or maintenance variables first, under the assumption that if a technique does not demonstrate acceptable levels of modification while it is in effect (during treatment), then it should be discarded in favor of more powerful means of modification.

Reviews within these pages have demonstrated a wide and rich variety of techniques that have had some degree of success when applied to the modification of certain kinds of behaviors. More techniques should probably be developed and tried with many different behaviors to test the range of their effectiveness. However, even with acceptably maintained levels of modification, there must be an increasing emphasis on outcome prospects, unless one is to introduce the issue of terminable versus interminable behavior therapy.

It is with the challenge of the study of outcome that problems become more rich and complex, as previous researchers in the study of this area (Meehl, 1955; Eysenck, 1952b, 1961a; Goldstein & Dean, 1966; Rubinstein & Parloff, 1959) have found. For the behavior therapist the challenge is to find reliable and valid measures of the rates of target behaviors in uncontrolled, natural environments. Frequently, the single-subject design will be inappropriate for this problem, since the desired modification in one individual maintained in one natural environment may not allow precise predictions about any other individuals in any other environments. The problem of subject generality in this context is a crucial one, and in its solution one would probably have to consider, at least, the history of reinforcement of the target behaviors, the behavioral repertoire at time of treatment (particularly high probability behaviors that might occur more frequently following reduction or elimination of pathological target behaviors), and variations in the natural environment (particularly the reinforcing practices of the community). Interaction between all these variables is assumed to occur. The challenge to the experimental clinician is to begin imaginative programs to approach this level of complexity.

Since the behavior therapist concentrates mainly upon rates of response, pathological as well as constructive, he will need more precise measures of base rates of change and stability in the kinds of behavior he treats. He will need more precise statements of the rates of relapse and spontaneous recovery, to use more clinical terms. This will necessitate the use of either more control groups of various kinds or matched temporal periods of nonspecific treatment within single subjects or groups.

To the extent that treatment methods occur in vitro, as in desensitization or covert sensitization, in vivo measures may have to be standardized and replicated for follow-up procedures. Thus, therapists attempting to modify phobic or avoidant responses may have to develop more and better measures of approach to formerly avoided situations or stimuli, perhaps in unstructured as well as in structured situations. In addition, especially if the therapist is teaching the subject to practice a technique at home, better measures are needed of the subject's progress.

EXTENSION OF THE LABORATORY MODEL
The model proposed in these pages has called for the gradual extension of conditioning and learning principles from the experimental laboratory to the natural environment. The viewpoint has been that this massive task might best be accomplished by the thorough study of pertinent variables under the controlled conditions that the laboratory can offer. In some areas (perhaps most notably those reviewed in sections on stimulus control, schedules of reinforcement, and aversive conditioning) this work has progressed to the point of great refinement and technological precision, based largely upon animal models. These advances in knowledge have been the cornerstone for similar advances in human behavior modification.

The suggestion has also been made repeatedly that greater dialogue and interaction between the laboratory and clinic could operate to the profit and ultimate gain of both. Thus, for example, we have traced historical strands showing the development of Wolpean desensitization out of the Pavlovian work on experimental neurosis and the later work of Masserman. Similarly, Ayllon and Azrin (1968) trace the roots of their token economy to work, some of it done years ago (Wolfe, 1936; Cowles, 1937), with animals in experimental laboratories. And several ongoing programs have been described (for example, Mendelson, 1968; Davidson, 1972b) that focus upon a particular behavior such as alcoholism and that maintain concurrently animal laboratories, in which models of etiology or acquisition are developed and experimental modes of modification are screened, and human laboratories in which the focus is upon modification.

As indicated earlier, most of the studies of behavior modification reviewed in this volume have been directed toward modification and maintenance under laboratory conditions, with very little direct extension into the natural environment. The next logical step will be the systematic study of those variables governing generalization from such programs to control in the natural environment. As mentioned in the discussion of generalization, there are several modes of approach to this problem. One is to attempt to design contingency programs that will have reinforcements and behaviors in common with the natural environment. This has been the function of most of the token economies.

In some proposed models, such as desensitization and covert sensitization, patients or clients are taught techniques in the laboratory and also instructed to practice them at home in private. This is another means of extending laboratory controls into the environment.

In addition, with many of the self-control models (Lindsley, 1971; Ferster *et al.*, 1962; Stuart, 1967, 1969) patients or clients are trained to record and measure their own behaviors and arrange their own contingencies, all within the context of the natural environment. Models such as these may help bridge the gap between the laboratory and the natural environment, for they offer a technology developed in the laboratory which is increasingly being applied directly in the home environment of the client. When behaviors are treated directly in this context, the problem of generalization may no longer be critical. In addition to this advantage, such a model allows the individual professional to contact many more persons than would otherwise be possible. In Lindsley's work (1971), for example, a single professional person may work with groups of persons engaged in modifying their own or others' behaviors, with none of the persons necessarily being maintained in special treatment institutions. This trend would seem to be in keeping with the current community psychology movement.

BEHAVIORAL ASSESSMENT
At various points in this text, assessment has been discussed tangential to other matters. Now is the time for extended comments on assessment and some extrapolation to an assessment of the future.

As behavior modification technology grows, behavioral assessment will have to expand and increasingly incorporate behavioral measures, in order to keep pace with the general movement. Some preferences have already been established, and many traditional assessment problems encountered in the past have again been encountered. Thus, when modification is directed at target behaviors and treatment is in vivo, the preferred assessment techniques may be direct measures of rates of the target behavior. Assessment problems may, in this case, consist largely of reliability and stability. That is, time samples and recording techniques may have to be adjusted until maximally stable base rates can be collected. Thus, if the target behavior is smoking and it is found to vary throughout the normal day, day-long measures may have to be obtained to provide stability. Obviously, if stimulus-control functions are suspected, such as smoking with coffee, at particular times or in specific places, measurements may have to cover such occasions or risk unreliability. As discussed previously, the power and resolution of the functional design, whether with individuals or groups, depends critically upon the stability of base-rate measures. Thus, for example, if measures are unstable prior to the introduction of treatment variables, it may be difficult or impossible to demonstrate any change, unless the change is of a large order of magnitude.

In conditions where stability of response rate is not obtained, the choice of which direction to go may be threefold: Measurement may be extended in the hopes that stability will eventually be observed; experimental control may be sought; or statistical control may be sought through the observation of the same response over groups of subjects. Taking the first choice always involves the risk of failing to find stability. Altering the time sampling of measurements may provide some resolution to the problem. Seeking experimental control may provide more information in the long run, but it may also be time-consuming. Obtaining experimental control may involve some analysis of variables actually maintaining the response, so that manipulation of deprivation and reinforcement variables may be in order. Thus, stability may result from approximations to laboratory control over the behavior, as Lindsley (1956) found with psychotic patients and Davidson (1972b) found with alcoholic patients.

If time is of the essence, statistical control may be the most appropriate choice. Procedures of this sort usually involve making observations over groups of subjects, so that stability of individual response rates may not be necessary. These procedures may involve observed stability for the group and within-group controls or between-group controls, and experimental and control groups may be compared for treatment effects. As Paul (1969a) has suggested, there are many variations of group-statistical designs which may be appropriate for problems of this sort.

As indicated earlier, analysis of treatment outcome may be much more complex than process or within-treatment types of analyses. Thus, for example, assessment of single-subject responses to treatment may be totally inappropriate for situations where prior knowledge indicates that posttreatment environments will differ between subjects. More specifically, aversive modification of addictive drug-taking behavior may produce measured long-lasting results in the patient who returns to a nondrug-taking culture following treatment, but the same treatment in the same person might produce other outcomes if the individual returns to a drug culture. Since the clinician cannot always control the environment the patient chooses to return to, it may be necessary to apply the same treatment to many individuals in order to resolve these differences or, at least, to observe the effects of the same treatment in several individuals who return to each of several kinds of posttreatment environment.

In many situations where treatment outcome is the experimental focus, it may be necessary to supplement direct measurement of rates of response with other types of measures, which may be used as predictive validity criteria. Thus, for example, Davidson (1972b) uses a questionnaire eliciting self-report measures, hospital records, and reports of other, hopefully unbiased, observers to supplement operant rates of alcohol consumption by alcoholic patients. These are correlated to obtain greater validity in the assessing of initial base rates of drinking probability prior to treatment and again in follow-up periods, and to assess treatment outcome via rates or probability of drinking following treatment.

Kanfer and Phillips (1969, 1970) have proposed programs of behavioral assessment designed to evaluate all the relevant variables (whether psychological, biological, or medical) that may contribute to maintenance and potential modification of a particular behavior. These proposals constitute a very ambitious program involving a multidisciplinary attack on the problem of assessment and may, therefore, not always be available to the clinician who does not work in multidisciplinary settings. However, the clinician should always be careful to eliminate the possibility of medical and other complications which may arise in behavior modification programs. A thorough medical is, of course, always advisable when complications are expected or when behavioral programs might interfere with the health of the patient. In the treatment of drug addiction or alcoholism, for example, a medical consultant may be most helpful in planning detoxification and in treating problems such as malnutrition and avitaminosis.

TRAINING

Issues related to the training of clinical and experimental psychologists have been mentioned briefly, but now a more complete training model will be proposed, along with a rationale to support it.

It would appear that throughout the history of psychology, the specialists in conditioning and learning have been too busy writing books or working in the laboratory to apply their principles and techniques to the training of their own students. With few exceptions, until recently, training models in clinical and experimental psychology have emphasized content and rarely technique. As a result of the Boulder Conference (APA, 1947), the model of clinician as scientist-professional was proposed. According to Albee (1969, 1970) and some other current writers, this model has not been practical, since few psychologists seem to have approximated it. Albee predicts an increasing, rather than decreasing, bifurcation and split between experimentalists and clinicians.

It was suggested earlier that part of the difficulty, if not impossibility, of the Boulder model was the lack of an appropriate research model, one geared specifically to the clinical situation. The case study seemed to fill the bill earlier, but lacked the power to resolve etiological historical variables or to differentiate effective from ineffective treatment variables. As revealed in the section on methodology, enough improvements have taken place in these areas in recent years to warrant some hope for an increasingly powerful and precise clinical-research model. With the availability of single-subject and within-subject-group control designs, it would seem that the clinician can now expect to collect rigorously controlled research data without violating ethical scruples which prohibit the nontreatment of people who need it. At this point, it would seem timely to provide a training model for those who would opt to work as scientist-professionals, with emphasis on behavior modification.

Borrowing from programmed instruction techniques (Skinner, 1968) and materials (Holland & Skinner, 1961) where appropriate, the authors of this text have organized a course of readings. This course has been organized in roughly spiral order, progressing from simple, introductory material to technical data in specialty areas. Areas of concentration have been divided as follows: general introduction to psychology and science, introduction to conditioning and learning, psychopathology, experimental analysis of pathological behavior, principles of behavior modification, techniques of behavior modification, and treatment of specific pathological behaviors.

The course has been organized to allow screening of any student from high school through graduate Ph.D. psychologist for skills, background, and competency in any of the areas outlined. It is offered to supplement or complement any standard, traditional graduate course in psychology. It could conceivably be coordinated with any training technique already in use, but a specific technology is recommended, since it has already been used successfully by the authors and others.

The proposed technology is a semiprogrammed one, which allows the student to progress through assigned material at his own rate, advancing to each step only as competence at the previous one is verbally demonstrated. Thus, a set of open-ended questions has been designed for each level and each assignment. These questions tap the appropriate information, including grasp of terminology, principles, techniques, and reported research. Once the student can verbally master this material, he is allowed to go on to the next step or level until he has covered all of the reading material.

Following demonstrated mastery at the introductory level, laboratory manuals (Reese, 1966; Michael, 1963) are provided, and the student is trained to care for and experiment with his own animal subjects. This is a highly recommended but not necessary step in clinical training. It is proposed that the rigorous control and technology available for working in the laboratory with animals is not yet available in most areas of clinical psychology. Seeing the principles of behavioral control in action at this level is usually extremely reinforcing to the student, providing him with a lasting impression of the power and precision of such control and often controlling a great deal of his own future behavior.

Following the student's mastery of the technical behavior modification section, another, extended laboratory experience is offered with human subjects. In a program that offers the maximum in training depth, the student is usually provided with a comprehensive orientation to behavioral assessment and measurement and with the assignment to propose a clinical research design. The student is then allowed to apply this methodology to one or two cases of human pathological behavior, each of which is to be regarded as a separate experiment. Within a preset period (two or three months is usually enough), the student is expected to collect base rates of well-defined target behavior(s), apply one to three proposed modification strategies until one appears sufficient for the task, devise a control technique to establish validity, and present the case. Such a comprehensive program allows the student the full reign of clinical practice and application of the skills and knowledge he should have acquired by this point. We have found that the challenge of such a comprehensive course serves to motivate students to the degree that they press for more material, more knowledge, and more experience.

ETHICS

A great deal has been said, even at this early date, regarding the ethical implications of behavioral systems and of behavior therapy in particular. There have too often been heated accusations from those on both sides of the issue, frequently couched in impassioned prose which has served to block or eliminate a healthy examination of the issues and its ramifications. Some of the major statements regarding such ethical problems appear in the famous encounter between Rogers and Skinner (1956); later comments include those of Kanfer (1965), Krasner (1962b), Lomont (1964), and Ulrich (1967).

Frequently, the major issues are formulated within the single dimension of freedom versus control. From the humanitarian point of view, the goal of human growth (and, therefore, of psychotherapy or behavior modification) should be an increase in freedom of choice. As long as the choices or alternatives available to an individual appear healthy and constructive, few might challenge this point of view. Should, however, institutional inmates be allowed the choice of wasting their lives on back wards or in crowded jail cells, staring at empty walls or bars, when they could be leading more constructive lives? Should alcoholics, drug addicts, compulsive head bangers, wife beaters, and rapists, to take only a few of the more colorful examples, be allowed to continue their pathological behaviors unchecked?

Most thoughtful persons would admit that one of the functions of civilized society is to form a system of laws, which specifies consequences for certain extreme behaviors, in an effort to control, reduce, or eliminate these behaviors and thereby protect others. Most of our societal institutions, ranging all the way from organized religion through the family to social clubs, are systems of control of one kind or another. Thus, the status symbols, positions of power, and other reinforcements dispensed by these institutions are usually contingent upon certain behavioral repertoires defined by the institution. Sometimes these contingencies very subtly shape the behaviors involved, and often the members say they enjoy membership in the society, no matter how conforming nonmembers may label them. Thus, behavioral control of some kind is probably a part of every known society. As Schaefer and Martin (1969) indicate:

> *The control of behavior takes place all the time. Certainly, therefore, studying the laws of control is bound to make for better mental health if for no other reason than avoiding any knowledge about control must inevitably lead to some misapplications. The study of behavioral control, surprisingly enough, reveals that all the punitive sort of control which dictators, benevolent or otherwise, have used is not at all that which is most powerful. Rather, the gentle, though lawful granting of the wishes and needs of the controlled exercises the greatest amount of control. For example, on the basis of behavioral laws, there are ways to teach animals to do nearly unbelievable acts—guiding missles, inspecting drugs, or reading simple numbers—all without ever punishing the animal or even touching him. All that is necessary is to arrange the animal's environment in such a way as to elicit the desired response. A basic exercise in undergraduate classes in behavioral science requires students to teach a laboratory animal to press a lever to obtain food, something the animal has never before done. Without knowledge of behavioral laws, students could not hope to accomplish this in the lifetime of the animal. Armed with an understanding of behavioral control, however, most students succeed in less than thirty minutes. (p. 12)*

It would seem to be more beneficial to all mental health personnel to be able to use some of the principles relating to the control of human behavior to help increase the number of healthy, constructive behaviors in their clients or patients than to deny the existence of such controls. In the sections on etiology or acquisition of pathological behavior and on its modification, the case has been made for the control of such behavior through various conditioning and learning techniques. To the extent that these techniques can be implemented wisely and with the goal of increasing the number of constructive behaviors in patients or clients, the mental health movement would seem to be that much further ahead systematically. At the very least, here is an entirely rational experimental framework based upon the guiding principles of conditioning and learning, originated within laboratory science, and providing a programmatic system of modification that can function self-correctively when coupled with rigorous assessment.

An added inducement to develop, rather than restrict, investigation of the principles and techniques of behavioral control is the contribution such a system can make to the behavioral self-control of any person, be he patient, professional, or layman. As discussed earlier, several behaviorists (notably Goldiamond, 1965a; Lindsley, 1971; Ferster *et al.,* 1962; Stuart, 1967, 1969; and Homme, 1965, 1966) have taken the tack that environmental events are the principal controllers of human behavior. To the extent, then, that people can be trained to reschedule or exchange some of these environmental determiners, they might consequently increase the amount of control over their own behaviors. In this way, the individual is allowed to vastly increase his own self-determination. Examples were given earlier of some of the innovative programs in which a person is trained to record and measure those target behaviors of interest to him and to try out various contingency arrangements designed to accelerate or decelerate particular response rates. To the extent that such a system works well for an individual, a technology has been placed in that individual's hands that allows him to be his own therapist. This might be one viable model that could enable mental health professionals to reach the ever-increasing number of individuals in need of help.

WHERE DO WE GO FROM HERE?

A number of writers have commented on the possibility that behavior therapy may be only a passing fancy or fad (Kanfer & Phillips, 1966, 1970; Breger & McGaugh, 1965). Certainly psychology, in its short history, has seen its share of passing fancies, in both clinical and experimental areas. Unfortunately, it would appear that something more akin to deprivation, stimulation, and satiation than to scientific thoroughness may govern the interests and activities of some research investigators. In regard to behavior therapy, to the extent that clinicians and practitioners of other forms of therapy call themselves behavior therapists without changing their own behavior, the practice and potential value of behavior therapy will be diluted. On the other hand, to the extent that interested experimentalists and clinicians alike formulate testable hypotheses, procedures, and techniques and submit them to experimental tests, the area will make a lasting contribution to psychology and science as a whole.

There are many avenues for healthy growth in behavior modification. However, it was no accident, and it may be prognostic of the future, that three decades of ground-breaking historical development took place in the laboratories prior to wholesale application of behavior modification techniques to clinical problems. Similarly, many of the current leaders of the behavior modification movement received their training in a laboratory situation, where techniques and variables could be studied under conditions of maximal control. The person who achieves his credentials in this fashion thus may not only be more skilled and knowledgeable regarding laboratory techniques and methodology, but may be exceptionally qualified once he has learned to apply similar techniques or methodology to cases in behavior modification.

Apropos of some of the remarks of George Albee (1969, 1970), the future of clinical psychology is uncertain, just as its past has clearly marked the meteoric rise of the private practitioner, at least in number. As Albee has commented, the major problem has been the apparent unworkability of the Boulder (APA, 1947) scientist-professional model, which specified that the same person should be capable of research and treatment. We have suggested that much of the difficulty may have arisen from the lack of a research model that was appropriate to a clinical treatment facility and that also had the necessary precision and power. Clearly, the clinical case study was not the answer. Nor, too frequently, was the factorial-group design in which a group of patients matched on pertinent variables (which usually included the request for treatment) would be used as an untreated control group.

One of the major themes of this book has been the reiteration of a variety of research designs that seem to be singularly appropriate to the clinical setting. No longer is the clinician expected always to obtain an untreated control group, which might be regarded as unethical. Now there are powerful designs that may be carried out with a single individual, as the clinician often prefers to work. There is, in addition, a multitude of group designs that may provide an equal or increased amount of control without the therapist's refusing treatment to anyone desiring it. With the availability of such designs, as well as the announced interest of behavior therapists in conditioning, learning, and laboratory methodology, a renaissance of the scientist-professional model may be evolving.

Perhaps the clinician of the future will not see treatment and research as the separate entities they have so often been considered in the past. Perhaps, also, the therapist of the future will engage in all the careful planning and extension, or extrapolation, from the relevant literature, all the precision of measurement and control that the laboratory investigator brings to bear upon each fresh experiment, and so approach each new patient. From this point of view the patient is the subject in an experiment with $N = 1$.

Critics (Breger & McGaugh, 1965) have suggested that this approach dehumanizes patients, making robots or guinea pigs out of them. However, it seems to the current authors that to treat patients without design, without careful measurement of their progress during and after therapy, and without the most modern, tested techniques available is unethical, if not harmful to the patient. It would seem ultimately to be in the best interests of the individual patient to make available to him all the rigor, all the power and precision that the new technology may offer.

There are not yet answers to every perplexing clinical problem. There are no ready-made techniques to fit the cases of existential crisis, of anomie, and of murderous rage. That cookbook has not been written yet. But a collection is forming of techniques which may become preferred treatment techniques for certain focalized behavioral pathologies. Many of these cases can now be treated by trained technicians, freeing the clinical investigators to look to the as-yet-unsolved riddles. Hopefully, the next generation of interns and trainees will be trained to do likewise.

References

Albee, G. W. Who shall be served first? *Professional Psychology,* 1969, *1,* 4–7.

Albee, G. W. The uncertain future of clinical psychology. *American Psychologist,* 1970, *25,* 1071–1080.

Alexander, F. *Fundamentals of psychoanalysis.* New York: Norton, 1948.

Alexander, F., & French, T. M. *Psychoanalytic therapy: Principles and application.* New York: Ronald, 1946.

Al-Issa, I., & Kraft, T. Personality factors in behavior therapy. *Canadian Psychologist,* 1967, *8,* 218–222.

Allen, K. E., Hart, B., Buell, J., Harris, F., & Wolf, M. Effects of social reinforcement on isolate behavior of a nursery school child. *Child Development,* 1964, *35,* 511–518.

American Psychiatric Association. *Diagnostic and statistical manual: Mental disorders with special supplement on plans for revision.* Washington, D.C.: APA, 1965.

American Psychological Association. Committee on training in clinical psychology. Recommended graduate training program in clinical psychology. *American Psychologist,* 1947, *2,* 539–558.

Amsel, A. Frustration, persistence and regression. In H. D. Kimmel (ed.), *Experimental psychopathology.* New York: Academic Press, 1971.

Anant, S. S. The use of verbal aversion technique with a group of alcoholics. *Saskatchewan Psychologist,* 1966, *2,* 28–30.

Anant, S. S. A note on the treatment of alcoholics by a verbal aversion technique. *Canadian Psychologist,* 1967a, *8,* 19–22.

Anant, S. S. Verbal aversion technique. *Interdiscipline,* 1967b, *4,* 1–14.

Anant, S. S. The use of verbal aversion (negative conditioning) with an alcoholic: A case report. *Behaviour Research and Therapy*, 1968, *6*, 395–396.

Anderson, O. D., & Liddell, H. S. Observations on experimental neurosis in sheep. *Archives of Neurology and Psychiatry*, Chicago, 1935, *34*, 330–354.

Anderson, O. D., & Parmenter, R. A long term study of experimental neurosis in the sheep and the dog. *Psychosomatic Medicine Monograph*, 1941, *2*, No. 5.

Angermeier, W. F., Schaul, L. T., & James, W. T. Social conditioning in rats. *Journal of Comparative and Physiological Psychology*, 1959, *52*, 370–372.

Ascough, J. C., & Sipprelle, C. N. Operant verbal conditioning of autonomic responses. *Behaviour Research and Therapy*, 1968, *6*, 363–370.

Ashem, B., & Donner, L. Covert sensitization with alcoholics: A controlled replication. *Behaviour Research and Therapy*, 1968, *6*, 7–12.

Atkinson, R. C. Computerized instruction and the learning process. *American Psychologist*, 1968, *23*, 225–239.

Atthowe, J. M., & Krasner, L. Preliminary report on the application of contingent reinforcement procedures (token economy) on a "chronic" psychiatric ward. *Journal of Abnormal Psychology*, 1968, *73*, 37–43.

Ayllon, T. Intensive treatment of psychotic behavior by stimulus satiation and food reinforcement. *Behaviour Research and Therapy*, 1963, *1*, 53–61.

Ayllon, T., & Azrin, N. H. Reinforcement and instructions with mental patients. *Journal of the Experimental Analysis of Behavior*, 1964, *7*, 327–331.

Ayllon, T., & Azrin, N. H. The measurement and reinforcement of behavior in psychotics. *Journal of the Experimental Analysis of Behavior*, 1965, *8*, 351–383.

Ayllon, T., & Azrin, N. H. Punishment as a discriminative stimulus and conditioned reinforcer with humans. *Journal of the Experimental Analysis of Behavior*, 1966, *4*, 411–419.

Ayllon, T., & Azrin, N. H. *The Token Economy: A motivational system for therapy and rehabilitation.* New York: Appleton-Century-Crofts, 1968.

Ayllon, T. & Haughton, E. Control of the behavior of schizophrenic patients by food. *Journal of the Experimental Analysis of Behavior*, 1962, *5*, 343–352.

Ayllon, T., & Haughton, E. Modification of symptomatic verbal behavior of mental patients. *Behaviour Research and Therapy*, 1964, *2*, 87–97.

Ayllon, T., & Michael, J. The psychiatric nurse as a behavioral engineer. *Journal of the Experimental Anaylsis of Behavior*, 1959, *2*, 323–334.

Azrin, N. H. Some effects of noise on behavior. *Journal of the Experimental Analysis of Behavior*, 1958, *1*, 183–200.

Azrin, N. H., & Holz, W. C. Punishment. In W. K. Honig (ed.), *Operant behavior: Areas of research and application.* New York: Appleton-Century-Crofts, 1966.

Azrin, N. H., Holz, W. C., Ulrich, R. and Goldiamond, I. The Control of the content of conversation through reinforcement. *Journal of the Experimental Analysis of Behavior*, 1961, *4*, 25–30.

Azrin, N. H., Hutchinson, R. R., & Hake, D. F. Extinction-induced aggression. *Journal of the Experimental Analysis of Behavior*, 1966, *9*, 191–204.

Azrin, N. H., & Lindsley, O. R. The reinforcement of cooperation between children. *Journal of Abnormal and Social Psychology,* 1956, *52,* 100–102.

Baer, D. M. Laboratory control of thumbsucking by withdrawal and re-presentation of reinforcement. *Journal of the Experimental Analysis of Behavior,* 1962, *5,* 525–528.

Baer, D. M. A case for the selective reinforcement of punishment. In C. Neuringer & J. L. Michael (eds.), *Behavior modification in clinical psychology.* New York: Appleton-Century-Crofts, 1970.

Baer, D. M., Peterson, R. F., & Sherman, J. A. The development of imitation by reinforcing behavioral similarity to a model. *Journal of the Experimental Analysis of Behavior,* 1967, *10,* 405–416.

Baer, D. M., & Sherman, J. A. Reeinforcement control of generalized imitation in young children. *Journal of Experimental Child Psychology,* 1964, *1,* 37–49.

Baer, D. M., Wolf, M. M., & Risley, T. R. Some current dimensions of applied behavior analysis. *Journal of Applied Behavior Analysis,* 1968, *1,* 91–97.

Baker, B. L. Symptom treatment and symptom substitution in enuresis. *Journal of Abnormal Psychology,* 1969, *74,* 42–49.

Bandura, A. Psychotherapy as a learning process. *Psychological Bulletin,* 1961, *58,* 143–159.

Bandura, A. Social learning through imitation. In M. R. Jones (ed.), *Nebraska symposium on motivation.* Lincoln: University of Nebraska Press, 1962. Pp. 211–269.

Bandura, A. Behavioral modifications through modeling procedures. In L. Krasner & L. P. Ullmann (eds.), *Research in behavior modification.* New York: Holt, Rinehart & Winston, 1965a. Pp. 310–340.

Bandura, A. Influence of models' reinforcement contingencies on the acquisition of imitative responses. *Journal of Personality and Social Psychology,* 1965b, *1,* 589–595.

Bandura, A. A social learning interpretation of psychological dysfunctions. In P. London & D. Rosenhan (eds.), *Foundations of abnormal psychology.* New York: Holt, Rinehart & Winston, 1968.

Bandura, A. *Principles of behavior modification.* New York: Holt, Rinehart & Winston, 1969.

Bandura, A., Blanchard, E. B., & Ritter, B. J. The relative efficacy of desensitization and modeling therapeutic approaches for inducing behavioral, affective, and attitudinal changes. Unpublished Manuscript, Stanford University, 1968.

Bandura, A., Grusec, J., & Menlove, F. L. Vicarious extinction of avoidance behavior. *Journal of Personality and Social Psychology,* 1967, *5,* 16–23.

Bandura, A., Lipsher, D. H., & Miller, P. E. Psychotherapists' approach-avoidance reactions to patients' expressions of hostility. *Journal of Consulting Psychology,* 1960, *24,* 1–8.

Bandura, A., & McDonald, F. J. The influence of social reinforcement and the behavior of models in shaping children's moral judgments. *Journal of Abnormal and Social Psychology,* 1963, *67,* 274–281.

Bandura, A., & Menlove, F. L. Factors determining vicarious extinction of avoidance behavior through symbolic modeling. *Journal of Personality and Social Psychology,* 1968, *8,* 99–108.

Bandura, A., & Perloff, B. Relative efficacy of self-monitored and externally imposed reinforcement systems. *Journal of Personality and Social Psychology,* 1967, *7,* 111–116.

Bandura, A., Ross, D., & Ross, S. A. Transmission of aggression through imitation of aggressive models. *Journal of Abnormal and Social Psychology,* 1961, *67,* 575–582.

Bandura, A., & Walters, R. H. *Social learning and imitation.* New York: Holt, Rinehart & Winston, 1962.

Bandura, A., & Whalen, C. K. The influence of antecedent reinforcement and divergent modeling cues on patterns of self-reward. *Journal of Personality and Social Psychology,* 1966, *3,* 373–382.

Barker, J. C., & Miller, M. E. Aversion therapy for compulsive gambling. *Lancet,* 1966a, *1,* 491–492.

Barker, J. C., & Miller, M. E. Aversion therapy for compulsive gambling. *British Medical Journal,* 1966b, *2,* 115.

Barker, J. C., & Miller, M. E. Aversion therapy for compulsive gambling. *Journal of Nervous and Mental Disorders,* 1968, *146,* 285–302.

Barrett, B. H. Reduction in rate of multiple tics by free operant conditioning methods. *Journal of Nervous and Mental Disease,* 1962, *135,* 187–195.

Baum, M. Extinction of an avoidance response motivated by intense fear: Social facilitation of the action of response prevention (flooding) in rats. *Behaviour Research and Therapy,* 1969, *7,* 57–62.

Baum, M., & Oler, I. D. Comparison of two techniques for hastening extinction of avoidance-responding in rats. *Psychological Reports,* 1968, *23,* 807–813.

Becker, W. C., Madsen, C. H., Arnold, C. R., & Thomas, D. R. The contingent use of teacher attention and praise in reducing classroom behavior problems. *Journal of Special Education,* 1967, *1,* 287–307.

Bekhterev, V. M. *General principles of human reflexology.* New York: International Publishers, 1932.

Bensberg, G. J. (ed.). *Teaching the mentally retarded: A handbook for ward personnel.* Atlanta: Southern Regional Education Board, 1965.

Benson, H., Shapiro, D., Tursky, B., & Schwartz, G. E. Decreased systolic blood pressure in patients with essential hypertension. *Science,* 1971, *173,* 740–742.

Bexton, W. H., Heron, W., & Scott, T. H. Effects of decreased variation in the sensory environment. *Canadian Journal of Psychology,* 1954, *8,* 70–76.

Bijou, S. W. Theory and research in mental (developmental) retardation, *Psychological Record,* 1963, *13,* 95–110.

Bijou, S. W., & Orlando, R. Rapid development of multiple-schedule performances with retarded children. *Journal of the Experimental Analysis of Behavior,* 1961, *4,* 7–16.

Black, A. H. Operant conditioning of autonomic responses. *Conditional Reflex,* 1968, *3,* 130.

Black, A. H. Autonomic aversive conditioning in infrahuman subjects. In F. R. Brush (ed.), *Aversive Conditioning and learning,* New York: Academic Press, 1971.

Blake, B. G. A follow-up of alcoholics treated by behaviour therapy. *Behaviour Research and Therapy,* 1967, *5,* 89–94.

Blakemore, C. B., Thorpe, J. G., Barker, J. C., Conway, C. G., & Lavin, N. I. The application of faradic aversion conditioning in a case of transvestism. *Behaviour Research and Therapy,* 1963a, *1,* 29–34.

Blakemore, C. B., Thorpe, J. G., Barker, J. C., & Lavin, N. I. Follow-up note to "The application of faradic aversion conditioning in a case of transvestism." *Behaviour Research and Therapy,* 1963b, *1,* 191.

Boren, J. J. The study of drugs with operant techniques. In W. K. Honig (ed.), *Operant behavior: areas of research and application.* New York: Appleton-Century-Crofts, 1966.

Boring, E. G. *A history of experimental psychology.* New York: Appleton-Century-Crofts, 1950.

Bostow, D. E., & Bailey, J. B. Modification of severe disruptive and aggressive behavior using brief timeout and reinforcement procedures. *Journal of Applied Behavior Analysis,* 1969, *2,* 31–37.

Boulougouris, J. C., Marks, I. M., & Marset, P. Superiority of flooding (implosion) to desensitization for reducing pathological fear. *Behaviour Research and Therapy,* 1971, *9,* 7–16.

Bowlby, J. Maternal care and mental health. *World Health Organization Monograph,* Series 1952, No. 2.

Brady, J. V. Assessment of drug effects on emotional behavior. *Science,* 1956, *123,* 1033–1034.

Brady, J. V. A comparative approach to the evaluation of drug effects upon behavior. In W. S. Fields (ed.), *Brain mechanisms and drug action.* Springfield, Ill.: Charles C Thomas, 1957.

Brady, J. V. Ulcers in executive monkeys. *Scientific American,* 1958, *199,* 95–100.

Brady, J. V. Psychophysiology of emotional behavior. In A. J. Bachrach (ed.), *Experimental foundations of clinical psychology.* New York: Basic Books, 1962.

Brady, J. V., & Hunt, H. F. An experimental approach to the analysis of emotional behavior. *Journal of Psychology,* 1955, *40,* 313–324.

Brawley, E., Harris, F., Allen, E., Fleming, R. S., & Peterson, R. F. Behavior modification of an autistic child. *Behavioral Science,* 1969, *14,* 87–97.

Breger, L., & McGaugh, J. L. Critique and reformulation of "learning theory" approaches to psychotherapy and neurosis. *Psychological Bulletin,* 1965, *63,* 338–358.

Brenner, J., Kleinman, R., & Goesling, W. The effects of different exposures to augmented sensory feedback on the control of heart rate. *Psychophysiology,* 1969, *5,* 510–516.

Bridger, H. W., & Birns, B. Experience and temperament in human neonates. In G. Newton & S. Levine (eds.), *Early experience and behavior.* Springfield, Ill.: Charles C Thomas, 1968.

Brigham, T. A., & Sherman, J. A. An experimental analysis of verbal imitation in preschool children. *Journal of Applied Behavior Analysis,* 1968, *1,* 151–158.

Broadhurst, P. Abnormal animal behavior. In H. J. Eysenck (ed.), *Handbook of abnormal psychology.* New York: Basic Books, 1961.

Brodsky, G. D. The relation between verbal and non-verbal behavior change. *Behaviour Research and Therapy,* 1967, *5,* 183–191.

Brown, E. C., & L'Abate, L. An appraisal of teaching machines and programmed instruction with special reference to the modification of deviant behavior. In C. M. Franks (ed.), *Behavior therapy: Appraisal and status.* New York: McGraw-Hill, 1969.

Brown, J. S., Martin, R. C., & Morrow, M. W. Self-punitive behavior in the rat: Facilitative effects of punishment on resistance to extinction. *Journal of Comparative and Physiological Psychology,* 1964, *57,* 127–133.

Bucher, B., & Lovaas, O. Use of aversive stimulation in behavior modification. In M. R. Jones (ed.), *Miami symposium on the prediction of behavior, 1967: Aversive stimulation.* Coral Gables, Fla.: University of Miami Press, 1968.

Burchard, J., & Tyler, V., Jr. The modification of delinquent behavior through operant conditioning. *Behaviour Research and Therapy,* 1965, *2,* 245–250.

Buss, A. H. *Psychopathology.* New York: Wiley, 1966.

Buss, A. H., & Durkee, A. Conditioning of hostile verbalizations in a situation resembling a clinical interview. *Journal of Consulting Psychology,* 1958, *22,* 415–418.

Cahoon, D. D. Symptom substitution and the behavior therapies. *Psychological Bulletin,* 1968, *69,* 149–156.

Caldwell, B. M. The effects of infant care. In M. L. Hoffman & L. W. Hoffman (eds.), *Review of child development research.* New York: Russel Sage Foundation, 1964.

Cameron, N., The functional psychoses. In J. McV. Hunt (ed.), *Personality and the behavior disorders, Vol. II.* New York: Ronald Press, 1944.

Campbell, D., Sanderson, R. E., & Laverty, S. G. Characteristics of a conditioned response in human subjects during extinction trials following a single traumatic conditioning trial. *Journal of Abnormal and Social Psychology,* 1964, *68,* 627–639.

Casler, L. Perceptual deprivation in institutional settings. In G. Newton & S. Levine (eds.), *Early experience and behavior.* Springfield, Ill.: Charles C Thomas, 1968.

Cautela, J. R. Treatment of compulsive behavior by covert sensitization. *Psychological Record,* 1966, *16,* 33–41.

Cautela, J. R. Covert sensitization. *Psychological Record,* 1967, *20,* 1115–1130.

Chittenden, G. E. An experimental study in measuring and modifying assertive behavior in young children. *Monographs of the Society for Research in Child Development,* 1942, 7 (1, Serial No. 31).

Chomsky, N. *Aspects of a theory of language.* Cambridge, Mass.: M.I.T. Press, 1965.

Church, R. M. Transmission of learned behavior between rats. *Journal of Abnormal and Social Psychology,* 1957, *54,* 163–165.

Church, R. M. The varied effects of punishment on behavior. *Psychological Review,* 1963, *70,* 369–402.

Clements, C. B., & McKee, J. M. Programmed instruction for institutionalized offenders: contingency management and performance contracts. *Psychological Reports,* 1968, *22,* 957–964.

Cohen, H. L. Educational therapy: The design of learning environments. In J. M. Shlien (ed.), *Research in psychotherapy.* Washington, D.C.: American Psychological Association, 1968. Pp. 21–53.

Cohen, H. L., Filipczak, J., Bis, J., Cohen, J., Goldiamond, I., & Larkin, P. *Case II-Model: A contingency-oriented 24-hour learning environment in a juvenile correctional institution.* Silver Spring, Md.: Educational Facility Press, 1968.

Coleman, J. C. *Abnormal psychology and modern life.* Glenview, Ill.: Scott Foresman, 1964.

Cooke, G. The efficacy of two desensitization procedures: An analogue study. *Behaviour Research and Therapy,* 1966, *4,* 17–24.

Cooper, A. J. A case of fetishism and impotence treated by behavior therapy. *British Journal of Psychiatry,* 1963, *109,* 645–652.

Corson, J. A. Observational learning of a lever pressing response. *Psychonomic Science,* 1967, *7,* 197–198.

Coulson, J. E. (ed.). *Programmed learning and computer-based instruction.* New York: Wiley, 1962.

Cowles, J. T. Food-tokens as incentives for learning by chimpanzees. *Comparative Psychological Monograph,* 1937, *14* No. 71.

Darby, C. L., & Riopelle, A. J. Observational learning in the Rhesus monkey. *Journal of Comparative and Physiological Psychology,* 1959, *52,* 94–98.

Davidson, R. S. Timeout from therapy as a reinforcer. Unpublished report, 1969.

Davidson, R. S. Conditioned reinforcing vs. punishment properties of electric shock. *Psychonomic Science,* 1970a, *18,* 155–157.

Davidson, R. S. Rapid shaping of fixed-interval verbal behavior. *Psychonomic Science,* 1970b, *18,* 349–350.

Davidson, R. S. Teaching speech to autistic children. Unpublished report, 1971.

Davidson, R. S. Aversive modification of alcoholic behavior: I. Punishment of an alcohol-reinforced operant. Submitted to *Behavior Therapy,* 1972a.

Davidson, R. S. Alcoholism: Experimental analyses of etiology and modification. Unpublished manuscript, 1972b.

Davidson, R. S. Aversive modification of alcoholic behavior: II. Punishment of an early component of a behavioral chain. Unpublished manuscript, 1972c.

Davis, H. V., Sears, R. R., Miller, H. C., & Brodbeck, A. J. Effects of cup, bottle, and breast feeding on oral activities of newborn infants. *Pediatrics,* 1948, *3,* 549–558.

Davis, R. C., & Berry, F. Gastrointestinal reactions during a noise avoidance task. *Psychological Reports,* 1963, *12,* 135–137.

Davison, G. C. A social learning therapy programme with an autistic child. *Behaviour Research and Therapy,* 1964, *2,* 149–159.

Davison, G. C. Anxiety under total curarization: Implications for the role of muscular relaxation under desensitization of neurotic fears. *Journal of Nervous and Mental Diseases,* 1966, *143,* 443–448.

Davison, G. C. Elimination of a sadistic fantasy by a client-controlled counterconditioning technique: A case study. *Journal of Abnormal Psychology,* 1968, *73,* 84–90.

Davison, G. C., & Valins, S. Maintenance of self-attributed and drug-attributed behavior change. *Journal of Personality and Social Psychology,* 1969, *11,* 25–33.

Davitz, J. R., & Mason, D. J. Socially facilitated reduction of a fear response in rats. *Journal of Comparative and Physiological Psychology,* 1955, *48,* 149–151.

Dekker, E., Pelser, H. E., & Groen, J. Conditioning as a cause of asthmatic attacks. *Journal of Psychosomatic Research,* 1957, *2,* 97–108.

DeMorsier, G., & Feldmann, H. Le traitement biologique de l'alcoolisme chronique par l'apomorphine. Etude de 200 cas. (The biological treatment of chronic alcoholism with apomorphine. Study of 200 cases.) *Schweizer Archiv fur Neurologie und Psychiatrie,* 1950, *65,* 472–473.

Dews, P. B. Modification by drugs of performance on simple schedules of positive reinforcement. *Annals of the New York Academy of Sciences,* 1956, *65,* 268–281.

Dews, P. B. Psychopharmacology. In A. J. Bachrach (ed.), *Experimental foundations of clinical psychology.* New York: Basic Books, 1962.

DiCara, L. V., & Miller, N. E. Instrumental learning of vasomotor responses by rats: Learning to respond differentially in the two ears. *Science,* 1968, *159,* 1485–1486.

DiCara, L. V. & Miller, N. E. Heart-rate learning in the noncurarized state, transfer to the curarized state, and subsequent retraining in the noncurarized state. *Physiology and Behavior,* 1969, *4,* 621–624.

Diefendorf, A. P. *Clinical psychiatry.* New York: Macmillan, 1921.

Dinsmoor, J. A. Punishment: I. The avoidance hypothesis. *Psychological Review,* 1954, *61,* 34–46.

Dinsmoor, J. A. Abnormal behavior in animals. In R. H. Waters, D. A. Rethlingshafer, & W. E. Caldwell (eds.), *Principles of comparative psychology.* New York: McGraw-Hill, 1960.

Dinsmoor, J. A. Variable-interval escape from stimuli accompanied by shocks. *Journal of the Experimental Analysis of Behavior,* 1962, *5,* 41–47.

Dinsmoor, J. A. Escape from shock as a conditioning technique. In M. R. Jones (ed.), *Miami symposium on the prediction of behavior 1967: Aversive stimulation.* Coral Gables, Fla.: University of Miami Press, 1968.

Dollard, J., & Miller, N. E. *Personality and psychotherapy.* New York: McGraw-Hill, 1950.

Drennan, W., & Greenspoon, J. Instructions and verbal conditioning. Unpublished research report, Florida State University, 1960.

Duke, M. P., Frankel, A. S., Sipes, M., & Stewart, R. W. The effects of different kinds of models on interview behavior and feelings about an interview situation. Unpublished manuscript, Indiana University, 1965.

Dulany, D. E. The place of hypotheses and intentions: An analysis of verbal control in verbal conditioning. In C. W. Eriksen (ed.), *Behavior and awareness—a symposium of research and interpretation.* Durham, N.C.: Duke University Press, 1962.

Dunlap, K. *Habits:* Their making and unmaking. New York: Liveright, 1932.

Dworkin, L. Conditioning neurosis in dog and cat. *Psychosomatic Medicine,* 1939, *1,* 388–396.

Ebbinghaus, H. *Memory: A contribution to experimental psychology,* 1885. (Translated by H. A. Ruger and C. E. Bussenius.) New York: Teachers College, Columbia, 1913.

Elliott, R., & Tighe, T. J. Breaking the cigarette habit: A technique involving threatened loss of money. *Psychological Record,* 1968, *18,* 503–513.

Ellis, A. An introduction to the principles of scientific psychoanalysis. *Genetic Psychology Monographs,* 1950, *41,* 147–212.

Eriksen, C. W., & Kuethe, J. L. Avoidance conditioning of verbal behavior without awareness: A paradigm of repression. *Journal of Abnormal and Social Psychology,* 1956, *53,* 203–209.

Estes, W. K., & Skinner, B. F. Some quantitative properties of anxiety. *Journal of Experimental Psychology,* 1941, *29,* 390–400.

Evans, D. R. An exploratory study into the treatment of exhibitionism by means of emotive imagery and aversive conditioning. *Canadian Psychologist,* 1967, *8,* 162.

Everett, P. B., & King, R. A. Schedule-induced alcohol ingestion. *Psychonomic Science,* 1970, *18,* 278–279.

Eysenck, H. J. *Dimensions of personality.* London: Routledge & Kegan Paul, 1947.

Eysenck, H. J. *Scientific study of personality.* London: Routledge & Kegan Paul, 1952a.

Eysenck, H. J. The effects of psychotherapy: An evaluation. *Journal of Consulting Psychology,* 1952b, *16,* 319–324.

Eysenck, H. J. *Structure of human personality.* London: Metheun, 1959.

Eysenck, H. J. The effects of psychotherapy. In H. J. Eysenck (ed.), *Handbook of abnormal psychology.* New York: Basic Books, 1961a. Pp. 697–725.

Eysenck, H. J. (ed.). *Handbook of abnormal psychology.* New York: Basic Books, 1961b.

Eysenck, H. J. Classification and the problem of diagnosis. In H. J. Eysenck (ed.), *Handbook of abnormal psychology.* New York: Basic Books, 1961c.

Eysenck, H. J. Extroversion and the acquisition of eyeblink and GSR conditioned responses. *Psychological Bulletin,* 1965, *63,* 258–270.

Eysenck, H. J., & Rachman, S. *The causes and cures of neurosis.* London: Routledge and Kegan Paul, 1965.

Fairweather, G. W. (ed.). *Social psychology in treating mental illness: An experimental approach.* New York: Wiley, 1964.

Fairweather, G. W. *Methods for experimental social innovation.* New York: Wiley, 1967.

Falk, J. L. Production of polydipsia in normal rats by an intermittent food schedule. *Science,* 1961, *133,* 195–196.

Falk, J. L. The motivational properties of schedule-induced polydipsia. *Journal of the Experimental Analysis of Behavior,* 1966, *9,* 19–25.

Feldman, M. P. Aversion therapy for sexual deviation: A critical review. *Psychological Review,* 1966, *65,* 65–79.

Feldman, M. P., & MacCulloch, M. J. The application of anticipatory avoidance learning to the treatment of homosexuality. I. Theory, technique and preliminary results. *Behaviour Research and Therapy,* 1965, *2,* 165–183.

Fenichel, O. *Outline of clinical psychoanalysis.* New York: Norton, 1934.

Fenichel, O. *The psychoanalytic theory of neurosis.* New York: Norton, 1945.

Ferster, C. B. Reinforcement and punishment in the control of human behavior by social agencies, *Psychiatric Research Reports,* 1958, *10,* 101–118.

Ferster, C. B. Suppression of a performance under differential reinforcement of low rates by a pre-time-out stimulus. *Journal of the Experimental Analysis of Behavior,* 1960, *3,* 143–153.

Ferster, C. B. Positive reinforcement and behavioral deficits of autistic children. *Child Development,* 1961, *32,* 437–456.

Ferster, C. B. Classification of behavior pathology. In L. Krasner & L. P. Ullmann (eds.), *Research in behavior modification.* New York: Holt, Rinehart & Winston, 1965.

Ferster, C. B. Arbitrary and natural reinforcement. *Psychological Record,* 1967a, *17,* 341–347.

Ferster, C. B. Perspectives in Psychology. XXV. Transition from animal laboratory to clinic. *Psychological Record,* 1967b, *17,* 145–150.

Ferster, C. B., & DeMyer, M. K. The development of performances in autistic children in an automatically controlled environment. *Journal of Chronic Diseases,* 1961, *13,* 312–345.

Ferster, C. B., & DeMyer, M. K. A method for the experimental analysis of the behavior of autistic children. *American Journal of Orthopsychiatry,* 1962, *32,* 89–98.

Ferster, C. B., Nurnberger, J. L., & Levitt, E. B. The control of eating. *Journal of Mathetics,* 1962, *1,* 87–109.

Ferster, C. B., & Perrott, M. C. *Behavior principles.* New York: New Century, 1968.

Ferster, C. B., & Simons, J. Behavior therapy with children. *Psychological Record,* 1966, *16,* 65–71.

Ferster, C. B., & Skinner, B. F. *Schedules of reinforcement.* New York: Appleton-Century-Crofts, 1957.

Findley, J. D. An experimental outline for building and exploring multi-operant behavior repertoires. *Journal of the Experimental Analysis of Behavior,* 1962, *5,* 113–166.

Findley, J. D. Programmed environments for the experimental analysis of human behavior. In W. K. Honig (ed.), *Operant behavior: Areas of research and application.* New York: Appleton-Century-Crofts, 1966.

Flanagan, B., Goldiamond, I., & Azrin, N. H. Operant stuttering: The control of stuttering behavior through response-contingent consequences. *Journal of the Experimental Analysis of Behavior,* 1958, *1,* 173–177.

Flanagan, B., Goldiamond, I., & Azrin, N. H. Instatement of stuttering in normally fluent individuals through operant procedures. *Science,* 1959, *130,* 979–981.

Fontana, A. F. Familial etiology of schizophrenia. Possible? *Psychological Bulletin,* 1966, *66,* 214–227.

Frank, G. H. The role of the family in the development of psychopathology. *Psychological Bulletin,* 1965, *64,* 191–205.

Franks, C. M. Conditioning and personality. *Journal of Abnormal and Social Psychology,* 1956, *52,* 143–150.

Franks, C. M. Conditioning and abnormal behavior. In H. J. Eysenck (ed.), *Handbook of abnormal psychology.* New York: Basic Books, 1961.

Franks, C. M. Behavior therapy, the principles of conditioning and the treatment of the alcoholic. *Quarterly Journal of Studies on Alcohol,* 1963, *24,* 511–529.

Franks, C. M. Conditioning and conditioned aversion therapies in the treatment of the alcoholic. *International Journal of the Addictions,* 1966, *1,* 61–98.

Freeman, G. L. A method of inducing frustration in human subjects and its influence on palmar skin resistance. *American Journal of Psychology,* 1940, *53,* 117–120.

Freud, S. *A general introduction to psychoanalysis.* New York: Boni & Liveright, 1920.

Freud, S. Three contributions to the theory of sex. (4th ed.) *Nervous and mental disease monograph series,* 1930, No. 7.

Frolov, Y. P. *Pavlov and his school.* New York: Oxford University Press, 1937.

Gambrill, E. Effectiveness of the counterconditioning procedure in eliminating avoidance behavior. *Behaviour Research and Therapy,* 1967, *5,* 263–274.

Gantt, W. H. The origin and development of nervous disturbances experimentally produced. *American Journal of Psychiatry,* 1942, *98,* 475–481.

Gantt, W. H. Experimental basis for neurotic behavior: Origin and development of artificially produced disturbances of behavior in dogs. New

York: Hoeber, 1944. Also *Psychosomatic Medicine Monograph,* 1944, *3,* Nos. 3 and 4.

Garfield, Z. H., Darwin, P. L., Singer, B. A., McBrearty, J. F. Effect of "in vivo" training on experimental desensitization of a phobia. *Psychological Reports,* 1967, *20,* 515–519.

Gelfand, D. M., Gelfand, S., & Dobson, W. R. Unprogrammed reinforcement of patients' behavior in a mental hospital. *Behaviour Research and Therapy,* 1967, *5,* 201–207.

Gendreau, P. E., & Dodwell, P. C. An aversive treatment for addicted cigarette smokers: Preliminary report. *Canadian Psychologist,* 1968, *9,* 28–34.

Gentry, W. D. Fixed-ratio schedule-induced aggression. *Journal of the Experimental Analysis of Behavior,* 1968, *11,* 813–818.

Gericke, O. L. Practical use of operant conditioning procedures in a mental hospital. *Psychiatric Studies and Projects,* 1965, *3,* 2–10.

Gewirtz, J. L., & Stingle, K. G. The learning of generalized imitation as the basis for identification. *Psychological Review,* 1968, *75,* 374–397.

Giles, D. K., & Wolf, M. M. Toilet training institutionalized, severe retardates: An application of operant behavior modification techniques. *American Journal of Mental Deficiency,* 1966, *70,* 766–780.

Girardeau, F. L., & Spradlin, J. E. Token rewards on a cottage program. *Mental Retardation,* 1964, *2,* 345–351.

Glynn, J. D., & Harper, P. Behavior therapy in transvestism. *Lancet,* 1961, *1,* 619.

Goffman, E. *Asylums: Essays on the social situation of mental patients and other inmates.* New York: Anchor Books, 1961.

Goldberg, S. R., Woods, J. H., & Schuster, C. R. Morphine: Conditioned increases in self-administration in rhesus monkeys. *Science,* 1969, *166,* 1306–1307.

Goldfried, M. R. & D'Zurilla, T. J. A behavioral-analytic model for assessing competence. In C. D. Spielberger (ed.), *Current Topics in clinical and community psychology.* Vol. I, New York: Academic Press, 1969.

Goldiamond, I. Self-control procedures in personal behavior problems. *Psychological Reports,* 1965a, *17,* 851–868.

Goldiamond, I. Stuttering and fluency as manipulative operant response classes. In L. Krasner & L. P. Ullman (eds.), *Research in behavior modification.* New York: Holt, Rinehart & Winston, 1965b. Pp. 108–156.

Goldstein, A. P., & Dean, S. J. (eds.). *The investigation of psychotherapy.* New York: Wiley, 1966.

Goodkin, R. Changes in word production, sentence production, and relevance in an aphasic, through verbal conditioning. *Behaviour Research and Therapy,* 1969, *7,* 93–99.

Gormezano, I. Classical conditioning. In J. B. Sidowski (ed.), *Experimental methods and instrumentation in psychology.* New York: McGraw-Hill, 1966.

Green, R. Sissies and tomboys: A guide to diagnosis and management. In C. W. Wohl (ed.), *Sexual problems.* New York: Free Press, 1967.

Greenspoon, J. The reinforcing effect of two spoken sounds on the frequency of two responses. *American Journal of Psychology,* 1955, *68,* 409–416.

Greenspoon, J. Verbal conditioning and clinical psychology. In A. J. Bachrach (ed.), *Experimental foundations of clinical psychology.* New York: Basic Books, 1962.

Grings, W. W., & Carlin, S. Instrumental modification of autonomic behavior. *Psychological Record,* 1966, *16,* 153–159.

Grünbaum, A. Causality and the science of human behavior. *American Scientist,* 1952, *40,* 665–676.

Guttman, N., & Kalish, H. I. Discriminability and stimulus generalization. *Journal of Experimental Psychology,* 1956, *51,* 79–88.

Hake, D. F., & Laws, D. R. Social facilitation of responses during a stimulus paired with electric shock. *Journal of the Experimental Analysis of Behavior,* 1967, *10,* 387–392.

Hall, C. S., & Lindzey, G. *Theories of personality.* New York: Wiley, 1957.

Harlow, H. F., Gluck, J. P., & Suomi, S. J. Generalization of behavorial data between human and nonhuman animals. *American Psychologist,* 1972, *27,* 709–716.

Harlow, H. F., & Harlow, M. K. Social deprivation in monkeys, *Scientific American,* 1962, *207,* 473–482.

Harlow, H. F., & Harlow, M. K. The affectional systems. In A. M. Schrier, H. F. Harlow, & F. Stollnitz (eds.), *Behavior of nonhuman primates.* Vol. 2. New York: Academic Press, 1965.

Harlow, H. F., & Zimmerman, R. R. Affectional responses in the monkey. *Science,* 1959, *130,* 421–432.

Harmatz, M. G., & Lapuc, P. Behavior modification of overeating in a psychiatric population. *Journal of Consulting and Clinical Psychology,* 1968, *32,* 583–587.

Harris, M. B. Self-directed program for weight control: A pilot study. *Journal of Abnormal Psychology,* 1969, *74,* 263–270.

Hart, B., Allen, E., Buell, J., & Harris, F. Effects of social reinforcement on operant crying. *Journal of Experimental Child Psychology,* 1964, *1,* 145–153.

Haughton, E., & Ayllon, T. Production and elimination of symptomatic behavior. In L. P. Ullmann & L. Krasner (eds.), *Case studies in behavior modification.* New York: Holt, Rinehart & Winston, 1965.

Hayes, K. J., & Hayes, C. Imitation in a home-raised chimpanzee. *Journal of Comparative and Physiological Psychology,* 1952, *45,* 450–459.

Herman, R. L. and Azrin, N. H. Punishment by noise in an alternative response situation. *Journal of the Experimental Analysis of Behavior,* 1964, *7,* 185–188.

Herrnstein, R. J. Superstition: A corollary of the principles of operant conditioning. In W. K. Honig (ed.), *Operant behavior: Areas of research and application.* New York: Appleton-Century-Crofts, 1966.

Herrnstein, R. J. Method and theory in the study of avoidance. *Psychological Review,* 1969, *76,* 49–69.

Hetzel, M. L., & Hetzel, C. W. *Relay circuits for psychology.* New York: Appleton-Century-Crofts, 1969.

Hogan, R. A. Implosive therapy in the short-term treatment of psychotics. *Psychotherapy: Theory, Research and Practice,* 1966, *3,* 25–32.

Hogan, R. A., & Kirchner, J. H. Preliminary report of the extinction of learned fears via short-term implosive therapy. *Journal of Abnormal Psychology,* 1967, *72,* 106–109.

Holland, G., & Skinner, B. F. *The analysis of behavior.* New York: McGraw-Hill, 1961.

Hollingworth, H. L. *Abnormal psychology.* New York: Ronald, 1930.

Holmes, D. S. Dimensions of projection. *Psychological Bulletin,* 1968, *69,* 248–268.

Holz, W. C., & Azrin, N. H. Discriminative properties of punishment. *Journal of the Experimental Analysis of Behavior,* 1961, *4,* 225–232.

Holz, W. C., & Azrin, N. H. Interactions between the discriminative and aversive properties of punishment. *Journal of the Experimental Analysis of Behavior,* 1962, *5,* 229–236.

Holz, W. C., Azrin, N. H., and Ayllon, T. A comparison of several procedures for eliminating behavior. *Journal of the Experimental Analysis of Behavior,* 1963, *6,* 399–406.

Holz, W. C., Azrin, N. H., & Allyon, T. Elimination of behavior of mental patients by response-produced extinction. *Journal of the Experimental Analysis of Behavior,* 1963, *6,* 407–412.

Homme, L. E. Perspectives in Psychology. XXIV. Control of coverants, the operants of the mind. *Psychological Record,* 1965, *15,* 501–511.

Homme, L. E. Contiguity theory and contingency management. *Psychological Reports,* 1966, *16,* 233–241.

Hsu, J. Electroconditioning therapy of alcoholics: A preliminary report. *Quarterly Journal of Studies on Alcohol,* 1965, *26,* 449–459.

Hull, C. L. *Principles of behavior.* New York: Appleton-Century-Crofts, 1943.

Humphrey, J. Behavior therapy with children: An experimental evaluation. Unpublished doctoral dissertation, University of London, 1966.

Hunt, J. G., & Zimmerman, J. Stimulating productivity in a simulated sheltered workshop setting. *American Journal of Mental Deficiency,* 1969, *74,* 43–49.

Immergluck, L. Determinism—Freedom in contemporary psychology: An ancient problem revisited. *American Psychologist,* 1964, *19,* 270–281.

Isaacs, W., Thomas, J., & Goldiamond, I. Application of operant conditioning to reinstate verbal behavior in psychotics. *Journal of Speech and Hearing Disorders,* 1960, *25,* 8–12.

Jacobson, E. *Progressive relaxation.* Chicago: University of Chicago Press, 1938.

Jahoda, M. *Current concepts of positive mental health.* New York: Basic Books, 1958.

Janis, I. L., & Mann, L. Effectiveness of emotional role playing in modifying smoking habits and attitudes. *Journal of Experimental Research in Personality,* 1965, *1,* 84–90.

Jersild, A., & Holmes, F. B. Methods of overcoming children's fears. *Journal of Psychology,* 1935, *1,* 75–104.

Johnson, R. F., Haughton, E., & Lafave, H. G. Behavior therapy—use in a sheltered workshop. *Diseases of the Nervous System,* 1965, *26,* 350–354.

Johnston, J. M. Punishment of human behavior, *American Psychologist,* 1972, *27,* 1033–1054.

Jones, E. *Life and work of Sigmund Freud.* Vol. I. New York: Basic Books, 1953.

Jones, M. C. A laboratory study of fear: The case of Peter. *Pedagogical Seminary,* 1924a, *31,* 308–315.

Jones, M. C. Elimination of children's fears. *Journal of Experimental Psychology,* 1924b, *7,* 382–390.

Justesen, D. R., Braun, E. W., Garrison, R. G., and Pendelton, R. B. Pharmacological differentiation of allergic and classical conditioned asthma in the guinea pig. *Science,* 1970, *170,* 864–866.

Kanfer, F. H. The effect of a warning signal preceding a noxious stimulus on verbal rate and heart rate. *Journal of Experimental Psychology,* 1958, *55,* 73–80.

Kanfer, F. H. Issues and ethics in behavior manipulation. *Psychological Reports,* 1965, *16,* 187–196.

Kanfer, F. H. Implications of conditioning techniques for interview therapy. *Journal of Counseling Psychology,* 1966, *13,* 171–177.

Kanfer, F. H. Verbal conditioning: A review of its current status. In T. R. Dixon & D. L. Horton (eds.), *Verbal behavior and general behavior theory.* Englewood Cliffs, N.J.: Prentice-Hall, 1968.

Kanfer, F. H., & Phillips, J. S. Behavior therapy: A panacea for all ills, or a passing fancy? *Archives of General Psychiatry,* 1966, *15,* 114–128.

Kanfer, F. H., & Phillips, J. S. A survey of current behavior therapies and a proposal for classification. In C. M. Franks (ed.), *Behavior therapy: Appraisal and status.* New York: McGraw-Hill, 1969.

Kanfer, F. H., & Phillips, J. S. *Learning foundations of behavior therapy.* New York: Wiley, 1970.

Kanfer, F. H., & Saslow, G. Behavioral diagnosis. In C. M. Franks (ed.), *Behavior therapy: Appraisal and status.* New York: McGraw-Hill, 1969.

Kant, F. Further modification in the technique of conditioned reflex treatment of alcohol addiction. *Quarterly Journal of Studies on Alcohol,* 1944, *5,* 229–232.

Kantorovich, N. V. An attempt at associative-reflex therapy in alcoholism. *Novoye Refleksologii nervnoy i Fiziologii Sistemy,* 1928, *3,* 436–445. Cited by Razran, G. H. S. Conditioned withdrawal responses with shock as the conditioning stimulus in adult human subjects. *Psychological Bulletin,* 1934, *31,* 111–143.

Karsh, E. B. Changes in intensity of punishment: Effect on running behavior of rats. *Science,* 1963, *140,* 1084–1085.

Karsh, E. B. Fixation produced by conflict. *Science,* 1970, *168,* 873–875.

Kazdin, A. E., & Bootzin, R. R. The token economy: an evaluative review. *Journal of Applied Behavior Analysis,* 1972, *5,* 343–372.

Keehn, J. D. Psychological paradigms of dependence. *International Journal of the Addictions,* 1969, *4,* 499–506.

Keehn, J. D. Ethanol consumption by rats on a differential probability of a reinforcement schedule. *Psychonomic Science,* 1970, *19,* 283–284.

Kelleher, R. T., & Morse, W. H. Schedules using noxious stimuli. III. Responding maintained with response-produced electric shocks. *Journal of the Experimental Analysis of Behavior,* 1968, *11,* 819–838.

Keller, F. S. "Goodbye, teacher . . .", *Journal of Applied Behavior Analysis,* 1968, *1,* 79–89.

Kellogg, W. N. "Positive" and "negative" conditioning, without contraction of the essential muscles during the period of training. *Psychological Bulletin,* 1939, *36,* 575.

Kennedy, T. D. Verbal conditioning without awareness: The use of programmed reinforcement and recurring assessment of awareness. *Journal of Experimental Psychology,* 1970, *84,* 487–494.

Keutzer, C. Case histories and shorter communications: Use of therapy time as a reinforcer. Application of operant conditioning techniques within a traditional psychotherapy context. *Behaviour Research and Therapy,* 1967, *5,* 367–370.

Kimble, G. A., Hilgard, E. R., & Marquis, D. G. *Conditioning and learning.* New York: Appleton-Century-Crofts, 1961.

Kimmel, H. D. Instrumental conditioning of autonomically mediated behavior. *Psychological Bulletin,* 1967, *67,* 337–345.

Kimmel, H. D. Introduction. In H. D. Kimmel (ed.), *Experimental Psychopathology.* New York: Academic Press, 1971.

Kimmel, H. D., & Hill, F. A. Operant conditioning of the GSR. *Psychological Reports,* 1960, *7,* 555–562.

Kimmel, H. D., & Kimmel, E. An instrumental conditioning method for the treatment of enuresis. *Journal of Behavior Therapy and Experimental Psychiatry,* 1970, *1,* 121–123.

King, G., Armitage, S., & Tilton, J. A therapeutic approach to schizophrenics of extreme pathology: An operant-interpersonal method. *Journal of Abnormal and Social Psychology,* 1960, *61,* 276–286.

Klein, B. Counterconditioning and fear reduction in the rat. *Psychonomic Science,* 1969, *77,* 150–151.

Koenig, K. P., & Masters, J. Experimental treatment of habitual smoking. *Behaviour Research and Therapy,* 1965, *3,* 235–244.

Krasner, L. Studies of the conditioning of verbal behavior. *Psychological Bulletin,* 1958, *15,* 148–171.

Krasner, L. Behavior control and social responsibility. *American Psychologist,* 1962a, *17,* 199–203.

Krasner, L. The therapist as a social reinforcing machine. In H. H. Strupp and L. Luborsky (eds.), *Research in psychotherapy,* Vol. II, Washington, D.C., APA, 1962b.

Krasner, L. Verbal conditioning and psychotherapy. In L. Krasner & L. P. Ullmann (eds.), *Research in behavior modification.* New York: Holt, Rinehart & Winston, 1965.

Krasner, L., & Ullmann, L. P. Variables affecting report of awareness in verbal conditioning. *Journal of Psychology,* 1963, *56,* 193–202.

Krasner, L., & Ullmann, L. P. *Research in behavior modification: New developments and implications.* New York: Holt, Rinehart & Winston, 1965.

Krasnogorski, N. I. The conditioned reflexes and children's neuroses. *American Journal of Diseases of Children,* 1925, *30,* 753–768.

Krumboltz, J. D., Varenhorst, B. B., & Thoresen, C. E. Nonverbal factors in the effectiveness of models in counseling. *Journal of Counseling Psychology,* 1967, *14,* 412–418.

Kushner, M., & Sandler, J. Aversion therapy and the concept of punishment. *Behaviour Research and Therapy,* 1966, *4,* 179–186.

LaBarba, R. C., & White, J. L. Maternal deprivation and the response to Ehrlich carcinoma in BALB/c mice. *Psychosomatic Medicine,* 1971, *33,* 458–460.

Lachenmeyer, C. W. Systematic socialization: Observations on a programmed environment for the habilitation of antisocial retardates. *Psychological Record,* 1969, *11,* 101–108.

Lal, H., & Lindsley, O. R. Therapy of chronic constipation in a young child by rearranging social contingencies. *Behaviour Research and Therapy,* 1968, *6,* 484–485.

Lang, P. J., Lazovik, A., & Reynolds, D. J. Desensitization, suggestibility, and pseudotherapy. *Journal of Abnormal and Social Psychology,* 1965, *70,* 395–402.

Lang, P. J., Stroufe, L. A., & Hastings, J. E. Effects of feedback and instructional set on the control of cardiac rate variability. *Journal of Experimental Psychology,* 1967, *75,* 425–431.

Lauer, D. W., & Estes, W. K. Successive acquisitions and extinctions of a jumping habit in relation to schedule of reinforcement. *Journal of Comparative and Psychological Psychology,* 1955, *48,* 8–13.

Lavin, N. I., Thorpe, J. G., Barker, J. C., Blakemore, C. B., & Conway, C. G. Behavior therapy in a case of transvestism. *Journal of Nervous and Mental Disease,* 1961, *133,* 346–353.

Lazarus, A. A. A preliminary report on the use of directed muscular activity in counterconditioning. *Behaviour Research and Therapy,* 1965, *2,* 301–303.

Lazarus, A. A. Aversion therapy and sensory modalities: Clinical impressions. *Perceptual and Motor Skills,* 1968, *27,* 178.

Lazarus, A. A. (ed.) *Clinical behavior therapy.* New York: Brunner-Mazel, 1972.

Lehrman, N. S. Precision in psychoanalysis. *American Journal of Psychiatry,* 1960, *116,* 1097–1103.

Leitenberg, H. Is time-out from positive reinforcement an aversive event? A review of the experimental evidence. *Psychological Bulletin,* 1965, *64,* 428–441.

Leitenberg, H., Agras, W. S., Barlow, D. H., & Oliveau, D. C. Contribution of selective positive reinforcement and therapeutic instructions to systematic desensitization therapy. *Journal of Abnormal Psychology,* 1969, *74,* 113–118.

Leitenberg, H., Agras, W. S., Thompson, L. E., & Wright, D. Feedback in behavior modification: An experimental analysis in two phobic cases. *Journal of Applied Behavior Analysis,* 1968, *1,* 131–137.

Lemere, F., & Voegtlin, W. L. An evaluation of aversion treatment of alcoholism. *Quarterly Journal of Studies on Alcohol,* 1950, *11,* 199–204.

Lemere, F., Voegtlin, W. L., Broz, W. R., & O'Hallaren, P. Conditioned reflex treatment of alcohol addiction. V. Type of patient suitable for this treatment. *Northwestern Medicine,* 1942a, *4,* 88–89.

Lemere, F., Voegtlin, W. L., Broz, W. R., O'Hallaren, P., & Tupper, W. E. The conditioned reflex treatment of chronic alcoholism. VIII. A review of six years' experience with this treatment of 1526 patients. *Journal of the American Medical Association,* 1942b, *120,* 269–270.

Lent, J. R., LeBlanc, J., & Spreidlin, J. E. Designing a rehabilitative culture for moderately retarded, adolescent girls. In R. Ulrich, T. Stachnik, and J. Mabry (eds.), *Control of human behavior.* Vol. Two. New York: Scott, Foresman and Co., 1970.

Lester, D. Self-maintenance of intoxication in the rat. *Quarterly Journal of Studies on Alcohol,* 1961, *22,* 223–241.

Levin, G. R., & Simons, J. J. Response to food and praise by emotionally disturbed boys. *Psychological Reports,* 1962, *11,* 539–546.

Levine, S. Infantile stimulation. *Scientific American,* 1960, *202,*81–86.

Levitt, E. E. Results of psychotherapy with children: An evaluation. *Journal of Consulting Psychology,* 1957, *21,* 189–196.

Levitz, L. S., & Ullmann, L. P. Manipulation of indications of disturbed thinking in normal subjects. *Journal of Consulting and Clinical Psychology,* 1969, *33,* 633–641.

Levy, D. Experiments on the sucking reflex and social behavior of dogs. *American Journal of Orthopsychiatry,* 1934, *4,* 203–224.

Libb, J. W. and Clements, C. B. Token Reinforcement in an exercise program for hospitalized geriatric patients. *Perceptual and Motor Skills,* 1969, *28,* 957–958.

Lichtenstein, F. E. Studies in anxiety. I. The production of a feeding inhibition in dogs. *Journal of Comparative and Physiological Psychology,* 1950, *43,* 16–29.

Liddell, H. S. Animal origins of anxiety. In M. C. Reymert (ed.), *Feelings and emotions.* New York: McGraw-Hill, 1950.

Liddell, H. S. The role of vigilance in the development of animal neurosis. In P. H. Hoch & J. Zubin (eds.), *Anxiety.* New York: Grune & Stratton, 1951.

Liddell, H. S. Conditioning and emotion. *Scientific American,* 1954, *190,* 48–57.

Liddell, H. S. *Emotional hazards in animals and man.* Springfield, Ill.: Charles C Thomas, 1956.

Lidz, T., Fleck, S., & Cornelison, A. R. *Schizophrenia and the family.* New York: International Universities Press, 1965.

Lindley, R. H., & Moyer, K. E. Effects of instructions on the extinction of a conditioned finger-withdrawal response. *Journal of Experimental Psychology,* 1961, *61,* 82–88.

Lindsley, O. R. Operant conditioning methods applied to research in chronic schizophrenia. *Psychiatric Research Reports,* 1956, *5,* 118–139.

Lindsley, O. R. Characteristics of the behavior of chronic psychotics as revealed by free-operant conditioning methods. *Diseases of the Nervous System,* 1960, *21,* 66–78.

Lindsley, O. R. Experimental analysis of social reinforcement: Terms and methods. *American Journal of Orthopsychiatry,* 1963a, *33,* 624–633.

Lindsley, O. R. Free-operant conditioning and psychotherapy. In J. H. Masserman (ed.), *Current Psychiatric Therapies,* 1963b, *3,* 47–56.

Lindsley, O. R. Direct behavioral analysis of psychotherapy sessions by conjugately programmed close-circuit television. *Psychotherapy: Theory, Research and Practice,* 1969, *6,* 71–81.

Lindsley, O. R. Direct behavioral analysis of psychotherapy sessions by conjugately programmed closed-circuit television. In R. Ulrich, T. Stachnik & J. Mabry (eds.), *Control of human behavior,* Vol. II. Glenview, Ill.: Scott Foresman, 1970.

Lindsley, O. R. Precision teaching workshop. Presented at the annual meeting of the Southeastern Psychological Association, Miami Beach, 1971.

Lippsett, L. P., Kaye, H., & Besack, T. N. Enhancement of neonatal sucking through reinforcement. *Journal of Experimental Child Psychology,* 1966, *4,* 163–168.

Littman, R. A., & Rosen, E. The molar-molecular distinction, *Psychological Revue,* 1950, *57,* 58–65.

Liversedge, L. A., Sylvester, J. D. Conditioning techniques in the treatment of writer's cramp. *Lancet,* 1955, *2,* 1147–1149.

Lloyd, K. E., & Abel, L. Performance on a token economy psychiatric ward: A two-year summary. *Behaviour Research and Therapy,* 1970, *8,* 1–9.

Lomont, J. F. The ethics of behavior therapy. *Psychological Reports,* 1964, *14,* 519–531.

London, P. *The modes and morals of psychotherapy.* New York: Holt, Rinehart & Winston, 1964.

Lovaas, O. I. Interaction between verbal and nonverbal behavior. *Child Development,* 1961, *32,* 329–336.

Lovaas, O. I. Control of food intake in children by reinforcement of relevant verbal behavior. *Journal of Abnormal and Social Psychology,* 1964, *68,* 672–678.

Lovaas, O. I. A behavior therapy approach to the treatment of childhood schizophrenia. In J. P. Hill (ed.), *Minnesota symposium on child psychology.* Vol. I. Minneapolis: University of Minnesota Press, 1967.

Lovaas, O. I., Berberich, J. P., Perloff, B. F., & Schaeffer, B. Acquisition of imitative speech by schizophrenic children. *Science,* 1966, *151,* 705–707.

Lovaas, O. I., Freitag, G., Gold, V. J., & Kassorla, I. C. Experimental studies in childhood schizophrenia: Analysis of self-destructive behavior. *Journal of Experimental Child Psychology,* 1965a, *2,* 67–84.

Lovaas, O. I., Freitas, L., Nelson, K., & Whalen, C. The establishment of imitation and its use for the development of complex behavior in schizophrenic children. *Behaviour Research and Therapy,* 1967, *5,* 171–181.

Lovaas, O. I., Schaeffer, B., & Simmons, J. Q. Building social behavior in autistic children by use of electric shock. *Journal of Experimental Research and Personality,* 1965b, *1,* 99–109.

Lovibond, S. H. Intermittent reinforcement in behavior therapy. *Behaviour Research and Therapy,* 1963, *1,* 127–132.

Lublin, I., & Joslyn, L. Aversive conditioning of cigarette addiction. Paper read at the meeting of the American Psychological Association, San Francisco, September 1968.

Luchins, A. S., & Luchins, E. H. Learning a complex ritualized social role. *Psychological Record,* 1966, *16,* 177–187.

Lumsdaine, A. A., & Glaser, R. (eds.). *Teaching machines and programmed learning: A source book.* Washington, D.C., National Education Association, 1960.

McAllister, W. R., & McAllister, D. E. Behavioral measurement of conditioned fear. In F. R. Brush (ed.). *Aversive conditioning and learning.* New York: Academic Press, 1971.

McAllister, L. W., Stachowiak, J. G., Baer, D. M., & Conderman, L. The application of operant conditioning techniques in a secondary school classroom. *Journal of Applied Behavior Analysis,* 1969, *2,* 277–285.

McBrearty, J. F., Dichter, M., Garfield, Z., & Heath, G. A behaviorally oriented treatment program for alcoholism. *Psychological Reports,* 1968, *22,* 287–298.

MacCorquodale, K., & Meehl, P. E. On a distinction between hypothetical constructs and intervening variables. *Psychological Review,* 1948, *55,* 95–107.

MacCulloch, M. J., Feldman, M. P., Orford, J. F., & MacCulloch, M. L. Anticipatory avoidance learning in the treatment of alcoholism: A record of therapeutic failure. *Behaviour Research and Therapy,* 1966, *4,* 187–196.

MacCulloch, M. J., Feldman, M. P., & Pinshoff, J. M. The application of anticipatory avoidance learning to the treatment of homosexuality. II. Avoidance response latencies and pulse rate changes. *Behaviour Research and Therapy,* 1965, *3,* 21–43.

McDavid, J. W. Imitative behavior in preschool children. *Psychological Monographs,* 1959, *73,* Whole No. 486.

McDavid, J. W. Effects of ambiguity of imitative cues upon learning by observation. *Journal of Social Psychology,* 1964, *62,* 165–174.

McGuire, R. J., Carlisle, J. M., & Young, B. G. Sexual deviations as conditioned behavior: A hypothesis. *Behaviour Research and Therapy,* 1965, *2,* 185–190.

McGuire, R. J., & Vallance, M. Aversion therapy by electric shock: A simple technique. *British Medical Journal,* 1964, *1,* 151–153.

McIntire, R., Davis, G., & Pumroy, D. Improved classroom performance by reinforcement outside the classroom. *Proceedings of the Annual Convention of the American Psychological Association,* 1970, *5* (Pt. 2), 747–748.

McKearney, J. W. Maintenance of responding under a fixed-interval schedule of electric shock presentation. *Science,* 1968, *160,* 1249–1251.

McQuitty, L. L. Theories and methods in some objective assessments of psychological well-being. *Psychological Monographs,* 1954, *68,* No. 385.

Maher, B. *Principles of psychopathology.* New York: McGraw-Hill, 1966.

Maier, N. R. F. *Frustration: The study of behavior without a goal.* New York: McGraw-Hill, 1949.

Maier, N. R. F., Glaser, N. M., & Klee, J. B. Studies of abnormal behavior in the rat. III. The development of behavior fixations through frustration. *Journal of Experimental Psychology,* 1940, *26,* 521–546.

Marks, I. M. *Fears and phobias.* New York: Academic Press, 1969.

Marks, I. M., & Gelder, M. G. Transvestism and fetishism: Clinical and psychological changes during faradic aversion. *British Journal of Psychiatry,* 1967, *113,* 711–729.

Martin, G. L., & Powers, R. B. Attention span: An operant analysis. *Exceptional Children,* 1967, *33,* 565–570.

Martin, M. L., Weinstein, M., & Lewinsohn, P. M. The use of home observations as an integral part of the treatment of depression: The case of Mrs. B. Unpublished manuscript, University of Oregon, 1968.

Mason, J. W., Brady, J. V., & Sidman, M. Plasma 17-hydroxy-corticosteroid levels and conditioned behavior in the rhesus monkey. *Endocrinology,* 1957, *60,* 741–752.

Masserman, J. H. *Behavior and neurosis: An experimental psychoanalytic approach to psychobiologic principles.* Chicago: University of Chicago Press, 1943.

Masserman, J. H. *Principles of dynamic psychiatry.* Philadelphia: Saunders, 1946.

Masserman, J. H. Experimental neuroses. *Scientific American,* 182, 1950, 38–50.

Masserman, J. H. *Modern therapy of personality disorders.* Dubuque, Iowa: William C. Brown, 1966.

Masserman, J. H., Jacques, M. G., & Nicholson, M. R. Alcohol as preventive of experimental neuroses. *Quarterly Journal of Studies on Alcohol,* 1945, *6,* 281–299.

Masserman, J. H., Yum, K. S., Nicholson, M. R., & Lee, S. Neurosis and alcohol: An experimental study. *American Journal of Psychiatry,* 1944, *101,* 389–395.

Max, L. W. Breaking up a homosexual fixation by the conditioned reaction technique: A case study. *Psychological Bulletin,* 1935, *32,* 734.

Meehl, P. E. Psychotherapy. *Annual Review of Psychology,* 1955, *6,* 357–378.

Mees, H. L. Sadistic fantasies modified by aversive conditioning and substitution: A case study. *Behaviour Research and Therapy,* 1966, *4,* 317–320.

Melzack, R., & Thompson, W. R. Effects of early experience on social behavior. *Canadian Journal of Psychology,* 1956, *10,* 82–90.

Mendelson, J. H. The national center for prevention and control of alcoholism, NIMH, *Psychiatric Research Reports,* 1968, No. 24, pp. 174–178.

Menninger, K. A. *The vital balance.* New York: Viking Press, 1963.

Michael, J. *Laboratory studies in operant behavior.* New York: Mc-Graw-Hill, 1963.

Miller, E. C., Dvorak, A., & Turner, D. W. A method of creating aversion to alcohol by reflex conditioning in a group setting. *Quarterly Journal of Studies on Alcohol,* 1960, *21,* 424–431.

Miller, M. M. Treatment of chronic alcoholism by hypnotic aversion. *Journal of the American Medical Association,* 1959, *171,* 1492–1495.

Miller, N. E. Experimental studies of conflict. In J. McV. Hunt (ed.), *Personality and the behavior disorders.* New York: Ronald Press, 1944.

Miller, N. E. Studies of fear as an acquirable drive. I. Fear as motivation and fear reduction as reinforcement in the learning of new responses. *Journal of Experimental Psychology,* 1948a, *38,* 89–101.

Miller, N. E. Theory and experiment relating psychoanalytic displacement to stimulus-response generalization. *Journal of Abnormal and Social Psychology,* 1948b, *43,* 155–178.

Miller, N. E. Liberalization of basic S-R concepts: Extensions to conflict behavior, motivation, and social learning. In S. Koch (ed.), *Psychology, a study of a science.* Vol. 2. New York: McGraw-Hill, 1959.

Miller, N. E. Learning resistance to pain and fear: Effects of overlearning, exposure, and rewarded exposure in context. *Journal of Experimental Psychology,* 1960, *60,* 137–145.

Miller, N. E. Learning of visceral and glandular responses. *Science,* 1969, *163,* 434–445.

Miller, N. E. Experiments relevant to learning theory and psychopathology. In W. S. Sahakian (ed.), *Psychopathology today: Experimentation, theory, and research.* Itasca, Ill.: Peacock, 1970.

Miller, N. E., & DiCara, L. Instrumental learning of heart rate changes in curarized rats: Shaping, and specificity to discriminative stimulus. *Journal of Comparative and Physiological Psychology,* 1967, *63,* 12–19.

Miller, N. E., & Dollard, J. *Social learning and imitation.* New Haven: Yale University Press, 1941.

Miller, N. E., & Kraeling, D. Displacement: Greater generalization of approach than avoidance in generalized approach-avoidance conflict. *Journal of Experimental Psychology,* 1952, *43,* 217–222.

Miller, R. E., Banks, J. H., Jr., & Ogawa, N. Role of facial expression in "cooperative avoidance conditioning" in monkeys. *Journal of Abnormal and Social Psychology,* 1963, *67,* 24–30.

Miller, R. E., Mirsky, I. A., Caul, W. F., & Sakata, T. Hyperphagia and polydipsia in socially isolated rhesus monkeys. *Science,* 1969, *165,* 1027–1028.

Minge, M. R., & Ball, T. S. Teaching of self-help skills to profoundly retarded patients. *American Journal of Mental Deficiencies,* 1967, *71,* 864–868.

Morrill, C. S. Teaching machines: A review. *Psychological Bulletin,* 1961, *58,* 363–375.

Morse, W. H. Intermittent reeinforcement. In W. K. Honig (ed.), *Operant behavior: Areas of research and application.* New York: Appleton-Century-Crofts, 1966.

Morse, W. H., & Kelleher, R. T. Schedules as fundamental determinants of behavior. Paper presented to American Psychological Association, September 1966.

Morse, W. H. & Kelleher, R. T. Schedules as fundamental determinants of behavior. In W. N. Schoenfeld (ed.), *The theory of reinforcement schedules*. New York: Appleton-Century-Crofts, 1970.

Morse, W. H., Mead, R. N., & Kelleher, R. T. Modulation of elicited behavior by a fixed-interval schedule of electric shock presentation. *Science,* 1967, *157,* 215–217.

Mowrer, O. H. An experimental analogue of "regression" with incidental observations on "reaction formation." *Journal of Abnormal and Social Psychology,* 1940, *35,* 56–87.

Mowrer, O. H. On the dual nature of learning—a reinterpretation of "conditioning" and "problem solving." *Harvard Educational Review,* 1947, *17,* 102–148.

Mowrer, O. H. Learning theory and the neurotic paradox. *American Journal of Orthopsychiatry,* 1948, *18,* 571–610.

Mowrer, O. H. *Learning theory and personality dynamics.* New York: Ronald Press, 1950.

Mowrer, O. H. Sin, the lesser of two evils. *American Psychologist,* 1960, *15,* 301–304.

Mowrer, O. H. Learning theory and behavior therapy. In B. Wolman (ed.), *Handbook of clinical psychology.* New York: McGraw-Hill, 1965.

Mowrer, O. H., & Jones, H. M. Habit strength as a function of the pattern of reinforcement. *Journal of Experimental Psychology,* 1945, *35,* 293–311.

Mulder, D. W., Lyon, D. O., & Pott, E. W. Conditioned suppression in humans. Paper presented at Midwestern Psychological Association, Chicago, 1967.

Munroe, R. *Schools of psychoanalytic thought.* New York: Dryden Press, 1955.

Murray, E. J. A content-analysis method for studying psychotherapy. *Psychological Monographs,* 1956, *70* (13, Whole No. 420).

Murphy, J. V., Miller, R. E., & Mirsky, I. A. Interanimal conditioning in the monkey. *Journal of Comparative and Physiological Psychology,* 1955, *48,* 211–214.

Narrol, H. G. Experimental application of reinforcement principles to the analysis and treatment of hospitalized alcoholics. *Quarterly Journal of Studies on Alcohol,* 1967, *28,* 105–115.

Nathan, P. E., Schneller, P., & Lindsley, O. R. Direct measurement of communication during psychiatric admission interviews. *Behaviour Research and Therapy,* 1964, *2,* 49–57.

Noelpp, B., & Noelpp-Eschenhagen, I Das experimentelle asthma bronchiale des meerschweinchens. III. Studien zur Bedeutung bedingte Reflexe. Bahrungs-bereitschaft and Haftfahigkeit unter "stress." *International Archives of Allergy,* 1952, *3,* 108–136.

Nolan, J. D. Self-control procedures in the modification of smoking behavior. *Journal of Consulting and Clinical Psychology,* 1968, *32,* 92–93.

O'Brien, F., Azrin, N. H., & Henson, K. Increased communication of chronic mental patients by reinforcement and by response priming. *Journal of Applied Behavior Analysis,* 1969, *2,* 23–29.

O'Connor, N. Children in restricted environments. In G. Newton & S. Levine (eds.), *Early experience and behavior.* Springfield, Ill.: Charles C Thomas, 1968.

O'Connor, R. D. Modification of social withdrawal through symbolic modeling. *Journal of Applied Behavioral Analysis,* 1969, *2,* 15–22.

O'Kelley, L. I., & Muckler, F. A. *Introduction to psychopathology,* Englewood Cliffs, N.J.: Prentice-Hall, 1955.

O'Leary, K. D., Becker, W. C., Evans, M. B., & Saudargas, R. A. A token reinforcement program in a public school: A replication and systematic analysis. *Journal of Applied Behavior Analysis,* 1969, *2,* 3–13.

O'Leary, K. D., O'Leary, S., & Becker, W. C. Modification of a deviant sibling interaction pattern in the home. *Behaviour Research and Therapy,* 1967, *5,* 113–120.

Orlansky, H. Infant care and personality. *Psychological Bulletin,* 1949, *46,* 1–48.

Ottenberg, P., Stein, M., Lewis, J., & Hamilton, C. Learned asthma in the guinea pig. *Psychosomatic Medicine,* 1958, *20,* 395–400.

Patterson, G. R. An empirical approach to the classification of disturbed children. *Journal of Clinical Psychology,* 1964, *20,* 326–337.

Patterson, G. R., & Brodsky, G. D. A behavior modification program for a child with multiple problem behaviors. *Journal of Child Psychology and Psychiatry,* 1966, *7,* 277–295.

Patterson, G. R., & Gullion, M. E. *Living with children: New methods for parents and teachers.* Champaign, Ill.: Research Press, 1968.

Patterson, G. R., & Reid, J. B. Reciprocity and coercion: Two facets of social systems. In Neuringer, C., & Michael, J. L. (eds.), *Behavior modification in clinical psychology.* New York: Appleton-Century-Crofts, 1970.

Paul, G. L. *Insight versus desensitization in psychotherapy: An experiment in anxiety reduction.* Stanford: Stanford University Press, 1966.

Paul, G. L. Behavior modification research: Design and tactics. In C. M. Franks (ed.), *Behavior therapy: Appraisal and status.* New York: McGraw-Hill, 1969a.

Paul, G. L. Physiological effects of relaxation training and hypnotic suggestion. *Journal of Abnormal Psychology,* 1969b, *74,* 425–437.

Pavlov, I. P. *Conditioned reflexes: An investigation of the physiological activity of the cerebral cortex.* London: Oxford University Press, 1927.

Pavlov, I. P. *Lectures on conditioned reflexes, Vol. 1.* (Translated by W. H. Gantt.) London: Lawrence & Wishart, 1928.

Pavlov, I. P. *Lectures on conditioned reflexes.* Vol. 2. *Conditioned reflexes and psychiatry.* New York: International Publishers, 1941.

Pavlov, I. P. *Selected works.* (Translated by S. Belsky; edited by J. Gibbons.) Moscow: Foreign Languages Publishing House, 1955.

Pemberton, D. A. A comparison of the outcome of treatment in female and male alcoholics. *British Journal of Psychiatry,* 1967, *113,* 367–373.

Perensky, J. J., Senter, R. J., & Jones, R. B. Induced alcohol consumption through positive reinforcement. *Psychonomic Science,* 1968, *4,* 109–110.

Peterson, G. L. The relationship between fixed-ratio schedules of reinforcement and aggression in children. Paper presented at Southeastern Psychological Association, Miami Beach, Fla., 1971.

Phelan, J. G., Hekmat, H., & Tang, T. Transfer of verbal conditioning to nonverbal behavior. *Psychological Reports,* 1967, *20,* 979–986.

Piercy, D. C., & Overall, J. E. Minimum adequate description of psychiatric disorder. *Proceedings of the 76th Annual Meeting of the American Psychological Association,* 1968, *3,* 475–476.

Pierrel, R., & Sherman, J. G. Train your pet the Barnabus way. *Brown Alumni Monthly,* 1963, February, 8–14.

Polin, A. T. The effect of flooding and physical suppression as extinction techniques on an anxiety-motivated avoidance locomotor response. *Journal of Psychology,* 1959, *47,* 235–245.

Powell, D. A., Francis, J., Braman, M. J., & Schneiderman, N. Frequency of attack in shock-elicited aggression as a function of the performance of individual rats. *Journal of the Experimental Analysis of Behavior*, 1969, *12*, 817–823.

Premack, D. Toward empirical behavioral laws. I. Positive reinforcement. *Psychological Review*, 1959, *66*, 219–233.

Premack, D. Reinforcement theory. In D. Levine (ed.), *Nebraska symposium on motivation, 1965.* Lincoln: University of Nebraska Press, 1965.

Pumpian-Mindlen, E. (ed.) *Psychoanalysis as science.* Stanford: Stanford University Press, 1952.

Quinn, J. T., & Henbest, R. Partial failure of generalization in alcoholics following aversion therapy. *Quarterly Journal of Studies on Alcohol,* 1967, *28*, 70–75.

Rachman, S. Aversion therapy: Chemical or electrical? *Behaviour Research and Therapy*, 1965, *2*, 289–300.

Rachman, S. Sexual fetishism: An experimental analogue. *Psychological Record*, 1966a, *16*, 293–296.

Rachman, S. Studies in desensitization: II. Flooding. *Behaviour Research and Therapy*, 1966b, *4*, 1–6.

Rachman, S. *Phobias: Their nature and control.* Springfield, Ill.: Charles C Thomas, 1968.

Rachman, S. Treatment by prolonged exposure to high intensity stimulation. *Behaviour Research and Therapy*, 1969, *7*, 295–302.

Rachman, S., & Eysenck, H. J. Reply to a "critique and reformulation of behavior therapy." *Psychological Bulletin*, 1966, *65*, 165–169.

Rachman, S., & Hodgson, R. J. Experimentally induced "sexual fetishism": Replication and development. *Psychological Record*, 1968, *18*, 25–27.

Rachman, S., & Teasdale, J. *Aversion therapy and behaviour disorders: An analysis.* Coral Gables, Fla.: University of Miami Press, 1969.

Raymond, M. J. Case of fetishism treated by aversion therapy. *British Medical Journal*, 1956, *2*, 854–857.

Raymond, M. J. The treatment of addiction by aversion conditioning with apomorphine. *Behaviour Research and Therapy*, 1964, *1*, 287–291.

Reese, E. P. *The analysis of human operant behavior.* Dubuque, Iowa: William C. Brown, 1966.

Renner, K. E. Delay of reinforcement: A historical review. *Psychological Bulletin*, 1964, *61*, 341–361.

Resnick, J. H. Effects of stimulus satiation on the over-learned maladaptive response of cigarette smoking. *Journal of Consulting and Clinical Psychology*, 1968, *32*, 501–505.

Ribble, M. A. *The rights of infants.* New York: Columbia University Press, 1943.

Rickard, H. C., Dignam, P. J., & Horner, R. F. Verbal manipulation in a psychotherapeutic relationship. *Journal of Clinical Psychology*, 1960, *16*, 364–367.

Rickard, H. C., & Dinoff, M. A follow-up note on "verbal manipulation in a psychotherapeutic relationship." *Psychological Reports*, 1962, *11*, 506.

Risley, T. R. The effects and side effects of punishing the autistic behaviors of a deviant child. *Journal of Applied Behavior Aanalysis*, 1968, *1*, 21–34.

Risley, T., & Hart, B. Developing correspondence between the nonverbal and verbal behavior of preschool children. *Journal of Applied Behavior Analysis*, 1968, *1*, 267–281.

Risley, T., & Wolf, M. Establishing functional speech in echolalic children. *Behaviour Research and Therapy,* 1967, *5,* 73–88.

Ritter, B. J. The group desensitization of children's snake phobias using vicarious and contact desensitization procedures. *Behaviour Research and Therapy,* 1968, *6,* 1–6.

Roberts, A. H. Self control procedures in modification of smoking behavior: A replication. *Psychological Reports,* 1969, *24,* 675–676.

Rogers, C. R. *Counseling and psychotherapy.* Boston: Houghton Mifflin, 1942.

Rogers, C. R. *Client-centered therapy: Its current practice, implications and theory.* Boston: Houghton Mifflin, 1951.

Rogers, C. R., & Skinner, B. F. Some issues concerning the control of human behavior. *Science,* 1956, *124,* 1057–1066.

Rosenblum, L. A., & Harlow, H. F. Approach-avoidance conflict in the mother-surrogate situation. *Psychological Reports,* 1963, *12,* 83–85.

Rosenhan, D. L. On being sane in insane places. *Science,* 1973, *179,* 250–258.

Ross, S. Sucking behavior in neonate dogs. *Journal of Abnormal and Social Psychology,* 1951, *46,* 142–149.

Rossi, A. M. General methodological considerations. In J. P. Zubek (ed.), *Sensory deprivation: Fifteen years of research.* New York: Appleton-Century-Crofts, 1969.

Rotter, J. B. Psychotherapy. In P. R. Farnsworth (ed.), *Annual review of psychology.* Vol. 11. Palo Alto, Calif.: Annual Reviews, 1960, 381–414.

Rubinstein, E. A., & Parloff, M. B. (eds.) *Research in psychotherapy.* Vol. I. Washington, D.C.: American Psychological Association, 1959.

Sachs, D. A., & May, J. G. The presence of a temporal discrimination in the conditioned emotional response with humans. *Journal of the Experimental Analysis of Behavior,* 1969, *12,* 1003–1007.

Salter, A. *Conditioned reflex therapy.* New York: Farrar-Straus, 1949.

Salzinger, K. Experimental manipulation of verbal behavior: A review. *Journal of General Psychology,* 1959, *61,* 65–94.

Salzinger, K., Feldman, R. S., Cowan, J. E., & Salzinger, S. Operant conditioning of verbal behavior of two young speech-deficient boys. In L. Krasner & L. P. Ullmann (eds.), *Research in behavior modification.* New York: Holt, Rinehart & Winston, 1965.

Salzinger, K., & Pisoni, S. Reinforcement of verbal affect responses of normal subjects during the interview. *Journal of Abnormal and Social Psychology,* 1960, *60,* 127–130.

Sandler, J. The effect of negative verbal cues upon verbal behavior. *Journal of Abnormal and Social Psychology,* 1962, *64,* 312–316.

Sandler, J. Masochism: An empirical analysis. *Psychological Bulletin,* 1964, *62,* 197–204.

Sandler, J., & Davidson, R. S. Punished avoidance behavior in the presence of a non-punished alternative. *Psychonomic Science,* 1967, *8,* 297–298.

Sandler, J., & Davidson, R. S. Psychopathology: An analysis of complex response consequences. In H. D. Kimmel (ed.), *Experimental psychopathology: Recent research and theory.* New York: Academic Press, 1971.

Sandler, J., Davidson, R. S., Greene, W. E., & Holzschuh, R. D. The effects of punishment intensity on signal instrumental avoidance behavior. *Journal of Comparative and Physiological Psychology,* 1966a, *61,* 212–216.

Sandler, J., Davidson, R. S., & Holzschuh, R. D. Effects of increasing punishment frequency on Sidman avoidance behavior. *Psychonomic Science,* 1966b, *5,* 103–104.

Sandler, J., Davidson, R. S., & Malagodi, E. F. Durable maintenance of behavior during concurrent avoidance and punished extinction conditions. *Psychonomic Science,* 1966c, *6,* 195–196.

Sandler, J., & Turner, W. Vocational preparation of the hard-core unemployed: The token economy. *Rehabilitation Counseling Bulletin.* (in press)

Sarbin, T. R. On the futility of the proposition that some people be labeled "mentally ill." *Journal of Consulting Psychology,* 1967, *31,* 447–453.

Sarbin, T. R. Ontology recapitulates philology: The mythic nature of anxiety. *American Psychologist,* 1968, *23,* 411–418.

Schaefer, H. H. Self-injurious behavior: Shaping "head-banging" in monkeys. *Journal of Applied Behavior Analysis,* 1970, *3,* 111–116.

Schaefer, H. H., & Martin, P. L. Behavioral therapy for "apathy" of hospitalized schizophrenics. *Psychological Reports,* 1966, *19,* 1147–1158.

Schaefer, H. H., & Martin, P. L. *Behavioral therapy.* New York: Mc-Graw-Hill, 1969.

Schneiderman, N. E. Personal communication, 1971.

Schneiderman, N. E., Pearl, L., Wilson, W., Metcalf, F., Moore, J. W., & Swadlow, H. A. Stimulus control in rabbits (Oryctolagus cuniculus) as a function of different intensities of intracranial stimulation. *Journal of Comparative and Physiological Psychology,* 1971, *76,* 175–186.

Schoenfeld, W. N. An experimental approach to anxiety, escape and avoidance behavior. In P. H. Hoch & J. Zubin (eds.), *Anxiety.* New York: Grune & Stratton, 1950.

Schultz, D. P. *Sensory Restriction: Effects on behavior.* New York: Academic Press, 1965.

Schwitzgebel, R., & Kolb, D. A. Inducing behavior change in adolescent delinquents. *Behaviour Research and Therapy,* 1964, *1,* 297–304.

Scott, W. A. Research definitions of mental health and mental illness. *Psychological Bulletin,* 1958, *55,* 29–45.

Seay, B., Alexander, B. K., & Harlow, H. F. Maternal behavior of socially deprived rhesus monkeys. *Journal of Abnormal and Social Psychology,* 1964, *69,* 345–354.

Sears, R. R. Survey of objective studies of psychoanalytic concepts. New York: *Social Science Research Council Bulletin,* 1943, No. 51.

Sears, R. R. Experimental analysis of psychoanalytic phenomena. In J. McV. Hunt (ed.), *Personality and the behavior disorders.* Vol. I. New York: Ronald Press, 1944.

Sears, R. R. *Survey of objective studies of psychoanalytic concepts.* New York: Social Science Research Council, 1951.

Shapiro, D., Tursky, B., & Schwartz, G. E. Differentiation of heart rate and systolic blood pressure in man by operant conditioning. *Psychosomatic Medicine,* 1970, *32,* 417–423.

Shaw, F. J. A stimulus-response analysis of repression and insight in psychotherapy. *Psychological Review,* 1946, *53,* 36–42.

Shenger-Krestovnikova, N. R. Contributions to question of differentiation of visual stimuli and the limits of differentiation by the visual analyser of the dog. *Bulletin of Lesgaft Institute of Petrograd,* 1921, *3,* 11–43.

Sherman, J. A. Use of reinforcement and imitation to reinstate verbal behavior in mute psychotics. *Journal of Abnormal Psychology,* 1965, *70,* 155–164.

Shoben, E. J. Psychotherapy as a problem in learning theory. *Psychological Bulletin,* 1949, *46,* 366–392.

Sibley, S. A., Abbott, M., & Cooper, B. Modification of the classroom behavior of a disadvantaged kindergarten boy by social reinforcement and isolation. *Journal of Experimental Child Psychology,* 1969, 7, 203–219.

Sidman, M. Avoidance conditioning with brief shock and no exteroceptive warning signal. *Science,* 1953, *118,* 157–158.

Sidman, M. Normal sources of pathological behavior. *Science,* 1960a, *132,* 61–68.

Sidman, M. *Tactics of scientific research.* New York: Basic Books, 1960b.

Sidman, M., & Stoddard, L. T. The effectiveness of fading in programming a simultaneous form discrimination for retarded children. *Journal of the Experimental Analysis of Behavior,* 1967, *10,* 3–15.

Silberman, H. F. Characteristics of some recent studies of instructional methods. In J. E. Coulson (ed.), *Programmed learning and computer-based instruction.* New York: Wiley, 1962.

Skinner, B. F. *The behavior of organisms.* New York: Appleton-Century-Crofts, 1938.

Skinner, B. F. *Walden two.* New York: Macmillan, 1948.

Skinner, B. F. *Science and human behavior.* New York: Macmillan, 1953.

Skinner, B. F. *Verbal behavior.* New York: Appleton-Century-Crofts, 1957.

Skinner, B. F. *Cumulative record.* New York: Appleton-Century-Crofts, 1959.

Skinner, B. F. *The technology of teaching.* New York: Appleton-Century-Crofts, 1968.

Skinner, B. F. *Contingencies of reinforcement.* New York: Appleton-Century-Crofts, 1969.

Soderberg, G. A. Delayed auditory feedback and stuttering. *Journal of Speech and Hearing Disorders,* 1968, 33, 260–267.

Solomon, R. L. Punishment. *American Psychologist,* 1964, *19,* 239–253.

Solomon, R. L., Kamin, L. J., & Wynne, L. C. Traumatic avoidance learning: The outcomes of several extinction procedures with dogs. *Journal of Abnormal and Social Psychology,* 1953, *48,* 291–302.

Solomon, R. L., & Wynne, L. C. Traumatic avoidance learning: Acquisition in normal dogs. *Psychological Monographs,* 1953, *67,* No. 354. P. 19.

Solyom, L., & Miller, S. A differential conditioning procedure as the initial phase of the behavior therapy of homosexuality. *Behaviour Research and Therapy,* 1965, *3,* 147–160.

Spielberger, C. D., & DeNike, L. D. Descriptive behaviorism vs. cognitive theory in verbal operant conditioning. *Psychological Review,* 1966, *73,* 306–326.

Spitz, R. A. Hospitalism: An inquiry into the genesis of psychiatric conditions in early childhood. *Psychoanalytic study of the child,* 1945, *1,* 53–74.

Staats, A. W., & Staats, C. *Complex human behavior.* New York: Holt, Rinehart & Winston, 1963.

Stampfl, T. G., & Levis, D. J. Essentials of implosive therapy: A learning-theory-based psychodynamic behavioral therapy. *Journal of Abnormal Psychology,* 1967, *72,* 496–503.

Stebbins, W. C., & Smith, O. A., Jr. Cardiovascular concomitants of the conditioned emotional response in the monkey. *Science,* 1964, *144,* 881–882.

Stevens, S. S. Psychology and the science of science. *Psychological Bulletin,* 1939, *36,* 221–263.

Stimbert, V. E., Schaeffer, R. W., & Grimsley, D. L. Acquisition of an imitative response in rats. *Psychonomic Science,* 1966, *5,* 339–340.

Stretch, R., Orloff, E. R., & Dalrymple, S. D. Maintenance of responding by fixed-interval schedule of electric shock presentation in squirrel monkeys. *Science,* 1968, *162,* 583–586.

Stuart, R. B. Behavioral control of overeating. *Behaviour Research and Therapy,* 1967, *5,* 357–365.

Stuart, R. B. Operant-interpersonal treatment for marital discord. *Journal of Consulting and Clinical Psychology,* 1969, *33,* 675–682.

Stuart, R. B. *Trick or treatment: How and when psychotherapy fails.* Champaign, Ill.: Research Press, 1970.

Szasz, T. S. The myth of mental illness. *American Psychologist,* 1960, *15,* 113–118.

Tate, B. G., & Baroff, G. S. Aversive control of self-injurious behavior in a psychotic boy. *Behaviour Research and Therapy,* 1966, *4,* 281–287.

Teplov, B. M. Problems in the study of general types of higher nervous activity in man and animals. In J. A. Gray (ed.), *Pavlov's typology.* London: Pergamon Press, 1964.

Terrace, H. S. Discrimination learning with and without "errors." *Journal of the Experimental Analysis of Behavior,* 1963, *6,* 1–27.

Thimann, J. Conditioned reflex treatment of alcoholism. II. The risks of its application, its indications, contraindications and psychotherapeutic aspects. *New England Journal of Medicine,* 1949, *241,* 406–410.

Thompson, T., Grabowski, J., Errickson, E., & Johnson, R. Operant conditioning program for chronically institutionalized profoundly retarded adult males. *Proceedings of the Annual Convention of the American Psychological Association,* 1970, *5* (Pt. 2), 783–784.

Thorne, F. C. A critique of nondirective methods of psychotherapy. *Journal of Abnormal and Social Psychology,* 1944, *39,* 459–470.

Thorpe, J. G., Schmidt, E., & Castell, D. A comparison of positive and negative (aversive) conditioning in the treatment of homosexuality. *Behaviour Research and Therapy,* 1963, *1,* 357–362.

Thorpe, J. G., Schmidt, E., Brown, P. T., & Castell, D. Aversion-relief therapy: A new method for general application. *Behaviour Research and Therapy,* 1964, *2,* 71–82.

Tighe, T. J., & Elliott, R. A technique for controlling behavior in natural life settings. *Journal of Applied Behavior Analysis,* 1968, *1,* 263–266.

Timmons, E. O. Weakening verbal behavior: A comparison of four methods. *Journal of General Psychology,* 1962, *67,* 155–158.

Tooley, J. T., & Pratt, S. An experimental procedure for the extinction of smoking behavior. *Psychological Record,* 1967, *17,* 209–218.

Truax, C. B. Reinforcement and nonreinforcement in Rogerian psychotherapy. *Journal of Abnormal Psychology,* 1966, *71,* 1–9.

Truax, C. B., Wargo, D. G., Carkhuff, R. R., Kadman, F., Jr., and Moles, E. A. Changes in self-concept during group psychotherapy as a function of alternate sessions and vicarious therapy pre-training in institutionalized mental patients and juvenile delinquents. *Journal of Consulting Psychology,* 1966, *30,* 309–314.

Turner, L. H., & Solomon, R. L. Human traumatic avoidance learning: Theory and experiments on the operant-respondent distinction and failures to learn. *Psychological Monographs,* 1962, 76 (40, Whole No. 559).

Tursky, B., Schwartz, G. E., & Crider, A. Differential patterns of heart rate and skin resistance during a digit-transformation task. *Journal of Experimental Psychology,* 1970, *83,* 451–457.

Tyler, V.·O., & Brown, G. D. The use of swift, brief isolation as a group control device for institutionalized delinquents. *Behaviour Research and Therapy,* 1967, *5,* 1–9.

Ullman, A. D. The experimental production and analysis of a "compulsive eating symptom" in rats. *Journal of Comparative and Physiological Psychology,* 1951, *44,* 575–581.

Ulrich, R. E. Behavior control and public concern. *Psychological Record,* 1967, *17,* 229–234.

Ulrich, R. E., & Azrin, N. H. Reflexive fighting in response to aversive stimulation. *Journal of the Experimental Analysis of Behavior,* 1962, *5,* 511–520.

Verhave, T. The functional properties of a time-out from an avoidance schedule. *Journal of the Experimental Analysis of Behavior,* 1962, *5,* 391–422.

Verhave, T. *The experimental analysis of behavior. Selected readings.* New York: Appleton-Century-Crofts, 1966.

Verplanck, W. S. The control of the content of conversation. *Journal of Abnormal and Social Psychology,* 1955, *51,* 668–676.

Verplanck, W. S. Unaware of where's awareness: Some verbal operants—notates, monents, and notants. In C. W. Eriksen (ed.), *Behavior and awareness.* Durham, N.C.: Duke University Press, 1962.

Voegtlin, W. L. The treatment of alcoholism by establishing a conditioned reflex. *American Journal of the Medical Sciences,* 1940, *149,* 802–809.

Voegtlin, W. L. Conditioned reflex therapy of chronic alcoholism. Ten years experience with the method. *Rocky Mountain Medical Journal,* 1947, *44,* 807–812.

Voegtlin, W. L., & Broz, W. R. The conditioned reflex treatment of chronic alcoholism. X. An analysis of 3125 admissions over a period of ten and a half years. *Annals of International Medicine,* 1949, *30,* 580–597.

Voegtlin, W. L., & Lemere, F. The treatment of alcohol addiction: A review of the literature. *Quarterly Journal of Studies on Alcohol,* 1942, *2,* 717–803.

Vogler, R. E., Lunde, S. E., Johnson, G. R., & Martin, P. L. Electrical aversion conditioning with chronic alcoholics. *Journal of Consulting and Clinical Psychology,* 1970, *34,* 302–307.

Wagner, M. K. A case of public masturbation treated by operant conditioning. *Journal of Child Psychology and Psychiatry and Allied Disciplines,* 1968, *9,* 61–65.

Wagner, M. K., & Cauthen, N. R. A comparison of reciprocal inhibition and operant conditioning in the systematic desensitization of a fear of snakes. *Behaviour Research and Therapy,* 1968, *6,* 225–227.

Wahler, R. G. Behavior therapy for oppositional children: Love is not enough. Paper read at Eastern Psychological Association meeting, Washington, D.C., April, 1968.

Walters, G. C. & Rogers, J. V. Aversive stimulation of the rat: Long term effects on subsequent behavior. *Science,* 1963, *142,* 70–71.

Walton, D. The relevance of learning theory to the treatment of an obsessive-compulsive state. In H. J. Eysenck (ed.), *Behaviour therapy and the neuroses.* New York: Pergamon Press, 1960.

Walton, D., & Mather, M. D. The application of learning principles to the treatment of obsessive compulsive states. *Behaviour Research and Therapy,* 1963, *1,* 163–174.

Ward, A. J. Infantile autism. *Psychological Bulletin,* 1970, *73,* 350–362.

Warden, C. J., Fjeld, H. A., and Koch, A. M. Imitative behavior in Cebus and Rhesus monkeys. *Pedagogical Seminary and Journal of Genetic Psychology,* 1940, *56,* 311–322.

Watson, J. B., & Rayner, R. Conditioned emotional reactions. *Journal of Experimental Psychology,* 1920, *3,* 1–14.

Weiner, H. Some effects of response cost upon human operant behavior. *Journal of the Experimental Analysis of Behavior,* 1962, *5,* 201–208.

Weiner, H. Conditioning history and human fixed-interval performance. *Journal of the Experimental Analysis of Behavior,* 1964, *7,* 383–385.

Weiner, H. Conditioning history and maladaptive human operant behavior. *Psychological Reports,* 1965, *17,* 935–942.

Weiner, H. Human behavioral persistence. *Psychological Record,* 1970, *20,* 445–456.

Weinstein, W. K., & Lawson, R. The effect of experimentally-induced "awareness" upon performance in free-operant verbal conditioning and on subsequent tests of "awareness." *Journal of Psychology,* 1963, *56,* 203–211.

Wickens, D. D. A study of voluntary and involuntary finger conditioning. *Journal of Experimental Psychology,* 1939, *25,* 127–140.

Wickens, D. D. Studies of response generalization in conditioning. I. Stimulus generalization during response generalization. *Journal of Experimental Psychology,* 1943, *33,* 221–227.

Wiest, W. M. Some recent criticisms of behaviorism and learning theory with special reference to Breger and McGaugh and to Chormsky. *Psychological Bulletin,* 1967, *67,* 214–225.

Wilcoxon, H. C. "Abnormal fixation" and learning. *Journal of Experimental Psychology,* 1952, *44,* 324–333.

Wilde, G. J. S. Behavior therapy for addicted cigarette smokers: A preliminary investigation. *Behaviour Research and Therapy,* 1964, *2,* 107–109.

Wilkins, W. Desensitization: Getting it together with Davison and Wilson. *Psychological Bulletin,* 1972, *78,* 32–36.

Williams, C. D. The elimination of tantrum behaviors by extinction procedures. *Journal of Abnormal and Social Psychology,* 1959, *59,* 269.

Williams, D. R., & Teitlebaum, P. Control of drinking behavior by means of an operant conditioning technique. *Science,* 1956, *124,* 1294–1296.

Willoughby, R. H. The effects of time-out from positive reinforcement on the operant behavior of preschool children. *Journal of Experimental Child Psychology,* 1969, *7,* 299–313.

Wilson, A., & Smith, F. J. Counter-conditioning therapy using free association: A pilot study. *Journal of Abnormal Psychology,* 1968, *73,* 474–478.

Wilson, F. S., & Walters, R. H. Modification of speech output of near-mute schizophrenics through social learning procedures. *Behaviour Research and Therapy,* 1966, *4,* 59–67.

Wolberg, L. R. *The technique of psychotherapy.* New York: Grune & Stratton, 1954.

Wolf, M. M., & Risley, T. Analysis and modification of deviant child behavior. Paper read at the American Psychological Association meeting, Washington, D.C., September 1967.

Wolfe, J. B. Effectiveness of token-rewards for chimpanzees. *Comparative Psychological Monograph,* 1936, *12,* No. 60.

Wolf, M. M., Gibs, D. K., & Hall, R. V. Experiments with token reinforcement in a remedial classroom. *Behaviour Research and Therapy,* 1968, *6,* 51–54.

Wolpe, J. Experimental neuroses as learned behavior. *British Journal of Psychology,* 1952, *43,* 243–268.

Wolpe, J. Reciprocal inhibition as the main basis of psychotherapeutic effects. *Archives of Neurology and Psychiatry,* 1954, *72,* 205–226.

Wolpe, J. *Psychotherapy by reciprocal inhibition.* Stanford: Stanford University Press, 1958.

Wolpe, J. Isolation of a conditioning procedure as the crucial therapeutic factor: A case study. *Journal of Nervous and Mental Disease,* 1962, *134,* 316–329.

Wolpe, J. For phobia: A hair of the hound, *Psychology Today,* 1969, *3* (1), 34–37.

Wolpe, J., & Lazarus, A. A. *Behavior therapy techniques: A guide to the treatment of neuroses.* New York: Pergamon Press, 1966.

Wolpin, M., and Raines, W. Visual imagery, expected roles and extinction as possible factors in reducing fear and avoidance behavior. *Behaviour Research and Therapy,* 1966, *4,* 25–37.

Woody, R. H. *Behavioral problem children in the schools.* New York: Appleton-Century-Crofts, 1969.

Yarrow, L. J. Separation from parents during early childhood. In M. L. Hoffman & L. W. Hoffman (eds.), *Review of child development research.* Vol. 1. New York: Russell Sage Foundation, 1964.

Yates, A. J. The application of learning theory to the treatment of tics. *Journal of Abnormal and Social Psychology,* 1958a, *56,* 175–182.

Yates, A. J. Symptoms and symptom substitution. *Psychological Review,* 1958b, *65,* 371–374.

Yerofeeva, M. N. Contribution a l'étude des reflexes conditionnels destructifs. Societe de biologie, Paris, comptes rendus, 1916, *79,* 239–240.

Zajonc, R. B. Social facilitation. *Science,* 1965, *149,* 269–274.

Zajonc, R. B. Social facilitation in cockroaches. In E. C. Simmel, R. A. Hoppe & G. A. Milton (eds.), *Social facilitation and imitative behavior.* Boston: Allyn & Bacon, 1968.

Zigler, E., & Phillips, L. Psychiatric diagnosis: A critique. *Journal of Abnormal and Social Psychology,* 1961, *63,* 607–618.

Zimmerman, J. Productive avoidance: A procedure for accelerating "productive" behavior in humans. Paper presented at the meeting of the American Psychological Association, Washington, D.C., 1969.

Zimmerman, E. H., Zimmerman, J., & Russell, C. D. Differential effects of token reinforcement on instruction-following behavior in retarded students instructed as a group. *Journal of Applied Behavior Analysis,* 1969, *2,* 101–112.

Zuckerman, M., & Cohen, N. Is suggestion the source of reported visual sensations in perceptual isolation? *Journal of Abnormal Psychology,* 1964, *68,* 655–660.

Index of Authors

A

Albee, G. W., 315, 320, 325
Alexander, F., 183
Al-Issa, I., 310
Allen, K. E., 221, 263, 271, 289
American Psychiatric Association, 22, 23
American Psychological Association, 320, 324
Amsel, A., 126
Anant, S. S., 203, 244
Anderson, O. D., 92
Angermeier, W. F., 283
Ascough, J. C., 266
Ashem, B., 203, 244
Atkinson, R. C., 269
Atthowe, J. M., 294
Ayllon, T., 112, 182, 213, 214, 215, 218, 219, 221, 229, 265, 267, 270, 275, 276, 277, 292–296, 305, 317
Azrin, N. H., 16, 110, 112, 126, 201, 233, 266, 267

B

Baer, D. M., 13, 79, 188, 231, 249, 256, 265, 274, 285, 286

Baker, B. L., 309
Bandura, A., 27, 43, 70, 76, 77–79, 173, 174, 187, 191, 201, 226, 228, 230, 262, 265, 275, 278, 283, 284, 285, 286, 307, 310
Barker, J. C., 259
Barrett, B. H., 225
Baum, M., 197
Becker, W. C., 264
Bekhterev, V. M., 180
Bensberg, G. J., 269
Benson, H., 266
Bexton, W. H., 171
Bijou, S. W., 28, 224
Black, A. H., 84, 266
Blake, B. G., 255, 258
Blakemore, C. B., 259
Boren, J. J., 193
Boring, E. G., 14
Bostow, D. E., 236, 256
Boulougouris, J. C., 197
Bowlby, J., 172
Brady, J. V., 16, 104, 136, 137, 138, 193
Brawley, E., 289
Breger, L., 66, 324, 325
Brenner, J., 222, 229

Bridger, H. W., 42
Brigham, T. A., 285, 309
Broadhurst, P., 87
Brodsky, G. D., 307
Brown, E. C., 268
Brown, J. S., 157–158, 264
Bucher, B., 242, 243, 245, 248, 258, 266, 300
Burchard, J., 270, 294
Buss, A. H., 17, 26, 136

C

Cahoon, D. D., 309
Caldwell, B. M., 41, 42
Cameron, N., 23
Campbell, D., 162, 194, 252, 254
Casler, L., 171
Cautela, J. R., 243, 244, 259, 300, 304, 310
Chittenden, G. E., 265
Chomsky, N., 132
Church, R. M., 232, 282
Clements, C. B., 295
Cohen, H. L., 265, 269, 294
Coleman, J. C., 17
Cooke, G., 206
Cooper, A. J., 259
Corson, J. A., 282
Coulson, J. E., 269
Cowles, J. T., 317

D

Darby, C. L., 282
Davidson, R. S., 163, 185, 221, 237, 244, 246, 248, 318, 319
Davis, H. V., 42
Davis, R. C., 138
Davison, G. C., 206, 224, 280, 292, 305
Davitz, J. R., 283
Dekker, E., 96
DeMorsier, G., 202
Dews, P. B., 16, 193
DiCara, L. V., 266
Diefendorf, A. P., 22
Dinsmoor, J. A., 12, 98, 248
Dollard, J., 67–69
Drennan, W., 308
Duke, M. P., 286
Dulany, D. E., 308
Dunlap, K., 181
Dworkin, L., 87

E

Ebbinghaus, H., 5
Elliot, R., 253, 254

Ellis, A., 39, 43
Eriksen, C. W., 133–134
Estes, W. K., 103–104, 163
Evans, D. R., 259
Everett, P. B., 141
Eysenck, H. J., 26, 48, 50, 51, 94, 181, 184, 316

F

Fairweather, G. W., 270
Falk, J. L., 121, 270
Feldman, M. P., 224, 232, 242, 249, 252, 253, 254, 256
Fenichel, O., 41, 113, 309
Ferster, C. B., 27, 61, 62, 63, 100, 164, 213, 216, 218, 238, 259, 264, 269, 271, 274, 280, 281, 282, 289, 318, 324
Findley, J. D., 275
Flanagan, B., 135, 222, 239
Fontana, A. F., 11
Frank, G. H., 9
Franks, C. M., 87, 96, 201, 231, 232
Freeman, G. L., 145–146
Freud ,S., 37–46, 182, 183
Frolov, Y. P., 87

G

Gambrill, E., 225
Gantt, W. H., 49, 191
Garfield, G. H., 206
Gelfand, D. M., 217
Gendreau, P. E., 250, 258
Gentry, W. D., 126–127
Gericke, O. L., 294
Gewirtz, J. L., 79, 228, 284, 287, 309
Giles, D. K., 269, 290
Girardeau, F. L., 269, 294
Glynn, J. D., 259
Goffman, E., 18
Goldberg, S. R., 138–141
Goldfried, M. R., 29
Goldiamond, I., 222, 239, 258, 279, 324
Goldstein, A. P., 316
Goodkin, R., 267
Gormezano, I., 193
Green, R., 43
Greenspoon, J., 132, 308
Grings, W. W., 266
Grünbaum, A., 5
Guttman, N., 302, 303

H

Hake, D. F., 283
Hall, C. S., 40

Harlow, H. F., 74–76, 168, 169, 170
Harmatz, M. G., 290, 291
Harris, M. B., 280
Hart, B., 223
Haughton, E., 130, 131
Hayes, K. J., 282
Herman, R. L., 256
Herrnstein, R. J., 252, 274
Hetzel, M. L., 269
Hogan, R. A., 199
Holland, G., 56, 269, 320
Hollingworth, H. L., 181
Holmes, D. S., 46
Holz, W. C., 111, 112, 228, 229, 234, 257
Homme, L. E., 296, 297, 298, 300, 324
Hsu, J., 254
Hull, C. L., 52
Humphrey, J., 265
Hunt, J. G., 270

I

Immergluck, L., 3, 6, 7
Isaacs, W., 265, 267, 270, 304

J

Jacobson, E., 203
Jahoda, M., 17
Janis, I. L., 227
Jersild, A., 181, 226, 289
Johnson, R. F., 270
Johnston, J. M., 238
Jones, E., 39
Jones, M. C., 180, 203, 208, 220, 226, 289
Justesen, D. R., 96

K

Kanfer, F. H., 27, 28, 66, 163, 205, 209, 267, 292, 320, 322, 324
Kant, F., 202
Kantorovich, N. V., 202, 258
Karsh, E. B., 46, 149, 164–165
Kazdin, A. E., 295
Keehn, J. D., 141
Kelleher, R. T., 117
Keller, F. S., 269
Kellogg, W. N., 306
Kennedy, T. D., 308
Keutzer, C., 237
Kimble, G. A, 40, 49, 55, 84, 96, 193, 196, 207
Kimmel, H. D., 138, 262, 266
King, G., 265, 270

Klein, B., 202
Koenig, K. P., 258
Krasner, L., 16, 186, 267, 308, 309, 322
Krasnagorski, N. I., 88–91
Krumboltz, J. D., 286
Kushner, M., 232, 242, 259

L

LaBarba, R. C., 171
Lachenmeyer, C. W., 294
Lal, H., 262
Lang, P. J., 138, 307
Lauer, D. W., 164
Lavin, N. I., 259
Lazarus, A. A., 206, 248, 256
Lehrman, N. S., 39
Leitenberg, H., 207, 222, 229, 233, 238, 288
Lemere, F., 200, 202, 209, 255
Lent, J. R., 269
Lester, D., 141
Levin, G. R., 265
Levine, S., 175
Levitt, E. E., 184
Levitz, L. S., 276
Levy, D., 42
Libb, J. W., 295
Lichtenstein, F. E., 148
Liddell, H. S., 92, 93, 191
Lidz, T., 78
Lindley, R. H., 194
Lindsley, O. R., 136, 181, 185, 222, 229, 267, 268, 270, 279, 280, 296, 318, 319, 324
Lippsett, L. P., 42
Littman, R. A., 186
Liversedge, L. A., 245
Lloyd, K. E., 294
Lomont, J. F., 322
London, P., 184
Lovaas, O. I., 77, 216, 221, 227, 228, 232, 243, 245, 248, 249, 258, 264, 266, 274, 278, 283, 284, 289, 307, 310
Lovibond, S. H., 274
Lublin, I., 258
Luchins, A. S., 285
Lumsdaine, A. A., 267

M

McAllister, L. W., 291
McAllister, W. R., 103, 198
McBrearty, J. F., 256
MacCorquodale, K., 24

MacCulloch, M. J., 249, 252, 253
McDavid, J. W., 283
McGuire, R. J., 98, 257, 258
McIntire, R., 292
McKearney, J. W., 117, 118, 160, 274
McQuitty, L. L., 26
Maher, B., 155, 156
Maier, N. R. F., 164
Marks, I. M., 197, 242, 259
Martin, G. L., 265
Martin, M. L., 270
Mason, J. W., 104
Masserman, J. H., 73, 93, 147, 148, 191, 193, 203
Max, L. W., 181
Meehl, P. E., 316
Mees, H. L., 225
Melzack, R., 167, 168
Mendelson, J. H., 318
Menninger, K. A., 25
Michael, J., 321
Miller, E. C., 256
Miller, M. M., 203
Miller, N. E., 46, 80, 138, 149, 150, 152–154, 156, 174, 181, 189, 266, 282
Miller, R. E., 168, 283
Minge, M. R., 269
Morrill, C. S., 268
Morse, W. H., 93, 116, 117, 118, 273, 275
Mowrer, O. H., 47, 70, 71, 72, 157, 159–160, 196, 307
Mulder, D. W., 104–105
Munroe, R., 44
Murray, E. J., 267
Murphy, J. V., 283

N

Narrol, H. G., 295
Nathan, P. E., 268
Noelpp, B., 96
Nolan, J. D., 281

O

O'Brien, F., 277, 278
O'Connor, N., 171
O'Connor, R. D., 227, 265, 286
O'Kelley, L. I., 19
O'Leary, K. D., 295
Orlansky, H., 40, 43
Ottenberg, P., 96–97

P

Patterson, G. R., 20, 21, 26, 176, 185, 269, 290
Paul, G. L., 14, 205, 319
Pavlov, I. P., 48, 49, 83, 85, 86, 180, 191, 193, 208
Pemberton, D. A., 255
Perensky, J. J., 141
Peterson, G. L., 128
Phelan, J. G., 307
Piercy, D. C., 26
Pierrel, R., 274
Polin, A. T., 197
Powell, D. A., 125
Premack, D., 32, 297, 313
Pumpian-Midlen, E., 38, 39

Q

Quinn, J. T., 300

R

Rachman, S., 66, 94–95, 194, 198, 201, 205, 231, 232, 248
Raymond, M. J., 256, 259
Reese, E. P., 100, 101, 321
Renner, K. E., 274
Resnick, J. H., 218, 229
Ribble, M. A., 172
Rickard, H. C., 223, 267, 289
Risley, T. R., 221, 227, 242, 243, 256, 264, 266, 283, 288, 300, 308
Ritter, B. J., 206, 226, 286
Roberts, A. H., 281
Rogers, C. R., 182, 183, 184, 322
Rosenblum, L. A., 170, 171
Rosenhan, D. L., 19
Ross, S., 42
Rossi, A. M., 171
Rotter, J. B., 25
Rubinstein, E. A., 184, 316

S

Sachs, D. A., 105
Salter, A., 88
Salzinger, K., 16, 132, 267
Sandler, J., 64–65, 85, 113–114, 115, 134, 195–196, 232, 273, 274, 295
Sarbin, T. R., 25, 175
Schaefer, H. H., 31, 118–120, 221, 270, 292–296, 305, 323
Schneiderman, N. E., 98, 192, 209
Schoenfeld, W. N., 103, 163, 175

Schultz, D. P., 171
Schwitzgebel, R., 310
Scott, W. A., 17
Sears, R. R., 41, 43, 44–45
Seay, 170
Shapiro, D., 222, 266, 267
Shaw, F. J., 181
Shenger-Krestovnikova, N. R., 85, 191
Sherman, J. A., 265, 267, 270
Shoben, E. J., 181, 292
Sibley, S. A., 291
Sidman, M., 4, 60, 102, 105–109, 221
Silberman, H. F., 269
Skinner, B. F., 6, 8, 14, 32, 40, 55–59, 136, 142, 174, 213, 268, 269, 274, 284, 320
Soderberg, G. A., 222, 240
Solomon, R. L., 124, 160–162, 194, 232, 252
Solyom, L., 224
Spielberger, C. D., 132, 308
Spitz, R. A., 172
Staats, A. W., 27
Stampfl, T. G., 198
Stebbins, W. C., 104
Stevens, S. S., 5
Stimbert, V. E., 282
Stretch, R., 117, 274
Stuart, 21, 24, 25, 175, 184, 259, 280, 281, 318, 324
Szasz, T. S., 24, 175

T

Tate, B. G., 216, 228, 232, 240, 258, 300
Teplov, B. M., 48, 49
Terrace, H. S., 220
Thimann, J., 255
Thompson, T., 290
Thorne, F. C., 183
Thorpe, J. G., 224, 249, 257, 259
Tighe, T. J., 253
Timmons, E. O., 158, 307
Tooley, J. T., 281
Truax, C. B., 267, 286, 292
Turner, L. H., 162, 254
Tursky, B., 222
Tyler, V. O., 237

U

Ullman, A. D., 122–123
Ulrich, R. E., 124–125, 322

V

Verhave, T., 238
Verplanck, W. S., 267, 308, 309
Voegtlin, W. L., 200, 201, 202, 209, 255
Vogler, R. E., 250

W

Wagner, M. K., 206, 263, 288
Wahler, R. G., 185, 265
Walters, G. C., 149
Walton, D., 259
Ward, A. J., 11
Warden, C. J., 282
Watson, J. B., 144–145, 180
Weiner, H., 128–130, 272
Weinstein, W. K., 308
Wickens, D. D., 194, 306
Wiest, W. M., 66
Wilcoxon, H. C., 46, 164
Wilde, G. J., 258
Wilkins, W., 205
Williams, C. D., 213
Williams, D. R., 120–121
Willoughby, R. H., 235, 256
Wilson, A., 206
Wilson, F. S., 265
Wolberg, L. R., 182, 183
Wolf, M. M., 270, 295
Wolfe, J. B., 317
Wolpe, J., 51–54, 149, 181, 199, 203, 204, 205, 208, 252, 288, 292, 304, 310, 315, 317
Wolpin, M., 81
Woody, R. H., 269

Y

Yarrow, L. J., 172, 173
Yates, A. J., 187, 216, 229
Yerofeeva, M. N., 75

Z

Zajonc, R. B., 191, 283
Zigler, E., 21, 25, 175
Zimmerman, E. H., 277
Zimmerman, J., 253, 298
Zuckerman, M., 171

Subject Index

A

Abnormal behavior. *See* Behavior, abnormal

Alcoholism. *See* Behaviors, alcoholic; Subjects, alcoholic

Analysis: behavioral, 279, 313; experimental, 14, 35, 47, 49, 66, 82, 147, 155, 176, 299, 315, 316; functional, 4, 11, 13–15, 30, 94, 110, 188, 209, 212, 269, 289, 292, 313; operant, *(see* Operant analysis)

Animal analogues, 5, 54, 317

Anxiety, 23, 38, 52, 53, 67–71, 103, 104, 106, 152, 162–164, 175, 198, 204, 206, 226, 250, 288

Anxiety hierarchy, 205

Assessment, 72, 120, 122, 184, 313, 316, 318–320, 324

Autism. See Behaviors, autistic; Subjects, autistic

Avoidance. See Behaviors, avoidance; Conditioning, avoidance; Techniques of behavior modification, avoidance

Awareness, 68, 133, 308

B

Behavior: abnormal, 17; pathological, *(see* Pathological behavior)

Behaviorism, 144, 312, 313

Behavior modification, 31, 179–180, 185–189, 228, 257, 261, 271, 279, 297, 301, 303, 304, 312, 314, 316, 317, 318, 320, 322, 324, 325

Behaviors: addictive, 138–141, 181; aggressive, 26, 123–128, 170, 173–174, 236, 237, 265, 284, 290, 307;alcoholic, 141, 148, 181, 200, 202, 203, 244, 253, 258; approach, 249, 286, 303, 310; asthmatic, 96–97; autistic, 29, 61, 170, 177, 221, 227, 249, 264, 271, 310, (see also Subjects, autistic); avoidance, 106, 107, 140, 147, 226, 232, 252–258; (see also Conditioning, avoidance; Response, avoidance); bedwetting, 262, 309; classroom, 277, 291; constructive, 242, 249, 272,

292, 300, 305, 311, 314, 323, 324; cooperative, 265, 266, 290; deficient, 27–29, 62, 78, 80, 262; delusional verbal, 214, 215, 223, 267, 289; depressed, 62, 74; eating, 122–123, 214, 250, 252, 280, 281, 290; excessive, 27, 29, 120–121, 163; headbanging, 118, 216–217, 232, 242; inappropriate, 78, 80, 109, 217, 289, 290, 291; incompatible, 203, 206, 262, 263, 288, 292, 296; maladaptive, 18, 115, 116, 290; neurotic, 23, 39, 52, 237; normal, 76, 258, 261, 265, 287, 314; phobic, 53, 144, 148, 160, 198, 203, 205, 222, 226, 250, 252, 285, 307, 310; self-injurious, 240, 241, 258; sexual, 94, 95, 194, 224, 242, 243, 249, 250, 253, 257–259, 263; smoking, 131, 218–219, 227, 280, 281, 319; social, 263, 269–271, 286, 289, 307; stuttering, 135, 216, 222; verbal, 132–136, 184, 214, 224, 268, 270, 308; withdrawal, 28, 31, 170, 227, 263, 265, 270
Behavior therapy, 180, 182, 184–185, 232, 309, 312, 324, (*see also* Techniques of behavior modification); broad-spectrum, 256, 257

C

Classification, 17–33, 63, 314; frequency model of, 21, 27–32; medical model, 21–25; statistical model, 26
Clinical psychology, 7, 8, 179, 180, 300, 314, 322, 325
Conditioned stimulus, 85, 197, 201, 276
Conditioned suppression, 103–110
Conditioning: aversive, 200–201, 254–258, (*see also* Stimulus, aversive; Stimulus, shock; Techniques of behavior modification, aversive); avoidance, 113, 121, 125, 137, 145, 160, 162, 217, 245, 252–256, 273, 283, 306, 310, (*see also* Be-

haviors, avoidance; Response, avoidance); classical, 47–49, 52, 54, 84–94, 96, 98, 144, 149, 162, 178, 184, 189–210, 276, 306; escape, 121, 159, 198, 202, 224, 239, 248–252, 253, 255, 282, 310; operant, 14–16, 184, 189, 264, 266, 290, 296, (*see also* Operant analysis; Operant paradigm); verbal, 132–133, 266, 307–309, (*see also* Behaviors, verbal)
Conflict, 49, 67–69, 73, 74, 81, 83, 89, 147, 150, 155, 156, 170
Contingency, 211, 269, 270, 293, 306, 328
Contingency management. *See* Techniques of behavior modification, contingency management
Control, 2, 290, 302, 312, 315, 322, 323–325
Counterconditioning. *See* Techniques of behavior modification, counterconditioning

D

Defense mechanisms. *See* Psychoanalytic defense mechanisms
Deprivation, 43, 73, 74, 166–173, 178, 217, 218, 313; maternal, 76, 168, 171
Design: ABA, 293, 306; functional, 30, 263, 319, (*see also* Analysis, functional); multiple baseline, 13, 30, 31, 215, 291, 292, 316; research, 184, 295, 309, 322, 325; reversal, 13, 30, 98, 184, 192, 209, 214, 216, 223, 292, 316; single subject, 31, 316; statistical, 14, 30, 290
Determinism, 4, 5, 16, 38, 184, 312, 313
Diagnosis, 21, 23, 24, 32, 175
Discrimination, 57, 85–90, 102, 119, 145, 164, 192, 282, 284
Discrimination training, 146, 147, 212, 220
Discriminative stimulus (S^D), 102, 111, 174, 216, 275, 276, 300
Drugs, 16, 191, 193, 201, 202, 255, 256, 280

E

Environment, 31, 304, 306, 318, 320; natural, 304, 305, 316–318

Ethics, 31, 231, 259, 315, 321–324

Etiology, 51, 53, 61, 63, 66, 143, 187–188, 232, 252, 274, 314, 318, 321, 323

Experimental neurosis, 84–93, 98, 149, 190, 193, 204

Extinction, 15, 56, 63, 94, 96, 100, 114, 152, 160, 161, 172, 173, 193–195, 199, 202, 207, 211–217, 222, 224, 225, 228, 241, 264, 290; resistance to, 157, 160, 164, 271

F

Fear, 68, 144, 152, 197–200, 204, 206, 226, 288, 304, 307

Follow-up, 251, 254, 255, 289, 290, 299, 310, 317

G

Generalization, 31, 102, 120, 145, 154, 223, 242, 289, 299–311, 318; response, 154, 202, 300, 304, 306–309; stimulus, 94, 194, 302–306

I

Imitation, 174, 226, 278, 284, 285, 298, 309, (*see also* Techniques of behavior modification, imitation); generalized, 228, 283–285; social, 226–228, 285

Imposive therapy. *See* Techniques of behavior modification, implosive therapy

L

Learning, 16, (*see also* Conditioning); contiguity, 77, 225, 283; social, 76–78

M

Measurement, 295, 298, 316, 317, 319, 325

Method: case study, 8, 321; field study, 9; statistical, 14, 26

Methodology, 313–317, 321, (*see also* Design)

Model, 262; medical, 21–25, 187; research, 321; scientist-professional, 320, 325

Modeling. *See* Techniques of behavior modification, modeling

O

Operant, 16, (*see also* Conditioning operant); multi-, 275

Operant analysis, 14–16, 113, 156, 210, 271, 300

Operant paradigm, 14–16, 118

P

Pathological behavior, 2, 3, 19, 28, 48, 49, 57–60, 70, 73, 74, 77, 81, 83, 92, 108, 110, 118, 130, 131, 142, 150, 155, 157, 159, 172, 179, 181, 185, 188, 190, 193–195, 209, 214, 225, 228, 231, 236, 237, 240, 242, 244, 253, 262, 264, 270, 272, 282, 285, 299, 300, 310, 314, 315, 322, 323, 326

Philosophy, 312–314

Principles, 321; conditioning, 181–182, 269, 317, 324; learning, 149, 181, 269, 317, 324; reinforcement, 55, 66, 77

Psychoanalysis, 37–47, 177, 303

Psychoanalytic defense mechanisms, 44–46; fixation, 45, 46, 163–166; regression, 45, 46, 158, 160; repression, 45, 58, 68, 133

Psychopathology, 2, 6–8, 10, 11, 18, 21, 22, 38, 41, 44, 49, 51, 55, 57–59, 66, 69, 70, 75, 80, 85, 95, 105, 113, 142, 143, 157, 168, 171, 178

Psychometrics. *See* Assessment; Measurement

Psychotherapy, 183, 184, 256, 267, 287, 289, 292, 303, 304, 314; nondirective, 183

Punishment, 15, 45, 56, 57, 61, 63, 69, 70, 102, 110, 114, 144, 146, 148, 149, 161, 164, 165, 175, 201, 211, 212, 222, 224, 228, 232, 233, 237, 238–248, 249, 254–259, 272, 274, 313

Q

Questionnaires, 244, 320

R

Rehabilitation, 269, 270

Reinforcement, 55, 211, 217, 224, 235, 244, 257, 266, 269, 270, 290, 292, 302, 308–310, 313; adventitious, 58, 62, 108, 109, 211, 274; delay of, 86, 89, 270, 274; negative, 15, 58, 64, 102, 140, 146, 210, 247, 248, 259; positive, 15, 64, 99, 116, 126, 156, 165, 172, 207, 210, 216, 233, 236, 238, 247, 262, 266, 274, 276, 288; Premack, 297, 313; social, 177, 213, 258, 267, 283, 284, 289

Reinforcement history, 61, 110, 129, 142, 184, 187–188, 276

Reinforcement schedules. *See* schedules of reinforcement

Reinforcement theory, 79, 176

Reinforcer, 211, 237, 293; conditioned, 292, 293; natural, 266, 271; token, 277, 279, 292–294

Reliability, 25, 289, 290, 293, 316

Research, 259, 325

Research design. *See* Design, research

Response: alternative, 234, 256; avoidance, 161, 168, 197, 216, 304, 307; bar press, 5, 103, 113, 141, 153, 233, 275, 285, 307; physiological, 16, 95, 137–138, 156, 198, 222, 266

Response hierarchy, 187, 191

Response priming, 277–278

Response rate, 244, 319, 320

S

Schedule of reinforcement, 61, 62, 64, 100, 128, 164, 176, 211, 221, 271–276; continuous, 100, 195, 211, 263, 271; DRL (differential reinforcement of low rate), 129, 257, 272; fixed interval, 101, 116, 128–130, 211, 263, 272, 274; fixed ratio, 100, 104, 118, 128, 211, 244, 248; intermittent, 100, 263, 266, 271; multiple, 275, 305, 316; variable interval, 101, 211, 235, 248; variable ratio, 101, 211, 242, 248, 274

Science, 3, 5, 6–8

Scientific method, 4, 12

Self-control. *See* Techniques of behavior modification, self-control

Shaping, 32, 277–278, 293, 296

Stability, 4, 14, 317, 319

Stimulus, 220, 302, 304; aversive, 232, 243, 248, 251, 252; shock (electric), 84, 85, 92, 103–109, 111, 116, 117, 122–125, 133, 135, 147, 149, 152, 157, 159–161, 165, 166, 197, 201, 202, 208, 216, 224, 239, 242–246, 249, 253–258, 274, 280, 306, 310

Stimulus control, 62, 212, 275, 281–282, 304, 319

Subjects: alcoholic, 244, 250, 253–255, 258, 300; animal, 84, 225, 314, 317, 321; autistic, 221, 227, 249, 264, 271, 283, 289; cat, 147, 149, 204; children, 88, 90, 126, 127, 185, 203, 212, 213, 221, 226, 227, 235, 240, 242, 249, 262–266, 269–271, 284, 286, 288–290, 292, 297, 307, 309; delinquent, 265, 269, 270, 294, 310; dog, 85, 86, 160, 161, 167; human, 128, 130, 132–136, 144, 162, 171, 194, 199, 216, 275, 280, 283, 306, 314, 322; monkey, 105–110, 113–114, 116–120, 136–140, 168–170, 275, 282; patient, 3, 185, 214, 218, 222, 234, 236, 244, 250, 253–257, 267, 270, 271, 277, 289, 292, 293, 298, 300, 304; pigeon, 111, 126, 220, 257; psychotic, 214, 240, 265, 267, 270, 289, 294, 304; rat, 103, 121–122, 124, 141, 151, 154, 157, 159, 164, 197, 202, 275, 282; retarded, 221, 227, 236, 265, 269, 277, 283, 290, 294, 297

Symptom, 21, 68

Symptom substitution, 186–187, 309

T

Target behavior, 184, 243, 253, 283, 296, 310, 311, 317, 319

Techniques of behavior modification: accelerative, 222, 261–298, 314; aversive, 203, 209, 225, 249, 231–259, 290; avoidance, 252–256, 310; contingency management, 296–298, 305; counterconditioning, 201–203, 223–225, 229, 242, 288–292; covert sensitization, 243, 244, 304, 311; decelerative, 213–230, 233, 288; desensitization, 204–209, 226, 255, 288, 303, 304, 307, 311; escape conditioning, 248–252, 253, 310; extinction, 193–195, 199, 202, 203, 207, 211–217, 223–225, 289, 290; fading, 203, 208, 220–221, 229, 272, 306; feedback, 221–223, 239, 240; flooding, 196–198; imitation, 230, 265, 278, 282–288, (*see also* Imitation); implosive therapy, 198–199; instructions, 276–278, 293, 298; modeling, 78, 226–228, 265, 285–287, 293, 307, 310; negative practice, 181, 216–217; precision teaching, 222, 279, 296; programmed instruction, 268, 297, 321; punishment, 212, 238–248, *(see also* Punishment); relaxation, 199, 203, 205–206, 255, 288, 297; satiation, 217–220, 229; self-control, 225, 250, 296, 298, 311, 324; systematic desensitiza-

tion, (*see* Techniques of behavior modification, desensitization); token economy, 269, 270, 279, 292–295, 305; time-out (TO), 233–238, 281, 290

Therapy outcome. *See* Treatment outcome

Therapy process, 316, 319

Token. *See* Reinforcer, token; Techniques of behavior modification, token economy

Training: avoidance, (*see* Conditioning, avoidance); clinical, 320, 322

Treatment, 299, 300, 313, 325

Treatment follow-up. *See* Follow-up

Treatment outcome, 258, 298, 309, 316, 319, 320

Two-factor theory of avoidance, 162, 252, 253, 307

Two-process theory of imitation, 283, 287

U

Ulcers, 136–138

V

Validity, 25, 316, 320, 322

Variable, 5; dependent, 4, 10, 15, 55, 186; independent, 4, 9, 10, 12, 30, 41, 55, 186, 316

73 74 75 7 6 5 4 3 2 1